Hinduism and the Ethics of Warfare in South Asia
From Antiquity to the Present

This book challenges the view, common among Western scholars, that precolonial India lacked a tradition of military philosophy. It traces the evolution of theories of warfare in India from the dawn of civilization, focusing on the debate between *dharmayuddha* (just war) and *kutayuddha* (unjust war) within Hindu philosophy. This debate centers around four questions: What is war? What justifies it? How should it be waged? And what are its potential repercussions? This volume provides evidence of the historical evolution of strategic thought on the Indian subcontinent that has heretofore been neglected by modern historians. Further, it provides a counterpoint to scholarship in political science that engages solely with Western theories in its analysis of independent India's philosophy of warfare. Ultimately, a better understanding of the legacy of ancient India's strategic theorizing will enable more accurate analysis of modern India's military and nuclear policies.

Kaushik Roy is a Reader in History at Jadavpur University in Kolkata, India, and Senior Researcher at the Centre for the Study of Civil War at the Peace Research Institute, Oslo, Norway. He is the author or editor of sixteen books and numerous journal articles, one of which won the Moncado Prize in 2006.

Hinduism and the Ethics of Warfare in South Asia

From Antiquity to the Present

KAUSHIK ROY

*Jadavpur University, Kolkata
Peace Research Institute, Oslo*

CAMBRIDGE UNIVERSITY PRESS
Cambridge, New York, Melbourne, Madrid, Cape Town,
Singapore, São Paulo, Delhi, Mexico City

Cambridge University Press
32 Avenue of the Americas, New York, NY 10013-2473, USA

www.cambridge.org
Information on this title: www.cambridge.org/9781107017368

© Kaushik Roy 2012

This publication is in copyright. Subject to statutory exception
and to the provisions of relevant collective licensing agreements,
no reproduction of any part may take place without the written
permission of Cambridge University Press.

First published 2012

Printed in the United States of America

A catalog record for this publication is available from the British Library.

Library of Congress Cataloging in Publication data
Roy, Kaushik, 1971–
Hinduism and the ethics of warfare in South Asia : from antiquity to the
present / Kaushik Roy.
pages cm
Includes bibliographical references and index.
ISBN 978-1-107-01736-8 (hardback)
1. Military art and science – India – Philosophy – History.   2. Military ethics – India –
History.   3. Hindu ethics – India – History.   I. Title.
U21.2.R68   2012
172'.420954–dc23   2011049734

ISBN 978-1-107-01736-8 Hardback

Cambridge University Press has no responsibility for the persistence or accuracy of URLs
for external or third-party Internet Web sites referred to in this publication and does not
guarantee that any content on such Web sites is, or will remain, accurate or appropriate.

Contents

Preface		*page* vii
Abbreviations		ix
Glossary		xi
	Introduction	1
1	Religious Ethics and the Philosophy of Warfare in Vedic and Epic India: 1500–400 BCE	13
2	Buddhism, Jainism and Asoka's *Ahimsa*	40
3	Kautilya's *Kutayuddha*: 300 BCE–300 CE	58
4	*Dharmayuddha* and *Kutayuddha* from the Common Era to the Advent of the Turks	106
5	Hindu Militarism under Islamic Rule: 900–1800 CE	161
6	Hindu Militarism and Anti-Militarism in British India: 1750–1947	211
7	The Hindu Military Ethos and Strategic Thought in Post-Colonial India	237
	Conclusion	261
Select Bibliography		267
Index		283

Preface

On an extremely cold day with heavy snowfall in January 2006, as I was wandering through the bunker-like labyrinths of the Peace Research Institute in Oslo and searching for the smoking room, I accidentally met Professor Gregory Reichberg. While chatting, he told me that he was interested in the interconnections between religious ethics and the conduct of warfare. Then he asked me if I had ever thought of the interconnections between one of the world's oldest religions (Hinduism) and the conduct of war. I showed my interest and said that I was willing to research it. And then Reichberg said, well then, you are 'in' the project. I am extremely grateful to him not only for introducing the idea of the interrelationship between religion and warfare but also for sustaining me financially and morally for about five years while I was engaged in writing this monograph. While I was writing the monograph, my friend and mentor at PRIO, Professor Scott Gates, always made me conscious of what Hinduism has to say about unconventional (intra-state) warfare. This volume builds upon the two essays I published in the *Journal of Military Ethics* (2007) and in a volume published by the United Nations Press (2009), and also on the 30,000-word piece on Hinduism and warfare I wrote for an anthology as part of Reichberg's project. I am also fortunate to have met Dr. Beatrice Rehl in Cyprus and then in Oslo; she kindly agreed to consider the volume for publication by Cambridge University Press. Thanks to the two unknown referees and my friend Torkel Brekke for their criticism and input. My special thanks to my wife, Suhrita, who accepted my continuous 'mindless' chattering about the *acharyas*' views on *yuddha* and *vigraha* during the last five years. As a final take, if this volume satisfies none of its readers but provokes them to think about the complex interstices between Hinduism and warfare, my work is done.

2012, Kolkata

Abbreviations

BJP	Bharatiya Janata Party, i.e., the right-wing Hindu party of independent India
COIN	Counter-insurgency
CTBT	Comprehensive Test Ban Treaty
EIC	East India Company
EWJN	*The Essential Writings of Jawaharlal Nehru*, ed. by S. Gopal and Uma Iyengar, 2 vols. (New Delhi: Oxford University Press, 2003)
EWMG	*The Essential Writings of Mahatma Gandhi*, ed. by Raghavan Iyer (1993; reprint, New Delhi: Oxford University Press, 2007)
HUMINT	Human intelligence, e.g., spies, undercover agents
IESHR	*Indian Economic and Social History Review*
INA	Indian National Army or the *Azad Hind Fauj*
INC	Indian National Congress
IOR, BL	India Office Records, British Library, London
IPKF	Indian Peace Keeping Force deployed in Sri Lanka in the 1980s
JME	*Journal of Military Ethics*
JMH	*Journal of Military History*
JSS	*Journal of Strategic Studies*
LOC	Line of Control, i.e., the boundary between India and Pakistan, especially in the disputed region of Kashmir
LTTE	Liberation Tigers of Tami Ealam (homeland)
MAS	*Modern Asian Studies*

MD	*Manava Dharmasastra*
M/F	Microfilm Collection
MODAR	*Ministry of Defence Government of India Annual Report*
NAI	National Archives of India, New Delhi
NPT	Non-Proliferation Treaty
POW	Prisoner of war
SIGINT	Signal Intelligence, e.g., the use of satellites

Glossary

Acharya Brahmin advisor, teacher

Ahimsa Doctrine of non-violence, the opposite of *himsa*

Akharas Centres in the countryside where Hindu military recruits were trained in various physical exercises, especially in wrestling

Amatya Civil bureaucrat

Amitra Deserters from the enemy's army; at times also a state in the *mandala* that harbours enmity towards the *vijigishu*

Anitya Uncertain, full of chance probability; result dependent on a random roll of dice

Ankush An iron rod with a curved point at the top; it was used by the *mahout* to pierce the brain of an elephant when the latter became uncontrollable due to injuries sustained on the battlefield

Artha Literal meaning: wealth; broadly, the term refers to anything connected to the material well-being of the people

Arthasastra Non-Vedic knowledge system concerned with *artha*

Aryaputra Literal meaning: sons of the Aryans; in early medieval India, the term referred to the Kshatriyas/*thakur*s and later to the Rajputs

Aryavarta Domains of the Aryans, i.e., north India for the ancient and medieval Hindu intellectuals

Aswamedha yagna Literal meaning: horse sacrifice; the conqueror sent a horse backed by his army. The horse traveled through the dominions of various kings. If these kings did not obstruct the horse, then theoretically they became tributaries of the conqueror. If any king stopped the horse as it was traveling through his dominion, then the army of the conqueror following the horse fought with that king. After victory, the horse was sacrificed in a *yajna*.

xii *Glossary*

Atavi Contingents provided by the tribal chieftains

Azad Hind Fauj Literal meaning: Independent India's Army; two such armies were created from the Indian POWs captured by Germany and Japan. The Japanese-sponsored *Azad Hind Fauj*, also known as the Indian National Army, was initially led by Mohan Singh and later by the ex–Indian National Congress politician Subhas Chandra Bose.

Bakshi Commander-in-chief of the army of a Muslim state

Bala Army/use of force

Bans Primitive rockets used during warfare in pre-modern India

Bargi A Maratha cavalier who was provided a warhorse or pony by the government or the Maratha *sirdar*

Bazaar Market

Bhaga Royal share of the produce from land

Bhalla Heavy spear made of wood or bamboo

Bhang A liquid drug made of hemp

Bharat Bharat Varhsa (the country of Bharat), the Sanskrit name of Jambudvipa, i.e., the subcontinent; Bharat is the mythical first ruler of the subcontinent

Bharatiya Indianness, the way of life in Bharat

Bheda Divide-and-rule policy

Bhikkus Ascetic Buddhist monks

Bhiksuki Female spy dressed as a mendicant woman

Bhrata Local volunteer auxiliaries or mercenaries

Brahmastra Astra means weapons in Sanskrit, and Brahma's *astra* means weapons of Lord Brahma (creator of the cosmos); it means weapons of mass destruction not to be used during *dharmayuddha*. Modern Indian commentators interpret *brahmastra* as nuclear weapons.

Cakkavattin/Cakravartin A just monarch following the policies of peace and moderation; he is the opposite of *vijigishu*

Chara Spy/secret agent

Charka A circular weapon with serrated edges that was thrown towards the enemy; like a boomerang, it returned to the person who threw it. In Hindu mythology, Lord Krishna used this weapon.

Chaturanga Bala/Chaturangabalam Four-limbed army comprising foot soldiers, cavalry, elephants and chariots

Chaturvarna The ideal society of the Hindu jurists comprised of four castes: Brahmins (priests), Kshatriyas (warriors), Vaishyas (businessmen and merchants) and Sudras (cultivators)

Chela Disciple of a *guru*

Glossary xiii

Danda Literal meaning: a staff or a rod; it refers to the coercion (including the army) that should be used moderately by a 'just' ruler to maintain peace, prosperity and stability. Basically, it means use of force in a legal manner for running the polity.

Dandaniti The theory of statecraft involving judicious use of force

Dar al Harb Region of darkness, i.e., territories under non-Islamic rule

Dar al Islam House of light, i.e., region into which Islam has spread

Darsana Traditional Indian philosophy

Dhamma Buddhist equivalent of Hindu *dharma*

Dharma Not religion, but morality, code of conduct; *dharma* operates at three levels: at the personal level, at the community level and at the cosmic level

Dharmasastra Sacred knowledge system concerned with *dharma*; it refers to the vast body of literature in Sanskrit produced in ancient India dealing with legal and juridical precepts

Dharmayuddha Righteous war; it means war according to the *sastras*. Such a war could be started only for just reasons. Moreover, such a war must be waged in accordance with certain rules and regulations. It involves a set piece battle/combat at a place and time previously decided by the combatants. In Sanskrit literature this is known as *prakasayuddha*. Such a war involves minimal damage, and the combatants are forced to obey certain constraints on their conduct: non-combatants, prisoners and retreating soldiers are not harmed; flank and surprise attacks and nocturnal raids are not allowed, etc.

Dharmik A righteous person/ruler; one who follows *dharma*

Duta Diplomatic envoy

Faqir Holy Muslim mendicant

Gada Club/mace

Gauda Ancient Sanskrit name of Bengal

Giridurga Hill fort, i.e., a fort situated at the summit of a hill or in a mountainous region

Govisthi Raids for acquiring cattle

Guptachar The word is derived from Kautilya's word *chara*. Literally, a *chara* means a spy, and *guptachar* means a secret spy.

Guptaghatak A mercenary who would commit murder secretly

Guru Literal meaning: master; the term refers to the *acharya* of a disciple

Harijan M. K. Gandhi's term for the untouchables, i.e., those outside the caste system such as the tribes (traditional term *nishada*s). Gandhi also brought out a newspaper with this name.

xiv *Glossary*

Himsa Violence, aggressiveness, anger, jealousy, all negative feelings that are the opposite of *ahimsa*

Howdah A box (made of wood and occasionally plated with iron) tied at the back of the war elephant with ropes. This box carried the *mahout* and the warriors. At times, the box was perforated to allow the archers inside to shoot their arrows.

Inam Literal meaning: reward; this term refers to a hereditary grant of land made by the Muslim rulers to both their Hindu and Muslim service elites as a reward for special service or display of merit

Jaladurga Water fort, i.e., a fort surrounded by water. It means a fort situated in a lake or lagoon or protected by wide, deep wet ditches.

Janapada An inhabited settlement; a region full of people who practice agriculture, trade and commerce and yield revenue

Jihad Islamic holy war against the infidels

Jizya A discriminatory poll tax that the Hindus had to pay to the Muslim ruler in return for security under the Muslim regime

Kalaha Serious struggle, tension, etc. that might escalate to war

Kalinga Ancient name for Orissa

Kama Desire, love and sex

Kamboja Kandahar and this region were considered famous by the *acharyas* for their horses

Kamrup Pre-modern name of Assam

Karma Action/activities in life; the classical Hindus accepted the *karma* theory, which means circle of births. One's activities, good or bad, determine the nature of rebirths.

Kavya Poem

Khanda Straight sword suited for slashing used by the Rajputs

Kliba Impotent, useless, cowardly, worthless, lacking *paurusha*; the term often refers to a ruler who fails to offer security to his subjects, hence he lacks dignity and honour and is unfit to rule

Kopa Internal rebellion, insurgency, popular uprising of subjects against an unjust ruler

Kosa Royal treasury

Koti Special units deployed at the outer flanks of an army deployed for battle

Kufr Also known as *kafir*, meaning infidel, unbeliever

Kuta Crookedness, evil genius; a component of *kutayuddha*

Kutayuddha Realpolitik is an essential component of *kutayuddha*. *Kutayuddha* is the opposite of *dharmayuddha*. The basic assumption is that in war everything is free and fair. *Kutayuddha* is waged by

Glossary

a powerful king for no valid reason, but just for the sake of power. *Kutayuddha* is also waged by a weaker king when faced with a strong adversary against whom he cannot wage *prakasayuddha*. The conduct of *kutayuddha* is free from moral or ethical restraints. The techniques of *kutayuddha* involve covert actions, commando raids, assassination, abduction, terrorist activities, guile, treachery, *bheda*, misinformation, disinformation, biological warfare (use of poison, smoke, etc.), nocturnal attacks, ambushes, tactical retreat and flank attacks. One component of *kutayuddha* is *mantrayuddha*, which involves diplomatic coercion, deceit, etc. An extreme form of *kutayuddha* is *asurayuddha*, which means execution of the defeated king and absorption of his territory by the victor.

Labha Literal meaning: greed; it means acquisition of things not one's own

Lashkar-i-Islam Army of Islam

Lok Sabha Lower house of the Indian Parliament, which makes laws

Madhyama Middle kingdom in the *mandala*. The attitude of the ruler of this kingdom is crucial for the *vijigishu*'s strategy. If *madhyama* becomes neutral, then it would aid the *vijigishu*, but if the *madhyama* turns against the *vijigishu*, then the latter's plan to become the hegemon of the *mandala* would be unsuccessful.

Magadha Traditional name of central Bihar

Mahajanapada Big localities inhabited by people; the precursor of the state

Mahout Elephant driver

Mandala The circle of the state system. The term denotes the classical Hindu conception of the inter-state system. The classical Hindu scholars conceptualized the international state system as circular (like a wheel), with the *vijigishu*'s state located at the centre of the circle and surrounded by allies and enemy states.

Mansab The term signifies a rank in the Mughal bureaucracy

Mansabdar Holder of a *mansab*; a Mughal imperial official

Mantri Minister, a crucial component (*prakriti*) of the polity

Matsanya Literal meaning: a pond where smaller fishes are gobbled up by a big fish; this term refers to an intense power struggle in the international arena where, in accordance with the principle of 'might is right', the weaker polities are absorbed by the stronger polity

Maula Regular soldiers of the standing army; at times the military service among them became hereditary

Mitra Troops of an ally; at times also refers to a state in the *mandala* that is friendly to the *vijigishu*

Mlechchas Literal meaning: unclean, and in the eyes of the orthodox Hindu intellectuals the term refers to the 'barbarians'; this term was used to denote non-Hindu foreigners like the Sakas, Parthians and Huns who entered India between the beginning of the Common Era and the sixth century CE through the north-west frontier passes

Moksa Salvation/liberation; breaking free from the cycle of births as propounded in the *karma* theory

Mujahideen Jihadi, soldier of Islam who is ready to sacrifice his life in order to kill the infidels and further the cause of Islam

Namak Halali Namak means salt, and *halali* means loyalty; the term means loyalty to the salt-giver, i.e., employer

Nawab After the death of Aurangzeb in 1707, the Mughal provincial governors became independent and took the title of *nawab*

Nayaka Vassal chief turned military commander of the king's army; a *nayaka* is a semi-autonomous warlord

Palana Protection and maintenance of subjects in order to ensure sustained growth; an essential function of a just ruler

Panchhazari mansabdar A *mansabdar* holding a 5,000 *mansab*, meaning he was under the obligation of maintaining 5,000 cavalry soldiers for service with the emperor

Panchsheel Literal meaning: five principles; it refers to the five principles of Jawaharlal Nehru's foreign policy, which emphasized peace and amity with neighbours

Patti Foot soldier of ancient India

Paurusha Manliness, an important aspect of a just ruler; it also involves the sexual prowess of the ruler. *Paurusha* is a symbolic component of *danda*.

Prakriti Kopa Internal rebellion that occurs due to malfunctioning of one or more of the components of the state

Raj Literal meaning: rule; the term refers to the British government of India between 1750 and 1947

Rajadharma Duties of the *raja*, i.e., ruler. It is somewhat similar to *dandaniti* as practiced by a just ruler.

Rajan Leader of the tribe in the early Vedic age and later became *raja/nripati*, i.e., monarch

Rajukas Mauryan government officials

Raksas Literal meaning: demons; in the ancient period, the term referred to the non-Aryan, most probably Dravidian, people of the subcontinent. During the medieval era, the term referred to the Muslim invaders.

Raksha Protection of the subjects; it is the caste duty of the Kshatriyas/ Rajputs and an essential function of *rajadharma*

Glossary

Ramrajya Literal meaning: kingdom of Rama where milk and honey flowed; actually it is a metaphor for good governance, i.e., a country with a just government that takes care of the people, who have to pay very low taxes

Rashtra State/polity, i.e., mostly a monarchical state

Ratha Chariot

Rathin Warrior on the chariot

Sadhu Hindu holy man engaged in worshipping the gods and goddesses

Saktism Worship of the feminine principle of *sakti* (absolute power) in Hinduism

Samanta Hindu feudal lord of early medieval India

Samantaraja Warden of the marches/tributary or vassal chieftain at the frontier

Sandhi Alliance for peacemaking or to avert war; occasionally it involves appeasement of the stronger party by the weaker party

Saptanga According to classical Hindu theory, a state comprising seven elements (*prakriti*): monarch, ministers, territory and people, fort, army, allies and the treasury

Sarvapath sambhav A key tenet of Hinduism; it means that all the paths/ religions lead to the same goal, i.e., God

Sastra Sacred system of knowledge; also refers to brahmanical customs and laws

Sastrasala Arms production centre (factory/workshop) in ancient India

Sataghni Literal meaning: hundred killer; it was a sort of stone-throwing machine that was used during siege operations. It is probably a sort of catapult/ballista.

Satyagraha Love force or truth force based on *ahimsa*; in M. K. Gandhi's eyes, it is a just instrument for achieving *swaraj*

Sena Army, also referred to as *vahini*

Senapati Commander of the *sena*, i.e., general of the army

Seniya One who possesses a *sena*

Shanti Peace, the opposite of *ashanti*, which means disorder, chaos

Shih Strategic power

Shuddhi Purification rituals to bring the unclean (non-Hindus) into the fold of Hinduism

Sindhu River Indus

Sreni Mercenary soldiers belonging to the private guilds and trading corporations; in general, the duty of the *sreni* was to protect the trading centres, commercial routes and caravans. But during emergencies, the rulers also hired them.

xviii   *Glossary*

Srenibala Military levies provided by the guilds

Suba/Subah Mughal province administered by a *subadar* (provincial governor). Independent *subadar* took the title of *nawab*.

Suta Driver of the chariot

Swaraj Self-rule, independence

Tamraparni West Bengal

Tanzeem Islamic militant outfits operating in Kashmir

Tapas/Tapasya Ascetic practice involving yoga for gaining spiritual and mental power. Such ascetic practice, including meditation, results in increasing the power of concentration and some believe results in acquiring supernatural power.

Trivarga Three objectives of life: *dharma, artha* and *kama*

Turangas Equivalent to *mlechchas*; the term *Turangas* is applied to all the non-Hindu groups along north-west India including the Huns, Sakas, Parthians and even the Persians

Uchchhvasa Chapter

Udasina A polity in the *mandala* that is neutral towards the *vijigishu*

Upayas Various means or mechanisms or different techniques; at times the term also refers to different policies

Ura Centre of the army deployed on a battlefield

Vahini Equivalent to *sena*, i.e., an army

Vahlika Bactria; a region considered by the *acharya*s to be famous for its supply of horses

Varna Caste; an order in the traditional Hindu system

Vigraha Inter-state war

Vijigishu The ideal ruler, the would-be hegemon of the *mandala* system

Vishakanyas Vish means poison, and *kanyas* means young ladies; the term *vishakanyas* refers to high-class prostitutes (scarlet women) who functioned as spies. They were educated and experts in dancing and singing. In other words, they had the skills to operate in elite society. They acquired information from their powerful clients while making love. At times, they also functioned as secret assassins. They would murder their powerful clients by administering poison in their food and drink.

Vyasanas Calamities that can occur in a state; these calamities could be caused by either human or divine factors (beyond human control, natural calamities such as flood, famine)

Vyuha Literal meaning: array; it means deployment or formation of troops in a specified manner. It is somewhat equivalent to the modern order of battle, i.e., ORBAT.

Glossary   xix

Yajna Also known as *yagna*; it is a vedic ritual conducted by the Brahmins. This ritual involved the use of *ghee* (clarified butter) for lighting the fire and sacrificing an animal (probably a horse).

Yantra Literal meaning: machine; for the *acharya*s the term refers to siege machine like a *sataghni*

Yavanas The Ionians, i.e., Greeks; the Bactrian Greeks who invaded India during the Common Era and settled on the subcontinent are called Indo-Greeks by historians. The ancient Hindu intellectuals called them *yavanas*; they were also considered *mlechchas*.

Yogis Hindu ascetic monks who were experts in practicing yoga and had renounced the world

Yuddha Inter-state war, i.e., conventional warfare

Introduction

The dominant view among Western scholars is that pre-British India had no tradition of strategic thinking. There have been some sporadic attempts by Western commentators to flesh out military ethics based on examination of Hindu religious texts. What we lack is a consistent analytical narrative, taking into account the opinions of different Indian *acharyas* (teachers) who wrote commentaries on *vigraha* (war) and justice throughout the ancient and medieval eras. To give an example, very few Western scholars know that Kamandaka (sixth century CE) speaks of the interrelationship between righteous war, people's support and a stable government, long before Carl Von Clausewitz came up with his famous trinity. And Kautilya (third century BCE) is probably the first authority on biological warfare. Again, Kautilya, Manu (Common Era) and Kamandaka wrote about the interconnections between conventional warfare (*vigraha*) and insurgencies (*kopa*). Modern historians dealing with South Asia completely neglect the historical evolution of military-strategic thought on the Indian subcontinent. And political scientists mostly engage with Western theories while trying to analyze the contours of independent India's philosophy of warfare and nuclear gaming.

The objective of this volume is to trace the effect of Hinduism on the evolution of theories of warfare[1] in India from the dawn of civilization until the present era. The focus is to bring out the complex debate between *dharmayuddha* and *kutayuddha* within Hindu philosophy. It must be noted that these two concepts are mere abstract and ideal

---

[1] In this volume the term "theory of warfare" is considered equivalent to the philosophy behind warfare.

I

2   Hinduism and the Ethics of Warfare in South Asia

types, and in pure form have never existed or operated in history. The terms are to be understood as a heuristic device for clarifying certain trends in history. Somewhat like Carl Von Clausewitz's concept of absolute war/total war, *dharmayuddha* and *kutayuddha* are ideal concepts that can never actually be realized due to 'frictions' in the real world. In fact, the two above-mentioned Hindu concepts were never frozen in time. Rather, they have evolved through the last two millennia. For instance, the concept of *dharmayuddha* in the two epics (*Ramayana* and *Mahabharata* around 400 BCE) is quite different from the *dharmayuddha* concept that emerged in the *Manavadharmasastra* (*Laws of Manu*) composed around the Common Era. This book attempts to show how these two key concepts have emerged gradually throughout the last two millennia.

The debate revolves around four questions: what is war, what are the justifications for starting it, how it should be waged, and finally, what could be the possible repercussions of using organized violence? The tension between the Lokayata (i.e., empiricist/positivist/materialist) and non-materialist/spiritual traditions within *darsana* (Indian philosophy) needs to be chiseled out. Hence, the comparative analysis of different religious-cultural streams within the heterogeneous Hindu tradition is undertaken. This monograph partly takes into account the religious traditions that emerged within India (i.e., Buddhism and Jainism) as well as the foreign inputs (Islam and Christian militarism) and how they have shaped the traditional Hindu view of the relationship between warfare, politics and good governance.

During the late twentieth century, as a reaction to technological determinism and Euro-American pragmatism in warfare and strategy, the strategic culture approach has evolved. The strategic culture approach emphasizes cultural factors in order to explain the origins, conduct and results of warfare.[2] Jack Snyder defines strategic culture as 'the sum total of ideas, conditioned emotional responses and patterns of habitual behaviour that members of a national strategic community have acquired through instruction or imitation.'[3] Ken Booth defines strategic culture as a nation's traditions, values, attitudes, patterns of behaviour, habits, customs, achievements and particular ways of adapting to the

---

[2] William H. Mott IV and Jae Chang Kim, *The Philosophy of Chinese Military Culture* (Houndmills, Basingstoke: Palgrave, 2006), p. x.

[3] Quoted from Lawrence Sondhaus, *Strategic Culture and Ways of War* (London/New York: Routledge, 2006), p. 3.

Introduction

environment and solving problems with respect to the threat of the use of force. Strategic culture is important, writes Booth, in order to understand the actions of another country on its own terms. Strategic culture helps us to understand the motivations, self-image and behavioral patterns of a particular country. Booth goes on to say that we live in a created world and that strategic realities are in part culturally constructed as well as culturally perpetuated.[4]

Several military historians also highlight the interrelationship between culture and warfare. Jeremy Black says that throughout history not all societies have been driven merely by the motivation to come up with the most combat-effective military machines. In fact, the acceptance and adoption of new technologies are shaped by cultural factors. Culture shapes how societies understand loss and suffering, at both the individual and collective levels of the soldier and the society.[5] In fact, the concepts of defeat and victory are partially shaped by culture, and this influences the style of military combat. Warfare is a product of culture, and combat is in turn a major factor in shaping culture.[6] Along with culture, the social fabric also shapes organized violence.

In the South Asian context, during the pre-British era war offered an avenue of social mobility for men of the lower classes. Successful military leaders effected a permanent, often inheritable elevation of social and material position. This upward mobility of able military men increased the stability of the stratification system. Stephen Peter Rosen claims that internal divisions (stratifications) are carried over into the military organization spawned by the host society. A state may occasionally, writes Rosen, go for a military system that reflects the dominant structures of the society, and such a military organization is not always the most effective.[7]

Social structures may or may not vary across cultural boundaries. By contrast, the culturalists argue that the concept of a culture remains constant within the cultural boundaries. The strategic culture approach focuses on the strategic behaviour of nations. Such behaviour varies

---

[4] Ibid., p. 5.

[5] Jeremy Black, 'Series Preface', in Everett L. Wheeler (ed.), *The Armies of Classical Greece* (Aldershot: Ashgate, 2007), p. ix.

[6] R. Brian Ferguson, 'A Paradigm for the Study of War and Society', in Kurt Raaflaub and Nathan Rosenstein (eds.), *War and Society in the Ancient and Medieval Worlds: Asia, the Mediterranean, Europe and Mesoamerica* (Washington, DC: Centre for Hellenic Studies, distributed by Harvard University Press, 1999), p. 409.

[7] Stephen Peter Rosen, 'Military Effectiveness: Why Society Matters', *International Security*, vol. 19, no. 4 (1995), pp. 5, 6, 19.

4   *Hinduism and the Ethics of Warfare in South Asia*

because the subjective ideas of the strategic elites vary. Hence, different ideas about the same reality result in different behaviours. In other words, strategic culture theory attempts to explain the complex behaviour of small groups of powerful individuals.[8]

Warfare is the product of both social and cultural forces, and Hinduism is a sort of socio-cultural system. Azar Gat assumes that religion fosters social cohesion among particular communities and that this in turn enables the community to survive in the big bad world. In fact, religion can be seen as part of the defence mechanism of a community. Gat rightly states that scarcity is partly relative. Competition and violent conflict intensify when opportunities and abundance increase. The potential for violent behaviour is innate, but such behavior is also socially learnt. Pugnacity and pacifism can be habituated by experience.[9]

The cultural relativist thesis claims that rationality is the product of Western culture and is not applicable to the non-Western societies.[10] Christopher Coker asserts that the West is unique in secularizing warfare. Since the West has instrumentalized war, it has turned its back on the ritualized aspects of combat. However, for non-Western societies, violence remains the moral essence of the warrior. Taking the example of the *Bhagavad Gita*, Coker asserts that for non-Western warriors, violence is existential. War for them is as much achieving one's humanity as achieving the objective of the state, but this is not the case for modern Western soldiers.[11] Coker's view is dominant among Western military historians, the majority of whom assert that classical Greek civilization gave rise to the Western Way of Warfare, which was further refined in Roman and medieval times. The Western tradition of warfare, characterized by technological innovations, rationality, and the absence of religious and cultural ethics as regards the application of violence, gave the West global military superiority during the early modern era.[12] In recent times, the

---

[8] Ibid., pp. 7, 14.

[9] Azar Gat, *War in Human Civilization* (Oxford: Oxford University Press, 2006), pp. 55, 139.

[10] Victoria Tin-Bor Hui, *War and State Formation in Ancient China and Early Modern Europe* (New York: Cambridge University Press, 2005), p. 18. According to Ken Booth, cultural relativism is the ideal that advocates scientific detachment on the part of the analyst. Sondhaus, *Strategic Culture and Ways of War*, p. 3.

[11] Christopher Coker, *Waging War without Warriors? The Changing Culture of Military Conflict* (London: Lynne Rienner, 2002), pp. 6–7.

[12] Geoffrey Parker (ed.), *The Cambridge Illustrated History of Warfare: The Triumph of the West* (Cambridge: Cambridge University Press, 1995). See the Introduction by Parker and the two essays by V. D. Hanson in this edited volume.

Introduction

paradigm of a monolithic and homogeneous Western Way of Warfare has been challenged by several historians.[13]

A complex relationship between rationalism and warfare has also existed in non-Western cultures. It would be wrong to assume that warfare is merely a cultural expression in non-Western societies. Warfare has been both existential and instrumental in China, India and the Islamic polities throughout history. Andrew Scobell asserts that China has a dualistic strategic culture. One strand is a Confucian one, which is conflict-averse and defensive-minded, and another strand is *realpolitik*, one that favours military solutions and is offensively oriented.[14]

A similar dualistic tradition, as exemplified by *dharmayuddha* (moderate, non-military, defensive-oriented statecraft) and *kutayuddha* (*realpolitik* in nature and aggressive in orientation) is also present in Hinduism. Manoj Kumar Sinha asserts that in ancient India, the proponents of *dharmayuddha* generated laws of armed conflict based on humanitarian considerations in order to limit the suffering caused by war.[15] Unlike the *jihad* of Islam and the crusade of Christianity, there is no justification in the *dharmayuddha* tradition for war against foreigners of other faiths. Surya P. Subedi notes that the concept of *dharmayuddha* in Hinduism is directed against the evil, whether they are nationals or aliens.[16] In contrast, the proponents of *kutayuddha* focus on overt militarism.[17]

A RAND Corporation analyst, George K. Tanham, writes that the fatalism inherent in Hinduism has discouraged sustained long-term strategic planning by Indian rulers throughout history. Tanham implies that Hindu India has no tradition of strategic thought.[18] One modern Indian scholar has challenged Tanham by arguing that, India being a country with an oral culture, strategic lessons have been imparted orally from generation to generation over thousands of years.[19]

---

[13] John A. Lynn, *Battle: A History of Combat and Culture* (Oxford: Westview, 2003).

[14] Andrew Scobell, *China's Use of Military Force: Beyond the Great Wall and the Long March* (Cambridge: Cambridge University Press, 2003), p. 15.

[15] Manoj Kumar Sinha, 'Hinduism and International Humanitarian Law', *International Review of the Red Cross*, vol. 87, no. 858 (2005), pp. 285–6.

[16] Surya P. Subedi, 'The Concept in Hinduism of "Just War"', *Journal of Conflict & Security Law*, vol. 8, no. 2 (2003), pp. 342–3.

[17] Biren Bonnerjea, 'Peace and War in Hindu Culture', *Primitive Man: Quarterly Journal of the Catholic Anthropological Conference*, vol. 7, no. 3 (1934), pp. 35, 44–5.

[18] George K. Tanham, 'Indian Strategic Thought: An Interpretive Essay', in Kanti P. Bajpai and Amitabh Mattoo (eds.), *Securing India: Strategic Thought and Practice, Essays by George K. Tanham with Commentaries* (New Delhi: Manohar, 1996), pp. 72–3.

[19] Waheguru Pal Singh Sindhu, 'Of Oral Traditions and Ethnocentric Judgements', in ibid., p. 174.

6   *Hinduism and the Ethics of Warfare in South Asia*

By analyzing the treatises of famous Hindu *acharya*s, we can get some idea of the Hindu theoreticians' attitude towards just and unjust wars. This volume does not attempt to provide a textual analysis of the various religious and quasi-religious texts generated under the rubric of Hinduism over the last two millennia. The objective of this volume is to elucidate the complex interaction between the evolution of the philosophy of warfare and Hindu religious ethics in South Asia during the last two and half millennia. Further, this volume follows the 'history from the top' approach and concentrates on texts generated by the elite 'grand' tradition rather than on the little tradition of folklore, local cults and regional deities. This is because, as it will become evident in the following chapters, the strategic managers and warlords throughout South Asian history have been influenced by the grand tradition.[20]

This volume has a broad scope both geographically and temporally. The genesis of military ethics in South Asia is studied in a global context by comparing and contrasting the Indian case with those of other civilizations. Major trends will become visible when sweeping cross-cultural analysis is undertaken across temporal periods. This is necessary in order to tackle the argument put forth by several historians that a Western Way of Warfare emerged in classical Greece and is still functioning. Also, some Western scholars occasionally group the Chinese and Indian military cultures as an Eastern Way of Warfare, which is posited as the polar opposite of the Western Way of Warfare. In fact, this volume tries to show that numerous similarities as well as dissimilarities have existed between the Indian and Chinese military cultures, on the one hand, and the Indian and Western military cultures, on the other. Michael I. Handel, in making a comparative analysis of Carl Von Clausewitz's and Sun Tzu's views, reaches the conclusion that the basic logic of strategy, like that of political behaviour, is universal.[21] In this book, Indian theorists and military theories are compared to Chinese and Western political philosophers and military thinkers in order to show that the binary concepts of Western and Eastern traditions of warfare are faulty.

Rather than engaging in abstract theorizing, this volume will attempt to historicize each theorist. For instance, Kautilya operated at a time when the pan-Indian Mauyran Empire was at its zenith. Kamandaka, by

---

[20] The grand tradition is the high Sanskrit culture as exemplified by texts like *Arthasastra*, *Nitisara*, etc. generated by persons close to the seat of state power for an elite audience.

[21] Michael I. Handel, *Masters of War: Classical Strategic Thought* (1992; reprint, London: Frank Cass, 1996), p. xiii.

Introduction

contrast, functioned at a time when the Hindu civilization was facing military threat from the Central Asian nomads. Hence, Kautilya could afford to be more aggressive than the defensive-minded Kamandaka. Chunks of the writings of the various *acharyas* are included to give the reader a feel for the theorists' thinking patterns. Dating and assigning authorship to the various classical Hindu texts is almost impossible. This is because ancient authors put their own views in the third person, presenting them as said by earlier writers.[22] We know something about Herodotus, Thucydides, St. Augustine and so on, but next to nothing about Kautilya, Manu and the author of the epics. In fact, we are not even sure whether Manu, Narayana (the author of *Hitopadesa*) and others were real individuals or not. In *darsana*, unlike in Western philosophy, the individual is unimportant. The individual author is merely recording truth, that is, the word of God. Secondly, most of the ancient Sanskrit works were written after the sixteenth century.[23] This was due to the domination of the oral tradition in South Asia. Before the late medieval era, most works were transferred orally from generation to generation. Hence, scholars continue to debate about the level of interpolation. Further, Sanskrit scholars debate whether these works are the product of a single author or several authors. The debates regarding date and composition of classical Sanskrit works are of interest to Indologists and linguistic experts. To an extent, Homer's *Iliad* is also characterized by this problem. While one group says that the *Iliad* represents a work of the early classical era, others argue that the *Iliad* comprises several layers: one going back to the archaic Greek era, another to the heroic era, and so on.

China's strategic culture, say William H. Mott IV and Jae Chang Kim, has emerged over two millennia. The problem as regards ancient Chinese history is the uncertainty regarding dates, numbers and facts, and especially motives, perceptions and feelings. Dates are important because they establish a sequence of what precedes and what follows that allows some inferences not only about cause and effect but also about the evolution of strategic thinking.[24] Many scholars doubt whether Sun Tzu was a historical figure.[25] Similar doubts are raised about the historicity of the classical

---

[22] P. V. Kane, *History of Dharmasastra (Ancient and Medieval Religious and Civil Law in India)*, vol. 1, Part 1 (1930; reprint, Poona: Bhandarkar Oriental Research Institute, 1968), p. 195.

[23] Irfan Habib and Vijay Kumar Thakur, *A People's History of India*, vol. 3, *The Vedic Age and the Coming of Iron, c. 1500–700 BC* (New Delhi: Tulika, 2003), p. 1.

[24] Mott IV and Kim, *Philosophy of Chinese Military Culture*, p. xi.

[25] Hui, *War and State Formation in Ancient China and Early Modern Europe*, p. 19.

8   *Hinduism and the Ethics of Warfare in South Asia*

Indian thinkers such as Kautilya, Manu and Kamandaka. Mott IV and Kim assert that the Chinese chroniclers used numbers not as data but as a literary technique to convey impressions. The same could be applied to ancient and medieval India's chroniclers. Mott IV and Kim claim that the ancient thinkers have deliberately recorded fiction and poetry and that their works are not constrained by historical facts. Unlike Euro-American philosophies, Chinese strategic culture has conceptualized the state not as an abstract or legalistic notion but as an organic link between *tao* and people.[26] Ancient Hinduism also considered society and *rashtra* (state) as an extension of the cosmic order.[27]

Jitendra Nath Mohanty asserts that all the classical schools of Hindu philosophy accept the idea that knowledge leads to desire, desire to effort, effort to action and action to success or failure. Success occurs if the object has been correctly determined in knowledge. Mohanty goes on to say that to a large extent Indian philosophy is theoretical. At the same time, the Indian mind assumed, a priori, that knowledge of truth must be practically beneficial. In the *Vedanta*, *Samkhya* and much of Buddhist literature, it is emphasized that knowledge of reality, by dispelling ignorance, shall remove suffering. It is knowledge upon which they focus because only knowledge can remove ignorance; no amount of practice can.[28] Over time ideas emerged through discourse, but ideas also evolved through practice. Andrea M. Gnirs says that the written sources of ancient Egypt are not strictly historical but are characterized by a propagandistic tradition. These texts reflect an elite ideology and describe the world as it should be rather than as it is.[29] The same applies to the texts generated in ancient India.

The practical conceptions of warfare comprise grand strategy (what the Americans call national security policy), military strategy, military doctrine and tactics. Grand strategy includes both military and non-military elements like foreign policy (diplomacy), economic aspects of warfare and military strategy. Military strategy refers to the planning and actions related to the use of military assets for conducting warfare. Andrew Scobell defines military doctrine in the following words: 'military

---

[26] Mott IV and Kim, *Philosophy of Chinese Military Culture*, pp. xii, 19.
[27] Subedi, 'Concept in Hinduism of "Just War"', p. 341.
[28] Jitendra Nath Mohanty, *Theory and Practice in Indian Philosophy* (published for the Centre for Studies in Social Sciences, Calcutta, by K. P. Bagchi & Co.: Kolkata, 1994), pp. 6–7, 12–13.
[29] Andrea M. Gnirs, 'Ancient Egypt', in Raaflaub and Rosenstein (eds.), *War and Society in the Ancient and Medieval Worlds*, p. 76.

Introduction

doctrine is devised to prepare for the kinds of wars that the armed forces anticipate from the threat environment and national objectives defined by the security policy.'[30] Rajesh Rajagopalan writes that military doctrine also throws light on the kind of war the military expects to fight and the manner in which it trains its soldiers. Military strategy, Rajagopalan continues, specifies how a particular objective is to be reached and is conditioned by various environmental factors that include the balance of opposing forces, the capabilities of the respective commanders and geography.[31] Rajagopalan's definition of military doctrine appears too broad. And at the same time, Rajagopalan appears to be a realist and does not take into account the cultural ethos shaping doctrine and strategy. Military doctrine could be defined as a set of views on war and the principles concerning its conduct that are adopted by the military leadership and taught in the military academies and that provide the basis for war plans. It is fruitful to define military tactics much more inclusively as military thought and practice regarding combat on the battlefield.

The evolution of the philosophy of warfare has involved a continuous interaction between the material culture and the ideas generated by the intellectual elites of the society. The material culture comprises the technological base, the mode of production of the society and the structure of the polity. Constant dialogue has occurred between the techniques and tools of warfare and the ideas about why and how to conduct warfare. In other words, the evolution of the ethics of warfare in South Asia cannot be understood without understanding the war-making tools and techniques available to communities during particular periods.

The term "military ethics" refers to the norms of behaviour of armies and polities during wartime and the collective set of ideas that gave birth to such norms. The just war concept in Western philosophy comprises *jus ad bellum* (just resort to war) and *jus in bello* (rules about battlefield behaviour). Torkel Brekke asserts that, unlike Western theoreticians, Hindu writers took very little interest in matters of *jus ad bellum* and in particular the principle of right authority. He maintains that this was because the Hindu theoreticians made no distinction between private duels and public violence or between internal and external enemies. According to Brekke, this was because pre-modern Indian polities were amorphous structures with fuzzy territorial borders. The power

---

[30] Scobell, *China's Use of Military Force*, p. 45.
[31] Rajesh Rajagopalan, *Fighting like a Guerrilla: The Indian Army and Counterinsurgency* (London/New York/New Delhi: Routledge, 2008), pp. 36–7.

Hinduism and the Ethics of Warfare in South Asia

and influence of the various kings overlapped and interpenetrated in such a way that it was difficult to distinguish between internal and external affairs.[32] By contrast, this volume argues that the Hindu *acharyas* realized the complex and nuanced inter-linkages between state and non-state violence. Because the *acharyas*, unlike many Western theoreticians, realized the linkages and close intermeshing of *vigraha* (conventional warfare) and *kopa* (unconventional warfare/insurgency), this volume throws light on the theory and praxis of both inter-state and intra-state warfare.

Scholars studying the interconnections between religion and violence have to grapple with the problem of whether monotheism has been more prone to violence. Hans Kung claims that long before the advent of monotheism, the world was full of violence associated with religion and that there is no evidence that violence associated with religion has increased since the advent of the monotheistic religions.[33]

Hinduism is not a monotheistic religion. It has neither a single prophet nor a single church nor a single authoritative text. In fact, there are 330 million gods and goddesses in the Hindu pantheon. One Western scholar correctly asserts that there is no single coherent body of beliefs in Hinduism.[34] Even within Hinduism, various branches like Brahmanism, Vedantism, Vaishnavism, Shakti and Tantra co-exist. Many scholars have questioned whether the concept of religion should be applied at all in the case of Hinduism, which is a way of life. According to them, Hinduism as it is understood today evolved in the nineteenth century due to the interaction between a classification and categorization scheme introduced by the British colonial state, Western education and indigenous reform movements.[35] There is much truth in this assertion.

However, it cannot be denied that Brahmanism as it has evolved from the dawn of Aryan civilization in South Asia constitutes the core of Hinduism even today. Tanham, like Stephen Peter Rosen, accepts that the core of Hinduism is the caste system, which has continued to operate on the

---

[32] Torkel Brekke, 'The Ethics of War and the Concept of War in India and Europe', *NUMEN*, vol. 52 (2005), pp. 59, 61, 80.

[33] Hans Kung, 'Religion, Violence and "Holy Wars"', *International Review of the Red Cross*, vol. 87, no. 858 (2005), p. 255.

[34] Coker, *Waging War without Warriors?*, p. 141.

[35] Torkel Brekke, *Makers of Modern Indian Religion in the Late Nineteenth Century* (Oxford: Oxford University Press, 2002), pp. 1–52; Romila Thapar, 'Imagined Religious Communities? Ancient History and the Modern Search for a Hindu Identity', in David N. Lorenzen (ed.), *Religious Movements in South Asia: 600–1800* (2004; reprint, New Delhi: Oxford University Press, 2006), pp. 333–59.

Introduction 11

subcontinent throughout two millennia.[36] Broadly, Hinduism during different historical periods has been based on certain texts. During the vedic and epic periods, Hinduism evolved around the *vedas* and the *Bhagavad Gita*. From the Common Era onwards, along with the *dharmasastra* literature, *Manusamhita/Manavadharmasastra* played an important role in the evolution of Hinduism. After 900 CE, various commentaries on the abovementioned texts mainly shaped the growth of Hinduism. From the fifteenth century onwards, the two epics, *Ramayana* and *Mahabharata*, acquired religious significance. One can argue that Hinduism from 1500 BCE onwards is the dominant religion of most of the people living between the Indus River and the Arakan Yomas. Hinduism is an amalgam of various strands of philosophy as well as a religion (based on certain rituals, beliefs, etc). Hence, Hinduism is best described as a culture, a way of life, that is, *dharma*.

Throughout history, India has remained a multi-lingual, multi-ethnic and multi-religious society. Along with Hinduism, other religions like Buddhism, Jainism, Sikhism, Islam and Christianity continue to exist side by side. In the 1990s, about 83 percent of India's population was Hindu, 11 percent Muslim, 2.6 percent Christian and slightly over 3 percent Sikhs, Jains, Parsis and Buddhists combined.[37] As this volume shows, *acharya*s as well as the rulers and warlords of the ancient and medieval periods were aware of the pervasive influence of the brahmanical order. And in modern India, politicians of different hues (M. K. Gandhi, Jawaharlal Nehru, etc.) as well as generals acknowledge the influence of Hinduism in statecraft.

This volume, in seven chapters, shows the interconnections between Hinduism and the theory and praxis of warfare in South Asia from the collapse of Indus Valley civilization until today. Whether it involved the use of chariots or nukes, the statesmen and warlords of South Asia have taken into account the Hindu social and cultural ethos. Broadly, the theory of warfare has revolved around two poles: *dharmayuddha* and *kutayuddha*. These two concepts, as used in this book, are not strictly equivalent to just/holy war and unjust war. In fact, the meaning of the two concepts has changed with time and place.

The first chapter deals with the development of military ethics in the *vedas* and the two epics and the constraints it imposed on the conduct of warfare on the subcontinent. The second chapter shows the influence of

---

[36] Tanham, 'Indian Strategic Thought: An Interpretive Essay', p. 42.
[37] Mark Jurgensmeyer, *Religious Nationalism Confronts the Secular State* (1993; reprint, New Delhi: Oxford University Press, 1996), p. 81.

Buddhism and Jainism on the evolution of the Asokan policy of *dhamma*, which in turn challenged the 'realist' tradition of *kutayuddha*. Chapter 3 deals with Kautilya, the father figure of the *Kutayuddha* school of thought. Strands of ideas in Kautilya *Arthasastra* are compared to the realist and liberal philosophers and political philosophies of the West and ancient China. While Chapter 3 is an example of critical philosophy, the rest of the chapters are examples of critical history. Chapter 4 shows the evolution of the *dharmayuddha* and *kutayuddha* concepts between the Common Era and the coming of the Turks in the tenth century. This chapter starts with Manu's *Manavadharmasastra*. Manu led the brahmanical reaction against Kautilya's *kutayuddha*. Kamandaka's *Nitisara* offered a watered-down version of *kutayuddha*. Kamandaka realized that in the real world, a mix of *dharmayuddha* and *kutayuddha* is most desirable. Kamandaka was supported by Bana, who argues in *Harsacharita* that at times it is necessary even for a righteous ruler to wage some form of *kutayuddha*. This chapter concludes by discussing some regional literature (*Hitopadesa*, *Panchatantra*, *Kathasaritsagara*, etc.) and by comparing the Tamil *kural* to the Sanskrit texts generated in north India. Chapter 5 discusses the response of Hinduism to the establishment of Islamic rule on the subcontinent. The Hindu response evolved from confrontation with Islam to gradual adaptation and coexistence and at times collaboration with the Islamic polities. Chapter 6 shows how British and Indian nationalists used Hinduism for their own purposes. This chapter focuses both on militant Hinduism and on non-violence as enunciated by Gandhi. Interestingly, both groups derived their ideas from the vedic texts. Finally, in the last chapter, the legacy of ancient India's philosophy in post-independence India's conduct of conventional and unconventional wars is studied. Further, India's nuclear policy is analyzed through the lens of Hindu strategic thought.

Along with the quasi-secular manuals on statecraft written by the *acharyas*, this volume also utilizes the brahmanical literature. The Brahmins were traditional advisors to the Indian rulers and sometimes occupied the highest echelons of the bureaucracy. The main sources for our project are the religious and *niti* (legal) literature of the Hindus; fables like *Hitopadesa* and *Kathasaritsagara*; histories written by the Muslim scholars of medieval India; the memoirs of the British and Indian political and military elite; Indian Defence Ministry Reports, articles written by Indian military officers in the various service journals; plus military files available at India Office Records, the British Library in London, and the National Archives of India at New Delhi. Now, let us have a flashback to the beginning of 'Aryan' civilization in India.

I

Religious Ethics and the Philosophy of Warfare in Vedic and Epic India

1500–400 BCE

Historians have reconstructed the political history of the vedic and epic ages and philosophers have studied the metaphysical aspects of the same. In this chapter, the objective is to show the interrelationship between war making (an integral part of state formation) and the quasi-religious vedic and epic philosophy. The vedic age extends roughly from 1500 BCE to 600 BCE.[1] The *Rig Veda* is the first of the four *vedas* (the other three are the *Yajur*, *Sama* and *Atharva Vedas*, respectively).[2] The *Rig Veda* was probably composed between 1300 and 1000 BCE.[3]

There are problems involved in historicizing the society that the two epics, *Ramayana* and *Mahabharata*, represent, just as there are problems in historicizing Homer's *Iliad* and *Odyssey*. While some say that Homer's *Iliad* and *Odyssey* represent the Greek Dark Age or the eighth century BCE, others argue that Homer is representing multi-layered materials from different eras.[4] Tradition ascribes the authorship of *Ramayana* to Valmiki,[5] but about his background we know nothing, just as we draw a complete blank as regards the background of Vyasa, the so-called author of the *Mahabharata*. John Brockington writes that from an analysis of

---

[1] Bimal Kanti Majumdar, *The Military System in Ancient India* (1955; reprint, Calcutta: Firma KLM, 1960), p. 7.

[2] Irfan Habib (ed.), *A People's History of India*, vol. 3, Irfan Habib and Vijay Kumar Thakur, *The Vedic Age and the Coming of Iron, c. 1500–700 BC* (New Delhi: Tulika, 2003), p. 1.

[3] Rev. H. Heras, S.J., 'The Age of the Mahabharata War', *Journal of Indian History*, vol. 26, Part 1, serial no. 76 (1948), p. 4.

[4] Everett L. Wheeler, 'Introduction', in Wheeler (ed.), *The Armies of Classical Greece* (Aldershot: Ashgate, 2007), p. xxxi.

[5] Amal Sarkar, *A Study on the Ramayanas* (Calcutta: Ridhi, 1987), p. 5.

14 *Hinduism and the Ethics of Warfare in South Asia*

the style and subject matter, it is clear that the *Ramayana* is the work of a conscious artist who worked within the limits and in the spirit of a living epic tradition.[6] The Valmiki *Ramayana* is an epic poem of some 50,000 lines describing in Sanskrit verse the career of Rama, the prince of Kosala in Awadh (the eastern part of north central India). The poem is divided into seven *kandas* (books) that chronologically chart the career of Rama.[7] There are hundreds of manuscripts about the *Ramayana*; most of them date from the sixteenth century CE, and the oldest among them goes back to 1020 CE.[8] Brockington identifies five stages in the growth of *Ramayana*. Stage 1 extended from the fifth to the fourth century BCE, and during that stage about 37.1 percent of the *Ramayana* was composed. This constitutes the Valmiki *Ramayana*. Stage 2 extended from the third century BCE untill the first century CE, a stage during which about 34.05 percent of the text was composed. During both of these stages, the *Ramayana* was orally transmitted. Stage 3 extended from the first to the third century CE; during that stage about 24.57 percent of the *Ramayana* was written down. Stage 4 extended from the fourth to the twelfth century CE, and Stage 5 started after 1200 CE.[9] Tulsidas' *Ramayana* came into existence during the last stage.

It seems that the *Mahabharata* was composed in Sanskrit between the fifth and the third century BCE.[10] B. A. van Nooten says that the *Mahabharata* represents society as it was around 1400 BCE.[11] The *Mahabharata* is the longest poem in the world, with more than 100,000 verses and seven to eight times the length of the *Iliad* and *Odyssey* combined.[12] The core of the *Mahabharata* is an account of the combat

---

[6] John Brockington, 'Stereotyped Expressions in the *Ramayana*', in Greg Bailey and Mary Brockington (eds.), *Epic Threads: John Brockington on the Sanskrit Epics* (2000; reprint, New Delhi: Oxford University Press, 2002), p. 125.

[7] *The Ramayana of Valmiki: An Epic of Ancient India*, vol. 1, *Balakanda*, Introduction and tr. by Robert P. Goldman (1984; reprint, New Delhi: Motilal Banarasidas, 2007), Introduction, pp. 4–5.

[8] Greg Bailey, 'Introduction', in Bailey and Brockington (eds.), *Epic Threads*, p. xvii.

[9] John Brockington, 'Stages of Composition of the *Ramayana*: Table', in Bailey and Brockington (eds.), *Epic Threads*, p. 353.

[10] Surya P. Subedi, 'The Concept in Hinduism of "Just War"', *Journal of Conflict & Security Law*, vol. 8, no. 2 (2003), p. 341.

[11] B. A. van Nooten, 'Introduction', in William Buck, *Mahabharata* (1981; reprint, New Delhi: Motilal Banarasidas, 2006), p. xiv.

[12] Nick Allen, 'Just War in the *Mahabharata*', in Richard Sorabji and David Rodin (eds.), *The Ethics of War: Shared Problems in Different Traditions* (Aldershot: Ashgate, 2006), p. 138; Ramashankar Tripathi, *History of Ancient India* (1942; reprint, New Delhi: Motilal Banarasidas, 1999), p. 65.

Vedic and Epic India

between the Kurus and the Pandavas for the fertile land at the confluence of the rivers Jamuna and Ganga. The Kurus were a tribe living along the upper reaches of the Jamuna, and the Pandavas were a comparatively newly emergent clan based around Indraprastha, about sixty miles southwest of the Kuru capital, Hastinapura. With the passage of time, peripheral stories that provide a social, moral and cosmological background to the climactic battle were added. Both the *Ramayana* and the *Mahabharata* portray the actions of the warriors in a heroic and moral context. To an extent, the *Mahabharata* also represents, writes Nooten, a re-enactment of a moral confrontation at the cosmic level. The *Mahabharata* is a moral and philosophical as well as an historical tale. Occasionally, the gods interact with the humans, give them weapons, influence the outcome of battles, make love with the queens, and so on.[13] The great Rig Vedic deities were all anthropomorphic in conception (idealized in human and superhuman forms).[14] Similarly, in the *Iliad*, the gods in human shape interact with humanity and determine the winners and losers in battle.[15]

The *Bhagavad Gita* was composed around 200 BCE.[16] Angelika Malinar and Steven J. Rosen claim that the *Bhagavad Gita* was composed not independently but in relation to and even for the epic *Mahabharata*. The *Bhagavad Gita* became part of the epic in the course of its own textual history.[17]

THE MATERIAL CONTEXT

Let us review the material context in which the vedic and epic philosophy flourished. The art of manufacturing arrowhead from stone was invented during the Neolithic era.[18] The chalcolithic age witnessed the replacement of stone arrowheads with bronze (an alloy of nine parts copper and one part tin) and copper arrowheads, which were used for both fighting

---

[13] Nooten, 'Introduction', pp. xiii–xv, xix.

[14] Irfan Habib (ed.), *A People's History of India*, vol. 2, Irfan Habib, *The Indus Civilization* (New Delhi: Tulika, 2002), p. 71.

[15] Wheeler, 'Introduction', p. xxxviii.

[16] Manoj Kumar Sinha, 'Hinduism and International Humanitarian Law', *International Review of the Red Cross*, vol. 87, no. 858 (2005), p. 286.

[17] Angelika Malinar, *The Bhagavadgita: Doctrines and Context* (Cambridge: Cambridge University Press, 2007), p. 33; Steven J. Rosen, *Krishna's Song: A New Look at the Bhagavad Gita* (Westport, Connecticut: Praeger, 2007), p. 23.

[18] G. N. Pant, *Indian Archery* (1978; reprint, New Delhi: Agam Kala Prakashan, 1993), pp. 12, 16.

and hunting.[19] In the Indus Valley civilization (2500–1500 BCE), combatants used arrows made of bronze and copper,[20] and double-edged swords and socket-hole axes also appeared.[21] Spoked wheels that transformed transportation emerged in Central Asia between 1700 and 1500 BCE. The Indus Valley civilization used carts with solid wheels, and in India spoked wheels came into use around 700 BCE.[22]

Between 1000 BCE and 600 BCE, the Aryans moved from north-west India and Punjab to the Ganga-Jamuna doab.[23] The location of the Aryan homeland and the very meaning of the term "Aryan" have generated debate among scholars, and the Aryan question is yet to be resolved. Initially, scholars argued that the Aryans were Sanskrit-speaking people who entered India through the north-western passes around 1500 BCE. However, a minority group claims that the Aryans were indigenous to India and identical to the people of the Indus Valley civilization. The Dravidian languages were prevalent in north India prior to Sanskrit, and this tends to support the hypothesis that a Dravidian language was the language of the Indus Valley civilization. The most recent view is that the Aryans did not represent any particular race but was instead a language group. As this particular language group moved into India and the Aryan-speaking people intermixed with local people, the Aryan language (a variation of the Indo-European language group) absorbed a large number of local Dravidian words. And instead of invasion, scholars are now more comfortable speaking of slow and gradual migration resulting in intermingling of the various communities.[24]

Romila Thapar asserts that early vedic society was a lineage society. A lineage meant a corporate group of unilineal kin with a formalized system of authority. It had rights and duties and accepted genealogical relationships as the binding factor. The basic unit in this system was the extended family based on a three- to four-generation lineage controlled by the eldest male, who represented it on both ritual and political occasions. The lineage was based on the system of marriage alliances, involving the circulation of women and the exchange of wealth associated with

---

[19] Pant, *Indian Archery*, p. 17; Habib, *Indus Civilization*, pp. 5, 15.
[20] Pradeep P. Barua, *The State at War in South Asia* (Lincoln/London: University of Nebraska Press, 2005), p. 4.
[21] G. N. Pant, 'The Saga of Indian Arms', *Journal of Indian History*, Golden Jubilee Volume (1973), p. 246.
[22] Habib and Thakur, *Vedic Age*, p. 9.
[23] Majumdar, *Military System in Ancient India*, p. 12.
[24] Thomas R. Trautmann, 'Introduction', in Trautmann (ed.), *The Aryan Debate* (New Delhi: Oxford University Press, 2005), pp. xiii, xxvii, xxxvi–xxxvii.

Vedic and Epic India

it, residence patterns and the rights relating to the wealth produced by the family as an independent unit as well as in its relationship with the clan. The power of the chiefs during the early vedic age was mostly based on legitimacy through lineage. The later vedic age represented the transition from pastoralism associated with cattle rearing to settled agriculture. Iron technology was essential for clearing the marshlands and monsoon forests of the middle Gangetic Valley.[25] The importance of agriculture is emphasized in the *Ramayana* as Janaka says:

Now one time, as I was plowing a field, a girl sprang up behind my plow. I found her as I was clearing the field, and she is thus known by the name Sita....

Sprung from the earth, she has been raised as my daughter, and since she was not born from the womb, my daughter has been set apart as one for whom the bride-price is great strength.[26]

Sita is the wife of Rama and the tragic heroine of the *Ramayana*.

A number of families constituted a *grama*, and the *gramani* was the village headman. A number of *gramas* constituted a *vis* (clan). The *vispati* was the chief of the clan. A number of *vis* constituted a *jana* (tribe). The territory that a *jana* occupied was known as a *janapada*. The boundaries between *janapadas* were topographical barriers like forests, rivers, streams and hills.[27] The *rajan* was the leader of the tribe. The *rajan's* power was not absolute.[28] Some hymns of the *Atharva Veda* speak of the election of kings.[29] The terms *gopa* and *gopati* (lord of cows) were used for *raja*, who later came to be called *nripati* (lord of men). This reflected the shift from cattle as the principal form of wealth to the rising importance of agricultural labourers required for cultivation. The *raja* or chief was the successful leader of a raid and, by extension, of a battle. The booty acquired after a successful raid was distributed among the clan, but the distribution was unequal. The priestly families claimed a substantial amount of the booty on the grounds that their rituals ensured success in battle. The heroic ideal was thus comprised of bravery and generosity in gift-giving, which strengthened the *raja-purohita* alliance, with the two

---

[25] Romila Thapar, *From Lineage to State: Social Formations in the Mid-First Millennium BC in the Ganga Valley* (1984; reprint, New Delhi: Oxford University Press, 1990), pp. 10, 18, 23, 68.

[26] *The Ramayana of Valmiki*, vol. 1, *Balakanda*, p. 249.

[27] Thapar, *From Lineage to State*, pp. 30, 34, 47.

[28] Majumdar, *Military System in Ancient India*, pp. 10–11.

[29] M. R. V. Swamy, 'Vedic *Rajadharma*', in Dr. Michael (ed.), *The Concept of Rajadharma* (New Delhi: Sundeep Prakashan, 2005), p. 13.

18   *Hinduism and the Ethics of Warfare in South Asia*

groups legitimizing each other. The Kshatriyas acquired legitimacy from the Brahmins by giving *dana* (gifts) to the latter.[30]

The hymns of *Rig Veda* expound the evolution of *varna* (caste) society in vedic India:

When they divided the Man, into how many parts did they apportion him? What do they call his mouth, his two arms and thighs and feet?

His mouth became the Brahmin; his arms were made into the Warrior, his thighs the People, and from his feet the Servants were born.[31]

It is to be noted that the warriors represent the Kshatriyas; the people are the Vaisyas; and the servants refer to the Sudras, the lowest caste, who tilled the land.

NATURE OF WARFARE IN THE VEDIC AND EPIC AGES

We do not have any historical chronicle for reconstructing the nature of warfare during the vedic and epic ages. Basically, we have to depend on the epics, which depict awesome battles and gruesome deaths.[32] We must remember that the two epics are not historical texts. They are a mixture of ballads, legends and myths along with some elements of historical memory. Brockington says that Valmiki's *Ramayana* is not a religious epic. In fact, the *Ramayana* projects the view that religion is to a great extent a social duty, in keeping with the Kshatriya background.[33] The *Ramayana* focuses on truth, valour and Kshatriya virtues. Only later did Tulsidas' *Ramayana* portray Rama as a religious hero.[34] The sixth *kanda* of the *Ramayana*, named *Yuddhakanda*, describes in detail the combat between Rama's forces and the *raksas* (literally meaning 'demons', but in the context of the *Ramayana* 'non-Aryans', probably Dravidians). The two epics borrowed from each other. A large proportion of the stereotyped phrases found in the *Yuddhakanda* of *Ramayana* are also found in the *Mahabharata*.[35] To an extent, the information supplied by the two epics could be supplemented by archaeological findings.

---

[30] Thapar, *From Lineage to State*, pp. 25–6, 63.
[31] *The Rig Veda: An Anthology, One Hundred and Eight Hymns*, selected, tr. and annotated by Wendy Doniger O' Flaherty (1981; reprint, New Delhi: Penguin, 1994), p. 31.
[32] Nooten, 'Introduction', pp. xxi–xxii.
[33] John Brockington, 'Religious Attitudes in Valmiki's *Ramayana*', in Bailey and Brockington (eds.), *Epic Threads*, pp. 218, 249.
[34] John Brockington, 'Ramo dharmabhrtam varah', in Bailey and Brockington (eds.), *Epic Threads*, pp. 261, 264.
[35] Brockington, 'Stereotyped Expressions in the *Ramayana*', pp. 99, 121.

Vedic and Epic India

As regards the actual conduct of war during the vedic and epic eras, we have two different interpretations. U. P. Thapliyal is of the view that even in Rig Vedic times, the troops were arrayed in *vyuhas* (prescribed formations) before being led into war, and that the troops were adept at maneuvers such as attack, encirclement and assault.[36] Thapliyal asserts that the *Rig Veda* mentions the troops being organized in formations of tens, hundreds and thousands.[37] Thapliyal continues that on the opening day of the Mahabharata War, Yudhistira, the eldest brother of the Pandavas, favoured *suci-vyuha*, which was formed according to the military thinker Brihaspati's doctrine. The *suci-vyuha* was an array suited to a numerically inferior army fighting a numerically superior enemy.[38] In a somewhat similar vein, Bimal Kanti Majumdar says that a standing army emerged in India around 600 BCE.[39] Pradeep P. Barua writes that despite their stage-managed appearance, battles in ancient India were extremely bloody affairs.[40] By contrast, a recent view put forward mostly by Western scholars asserts that ancient Indian warfare was comprised of 'Flower Wars'.[41] The reality probably lies somewhere between these two extreme viewpoints.

Heroic duels abound in the epics. For instance, Parasurama challenges Rama in the following words: 'If I see that you have strength enough to put an arrow to this bow, then I shall challenge you to single combat, which is praised by men of might.'[42] Again, Rama kills Ravana, the chief of the *raksas* and the ruler of Lanka, in single combat.[43] At the same time, the *Ramayana* speaks of the *chaturanga bala* (four-limbed army comprising infantry, cavalry, chariots and elephants): 'He also gave them beautifully adorned and godlike troops, including elephants, horses, chariots, and

---

[36] U. P. Thapliyal, 'War in Ancient India – Concepts', in S. N. Prasad (ed.), *Historical Perspectives of Warfare in India: Some Morale and Material Determinants* (New Delhi: Motilal Banarasidas, 2002), p. 48.

[37] U. P. Thapliyal, 'Military Organization in the Ancient Period', in Prasad (ed.), *Historical Perspectives of Warfare in India*, p. 77.

[38] Thapliyal, 'War in Ancient India – Concepts', p. 53.

[39] Majumdar, *Military System in Ancient India*, p. 15.

[40] Barua, *State at War in South Asia*, p. 8.

[41] For instance, T. A. Heathcote writes that '[b]attle was considered to be merely a series of individual combats, with the courage and morale of the mass depending upon the visible performance of their leaders. If a leader fell … the rest made their escape as best as they could.' Heathcote, *The Military in British India: The Development of British Land Forces in South Asia, 1600–1947* (Manchester: Manchester University Press, 1995), p. 3.

[42] *The Ramayana of Valmiki*, vol. 1, Balakanda, p. 264.

[43] Ibid., vol. 1, Balakanda, p. 12.

20   *Hinduism and the Ethics of Warfare in South Asia*

foot soldiers.'[44] The *Mahabharata* frequently mentions *dvairatha* (chariot duels among the heroes).[45] The Rig Vedic age forces were comprised of *pattis* (foot soldiers) and *rathins* (chariot warriors).[46] The *chaturanga bala* probably emerged during the later vedic age or during the epic age.

The advent of the Aryans in India saw the use of iron in warfare, beginning around 1000–800 BCE. The Aryans' success against the non-Aryans in the Gangetic basin was primarily due to the use of bows, horse-drawn chariots and iron weapons.[47] The use of iron weapons, asserts Richard A. Gabriel, increased the frequency, scope and intensity of warfare. This is because the tin required to fashion bronze was costly and not easily available. By contrast, large quantities of iron weapons could be produced cheaply, iron deposits being easily accessible. The Assyrian army during the eighth century BCE was comprised of about 200,000 men. It was the first army in the world to be entirely equipped with iron weapons.[48]

Until 1200 BCE, Mycenaean war making was undertaken by light-armed skirmishers and missile men who clustered around chariots carrying men armed with javelins and bows.[49] Between 1200 BCE and 750 BCE, when the bronze age Mycenaean civilization collapsed – the period of the so-called Dark Age in Greece – warfare consisted of raids against neighbouring lands and coasts conducted by warrior bands under the leadership of local and regional leaders. In Archaic Greece (750–480 BCE), warfare consisted of private and semi-private raids for cattle and booty. Some fighting also involved contests among the *polis* (city-states) for control of the fertile borderland.[50] In Archaic Greek warfare, individual bravery mattered a lot; its role declined somewhat during the battles fought in the Hoplite warfare of the Classical Age.[51] Everett L. Wheeler writes that Greek warfare of the Dark Age and Geometric periods was

[44] Ibid., vol. 1, *Balakanda*, p. 263.

[45] John Brockington, 'Fashions in Formulae: Sanskrit Epic Tradition III', in Bailey and Brockington (eds.), *Epic Threads*, p. 344.

[46] Majumdar, *Military System in Ancient India*, p. 16.

[47] Habib and Thakur, *Vedic Age*, pp. 43, 88.

[48] Richard A. Gabriel, *The Great Armies of Antiquity* (Westport, Connecticut: Praeger, 2002), pp. 5–6, 20.

[49] Victor Davis Hanson, *The Wars of the Ancient Greeks* (1999; reprint, London: Cassell, 2000), p. 31.

[50] Kurt Raaflaub, 'Archaic and Classical Greece', in Raaflaub and Nathan Rosenstein (eds.), *War and Society in the Ancient and Medieval Worlds: Asia, the Mediterranean, Europe, and Mesoamerica* (Washington, D.C., Centre for Hellenic Studies, distributed by Harvard University Press, 1999), pp. 129, 131.

[51] Peter Krentz, 'Fighting by the Rules: The Invention of the Hoplite Agon', in Wheeler (ed.), *Armies of Classical Greece*, p. 122.

Vedic and Epic India

characterized by combat among small group of aristocrats who relied mainly on missile weapons and swords. In the *Iliad*, we find the heroes fighting by throwing spears at their opponents.[52]

The Aryans engaged in warfare in order to acquire captives, land and pasture for their cattle. The accumulation of cattle was known as *govisthi*. Most of the Aryans desired more cows.[53] The Panis were a wealthy non-Aryan tribe who frequently raided the Aryan settlements and carried away their cattle.[54] Among the Aryans, the winner of the cows is known as the *gojit*, which is an epithet for hero.[55] The Aryans also engaged in inter-tribal warfare. The *Dasarajna* (Battle of Ten Kings) was an engagement fought on the bank of the river Parusni (Ravi). Sudasa, the leader of the Bharata tribe, inflicted a defeat on a confederacy of ten kings. Many of the latter kings came from the north-west region of the subcontinent. Sudasa emerged victorious, and the Bharata tribe became predominant among the Aryans in India.[56] As regards close-quarter weapons, the *Ramayana* says of Parasurama: 'With his battle-axe slung over one shoulder'.[57] Combat in the Battle of Ten Kings (500 BCE?) involved encounters between chariots and foot soldiers equipped with axes, with both parties also trying to alter the course of the river by constructing earthen embankments and cutting channels.[58]

Combat in vedic and epic India was not merely a clash between indisciplined masses that milled around the heroes in *rathas*. Training of the warriors was carried out in the *asramas* under the direction of the *rishis* (warrior sages).[59] The *Shiva Dhanurveda* (the science of archery) was composed around 600 BCE.[60] Both Rama (the Aryan hero of *Ramayana*) and Arjuna (the star warrior of the Pandavas in *Mahabharata*) wreaked havoc among their enemies with the aid of archery.[61] The mace was the

---

[52] Everett L. Wheeler, 'Ephorus and the Prohibition of Missiles', in Wheeler (ed.), *The Armies of Classical Greece*, pp. 169–70.

[53] Majumdar, *Military System in Ancient India*, p. 7; Habib and Thakur, *The Vedic Age*, p. 15.

[54] V. M. Mohanraj, *The Warrior and the Charioteer: A Materialist Interpretation of the Bhagavad Gita* (New Delhi: LeftWord, 2005), p. 24.

[55] Thapar, *From Lineage to State*, p. 24.

[56] Majumdar, *Military System in Ancient India*, pp. 8–9.

[57] *The Ramayana of Valmiki*, vol. 1, *Balakanda*, p. 264.

[58] R. N. Nandi, 'Aryan Settlements and the *Rig Veda*', *Indian Historical Review*, vol. 21, nos. 1–2 (1994 and 1995), p. 24.

[59] U. P. Thapliyal, 'Weapons, Fortifications and Military Training in Ancient India', in Prasad (ed.), *Historical Perspectives of Warfare in India*, p. 125.

[60] Pant, *Indian Archery*, p. 5.

[61] Pant, 'Saga of Indian Arms', p. 248.

22 *Hinduism and the Ethics of Warfare in South Asia*

direct descendant of the club. The defenders of Catal Huyuk around 6000 BCE used it.[62] *Gadas* (maces) are mentioned in the *Mahabharata*.

The hymns of the *Bhagavad Gita* vividly describe the battlefield of Kurukshetra in all its glory and grandeur just before combat started. The hymns of *Rig Veda* describe the heroic warrior armed with bow and arrow going to the battlefield on his *ratha* (chariot).[63] The bow was made from bamboo, cane or wood. It was composed of a stout staff bent into a curved shape and a bowstring made of a strip of cowhide. During the vedic period, the bowstring was drawn back to the ear, whereas in Homeric Greece the bowstring was drawn to the breast before discharging the arrow.[64] Pachugopal Bhattacharya claims that the *Ramayana* informs us that Rama used *narach* (iron arrows) against Ravana, the *raksa* (non-Aryan, probably Dravidian) ruler of Lanka.[65]

In China, during the Western Zhou period (1045–770 BCE), the warrior elites primarily used bows and arrows.[66] The Assyrians were using composite bows around 2200 BCE. The composite bow generated greater power from a shorter draw. Arrows shot from the composite bow were able to penetrate leather armour. The composite bow spread to Palestine around 1800 BCE and then into Egypt around 1700 BCE. The Egyptian bow had a central wooden core with thin strips of horn and leather laminated onto it. Gabriel asserts that the killing power of the composite bow was further enhanced by the Egyptian innovation of placing the archer in a chariot.[67]

In the eighteenth century BCE, the Mesopotamian states introduced horse-drawn chariots. The Egyptian chariot was constructed of a light wooden frame covered by stretched fabric or hide. The platform that supported the driver and the warrior was made of stretched leather thongs covered with hide. Two horses, held by a central yoke pole, pulled the vehicle. In addition to bows, the warriors also carried axes, spears and quivers filled with arrows. The Egyptian chariot was mainly a mobile firing platform.[68] By contrast, the Hittite chariot was heavier as it was used

---

[62] Gabriel, *Great Armies of Antiquity*, p. 51.
[63] *The Bhagavad Gita*, tr. from the Sanskrit with an Introduction by Juan Mascaro (London: Penguin, 1962), p. 3.
[64] Pant, *Indian Archery*, pp. 21, 245.
[65] Pachugopal Bhattacharya, *Ramayana Yuddhbidhya* [in Bengali] (Kolkata: Sanskrit Pustak Bhandar, 1399), pp. 34–5, 40–1. Translation by the author.
[66] Robin D. S. Yates, 'Early China', in Raaflaub and Rosenstein (eds.), *War and Society in the Ancient and Medieval Worlds*, pp. 18–19.
[67] Gabriel, *Great Armies of Antiquity*, pp. 28, 57, 67.
[68] Ibid., pp. 52, 65, 78.

Vedic and Epic India

as a shock weapon; it was designed to shatter enemy formations using the sheer weight of the vehicle.[69] The warrior in Hittite chariot was armed with a six-foot-long stabbing spear. The crew also dismounted and functioned as infantry and engaged in close-quarter combat.[70]

Around 500 BCE, chariots entered China from Mesopotamia through Central Asia.[71] However, Edward L. Shaugnessy asserts that chariots had already entered China from trans-Caucasia around 1200 BCE. The horses were fastened to the yoke saddle by leather straps that ran across the neck of the horse and also to its mouth. The harness was joined at the mouth with a bit and cheek pieces, usually made of iron or bone or horn. By the second half of the ninth century BCE, China witnessed mass chariot battles, which also occurred in the Middle and Near East.[72] Chariots were also used in Homeric battles.[73]

The Rig Vedic *ratha* was a two-wheeled vehicle. The body of the *ratha* was light and consisted of a wooden framework fixed on an axle tree and fastened by cowhide thongs. The pole of the chariot was attached to the middle of the axle, and at the end of the pole was the yoke. The yoke was placed at the neck of the horses. The reins were fastened to the bit in the horse's mouth. By the fourth century BCE, the Aryans on the subcontinent used the bit, but not the curb bit as the *suta* (chariot driver) directed the horse using a spike outside (i.e., behind the jaw). The *suta* controlled the horses with the reins and spurred them on with a whip. Initially, solid wheels were used, but gradually wheels with spokes replaced them. The vedic war chariot carried a *rathin* (warrior) and a *suta*.[74] Some of the epic war chariots were big, as each of them was pulled by four horses. A flagstaff was attached to the *ratha* where the standard of the hero warrior was tied.[75]

Unlike the *Rig Veda*, the *Mahabharata* describes the use of elephants in warfare.[76] The *Yajur Veda* (composed between 900 and 800 BCE) describes

---

[69] Doyne Dawson, *The First Armies* (London: Cassell, 2001), p. 122.

[70] Gabriel, *Great Armies of Antiquity*, p. 79.

[71] Yates, 'Early China', p. 11.

[72] Edward L. Shaugnessy, 'Historical Perspectives on the Introduction of the Chariot into China', in Peter Lorge (ed.), *Warfare in China to 1600* (Aldershot: Ashgate, 2005), pp. 1–39.

[73] A. M. Snodgrass, 'The "Hoplite Reform" Revisited', in Wheeler (ed.), *Armies of Classical Greece*, p. 10.

[74] Pant, *Indian Archery*, p. 265; Thapliyal, 'Weapons, Fortifications and Military Training in Ancient India', p. 108.

[75] Pant, *Indian Archery*, p. 266.

[76] Ibid., p. 279.

24   *Hinduism and the Ethics of Warfare in South Asia*

the taming of elephants.[77] The epic's warriors would shoot arrows at their enemies from the backs of the elephants.[78] The *Mahabharata* tells us that the inhabitants of Magadha were famous for fighting from the backs of elephants, while the *Yavana*s (unclean foreigners, i.e., Central Asian steppe nomads) and Kambojas (i.e., people from Afghanistan) were good cavalry soldiers. And the south Indians were good as swordsmen.[79]

The vedic and epic age forces were not all-weather forces. In the *Ramayana*, autumn and winter are considered the best seasons for campaigning.[80] Peter Krentz says that battles conducted by the farmers in Archaic Greece occurred during summer only.[81] The pay of the soldiers was comprised of booty collected from the defeated enemy.[82] We are not sure about the nature of the armour used by the vedic and epic warriors. Ramashankar Tripathi claims that the vedic and epic warriors used coats of mail and metal helmets.[83] By way of comparison, it might be mentioned that the Celts introduced iron chain mail armour around the third century BCE.[84] The *Ramayana* mentions that Rama's father, Dasaratha, settled artisans in his kingdom for the purpose of manufacturing weapons. And the *Mahabharata* refers to artisans being supplied with raw materials for manufacturing weapons by the rulers.[85] Communication on the battlefield was an important aspect of warfare. The *dundubhi* was used during the vedic period. The *Atharva Veda* says that it was made of wood and covered with either cowhide or deer skin. The conch came into existence during the later vedic age.[86] The hymns of the *Bhagavad Gita* note that conch shells and drums were used for signaling purposes on the battlefield.[87]

The battering rams used for overcoming fortifications came into existence around 2500 BCE. Spear blades were attached to long beams which allowed stones to be pried loose from a wall until it was breached. The

---

[77] Habib and Thakur, *Vedic Age*, pp. 49, 65. D. D. Kosambi, in *The Culture and Civilisation of Ancient India in Historical Outline* (n.d.; reprint, New Delhi: Vikas, 2001), p. 85, puts the date of composition of *Yajur Veda* around 600 BCE.

[78] Pant, *Indian Archery*, p. 201.

[79] Thapliyal, 'Military Organization in the Ancient Period', p. 70.

[80] Ibid., p. 84.

[81] Krentz, 'Fighting by the Rules', p. 115.

[82] Thapliyal, 'Military Organization in the Ancient Period', p. 81.

[83] Tripathi, *History of Ancient India*, p. 33.

[84] Gabriel, *Great Armies of Antiquity*, p. 21.

[85] Thapliyal, 'Military Organization in the Ancient Period', p. 82.

[86] U. P. Thapliyal, 'Early Indian Heraldry and Ceremonials', in Prasad (ed.), *Historical Perspectives of Warfare in India*, pp. 143, 145.

[87] *Bhagavad Gita*, p. 4.

Vedic and Epic India

Hittites used the technique of building an earthen ramp at a low spot on the wall and then rolling large covered battering rams into place. The Assyrians constructed large wooden siege towers, taller than the defensive walls, and used archers in the siege towers to provide covering fire for the crews of the battering rams working below. The Assyrians also used scaling ladders to insert assaulting parties across the wall.[88]

The Indus Valley civilization's system of warfare was defensive in nature and relied mostly on fortifications.[89] Defensive walls were present at various Indus Valley civilization sites (Kot-Diji, Kalibangan, etc.). Sundried bricks as well as bricks hardened by fire were used for building the citadel walls.[90] In general, the walls were raised by laying the bricks either in mud or in both mud and gypsum mortar.[91] The Dravidians (the *Dasas* and *Dasyus* of the vedic and epic literature) constructed forts consisting of ramparts of hardened earth with palisades and ditches.[92] Some of the forts constructed by non-Aryans inside India were also made of stone and unbaked bricks.[93] The *raksas*, the enemies of the Aryans (says the *Ramayana*) were familiar with urban culture.[94] Canto 58 of *Kiskindhakanda* of the *Ramayana* says: 'On a well known island in the sea, situated at a distance of full one hundred *yojanas* [eight hundred miles] from this shore, lies the lovely city of Lanka, constructed by Viswakarma [the architect of the gods], abounding in wonderful gates of Jambunada [gold found on the banks of the Jammu River] and stately mansions of golden hue with terraces of gold and enclosed by a massive fortification wall bright as the sun.'[95] In contrast to the conduct of land battles, the siege warfare of the Aryans was quite brutal. It involved setting fire to the walls of the enemy forts. The *Rig Veda* mentions *pur charisnu*, which means a mobile engine used for assaulting strongholds. It was probably a battering ram.[96]

As regards pre-Mauryan warfare in India, Barua claims: 'These stagnant battle tactics differed dramatically from the lessons being learned

---

[88] Gabriel, *Great Armies of Antiquity*, p. 15.

[89] Barua, *State at War in South Asia*, p. 4.

[90] Habib, *Indus Civilization*, pp. 12, 34–5.

[91] Tripathi, *History of Ancient India*, p. 17.

[92] Thapliyal, 'Weapons, Fortifications and Military Training in Ancient India', p. 115.

[93] Habib and Thakur, *Vedic Age*, p. 17.

[94] Sarkar, *Ramayanas*, p. 7.

[95] *Srimad Valmiki-Ramayana (with Sanskrit Text and English Translation)*, Part I [*Balakanda, Ayodhaykanda, Aryanyakanda and Kiskindhakanda*] (1969; reprint, Gorakhpur: Gita Press, 2001), verse 19, p. 927.

[96] Majumdar, *Military System in Ancient India*, pp. 17, 19.

26   Hinduism and the Ethics of Warfare in South Asia

outside India and could only develop in sheltered isolation from external influences.'[97] In fact, the somewhat choreographed nature of Indian land warfare was also due to the complex philosophy of warfare developed in the religious and quasi-religious texts, an issue that is the subject of the next section.

MILITARY ETHICS IN THE *VEDAS* AND THE EPICS

W. R. Connor writes in the context of early Greek warfare:

Military conduct in many cultures is governed by elaborate codes or standards of behaviour; it can also be encoded in another and more interesting sense – as an encapsulation of social roles and values. Such codes may represent relationships within the society and sometimes help resolve conflicts and tensions between social groups or values.... The code was incorporated in a series of unwritten "laws of the Greeks", widely recognized, although not universally followed.[98]

The same assertion, as we will see, could be made in the case of warfare as depicted in the *Ramayana* and the *Mahabharata*.

In Homer's Trojan War, ambassadors were traditionally priests, and they were considered to be immune from harm. Battles were followed by the burial of the dead.[99] In Homer, we find *monomachia* (a duel of the champions). The general rule was that heroes would throw spears at each other before closing in for close-quarter combat with swords.[100] Border wars between the *polis* were also decided by duels among the champions or by duels among a limited number of individuals from both sides.[101] There was continuous tension in Classical Greek warfare as to whether the contest would be an *agon* (regulated contest) or a *polemos* (in which each side acted as it saw fit). In response to numerous wars and political violence, Isocrates became the chief proponent of Panhellenism, which attempted to limit warfare among the Greeks and to direct aggression against the 'barbarian' Persia. Plato in his *Republic* emphasizes that when fighting among themselves the Greeks should not

---

[97] Barua, *State at War in South Asia*, p. 8.

[98] W. R. Connor, 'Early Greek Land Warfare as Symbolic Expression', in Wheeler (ed.), *Armies of Classical Greece*, p. 99.

[99] G. Scott Davis, 'Introduction: Comparative Ethics and the Crucible of War', in Torkel Brekke (ed.), *The Ethics of War in Asian Civilizations* (London/New York: Routledge, 2006), p. 3.

[100] Wheeler, 'Ephorus and the Prohibition of Missiles', p. 171.

[101] Wheeler, 'Introduction', p. xxxiii.

Vedic and Epic India

enslave their defeated opponents and should not hinder the burial of their dead enemies.[102] In Connor's view, there was a tacit understanding among the *polis* that ambush and surprise should not be resorted to. Surprise attack (*apate*) was considered deception and thus illegitimate. The hoplite forces of the opposing cities decided where and when to meet and fight it out.[103]

The ethics of war in Judaism emphasize that fruit trees should not be cut during sieges. Norman Solomon rightly says that this norm reflects not only environmental concern of the besieging army and the besieged but also the prudential motive of not destroying the food resources required by the combatants themselves.[104] In ancient Chinese literature, the concept of *yi bing* reflected the notion of just or justifiable war. The *yi bing* concept emerged between the fifth and the second century BCE. According to this concept, war is considered necessary and proper as long as it is used by a legitimate ruler to curb violence. And war is resorted to only when a ruler's policy based on benevolence and justice has failed.[105] Frank A. Kierman Jr. writes that the ancient Chinese military code of conduct valued restraint and humanity even in the midst of war.[106]

By contrast, the political ideology of ancient Egypt represented the inhabitants of the outside world as evil, hostile and cowardly by nature, a constant threat to Egypt and the cosmic order it represented. The superiority of the Egyptian polity was emphasized. As a result, warfare was not ritualized. Against outsiders, writes Andrea M. Gnirs, the Egyptians followed the techniques of 'Total War', which involved a scorched-earth policy and large-scale deportation of hostile populations.[107]

As regards ancient Hindu India, Torkel Brekke asserts that the two epics, *Ramayana* and *Mahabharata*, espouse the heroic ideal. He goes on to say that in the Hindu epics there is a lack of clear-cut rules for conducting just war. And the Hindu epics, unlike the works of European writers, did not differentiate between violence projected against external

---

[102] Wheeler, 'Ephorus and the Prohibition of Missiles', pp. 179–80.

[103] Connor, 'Early Greek Land Warfare as Symbolic Expression', pp. 91–2.

[104] Norman Solomon, 'The Ethics of War in Judaism', in Brekke (ed.), *Ethics of War in Asian Civilizations*, p. 40.

[105] Mark E. Lewis, 'The Just War in Early China', in Brekke (ed.), *Ethics of War in Asian Civilizations*, pp. 185, 188.

[106] Frank A. Kierman, Jr., 'Phases and Modes of Combat in Early China', in Kierman Jr. and John K. Fairbank (eds.), *Chinese Ways in Warfare* (Cambridge, Massachusetts: Harvard University Press, 1974), p. 45.

[107] Andrea M. Gnirs, 'Ancient Egypt', in Raaflaub and Rosenstein (eds.), *War and Society in the Ancient and Medieval Worlds*, pp. 72–3.

28   *Hinduism and the Ethics of Warfare in South Asia*

and internal enemies.[108] As regards the duties of the king in *Mahabharata*, Brekke continues, there is no clear discussion of the right authority to initiate war or of what constitutes a just cause for war. On the other hand, the means by which the war is fought (i.e., *jus in bello*) is important in the epic worldview because war is the private business of the heroes. The epics do not differentiate between public violence (war proper) and private duels. In fact, the Mahabharata War is a conglomeration of heroic duels.[109]

In the earlier section, we have seen that vedic and epic age warfare was something more complex than heroic duels. And the following discussion shows that the ancient Hindu concept of war as regards its causes, courses and consequences is much more complex, involving an amalgamation of the public and private spheres, the individual ethos and collective duty simultaneously. Discussions of the ethics of war and peace are found in the *Udyogaparva* (the fifth book of the *Mahabharata*) and the *Bhagavad Gita*.[110]

In the vedic and epic literature, the concept of *dharmayuddha* (just war or civilized warfare) is elaborated, and some traces of *kutayuddha* (unjust war) can also be found. The issue of *dharmayuddha*, writes M. A. Mehendale, depends on both the ends and the means. In general, fighting against injustice is *dharmayuddha*.[111] Bhisma, the senior advisor in the court of the Kauravas in the *Mahabharata*, says that a just cause is based on truth and that this can only lead to victory in war.[112]

It could be argued that *dharmayuddha* is concerned with the just causes for waging war, the just means to be employed while waging war and also with the establishment of a just peace after the war. The *Mahabharata* classifies warfare into two categories: *dharmayuddha* and *asurayuddha* (equivalent to *kutayuddha*). The *Mahabharata* notes the conditions that lead to a *dharmayuddha*. War is to be resorted to only as a last option, when all the other paths are closed. Initially, the aggrieved party has to go for *sama* (peaceful conciliation), and then he should try to create *bheda* (internal dissension) among the enemy camp. Some contingents within

---

[108] Torkel Brekke, 'Between Prudence and Heroism: Ethics of War in the Hindu Tradition', in Brekke (ed.), *Ethics of War in Asian Civilizations*, pp. 113, 115, 119.
[109] Torkel Brekke, 'The Ethics of War and the Concept of War in India and Europe', *NUMEN*, vol. 52 (2005), pp. 72–3.
[110] Malinar, *The Bhagavadgita: Doctrines and Contexts*, p. 34.
[111] M. A. Mehendale, *Reflections on the Mahabharata War* (Shimla: Indian Institute of Advanced Study, 1995), p. 2.
[112] Buck, *Mahabharata*, p. 355.

Vedic and Epic India

the enemy camp are also to be won over through *dana* (in this context the term means bribery and not a gift). Only then, if the enemy does not turn around, should the option to use *danda* (force) be considered.[113] Both the *Ramayana* and the *Mahabharata* show that war broke out after the aggrieved party failed to negotiate a compromise peace. Rama's wife, Sita, was abducted by Ravana. Then Rama sent a *duta* (ambassador) to Ravana requesting that he return Sita. When Ravana refused, Rama decided to invade Lanka. Similarly, Krishna, acting as a *duta* of the Pandavas, requested that Duryodhana, the chief of the Kauravas, hand over at least five villages to the five Pandava brothers. Duryodhana refused, and the Pandavas then decided that the only option before them was to fight it out.[114]

To recover the unlawfully usurped kingdom even if it means having recourse to violence and slaying the enemy in battle is an example of *dharmayuddha*, according to the *Mahabharata*.[115] *Dharmayuddha* could also be resorted to for the protection of a kingdom's subjects. Rama and Bhisma say that the king should take one-sixth of the produce to provide revenue for the purpose of protecting the people under him.[116] Both the *Ramayana* and the *Mahabharata* discuss the evils that result if a king fails to protect his subjects properly.[117] The principal duty of the Kshatriyas, in accordance with *rajadharma* (the duties of the ruler), was to punish the wicked and protect the good, and this policy was controlled, regulated, supported and guided by the Brahmins. It was the duty of the Brahmins to define and interpret *dharma* (the Hindu code of conduct). And the Kshatriyas had to implement the rules and regulations laid down by the Brahmins in accordance with *dharma*.[118] Since the *Mahabharata* was largely composed by Brahmins, the peripheral quasi-historical stories also emphasize the power and glory of the Brahmins.[119] The pursuit of *rajadharma* (the duties of the king, which involved fighting) in turn legitimized the power structure of the Kshatriyas.[120]

---

[113] Allen, 'Just War in the *Mahabharata*', p. 140.
[114] Indra, *Ideologies of War and Peace in Ancient India* (Hoshiarpur: Vishveshvaranand Institute Publications, 1957), p. 40.
[115] Mehendale, *Reflections on the Mahabharata War*, p. 1.
[116] C. Rajendran, '*Rajadharma* according to *Mahabharata*', in Michael (ed.), *Concept of Rajadharma*, p. 37; Brockington, '*Ramo dharmabhrtam varah*', p. 259.
[117] John Brockington, 'Stereotyped Expressions in the *Ramayana*', in Bailey and Broockington (eds.), *Epic Threads*, p. 122.
[118] Swamy, 'Vedic *Rajadharma*', p. 14.
[119] Nooten, 'Introduction', p. xvi.
[120] Swamy, 'Vedic *Rajadharma*', p. 14.

Participation in *dharmayuddha* was considered meritorious, and a victory in it was regarded as a matter of honour.[121] The *varna* system developed in the later vedic age. Due to the *varna* system, only the Kshatriyas could bear arms. So Hindu *dharma* never conceptualized the entire body of people in a Hindu polity as a general levy.[122] By contrast, the armies of the *polis* could be described as the citizen body under arms.[123] Athenian citizens were liable for military service from the age of eighteen to sixty.[124] Participation in *dharmayuddha* was confined only to the Kshatriyas.

In the *Ramayana*, Rama is considered the best upholder of *dharma*.[125] For Rama, *dharma* is truth and one's duty in life.[126] *Dharma* is referred to as *rita* (standing upright) in the *vedas*. It encompasses all the good actions that are required to support the cosmic order against the evil forces threatening that order.[127] The concept of *dharma* underwent modifications in the epics. Sita comes up with the doctrine of *ahimsa*, saying that it is not necessary to attack the *raksas*. Then Rama explains that his *dharma* is to protect the Brahmin sages from the depredations of the *raksas*.[128] Nooten claims that *dharma* in the *Mahabharata* is the doctrine of the religious and ethical rights and duties of each individual. At times, *dharma* might refer to duty as ordained by religion, but it also means simply virtue or right conduct. So one would have caste *dharma* (in accordance with one's hereditary occupation), personal *dharma* (in accordance with one's age), and so on.[129] *Dharma* means maintenance of the correct social order (i.e., *varna* society), and for the Kshatriyas *dharma* also means maintenance of political stability.[130]

Mehendale defines *dharmayuddha* as war fought as a duty (*dharma*) by a Kshatriya.[131] *Kshatra* means valour.[132] In the vedic age, death on the

[121] Thapliyal, 'Military Organization in the Ancient Period', p. 89.
[122] Majumdar, *Military System in Ancient India*, pp. 14–15.
[123] Matthew F. Trundle, 'Identity and Community among Greek Mercenaries in the Classical World: 700–322 BCE', in Wheeler (ed.), *Armies of Classical Greece*, p. 484.
[124] Ronald T. Ridley, 'The Hoplite as Citizen: Athenian Military Institutions in Their Social Context', in Wheeler (ed.), *Armies of Classical Greece*, p. 156.
[125] Brockington, '*Ramo dharmabhrtam varah*', p. 250.
[126] Sumitra V. Bhat, 'Ethical Values in the *Ramayana*: A Reflection', in K. B. Archak (ed.), *Ethics for Modern Man in Sanskrit Literature* (New Delhi: Sundeep Prakashan, 2007), p. 29.
[127] Subedi, 'Concept in Hinduism of "Just War"', p. 341.
[128] Brockington, '*Ramo dharmabhrtam varah*', p. 259.
[129] Nooten, 'Introduction', pp. xv–xvi.
[130] Greg Bailey, 'Introduction: An Empirical Approach to the *Ramayana*', in Bailey and Brockington (eds.), *Epic Threads*, p. xiv.
[131] Mehendale, *Reflections on the Mahabharata War*, p. 1.
[132] Swamy, 'Vedic *Rajadharma*', p. 17.

Vedic and Epic India 31

battlefield was considered glorious. The *Rig Veda* says that a dead warrior had earned the same merit as the donor of 1,000 cows.[133] Similarly, the Spartans considered it better to die than to retreat in the face of the enemy.[134] Lasting fame and a glorious death in battle, asserts Everett L. Wheeler, represented the epitome of the hoplite ideal in Classical Greece.[135] The *Ramayana* notes that a king (Kshatriya) has to display the following qualities: fierceness, heroism, gentleness, self-control and purity.[136] However, unnecessary brutality in war was not allowed. It is to be noted that in the *Brhadaranyaka Upanishad*, the emphasis is on practicing self-restraint and generosity and exhibiting compassion.[137] The *Ramayana* implies that the heroes, by performing glorious deeds, influenced the chain of events. Lakshmana tells his elder brother Rama that weaklings are ruled by fate, but heroes scorn it and by their heroic actions challenge the inevitability of fate.[138]

Let us shift the focus to the *Bhagavad Gita* in order to expound on the duties of a Kshatriya fighting a *dharmayuddha*. The blind king Dhritarashtra (chief of the Kauravas) asks his minister Sanjaya to tell him what is happening on the battlefield of Kurukshetra. Sanjaya repeats verbatim the dialogue between Krishna (god cum *suta* of Arjuna) and Arjuna (the most famous warrior on the side of the Pandavas). The dialogue between Arjuna and Krishna took place on the first day of the war, just before combat started. Before the beginning of the battle, Arjuna said to Krishna that he wanted to see all those who had come to fight. Krishna then drove forward and pulled up the *ratha* between the two armies. Arjuna then looked forward and saw his kith and kin armed to the teeth, ready to kill and be killed. He was overwhelmed with grief and despair. With tears in his eyes, Arjuna said that fratricide was repugnant to him and that he did not want wealth and kingdom at the cost of killing his kinsmen. Probably, Arjuna was unnerved by the sight.[139]

Angelika Malinar states that though the *Bhagavad Gita* emphasizes disinterested action, the dialogue between Krishna and Arjuna also

---

[133] Thapliyal, 'Early Indian Heraldry and Ceremonials', p. 140.

[134] W. S. Ferguson, 'The Zulus and the Spartans: A Comparison of Their Military Systems', in Wheeler (ed.), *Armies of Classical Greece*, p. 81.

[135] Wheeler, 'Introduction', p. xxxix.

[136] John Brockington, 'Religious Attitudes in Valmiki's *Ramayana*', in Bailey and Brockington (eds.), *Epic Threads*, p. 228.

[137] Sindhu S. Dange, 'Ethical Codes in the Vedic Literature', in Archak (ed.), *Ethics for Modern Man in Sanskrit Literature*, p. 19.

[138] Brockington, 'Religious Attitudes', p. 243.

[139] Mohanraj, *Warrior and the Charioteer*, pp. 39, 61–2.

represents a tension between *kuladharma* (kinship law) and *kshatriyadharma* (the law of the warriors/Kshatriyas). In accordance with *kuladharma*, Arjuna is not supposed to kill his relatives and clan members who have sided with Duryodhana. But in accordance with *kshatriyadharma*, Arjuna is supposed to kill the enemies without regard to whether they have any blood relations with him. Duryodhana represents the warriors' *dharma*. The *Udoygparva* of *Mahabharata* says that he is trying to build himself up as an absolute ruler, high above all the existing family relationships. Duryodhana's loyalty is to his kingdom and kingship and not to kinship. Duryodhana claims for himself the highest possible position, the over-lordship of all human beings on the subcontinent. This is a concept of absolute kingship and resembles the concept of god-king. Malinar and Steven J. Rosen claim that in the context of ancient Indian culture, such absolute kings are not regarded as role models but are depicted as evildoers and demonic figures. Duryodhana is portrayed as the *Kali Purusha*, the demon Kali in human form. In general, ancient Indian texts push the concept of the king as subordinate to the highest god. Thus, though the king enjoys a special position within the socio-cosmic order, his power is limited. The king becomes the instrument and sign of the god, and ascetic power is also demanded from him. This does not mean that the king renounces the world, but rather that the king must follow the rules of *dharma* and *sastra* (Hindu laws) and must see that his subjects also follow these rules.[140]

Krishna emphasized Arjuna's duty as a Kshatriya. A Kshatriya who dies fighting attains *veeraswarga* (the Heaven of the Heroes).[141] It should be noted that even if an evil Kshatriya fights courageously, he attains heaven. After the war, the *Mahabharata* tells us, Yudhistira (the eldest of the Pandava brothers) was shocked to learn from God Indra that Duryodhana had attained heaven due to his courageous behaviour on the battlefield.[142]

Further, Krishna emphasized the *karma* theory (i.e., the laws of action). According to this theory, the soul is immortal. Hence, after the destruction of the body, the soul remains. Thus, nobody dies. While the soul is immortal, the body is transient. Also, one who is born is bound to die one day (i.e., destruction of the body and not the soul) and is bound to

---

[140] Malinar, *The Bhagavadgita: Doctrines and Contexts*, pp. 226–7, 233; Rosen, *Krishna's Song*, p. 24.
[141] Mohanraj, *Warrior and the Charioteer*, pp. 63–4.
[142] Buck, *Mahabharata*, p. 367.

Vedic and Epic India

be reborn again. Krishna emphasized to Arjuna the concept of *nishkama-karma*, that is, doing one's duty selflessly. The right way of doing *karma* is to perform one's duty without thinking about the possible rewards, in order to maintain the social structure. Krishna continues that if Arjuna fought with detachment (i.e., doing his *karma*), then he would not be committing any sin.[143] In other words, a Kshatriya fights only for a just cause and not for the prospect of any material gain from fighting or because combat excites his passion.[144]

Krishna urges Arjuna to apply *buddhi* (the faculty of discrimination) as taught in Samkhya philosophy and apply it to yogic practice. Krishna refutes Arjuna's opinion that non-action, that is, non-violence on the battlefield, is a sign of insight as a method of ending *karmic* bondage. A *yogin* (one who performs *yogic* practice) achieves self-control, which implies a conquest of cosmological realms and power that culminates in his reaching *Brahman* (cosmic soul). Becoming *Brahman* means replacement of the individual ego-bound agency with that of *Brahman* and *prakriti* (the Samkhya concept of nature). The *yogin* thus reaches a position where he controls and directs the activities of his cognitive and physical powers without identifying with them and becoming attached.[145] Unlike in the *Bhagavad Gita*, Plato and Aristotle stipulate that war should always remain instrumental and not an end in itself.[146]

Krishna, in the *Bhagavad Gita*, says:

Interwoven in his creation, the Spirit is beyond destruction....

For beyond time he dwells in these bodies, though these bodies have an end in their time; but he remains immeasurable, immortal. Therefore, great warrior, carry on thy fight.

....

As a man leaves an old garment and puts on one that is new, the Spirit leaves his mortal body and then puts on one that is new.[147]

....

Think thou also of thy duty and do not waver. There is no greater good for a warrior than to fight a righteous war.

There is a war that opens the doors of heaven, Arjuna! Happy the warriors whose fate is to fight such war.

---

[143] Mohanraj, *Warrior and the Charioteer*, pp. 64–6, 71.

[144] S. Revathy, 'The Ethics of the *Bhagavad Gita*', in Archak (ed.), *Ethics for Modern Man in Sanskrit Literature*, p. 52.

[145] Malinar, *The Bhagavadgita: Doctrines and Contexts*, pp. 228–30.

[146] Neal Wood, 'Xenophon's Theory of Leadership', in Wheeler (ed.), *Armies of Classical Greece*, p. 458.

[147] *Bhagavad Gita*, tr. by Mascaro, p. 11.

34   *Hinduism and the Ethics of Warfare in South Asia*

But to forego this fight for righteousness is to forego thy duty and honour: is to fall into trangression.

Men will tell of thy dishonour both now and in times to come. And to a man who is in honour, dishonour is more than death.

The great warriors will say that thou hast run from the battle through fear; and those who thought great things of thee will speak of thee in scorn.

....

In death thy glory in heaven, in victory thy glory on earth....

Prepare for war with peace in thy soul. Be in peace in pleasure and pain, in gain and in loss, in victory or in the loss of a battle. In this peace there is no sin.[148]

However, *kutayuddha* could be practiced against non-Aryan tribes. Because of 'racial' and cultural differences, war between Aryans and non-Aryans was more brutal than conflict among the Aryans.[149] The *Rig Veda* tells us that the Aryan war god Indra executed 50,000 members (including pregnant women) of a non-Aryan tribe.[150] Similarly, the Greeks followed the rules of warfare while fighting among themselves but not when they fought the 'other', that is, the 'barbarian' Persians. The Greek mercenaries under Xenophon resorted to war without rules of conduct against the Persians.[151]

Unlike the Mahabharata War, which seemed to be an intra-Aryan war, the *Ramayana* portrays war against non-Aryans. Even then, combat in *Ramayana* is not totally free of the constraints of military ethics. Rama resorted to war against Ravana for a just cause, that is, to regain his wife.[152] The conflict between Rama and Ravana also contains a moral allegory. It represents the struggle between good and evil. From another angle, the *Ramayana* represents the spread of Aryan political and cultural domination from north India into peninsular India. The expansion of Aryan culture into peninsular India was the product of cooperation between the Brahmins and the Kshatriyas, who carried the flag of Aryanization. Amal Sarkar rightly says that the Aryan penetration into south India was the product not of peaceful cultural interaction but of the military exploits of Aryan chieftains. Lanka may be south of Vindhya Mountain (in present-day Madhya Pradesh) or may be Sri Lanka (known as Serandip). The language of the *raksas* was Andhra (Telegu).[153]

---

[148] *Bhagavad Gita*, tr. by Mascaro, p. 12.
[149] Tripathi, *History of Ancient India*, p. 30.
[150] Mohanraj, *Warrior and the Charioteer*, pp. 45–6.
[151] Wheeler, 'Introduction', p. xlv.
[152] Mehendale, *Reflections on the Mahabharata War*, p. 58.
[153] Sarkar, *Ramayanas*, pp. 2, 8–9, 14, 16, 19, 45.

Vedic and Epic India 35

The code of conduct for *dharmayuddha* (righteous war) as developed in the two epic poems involved the declaration of war and the practice of ending combat at sunset.[154] In accordance with the code of *dharmayuddha*, it is better to die fighting than to win a victory by unfair means.[155] Both the *Ramayana* and the *Mahabharata* say that non-combatants, those warriors who have lost their weapons or want to surrender or are hiding and those who are retreating, are not to be killed.[156]

During the Eastern Chou period (770–403 BCE), the idea that one should not take advantage of an adversary in distress became deeply rooted.[157] In Archaic Greece, after the battles, the captives were generally ransomed by their friends and relatives.[158] During the sixth and fifth centuries BCE, the Spartans always consulted the oracle at Delphi before going to war. In case of bad omens and at the times of certain festivals, the Spartans aborted expeditions.[159] The Greeks during the Classical Age did not usually pursue the defeated foe. The reason for this was partly ideological and partly tactical. The ideological factor was that it was ungentlemanly to kill fleeing fellow Greeks, and the tactical factor was that if the victorious hoplites broke ranks to pursue the defeated foe, then the former were vulnerable to a counter-attack by the enemy.[160]

Even during *dharmayuddha* among the Aryans, spies were used. Bhisma, in the *Mahabharata*, asserts that a king should employ spies. The spies should appear as blind and deaf. The spies should be set even against the councilors, princes and subordinate chiefs, both in the capital and in the provinces.[161] The *Mahabharata* informs us that the news of Arjuna's vow that he would kill Jayadratha the next day before sunset was brought to the Kauravas by their spies.[162]

In several instances during the Mahabharata War, the rules of war were broken by both sides. After the slaying of Jayadratha, the Kaurava general Drona ordered that the Kaurava army continue to fight the Pandavas even after sunset. And Aswathama, Drona's son and the last general on

---

[154] Sinha, 'Hinduism and International Humanitarian Law', p. 288.
[155] Thapliyal, 'Military Organization in the Ancient Period', p. 90.
[156] Mehendale, *Reflections on the Mahabharata War*, pp. 5, 59.
[157] Kierman, Jr., 'Phases and Modes of Combat in Early China', p. 44.
[158] Connor, 'Early Greek Land Warfare as Symbolic Expression', p. 95.
[159] M. D. Goodman and A. J. Holladay, 'Religious Scruples in Ancient Warfare', in Wheeler (ed.), *Armies of Classical Greece*, pp. 134–6.
[160] Peter Krentz, 'Casualties in Hoplite Battles', in Wheeler (ed.), *Armies of Classical Greece*, p. 356.
[161] Rajendran, '*Rajadharma* according to *Mahabharata*', p. 37.
[162] Mohanraj, *Warrior and the Charioteer*, p. 48.

36   *Hinduism and the Ethics of Warfare in South Asia*

the Kaurava side, attacked the Pandava camp during the night and killed the Pandava soldiers, who were deep in slumber. Those Pandava soldiers who tried to escape from the camp were ambushed by Kripa (Drona's brother) and Kirtavarman.[163]

Krishna's credo was to win at all cost. Krishna asked Yudhistira (the eldest of the Pandava brothers) to tell Drona that Aswathama had been killed. However, Yudhistira, who was famous for his honesty, refused to tell such an outright lie. An elephant named Aswathama was then killed. Yudhistira then went to Drona and told him that Aswathama the elephant had been killed. The exact words used by Yudhistira are as follows: *Aswathama hatha, iti nara nahi gaja* (Aswathama is dead, but it is an elephant and not a human). However, Krishna managed to have several drums beaten loudly at that moment, and the phrase 'Aswathama the elephant' was drowned in the ensuing noise. Drona thought that his son Aswathama had been killed. Totally disheartened, he gave up fighting. Then Arjuna, on Krishna's advice, attacked and killed Drona. Krishna also gave unethical advice to Arjuna for killing Karna. During the duel between Arjuna and Karna, the latter's *ratha* got stuck. Then Karna left his weapon and struggled to move the wheel of his *ratha* out of the mud. It was considered unethical to engage an unarmed enemy. However, Krishna advised Arjuna to take advantage of Karna's vulnerability and kill him. Again, when Duryodhana and Bhima were fighting with *gadas*, the former was on the point of winning. Krishna then advised Bhima to attack the former's thigh. Generally, it was considered unethical to attack an opponent's thigh. The rules of *gadayuddha* (combat between two fighters equipped with maces) noted that an opponent could not be struck below the navel. Bhima followed Krishna's advice and wounded Duryodhana.[164]

Krishna justified his actions by arguing that the end justifies the means (an instrumental view of war that is in tune with *kutayuddha*). Krishna says that the Pandava's war against the Kauravas was fought for a just cause. Hence, in order to win such a war, there was no *aniti* (immorality) involved if a minimum of *adharma* (unjust techniques) were used. Mehendale says that the *Mahabharata* shows that, due to the operation of *dharma* on a cosmic scale, nemesis or retributive justice overtook even Krishna in the end. Krishna was killed accidentally by a hunter.[165]

---

[163] Mehendale, *Reflections on the Mahabharata War*, pp. 53, 57.
[164] Mohanraj, *Warrior and the Charioteer*, pp. 50–2; Mehendale, *Reflections on the Mahabharata War*, p. 40.
[165] Mehendale, *Reflections on the Mahabharata War*, pp. 45, 57.

Vedic and Epic India

In the *Ramayana* we also find that in order to win a just war, Rama resorted to several unjust measures. In order to defeat the 'wicked' Ravana, Rama needed an army. So Rama decided to interfere in the internal affairs of the kingdom of the *hanuman*s. The literal translation of this term is 'monkeys', but in the *Ramayana* it probably refers to the Dravidians, who were considered by the Aryans to be somewhat lower on the scale of civilization. Even today, in popular usage, an uncultured and rude person is called by the abusive term *hanuman*. Rama made a pact with Sugriva that while Sugriva was fighting with his brother, the *hanuman* king Valin, Rama would ambush the latter. And after the death of Valin, Sugriva would take both Valin's kingdom and his wife and in return would provide Rama with an army for invading Lanka.[166]

Rama, the Aryan chief, used guile and treachery while fighting Ravana. This is especially evident in the killing of Meghnada (the son of Ravana, also known as Indrajit) by Lakshmana. Rama and Lakshmana occasionally waged *mantra yuddha* (which was characterized by deceit and subterfuge) against the *raksas*.[167] Simultaneously, Indrajit, Ravana's son, also used *maya* (subterfuge), while fighting Rama and Lakshmana.[168] *Mantrayuddha* and *mayayuddha* constitute *kutayuddha*.

Despite the presence of laws, in the heat of battle the Greeks broke them occasionally as well. Mutilation of dead enemy soldiers was common among the Classical Greeks. In the *Iliad*, we come across the fact that the Greek warriors stabbed Hector's lifeless body before Achilles dragged it around Troy. Xenophon's Greeks mutilated the Persians in order to terrify the suviving enemy soldiers.[169]

Dharmayuddha also involved construction of a just peace. After the end of the Mahabharata War, Dhritarashtra was deposed and sent to the jungle. He then advised Yudhistira on the establishment of good governance for the maintenance of peace. One of the principles of good governance, according to Dhritarashtra, was to be mild to the peaceful and harsh towards the wicked. Further, Dhritarashtra advised Yudishtira to send out spies disguised as morons and blind men,[170] in order to get information about possible rebellious tendencies, which were to be nipped in the bud. And the *Ramayana* asserts that even after the victory over

---

[166] *The Ramayana of Valmiki*, vol. 1, *Balakanda*, p. 10.
[167] Sarkar, *Ramayanas*, pp. 15, 25.
[168] Mehendale, *Reflections on the Mahabharata War*, p. 63.
[169] Lawrence A. Tritle, 'Hector's Body: Mutilation of the Dead in Ancient Greece and Vietnam', in Wheeler (ed.), *Armies of Classical Greece*, pp. 339, 341.
[170] Buck, *Mahabharata*, p. 397.

38   *Hinduism and the Ethics of Warfare in South Asia*

Ravana, Rama's governance in Kosala was subject to the wishes of the *loka* (common people).[171]

Just peace after warfare, says the *Mahabharata*, means that no enmity should be displayed towards the descendants and relatives of the dead enemy king. Further, if possible, the victor should put on the throne the descendant of the dead enemy ruler.[172] However, the establishment of a just peace after a just war reflects the presence of some streaks of imperialism. After killing Ravana, Rama put the latter's brother Bibhisana on the throne of Lanka. The argument is that Lanka is saved from the depredations of the tyrant Ravana, and now the people of Lanka will rejoice when placed under the rule of a 'good' ruler. However, the underlying imperial logic is also clear. Bibhisana had deserted Ravana early during the war. Bibhisana's argument was that he was dissatisfied with the tyranny of his brother Ravana.[173] Bibhisana functioned as a client ruler of Rama and accepted the over-lordship of the ruler of Kosala. So Lanka from an independent kingdom was turned into a tributary of a hegemonic Aryan state of north India. At the popular level even today, Bibhisana is regarded as a fifth columnist and as an enemy within the gates.

CONCLUSION

The elaborate code of military ethics for limiting the lethality of warfare was present to some degree in most of the civilizations of ancient Eurasia but was probably most developed in ancient Greece and China. Vedic and epic philosophy was not pacific. Sita's emphasis on *ahimsa* is marginal in the overall context of the *Ramayana*. Interestingly, vedic and epic India did not generate any discussion of the military ethics of siege warfare. Ideas about restraint in warfare develop when fighting occurs within an ethnic group. The early Aryans were mostly pastoral and not urban dwellers. Hence, siege warfare was uncommon during conflicts among the various Aryan tribes. Siege warfare was conducted only against non-Aryans. Hence, there was not adequate motivation for limiting the lethality of siege warfare by establishing elaborate rules and regulations. The *varna* system, the *karma* theory and the discussion regarding the establishment of a just peace after a just war are probably the unique contributions of

---

[171] Bhat, 'Ethical Values in the *Ramayana*', p. 33.
[172] Gauri Mahulikar, 'Ethical Teachings in the *Santiparva* of the *Mahabharata*', in Archak (ed.), *Ethics for Modern Man in Sanskrit Literature*, p. 37.
[173] *Ramayana of Valmiki*, vol. 1, *Balakanda*, Introduction, p. 10.

Vedic and Epic India

vedic and epic India to the literature on just war theory. The *varna* system, by emphasizing the carrying of arms as the vocation of a few, limited the scope and intensity of warfare in the vedic and epic ages. And the concept of reincarnation inherent in *karma* theory not only maintained the *varna* system but also strengthened the morale of the Kshatriyas on the blood-filled battlefield. In contrast to Brekke's opinion, we have seen that the *Ramayana* and the *Mahabharata* consider the just causes for starting a war. In fact, war is to be undertaken only when all attempts to reach a compromise peace fail. Overall, in inter-tribal fighting, the Aryans conducted symmetrical warfare. The *Ramayana* and to a greater extent the *Mahabharata* portray the continuous tension between constructing an elaborate code of conduct for resorting to and waging battle and the breaking of the rules by the principal combatants. By around 300 BCE, Asoka elaborated on the concept of *dharmayuddha*, which is the subject of the next chapter.

2

Buddhism, Jainism and Asoka's *Ahimsa*

The general view both within India and outside the subcontinent is that the Maurya Emperor Asoka (emperor from 268/270 to 234/233 BCE) abjured violence under the influence of Buddhism. His demilitarization policy, it is argued, was far too advanced for his time. Asokan anti-militarism was revived by Mohandas Karamchand Gandhi when he practiced *ahimsa*-oriented *satyagraha* against the British between 1920s and the 1940s. This chapter attempts to show the historical context that shaped Asoka's policy of limited violence as propounded in his *dhamma*. Further, this chapter will try to put Asoka's *dhamma* in a cross-cultural comparative perspective. Asoka certainly broke out of the 'realist' *kut-ayuddha* tradition, but he was neither a visionary nor an ideologue but rather a pragmatist who attempted to consolidate his empire using minimum force. Neither Buddhism nor Asoka's *ahimsa* was the equivalent of Gandhi's non-violent struggle against the British during the first half of the twentieth century.

THE RISE OF BUDDHISM AND JAINISM

When Buddhism and Jainism emerged on the subcontinent, there were sixteen great *mahajanapadas*. They were Kasi (Benaras), Kosala (Gonda region), Anga (eastern Bihar), Magadha (central Bihar), Vajji, Malla, Cedi (Bundelkhand), Vatsa (Allahabad), Kuru (Delhi region), Pancala (Rohilkhand), Matsya (Jaipur), Surasena (Mathura), Assaka (Godavari region), Avanti (western Malwa), Gandhara with its capital at Taxila (eastern Afghanistan), and Kamboja (north-west frontier province of

Buddhism, Jainism and Asoka's Ahimsa   41

Pakistan). Of these *mahajanapadas*, Magadha was on the point of becoming dominant and the core of a north Indian empire that was to emerge in the fourth century BCE.[1]

Initially, Buddhism began as a schismatic movement against the orthodox brahmanical outlook. To a great extent, Buddhism was a protest against the various malpractices that had crept into Hindu ritual and thought. The latter development, argued the Buddhists, was due to the increasing power of the Brahmins. The artisans and the traders known as *setthis* constituted a great proportion of the populace of the cities – Kausambi (near Allahabad), Sravasti, and others – and they supported Buddhism. The Buddhist *sanghas* (assemblies) were supported by the traders and merchants. The commercial class provided support to Buddhism because, in accordance with strict brahmanical orthodoxy, the traders and merchants, despite possessing economic wealth, were regarded as social and cultural inferiors to the Brahmins and the Kshatriyas. Both Mahavira and Buddha challenged the hereditary caste system. And unlike brahmanism, Buddhism encouraged sea voyages, which the merchants engaged in overseas trade undertook frequently.[2] Loans and debts were taken on interest. At times letters of credit functioned as substitutes for money. The *Gautama dharmasutra* prescribes a limit on the interest chargeable by the creditor. The lawful limit was 1.25 percent per month or 15 percent per year. The interest could not exceed the principal, however long the debt remained unpaid. Again, in Buddhism, the interests of the creditors and the moneylenders were protected, and the debtors were reminded of their obligations. By contrast, the brahmanical lawgivers despised the moneylenders. The emphasis on truth, justice, honesty, and so on, present in the Buddhist system supported the concept of private individual property. Such ethics suited the activities of the traders and moneylenders.[3]

Sacrifice was an integral part of the brahmanical system.[4] The Buddhist critique of Brahmin-mediated sacrifices suited the mentality of the profit-

---

[1] Ramashankar Tripathi, *History of Ancient India* (1942; reprint, New Delhi: Motilal Banarasidas, 1999), pp. 82–5.

[2] Romila Thapar, *Asoka and the Decline of the Mauryas* (1963; reprint, New Delhi: Oxford University Press, 1989), pp. 140–1; R. S. Sharma, 'Material Background of the Origin of Buddhism', in Bhairabi Prasad Sahu (ed.), *Iron and Social Change in Early India* (New Delhi: Oxford University Press, 2006), p. 44.

[3] Kailash Chand Jain, *Lord Mahavira and His Times* (1974; reprint, New Delhi: Motilal Banarasidas, 1991), pp. 238, 313.

[4] John Ferguson, *War and Peace in the World Religions* (New York: Oxford University Press, 1978), p. 29.

42   *Hinduism and the Ethics of Warfare in South Asia*

oriented commercial class.[5] Then, the doctrine of *ahimsa* was invoked by the heads of the peasant communities, which were expanding into the domains of the forest tribes who lived by hunting and killing. The latter occupation was considered blameworthy by the *ahimsa* preachers, and this justified the subjugation of the forest dwellers at the hands of the expanding rural peasant society. Thus, the rural *gahapatis* (householders) found the *ahimsa* of Buddhism, and to an extent that of Jainism, attractive.[6] Again, the brahmanical rituals involved killing as many as 600 bulls at a time for a particular *yagna*. The vedic religious philosophies, writes R. S. Sharma, did not suit the newly established plough agriculture, which was dependent on animal husbandry. By contrast, the Buddhist emphasis on non-injury to animals was attractive to the practitioners of plough agriculture. The Pali canons stressed non-violence towards animals rather than towards men. The early Buddhist text *Sutta-nipata* states that cattle should be protected because they provide *annada*, *vannada* and *sukhada* (food, beauty and happiness/peace).[7] At least some streams within the brahmanical tradition also opposed the unnecessary waste of animal lives. For instance, the *Chandogya Upanishad* points out the importance of not killing any living creature unnecessarily.[8] So Buddhism and Jainism probably derived some ideas from these brahmanical strands.

Mahavira was born around 550 BCE and died around 480 BCE, while Buddha (Gautama/Siddhartha) was born roughly around 480 BCE. According to another tradition, Buddha was born about 560 BCE and died around 486/484 BCE.[9] He left his wife and son and became a wandering ascetic. Buddha first sought enlightenment in Hindu philosophy and then in ruthless asceticism. Neither brought him liberation. Then he sat for meditation under the Pipal tree (later known as Bodhi tree or tree of wisdom) on the outskirts of the town of Gaya in Magadha and found enlightenment.[10] Buddha preached for over forty years. He spent his last

---

[5] Burton Stein, *A History of India* (1998; reprint, New Delhi: Oxford University Press, 2004), pp. 74–5.

[6] Krishna Mohan Shrimali, *A People's History of India*, 3A, *The Age of Iron and the Religious Revolution, c. 700–c. 350 BC* (New Delhi: Tulika, 2007), pp. 138–9.

[7] Sharma, 'Material Background of the Origin of Buddhism', p. 43.

[8] Laurie L. Patton, 'Telling Stories about Harm: An Overview of Early Indian Narratives', in John R. Hinnells and Richard King (eds.), *Religion and Violence in South Asia: Theory and Practice* (London/New York: Routledge, 2007), p. 20.

[9] The debate regarding their dates of birth and the dates on which these two *acharyas* passed away is still continuing. Stein, *A History of India*, p. 38; Jain, *Lord Mahavira and His Times*, pp. 76, 80; Ferguson, *War and Peace in the World Religions*, p. 41.

[10] Ferguson, *War and Peace in the World Religions*, p. 41; Shrimali, *The Age of Iron and the Religious Revolution*, p. 125.

Buddhism, Jainism and Asoka's Ahimsa

year in Kusinara near Gorakhpur and then passed away.[11] Buddha frequently reminded his disciples of the importance of travelling in order to facilitate preaching and spreading Buddhism.[12] The early (Theravadin) Buddhist tradition enumerates several councils that were held in order to recite and codify the Pali canon. The First Council was held just after the death of Buddha, and between that time and the death of Asoka, two more councils were held. King Ajatasatru of Magadha (accession to kingship 491 BCE) gave patronage to the First Council, which was held at Rajagriha and attended by 500 *bhikkus*.[13] During the First Council, while some leading brethren expounded the *dhamma*, other monks repeated their formulations. This was the beginning of the system of *bhanakas* (reciters), which has been instrumental in the making of the Buddhist (Pali) canon. The Second Council was held at Vaishali about 100 years after the First Council. The Third Council was held at Pataliputra and presided over by a monk named Moggaliputta Tissa. The division between Theravada and Mahayana Buddhism occurred during the early centuries of the Christian era.[14] The term 'Theravada' means 'School of Elders'. *Thera* means elder; *stha* means to stand over; and *vada* refers to theory, doctrine or school.[15]

In the Buddhist tradition, *dhamma* refers to Buddha's doctrine and teaching.[16] Buddha's philosophy is the middle way between rigorous asceticism involving mortification of the flesh, as propounded by a branch of Jainism, and the extreme sensuality of the Carvakas (a branch of materialist philosophy that gave rise to the realist *kutayuddha* tradition). Buddhism lays stress on service on behalf of others in order to help them to escape the endless cycles of rebirth.[17] Buddhism placed the inculcation of ethical values on a high practical pedestal.[18] Buddha advised his disciples to work for the welfare of society. The attempt to work for the welfare of society is embedded in the Buddhist concept of *karuna* (compassion). It is the sentiment that inclines one to help those who are in

---

[11] Shrimali, *The Age of Iron and the Religious Revolution*, p. 125.
[12] Mahinda Deegalle, *Popularizing Buddhism: Preaching as Performance in Sri Lanka* (New York: State University of New York Press, 2006), p. 24.
[13] Shrimali, *The Age of Iron and the Religious Revolution*, p. 132; Jain, *Lord Mahavira and His Times*, p. 75.
[14] Shrimali, *The Age of Iron and the Religious Revolution*, pp. 132–4.
[15] Deegalle, *Popularizing Buddhism*, p. 189.
[16] Irfan Habib and Vivekanand Jha, *A People's History of India*, vol. 4, *Mauryan India* (New Delhi: Tulika Books, 2004), p. 63.
[17] Ferguson, *War and Peace in the World Religions*, p. 42.
[18] Shrimali, *The Age of Iron and the Religious Revolution*, p. 130.

44   *Hinduism and the Ethics of Warfare in South Asia*

distress.[19] The basic virtues are benevolence, compassion, joy and equanimity.[20] Buddha encouraged mildness in justice and attempts to establish peace in times of war. According to one story, Buddha intervened when the Sakyas and the Koliyas were fighting and persuaded them to hold diplomatic parleys. The *Dhammapada*, an early collection of Buddhist verse, notes that enmity can never be appeased by enmity but only by non-enmity. This is the eternal law. Secondly, victory breeds hatred. Calmness and happiness require giving up thoughts of victory and defeat.[21]

Rupert Gethin claims that even within the Buddhist framework of *dhamma*, limited violence is allowed in certain contexts. The advice to rulers is to pass judgement not in haste or anger but appropriately, so that the punishment fits the crime. If war is necessary, then care should be taken to minimize and contain the acts of violence. Buddhism accepted the idea that the duties of the king involved the implementation of a limited amount of violence for the purpose of deterring external enemies and to maintain law and order in the society. Even when violence on the part of the king becomes necessary, his mind must still be motivated by aversion.[22] The person killing must act out of compassion and charity, so that inner peace is not disturbed. Another argument within Buddhism is that since destiny is pre-determined, it is no sin to put someone to death.[23] One *sutta* notes that someone who kills another person is not necessarily reborn in hell. In fact, at times, a soldier might be reborn in the heavenly realm. This point seems to be taken from the *Bhagavad Gita*. In the Pali commentaries, the victim's lack of virtuous qualities diminishes the burden of killing on the part of the person who kills.[24] In one story from the *Mahaparinirvana Sutra* of Mahayana Buddhism, Buddha is said to have encouraged his followers to take up arms in defence of the Buddhist Order. Having recourse to violence in order to protect the doctrine against aggressors is acceptable in the Buddhist framework. At times, it is necessary to kill one in order to save two or more persons.[25] It seems that Buddhism could justify defensive warfare, which can be categorized as a sort of *dharmayuddha*.

[19] Deegalle, *Popularizing Buddhism*, p. 24.
[20] Ferguson, *War and Peace in the World Religions*, p. 46.
[21] Shrimali, *The Age of Iron and the Religious Revolution*, pp. 130–1.
[22] Rupert Gethin, 'Buddhist Monks, Buddhist Kings, Buddhist Violence: On the Early Buddhist Attitude to Violence', in Hinnells and King (eds.), *Religion and Violence in South Asia*, pp. 71–3.
[23] Ferguson, *War and Peace in the World Religions*, p. 56.
[24] Gethin, 'Buddhist Monks, Buddhist Kings, Buddhist Violence', p. 77.
[25] Ferguson, *War and Peace in the World Religions*, p. 55.

Buddhism, Jainism and Asoka's Ahimsa

According to one view, Mahavira was not the founder of the Jaina religious system. He was the twenty-fourth and last *tirthankara* of the Jaina faith. The other important *tirthankaras* were Rishbhanatha and Arishtanemi. Their names appear in the *Rig Veda*. The twenty-third *tirthankara* was Parshvanatha/Parsva, who came some 250 years before Mahavira.[26] According to one tradition, under Parasva (877–777 BCE), the kings of Gandhara, Videha, Pancala, Vidharbha and Kalinga accepted Jainism.[27] Mahavira's childhood name was Vardhamana. He was the son of Siddhartha (not to be confused with Gotama or Gautama Buddha), a chief of the clan associated with the Lichchavis of Vaishali (Bihar). Vardhamana, like Buddha, left home at the age of thirty, leaving his wife and daughter behind him. He moved with the ascetic group called *nirganthas* (free from bonds). He was with them for twelve years. In the thirteenth year, Vardhamana became *Jina* (the conqueror). For thirty years he taught and journeyed. He starved himself to death at the age of seventy-two in the town of Pava near the Magadhan capital of Rajagriha.[28]

Had Mahavira insisted on rigorous asceticism on the part of all his followers, then Jainism would have become the religion of a microscopic minority. Mahavira's Third Order was comprised of numerous laymen. Sankha Sataka headed this order. These laymen were householders who could not actually renounce the world, but they could at least observe five small vows called *anuvrata*. The similarity of their religious duties, not in kind but in degree, resulted in a close union between the laymen and the monks. Most of the regulations meant to govern the conduct of the laymen were apparently intended to make them participate, to an extent and for some time, in the merits and benefits of monastic life without obliging them to renounce the world altogether.[29]

Paul Dundas asserts that world renunciation of the sort followed by the Jains and the Buddhists was an institution that entailed not so much as the abandonment of social ties for a career of mendicant quietism as an entry into a heroic way of life that involved raiding and plundering and the purificatory practice of celibacy by the Kshatriyas, at least in north India during the seventh and sixth centuries BCE. The Mallas (a community of wrestlers), despite engaging intensively in martial arts,

---

[26] Shrimali, *The Age of Iron and the Religious Revolution*, p. 114.
[27] Jain, *Lord Mahavira and His Times*, p. 16.
[28] Shrimali, *The Age of Iron and the Religious Revolution*, pp. 114–15.
[29] Jain, *Lord Mahavira and His Times*, p. 60.

46 *Hinduism and the Ethics of Warfare in South Asia*

were supporters of Mahavira and Gautama Buddha (both members of the Kshatriya, i.e., warrior class).[30] Again, the Gangas, the Rashtrakutas and the Hoysalas, powerful dynasties in medieval south India, were supporters of Jainism.[31] According to Jaina tenets, violence in self-defence is justifiable under certain circumstances. This is elucidated clearly in the *Uttaradhyayana Sutra*, a text composed around the third century BCE. The *Bhagavati Sutra*, composed at the beginning of the Common Era, does not condemn war. This text makes clear that going to war when commanded by one's leader is obligatory. However, when going to war it is necessary for soldiers to observe Jain values.[32]

A Jain Digambara monk founded the Hoysala Dynasty in the twelfth century in Karnataka and recommended a defensive form of violence. The Digambara sect of Jains, which flourished in early medieval south India, preached that a warrior who died in battle became a true Jain ascetic. Medieval Jain poetry extolled heroic action and compared the heroism of the warrior to that of the ascetic striving monk.[33]

Robert J. Zydenbos writes that Jainism accepted the idea that for lay people, who are involved in the working of day-to-day life, some *himsa* is unavoidable. If the attitude of the person is right, then such *himsa* is considered accidental and will have a minimal *karmic* effect on him. So *himsa* with proper self-control is acceptable, but not any violent act that is premeditated. Somewhat like the *Bhagavad Gita*, the Jain doctrine assures the lay follower that if violence is associated with his or her occupation, and if such acts are carried out dispassionately with a sense of inner detachment, then the person can still be a good Jain. But violence inspired by self-interest leads to evil and darkness. Zydenbos concludes that *ahimsa* is not a goal in itself. It is a way of manipulating the flow and working of *karma*. *Ahimsa* is a persuasive device in Jainism. The objective is to cultivate restraint, conscious self-control, in order to improve the overall conduct of the people.[34]

---

[30] Paul Dundas, 'The Non-Violence of Violence: Jain Perspectives on Warfare, Asceticism and Worship', in Hinnells and King (eds.), *Religion and Violence in South Asia*, pp. 42–3.

[31] Robert J. Zydenbos, 'Jainism as the Religion of Non-Violence', in Jan E. M. Houben and Karel R. Van Kooij (eds.), *Violence Denied: Violence, Non-Violence and the Rationalization of Violence in South Asian Cultural History* (Leiden: Brill, 1999), pp. 188–9.

[32] Dundas, 'The Non-Violence of Violence', pp. 46–8.

[33] Robert Elgood, *Hindu Arms and Rituals: Arms and Armour from India, 1400–1865* (Ahmedabad: Mapin, 2004), pp. 43–4.

[34] Zydenbos, 'Jainism as the Religion of Non-Violence', pp. 197–207.

Buddhism, Jainism and Asoka's Ahimsa

A similar strand of thought for the purpose of limiting violence emerged in ancient China. Confucius lived from 551 to 479 BCE. The Confucian emphasis on benevolence functioned as a corrective to the self-destructive brutality of the Legalists. The Legalists focussed on inflexible bureaucratic regimentation. Confucius claimed that government should be based on the benevolent sentiments of educated gentlemen, while the Legalists derided benevolence. Confucius accepted the existence of armed forces and the necessity that rulers would occasionally have to use them. The three essentials of a state for him are food, the confidence of the people and the soldiers.[35] Confucian thought probably emerged in reaction to the indiscriminate and continuous violence of the Warring States Era (403–221 BCE).

Buddhism and Jainism both emphasize *ahimsa*, each in its own way. *Ahimsa* is connected to sacrifice in the *Chandogya Upanishad*. *Ahimsa* is equated with *tapas* (austerity), *danam* (generosity/gift), *daksina* (sacrificial gifts), truthfulness and integrity.[36] In Buddhism and Jainism, *ahimsa* retains the other qualities presented in the *Chandogya Upanishad* but is otherwise completely delinked from sacrifice. The *ahimsa* of Jainism and Buddhism should not be confused with passive non-violence, which Gandhi followed between the 1920s and the 1940s.[37] Now, let us see how Buddhism operated in practice under its greatest practitioner, Asoka.

ASOKA'S *DHAMMA*

As far as governance was concerned, Romila Thapar rightly says that there were two options before Asoka. One option was ruthless control of the subject populace with the aid of the army, self-deification of the emperor, and so on, as practiced by Asoka's near-contemporary Emperor Huang-Ti in China. The other option was that of the king declaring himself in favour of a new belief, an eclectic collection of views from varying groups; the dominance of other groups could thus be undermined, and the central authority could increase its power and sway. Asoka followed the second policy, and such a policy was also followed by the Mughal Emperor Akbar 1,800 years later, when the latter introduced *Din-i-Ilahi*.[38] In fact, it could be argued that Asoka, like Plato (427–347 BCE), was no

---

[35] Thomas M. Kane, *Ancient China on Postmodern War: Enduring Ideas from the Chinese Strategic Tradition* (London/New York: Routledge, 2007), pp. 12, 15, 53, 115.

[36] Patton, 'Telling Stories about Harm', p. 21.

[37] Dundas, 'The Non-Violence of Violence', p. 43.

[38] Thapar, *Asoka and the Decline of the Mauryas*, p. 144.

48   *Hinduism and the Ethics of Warfare in South Asia*

pacifist, although both believed that politics and philosophy should be pursued for the sake of peace and not war.[39]

Asoka assumed that the adoption of a new faith and its propagation through the state apparatus would produce some sort of ideological unity among the various cultural groups that inhabited his empire. A new religion could be used as an emblem or symbol of a new unity, and it could be an effective means of propaganda. Thus, such a measure would aid in the consolidation of the Mauryan Empire. Asoka emphasized good communication not only for the purpose of quickly transferring military assets during times of trouble and for encouraging trade and commerce, but also for the propagation and infiltration of his *dhamma*.[40] The *Uttarapatha* (northern road) extended from Bengal to Taxila; another road branched from the juncture of the Ganga and Jamuna rivers and continued to the Narmada basin and from there to the Arabian seaport of Broach in Gujarat in west India. The *Dakshinapatha* (southern road) branched southward from Ujjain to the provincial capital of Suvarnagiri.[41] Asoka included his message – i.e., his *dhamma* – in the various rock and pillar edicts that he constructed in different parts of his empire. Some sort of ceremonial, congregational reading of the edicts on certain occasions, either in select gatherings comprised of high-level Mauryan bureaucrats or in larger gatherings in which the state's officials played an important role, was common during Asoka's reign. His rock and pillar edicts are somewhat similar to the pillar edicts of Darius. For instance, the polished nature of the Mauryan and Achaemenid pillars and the use of certain common sculptural motifs, such as the lotus, was to an extent a product of cultural interaction between India and Iran. However, there is a difference. While Darius's pillars propagated military victories and the military might of the Achaemenid monarch, Asoka's rock and pillar edicts portray his quasi-benevolent message of a 'caring' emperor. In other words, while Darius's pillars portray a kingship that was martial in nature, the Asokan pillars portray a kingship that was moral and didactic in nature. Upinder Singh points out the Buddhist influence on the Asokan pillars. In her eyes, the lion emblem included in the Asokan pillars is a motif taken from Buddhism.[42]

---

[39] Gregory M. Reichberg, Henrik Syse and Endre Begny (eds.), *The Ethics of War: Classic and Contemporary Readings* (Malden, MA and Oxford: Blackwell, 2006), p. 18.

[40] Thapar, *Asoka and the Decline of the Mauryas*, pp. 145, 152.

[41] Stein, *A History of India*, p. 79.

[42] Upinder Singh, 'Texts on Stone: Understanding Asoka's Epigraph-Monuments and Their Changing Contexts', *Indian Historical Review*, vol. 24, nos. 1–2 (July 1997 and Jan. 1998), pp. 2, 5, 9; Habib and Jha, *Mauryan India*, pp. 61–2.

Buddhism, Jainism and Asoka's Ahimsa

In Burton Stein's view, Asoka became a devotee of Buddhism around 250 BCE.[43] However, Asoka did not become a monk but remained the ruler, albeit a changed ruler, emphasizing righteousness, social justice and peace. John Ferguson rightly says that there is no evidence of any account of *nirvana* or the Four Noble Truths or the Eightfold Path in the edicts of Asoka.[44] Krishna Mohan Shrimali points out that though the Third Buddhist Council was held during the reign of Asoka (270–34 BCE), the emperor's edict does not mention it.[45] Andre Wink notes that as far as the formulation of Asoka's policies was concerned, the Buddhist *sanghas* remained passive, and the emperor had no Buddhist religious advisors.[46] Further, Asoka also patronized other religious orders like the Ajivikas.[47] Asoka's *dhamma* was an amalgamation of ideas from different religions including Buddhism, Jainism, and others.

Dhamma is the Prakrit equivalent of the Sanskrit word *dharma*.[48] The term *dhamma* in Asoka's paradigm refers not to religion but to sacred and filial duties plus ethical values.[49] D. N. Jha writes that *dhamma* is an ethical code aimed at fostering an attitude of social responsibility among the people. One of the basic principles of *dhamma* is toleration.[50] Asoka proclaimed religious toleration.[51] This was necessary to prevent religious strife among the various sects. As a point of comparison, it could be said that to a great extent, the Western Roman Empire was brought to ruin by continuous conflict between the various sects of Christianity and between Christians and pagans.[52] Asoka exhorts his subjects to avoid anger and killing and injuring human beings and animals.[53] The Second Minor Rock Edict urges compassion towards and avoidance of injury to living beings. The Second Pillar Edict advocates avoidance of fierceness, cruelty, anger, pride and envy.[54]

---

[43] Stein, *A History of India*, p. 80.

[44] Ferguson, *War and Peace in the World Religions*, p. 50.

[45] Shrimali, *The Age of Iron and the Religious Revolution*, p. 133.

[46] Andre Wink, *Al-Hind: The Making of the Indo-Islamic World*, vol. 2, *The Slave Kings and the Islamic Conquest 11th–13th Centuries* (1997; reprint, New Delhi: Oxford University Press, 2001), p. 341.

[47] Shrimali, *The Age of Iron and the Religious Revolution*, p. 112.

[48] D. N. Jha, *Early India: A Concise History* (New Delhi: Manohar, 2004), p. 109.

[49] Romila Thapar, *The Mauryas Revisited* (1987; reprint, Calcutta: K. P. Bagchi, 1993), p. 22.

[50] Jha, *Early India*, p. 110.

[51] Ferguson, *War and Peace in the World Religions*, p. 51.

[52] Michael Grant, *The Fall of the Roman Empire* (1976; reprint, London: Phoenix, 2005), pp. 155–71.

[53] Gethin, 'Buddhist Monks, Buddhist Kings, Buddhist Violence', p. 74.

[54] Habib and Jha, *Mauryan India*, p. 64.

50   *Hinduism and the Ethics of Warfare in South Asia*

The *Ssu-ma Fa* is a Chinese text that could be dated around the fourth century BCE. It says that the important virtues on which the government should rely are benevolence, righteousness, faith, trust, loyalty and wisdom.[55] The *Ssu-ma Fa* notes: 'In general, with regard to the people: rescue them with benevolence; engage them in battle with righteousness; make decisions through wisdom ... exercise sole authority through credibility.... Thus the mind must embody benevolence and actions should incorporate righteousness.'[56]

Megasthenes, the Greek ambassador to the Maurya capital at Pataliputra, tells us that the Mauryas practiced a form of limited or just warfare. Even when battles raged between two armies, the peasants in the vicinity of the battlefield continued to cultivate their land, and the soldiers were strictly instructed not to molest the peasants.[57] However, the Kalinga (Orissa) expedition (262 BCE)[58] was an exception. Kalinga rebelled during the later part of Bindusara's (the father of Asoka) reign. Asoka conquered Kalinga because this region bred war elephants. Further, he wished to secure the trade route to central and south India, and to reconquer a territory that had rebelled against the imperial government.[59] The inability to recover lost territory would have encouraged further rebellions. About 150,000 people were deported from Kalinga after the war.[60]

In the Thirteenth Major Rock Edict, Asoka speaks of his remorse at the death of over 100,000 people as a result of the military campaign and bemoans the sufferings caused by war.[61] In the dialogues between Socrates and Alcibiades, which are authored by Plato, Socrates' message is that warfare cannot be judged in isolation from the issue of justice. And the preservation of virtue stands above the purely physical results of war. The overall message of the dialogue, according to Henrik Syse, is that when war is undertaken for personal reasons, it brings ruin.[62] Again, Socrates claimed that besides courage, the soldiers must learn other virtues like moderation, justice and prudence (practical wisdom) for waging

[55] *The Seven Military Classics of Ancient China*, tr. and Commentary by Ralph D. Sawyer with Mei-chun Sawyer (Boulder/San Francisco: Westview Press, 1993), pp. 111, 118.
[56] *The Seven Military Classics of Ancient China*, p. 141.
[57] Thapar, *The Mauryas Revisited*, pp. 8–9.
[58] Habib and Jha, *Mauryan India*, p. 97.
[59] Thapar, *The Mauryas Revisited*, p. 6.
[60] Jha, *Early India*, p. 100.
[61] Gethin, 'Buddhist Monks, Buddhist Kings, Buddhist Violence', p. 74.
[62] Henrik Syse, 'Plato, Thucydides, and the Education of Alcibiades', *JME*, vol. 5, no. 4 (2006), pp. 297, 299.

Buddhism, Jainism and Asoka's Ahimsa

'just' war.[63] The Thirteenth Rock Edict proclaims Asoka's remorse over the human suffering caused by his own action, that is, the Kalinga campaign.[64] T'ai Kung's *Six Secret Teachings* dates from the Warring States period (403–221 BCE). T'ai Kung notes that the ruler, and by implication all the members of the government, should intensively cultivate universally acknowledged virtues like benevolence, righteousness, loyalty, credibility, sincerity, wisdom and so on.[65]

Socrates views true courage as pursuing the right course in spite of unwanted consequences. Socrates goes on to say that waging war against those who act justly is unlawful.[66] In the Thirteenth Rock Edict, Asoka says that there should be no more territorial conquests and that his descendants should also abjure conquest by arms. However, being a realist, write Irfan Habib and Vivekanand Jha, he does not make the ban on conquest by arms absolute. If conquest by arms becomes necessary, it should be undertaken with mildness and light punishment.[67] Asoka speaks of conquest by means of *dhamma* as opposed to military violence.

Immanuel Kant's *Perpetual Peace* (1795) aspires to an ideal and views peace as a moral objective.[68] Asoka, somewhat like Rousseau and Kant, seems to have believed that war is antithetical to the rational order of the polities.[69] Asoka – despite his emphasis on *ahimsa*, derived from Buddhism and Jainism – did not disband his large army. Asoka may not have engaged in any further military adventures after the conquest of Kalinga, but the army remained the principal instrument for deterring enemies, both inside and outside the frontiers of the Mauryan Empire. Nor did Asoka emphasize general disarmament. Soldiers occupied an important place in the Maurya society. Megasthenes tells us that Indian society was divided into seven classes, of which soldiers constituted one of the most important.[70] Military power remains the last option for pacification, if persuasion fails.[71]

---

[63] Reichberg, Syse and Begby (eds.), *The Ethics of War*, p. 23.

[64] Habib and Jha, *Mauryan India*, p. 65.

[65] *The Seven Military Classics of Ancient China*, p. 32.

[66] Syse, 'Plato, Thucydides, and the Education of Alcibiades', pp. 294–5.

[67] Habib and Jha, *Mauryan India*, p. 82.

[68] Hew Strachan, *Clausewitz's On War: A Biography* (New York: Atlantic Monthly Press, 2007), p. 90.

[69] Julian Reid, 'Foucault on Clausewitz: Conceptualizing the Relationship between War and Power', *Alternatives*, vol. 28, no. 1 (2003), p. 10.

[70] Thapar, *The Mauryas Revisited*, p. 33.

[71] Habib and Jha, *Mauryan India*, p. 82.

52   *Hinduism and the Ethics of Warfare in South Asia*

Buddhism pushed the concept of *cakravattin/cakavattin*, that is, the universal monarch who is defined as a just ruler and who rules in accordance with the regulations of *dhamma*. If he fails to rule justly, then the wheel (the symbol of royalty) sinks to the ground and disappears.[72] The *cakravartin* is the moral center of the political world, and the ruler is seen as regulating the wheel of righteousness.[73] The symbols accompanying the image of the *cakravartin* are known as the seven jewels and consist of the wheel – signifying universal power – the goddess of fortune, the queen, the *yuvaraj* (crown prince), *mantra* (minister), imperial *hasti* (elephants) and *asva* (horse). The Buddhist and Jain concept of *cakravartin* was an integral part of Asoka's *dhamma*. The *cakravartin* is regarded as a universal emperor whose dominion included the whole of Jambudipa (the subcontinent). Such a ruler is just, and his reign is prosperous. He is so virtuous that he is regarded as having the power of divinity.[74]

Asoka rejected or modified certain elements of Buddhism while formulating his *dhamma*. Early Buddhism preached the theory of *Mahasammatta*, the Great Elect, a contractual theory based on an agreement between the population and the person whom they elect as king. The king was regarded as serving the state, the collection of taxes being his due. In his edicts, Asoka did not regard himself as the Great Elect in his relations with his subjects, but rather portrayed himself as a father-figure. He stressed the father-child relationship between the king and the populace. The monarch was portrayed as a powerful paternal benefactor and not as the servant of the state. This paternal attitude was a new feature of kingship and replaced the *Mahasammatta* theory, reflecting the trend in governance towards centralization.[75] The paternal concept of kingship becomes more rigid and elaborate in Kautilya's *Arthasastra* and Kamandaka's *Nitisara*.

T'ai Kung in China emerges as a strong proponent of the doctrine of the benevolent ruler, with its consequent administrative emphasis on the people's welfare. Wei Liao-tzu, in a book composed around the fourth century BCE, writes that the policies of the king must be directed towards aiding and sustaining the people rather than towards self-aggrandizement and the glorious exercise of power. Confucius (551–479 BCE) in his *Analects* demands courage and resoluteness in the practice of

---

[72] Thapar, *The Mauryas Revisited*, pp. 17–18.
[73] Stein, *A History of India*, p. 81.
[74] Thapar, *Asoka and the Decline of the Mauryas*, p. 146.
[75] Ibid., p. 147.

Buddhism, Jainism and Asoka's Ahimsa

righteousness. Warfare is considered inappropriate for civilized men.[76] According to Confucian thought, which became the state philosophy under the Former Han Dynasty (206 BCE–8 CE), the ruler need only cultivate his virtue and implement benevolent policies.[77] Asoka's *dhamma*'s emphasis on the welfare of the subjects was related to the Buddhist idea that serving others secures one's path to salvation.[78]

In addition, there were instrumental reasons for pushing the welfare concept in the *dhamma*. Asoka realized that his centralized monarchy would be strengthened if the subjects' welfare at all levels was attended to by the monarch, in particular, and by the state in general. In one of his edicts, Asoka speaks of the welfare of the state's prisoners. Prison was considered not as a house of torture and terror but as a reformatory (quite a modern concept). Until the prisoner was released, his family was cared for by the state.[79] However, Asoka never banned capital punishment. In the Thirteenth Rock Edict, he exhorts the forest dwellers to behave properly so that they do not have to be killed. The same rock edict says that obedience to persons placed above oneself is a crucial part of *dhamma*. As regards internal pacification, in the Fourth Pillar Edict, Asoka says that if any of his subjects breaks *dhamma*, that person sins against other persons and needs to be punished. In such a scenario, the *rajukas* should exercise *samata* (moderation) when awarding punishment.[80] The Sixteenth Rock Edict notes: 'An officer fails to act impartially owing to the following dispositions, viz., jealousy, anger, cruelty, hastiness, want of perseverance, laziness and fatigue.... The root of the complete success of an officer lies in the absence of anger and avoidance of hastiness.'[81]

[76] *The Seven Military Classics of Ancient China*, pp. 31, 232–3, 377–8.
[77] *The Seven Military Classics of Ancient China*, General Introduction and Historical Background, p. 2.
[78] Ferguson, *War and Peace in the World Religions*, p. 45.
[79] Thapar, *Asoka and the Decline of the Mauryas*, p. 156.
[80] Habib and Jha, *Mauryan India*, pp. 64, 77–8. I differ from Irfan Habib and Vivekanand Jha in translating *samata* as "equity." There is no equivalent word in English for *samata*. *Samata* is somewhat equivalent to *Khama* in Bengali (which is derived from the Sanskrit *Kshama*), which means at least partial pardon for committing an offence. This concept is in contrast to the harsh punishment advocated by the Legalist School and the *Arthasastra*. In my understanding, *samata* means maintaining benevolence and toleration while punishing the sinner. It is an attempt to establish punishment in proportion to the crime committed under specific conditions rather than relying on rigid adherence to abstract rules. The objective is to punish the sin and not the sinner. This is the idea that M. K. Gandhi later followed. The underlying idea is: 'To err is human/normal; partial forgiveness is divine'.
[81] D. C. Sircar, *Inscriptions of Asoka* (1957; reprint, New Delhi: Publications Division, 1998), Inscriptions.

54   Hinduism and the Ethics of Warfare in South Asia

These measures are in accordance with the Buddhist ideal of maintaining a balance between sin and punishment. Lambert Schmithausen notes that Asoka became a Buddhist lay follower. Not only Asoka, but before him Ajatasatru was also influenced by Buddhism. Schmithausen continues that it is possible to an extent to reconcile the Buddhist emphasis on *ahimsa* with good governance. Buddha did not apply *ahimsa* to the specific situation of a king or to the case of an invasion. Defensive military measures are allowed to an extent. One Buddhist text notes that soldiers are asked not to retreat but are warned not to kill indiscriminately. Schmithausen says that according to the Buddhist *cakravartin* ideal, neighbouring kings should submit to the righteous ruler. Here, Buddhism is probably referring to what modern-day international theorists call deterrence. The implication is that if these kings do not submit, then the righteous ruler is justified in attacking and subduing them. If deterrence fails, then military attacks are allowed. Overall, it is left to the ruler to decide whether and to what extent the concept of non-violence is to be applied in the domain of politics (i.e., public violence, like warfare and capital punishment). The warrior is to observe the Buddhist norms wherever they do not conflict with his specific duties as a ruler. In case a warrior has to indulge in limited warfare, he can compensate for his sin through lavish donations to the Buddhist order. In fact, one text notes that it is a sin for a good ruler not to censure, punish or exile those who deserve it. *Milindapanha* notes that corporal punishment should be applied to thieves because they deserve it owing to their bad *karma*. The Mahayana and Vajrayana texts view the killing of 'bad' persons as compassionate.[82]

This trend of justifying the use of minimal violence for good governance is also in line with Confucianism. Mencius (371–289 BCE), the second great Confucian, advocated punitive military expeditions to chastize evil rulers and relieve the people's sufferings. Hsun-tzu, a Confucian of the late Warring States era, wrote about the inescapable necessity of armies and warfare.[83]

The concept of aggressive expansion was inherent in brahmanical ideology, with the central role of sacrificial rituals like the *asvamedha* and *rajasuya* ceremonies eulogizing wars of aggrandizement. Buddhism, by contrast, eulogized the role of *dharmaraja*, which made such rituals irrelevant.[84] In accordance with the principles of *dhamma*, Asoka

---

[82] Lambert Schmithausen, 'Aspects of the Buddhist Attitude towards War', in Houben and Van Kooji (eds.), *Violence Denied*, pp. 50–9.

[83] *The Seven Military Classics of Ancient China*, pp. 2, 378.

[84] Thapar, *The Mauryas Revisited*, p. 17.

Buddhism, Jainism and Asoka's Ahimsa

banned the ritual sacrifice of animals, a move that hit the class interests of the Brahmins. Both the Roman Emperor Constantine and the Mauryan Emperor Asoka used religion for political purposes. Asoka's *dhamma* and Constantine's Christianity forbade sacrifices at home and festive meetings and gatherings, reflecting the fear that such religious gatherings might transform themselves into politically subversive groups.[85]

In two rock edicts, Asoka says that the inhabitants of his empire are like his children and that he would strive for their welfare just as he would for his own siblings'. Asoka's public welfare measures involved providing medical assistance and other sorts of relief for the travellers and animals on the roads.[86] He constructed rest houses and veterinary establishments.[87] The Buddhist monks studied medical lore and treated fellow monks and laymen. Buddha himself is called *mahabhisaja*, that is, the great physician.[88] Asoka ordered the digging of wells and planting of trees along the roads.[89]

Asoka appointed a special class of officers known as *dhamma mahamattas*. Superficially, they were supposed to attend to the welfare of the subjects and to bring about an infiltration of *dhamma* into all levels of the society. In reality, they were organs of surveillance. They had the power to enter the homes of people of all classes of society, even members of the royal family and their relatives. With the passage of time, the power of the *dhamma mahamattas* to interfere in the lives of the people increased. These officials operated not only in the heart of the empire but also in the distant frontier regions and among neighbouring peoples (of the vassal states). The *dhamma mahamattas* worked among both religious communities and secular groups. Besides the *dhamma mahamattas*, Asoka had another class of officers known as *pativedikas* who bought news of the people to the monarch.[90] The Sixth Rock Edict tells us that Asoka appointed *pativedakas* (reporters) who would report to him about conditions among the people. The Third Rock Edict and First Rock Edict inform us that officials were ordered to make tours of inspection every three to five years.[91] One could surmise that the *pativedakas* also

---

[85] Thapar, *Asoka and the Decline of the Mauryas*, pp. 145, 151; Jha, *Early India*, p. 111.
[86] Habib and Jha, *Mauryan India*, pp. 76, 80.
[87] Ferguson, *War and Peace in the World Religions*, p. 51.
[88] Shrimali, *The Age of Iron and the Religious Revolution*, p. 130.
[89] Habib and Jha, *Mauryan India*, p. 35.
[90] Thapar, *Asoka and the Decline of the Mauryas*, pp. 156–8.
[91] Habib and Jha, *Mauryan India*, p. 35.

56   Hinduism and the Ethics of Warfare in South Asia

functioned as news writers/intelligence agents, that is, as spies. Kautilya *Arthasastra* also put forward the scheme that the *vijigishu* should made use of monks, religious mendicants and nuns plus professional spies as *chara*s.

Asoka also started the practice of *dhamma yatras*. He toured the country for the furtherance of *dhamma* and to gain firsthand knowledge regarding the state of affairs in his empire. Before Asoka, monarchs toured their domain during military expeditions, hunting excursions and pleasure trips. Hunting expeditions were ended by Asoka.[92] In the pre-modern era, an army gained collective training for warfare while conducting hunting expeditions. One can surmise that Asoka's ban on hunting expeditions reduced the combat effectiveness of the Mauryan Army in the long run.

CONCLUSION

Asoka's policy of *dhamma* shows that for the first time in South Asian history, the state was systematically trying to regulate religion within its dominions. Asoka's *dhamma* means rules of conduct. The *ahimsa* of Buddhism and Jainism suited Asoka, who followed the policy of strategic defence: no more aggressive campaigns for annexation of foreign territories, but continued use of the army for deterring external and internal enemies. Asoka followed a moderate form of militarism. Force was to be used as a last option for maintaining the borders and keeping the 'peace' among the forest dwellers. This was possible because of certain beliefs within Buddhism and Jainism that tend to relativize the norm of not killing.[93] Asoka, like Plato, accepted that war should not be considered apart from morality and justice.[94] Truly, Asoka breathed a humanitarian spirit into the rigid Mauryan administration. However, Asoka's welfare policy is a double-edged sword. On the one hand, his welfare mechanism's objective was to look after the material well-being of the inhabitants of his empire; on the other hand, it functioned as a surveillance mechanism. Asoka's *dhamma* had many similarities to Confucianism and certain other political philosophies of ancient China. However, Asoka's *dhamma* died an early death. The brahmanical reaction was not long in coming. The last Maurya emperor was

---

[92] Thapar, *Asoka and the Decline of the Mauryas*, p. 160.
[93] Schmithausen, 'Aspects of the Buddhist Attitude towards War', p. 56.
[94] Reichberg, Syse and Begby (eds.), *The Ethics of War*, p. 19.

Buddhism, Jainism and Asoka's Ahimsa   57

assassinated by Pusyamitra Sunga, the Brahmin commander-in-chief of the Mauryan army, who founded the Sunga Dynasty.[95] As a reaction to the elaborate code of *dharmayuddha*, Kautilya, as the next chapter shows, expounded the theory of *kutayuddha* in his *Arthasastra* and changed the rules of warfare.

---

[95] Thapar, *The Mauryas Revisited*, p. 25.

3

Kautilya's *Kutayuddha*

300 BCE–300 CE

The debate regarding the dating and authorship of the *Arthasastra* continues. Thomas Trautmann argues that the Kautilya *Arthasastra* is actually a composite product of three or four different individuals. In Trautmann's view, Kautilya is at best a compiler and editor of the teachings of previous teachers belonging to the *arthasastra* tradition.[1] In a somewhat similar vein, D. N. Jha writes that computer analysis shows that there are three distinct styles in the *Arthasastra*, but that Books 2, 3 and 4 have a distinct Mauryan touch and constitute the kernel of the *Arthasastra*.[2]

Related to the problem of authorship, the author's background is also shrouded in mystery. According to one tradition, Kautilya (also known as Chanakya and Vishnugupta) was a learned Brahmin of eastern India who served the Nanda Dynasty of Magadha but left the Nandas due to some personal problems. According to another version, Kautilya hailed from Taxila, an important cultural centre in Pakistan's Punjab, about twenty miles north-west of Rawalpindi. On his own initiative, he became a councilor of Chandragupta Maurya, the founder of the Maurya Empire.[3] P. V. Kane, following the Buddhist and Jain traditions, suggests that Kautilya probably hailed from Gandhara.[4] The

---

[1] Surendra Nath Mital, *Kautilya Arthasastra Revisited* (2000; reprint, Centre for Studies in Civilizations, distributed by Munshiram Manoharlal: New Delhi, 2004), pp. 106, 111.

[2] D. N. Jha, *Early India: A Concise History* (New Delhi: Manohar, 2004), p. 96.

[3] Narasingha P. Sil, *Kautilya's Arthasastra: A Comparative Study* (Calcutta/New Delhi: Academic Publishers, 1985), p. 19.

[4] P. V. Kane, *History of Dharmasastra (Ancient and Medieval Religious and Civil Law in India)*, vol. 1, Part 1 (1930; reprint, Poona: Bhandarkar Oriental Research Institute, 1968), pp. 173, 214–15.

Bhagavata Purana says that a Brahmin named Chanakya destroyed the Nandas and coronated Chandragupta, whose son was Bindusara and whose grandson was Asoka.[5] Overall, the *Puranas* and *Mahavamsa* equate Chanakya with Kautilya. In general, historians agree that Kautilya played a very important part in the success of Chandragupta (320–297/6 BCE). P. V. Kane claims that the *Arthasastra* was composed between 320 and 300 BCE. Some scholars point out that if the *Arthasastra* was the product of Kautilya, why does Megasthenes, the Seleucid ambassador to the Maurya court, never mention Kautilya? Kane says that it is because in 302 BCE, when Megasthenes came to India, Kautilya had retired from public life.[6] Narasingha P. Sil assumes that towards the end of Chandragupta's reign, Kautilya fell out with his royal master and left the Maurya capital of Pataliputra (near Bankipur on the river Ganga in Bihar) and retired to private life. The *Arthasastra* was probably composed during Kautilya's retirement from the court at Pataliputra.[7] Secondly, only fragments of Megasthenes' work has survived. So we cannot be sure whether Megasthenes did know of Kautilya *Arthasastra*.

ORIGIN AND SCOPE OF *ARTHASASTRA*

Kautilya's work did not develop in a vacuum. The theory of polity – that is, the genre known as *arthasastra* – emerged as early as 600 BCE.[8] Kautilya quotes several individual predecessors, including Pisuna, Bharadvaja, Kaninka, Vatavyadhi, and Visalaksa, most of whom belonged to the *arthasastra* tradition. *Arthasastra* is the name of the work composed by Kautilya, but it also refers to a genre of classical Hindu literature. In Kane's view, *arthasastra* is narrower in scope than *dharmasastra* but broader than *dandaniti*. Overall, *arthasastra* comprises politics, economics, law and justice.[9] *Arthasastra* means *labha* (the theory of politics for acquisition, i.e., the theory of the acquisition of political power and economic resources) and *palana* (good governance, i.e., the protection of material goods and the king's subjects).[10] 'Economics and the theory

---

[5] Mital, *Kautilya Arthasastra Revisited*, p. 60.

[6] Kane, *History of Dharmasastra*, vol. 1, Part 1, pp. 172, 184–5, 215.

[7] Sil, *Kautilya's Arthasastra*, pp. 19–20.

[8] *The Kautilya Arthasastra* (hereinafter *KA*), Part III, *A Study*, by R. P. Kangle (1965; reprint, New Delhi: Motilal Banrasidas, 2000), p. 11.

[9] Kane, *History of Dharmasastra*, vol. 1, Part 1, pp. 152–3.

[10] Mital, *Kautilya Arthasastra Revisited*, p. 65.

Hinduism and the Ethics of Warfare in South Asia

of politics are the only sciences', say the followers of Brihaspati.[11] 'The theory of politics is the true knowledge', say the followers of Usanas (a pre-Kautilyan political thinker). The school of the Usanas continues: 'For with it are bound up undertakings connected with all the knowledge systems.'[12] Kautilya says: 'Since with their help one can learn what is spiritual good and material well-being, therefore the knowledge systems (*vidyas*) are so called. Samkhya, Yoga and Lokayata – these constitute philosophy.'[13] Kautilya attempts to put forward the timeless laws of politics, economy, diplomacy and war.[14]

Kautilya's work contains fifteen *adhikaranas* (books). The first five books deal with the internal administration of the polity, and the next eight deal with foreign relations. The last two books are miscellaneous in character. Book 7 deals especially with foreign policy and the use of stratagems and force for gaining objectives. Books 9 and 10 deal with military preparations for the *vijigishu* (ruler with hegemonic ambitions). Book 12 shows how a weak king should survive against a strong king. Book 13 mainly describes siege warfare.[15]

The *Arthasastra* is written in prose, with verses scattered at the middle or end of chapters.[16] The geographical scope of Kautilya's theory encompasses the whole subcontinent. Kautilya praises high-value commodities from different parts of South Asia. He refers to silk from Magadha (Bihar) and Kasmira (Kashmir), cloth from Vanga (West Bengal and Bangladesh), and gems and diamonds from Vidharbha, Kalinga (Orissa), Kosala and Kasi.[17] Kautilya was also aware of the neighbouring countries of India. The *Arthasastra* speaks of silk from Cinas (China) and blankets from Nepal.[18]

Kautilya's work does not refer to any particular historical event. This is because in ancient India, according to the tradition of the *sastras*, great works expounding timeless principles were always compiled by some

---

[11] *The Kautilya Arthasastra*, Part II, *An English Translation with Critical and Explanatory Notes*, by R. P. Kangle (1972; reprint, Delhi: Motilal Banarasidas, 1992), p. 6.

[12] My translation differs from that of Kangle. *KA*, Part II, by Kangle, p. 6.

[13] My translation differs from that of Kangle. *KA*, Part II, by Kangle, p. 6. In the manuscript, the term *vidya* is used. Instead of the term 'science' which Kangle uses, I prefer the term 'knowledge system'.

[14] Roger Boesche, 'Kautilya's *Arthasastra* on War and Diplomacy in Ancient India', *JMH*, vol. 67 (Jan. 2003), p. 15.

[15] *KA*, Part III, by Kangle, pp. 19–20.

[16] Kane, *History of Dharmasastra*, vol. 1, Part 1, p. 197.

[17] Mital, *Kautilya Arthasastra Revisited*, p. 25.

[18] Kane, *History of Dharmasastra*, vol. 1, Part 1, p. 211.

Kautilya's Kutayuddha   61

mythical sage. In such works, any reference to historical individuals or events is inconceivable, as any such reference would reduce the value of the work.[19] Kautilya may not have mentioned historical events but no theorist could remain unaffected by the surrounding historical context and the contemporary material culture. In addition to the pre-existing political theories in India, Kautilya's ideas are also shaped by his immediate historical background, which is the focus of the next section.

THE ECONOMIC, POLITICAL AND MILITARY BACKGROUND

After late in the sixth century BCE, Magadha emerged as the most powerful *mahajanapada*. Bimbisara, the ruler of Magadha (546–494 BCE), was known as *seniya* (one with *sena*). D. N. Jha asserts that Bimbisara was probably the first ruler in India with a regular standing army. Bimbisara annexed Anga. Bimbisara's son and successor, Ajatasatru, not only fortified Rajagriha (the capital of Magadha) with a forty-kilometer-long wall but also sent one of his ministers (a Brahmin named Vassakara) to sow dissension among the Lichchhavi tribes.[20] Ajatasatru was able to overthrow the Vajjis through the policy of *bheda* followed by Vassakara.[21] Kautilya's concept of *kutayuddha* was probably shaped by such historical events.

In 413 BCE, Shishunaga, the viceroy/governor of Benaras, became the ruler, and in 321 BCE the Shishunaga dynasty was overthrown by Mahapadma Nanda. Mahapadma, a Sudra, not only annexed Kalinga but also increased the strength of the army.[22] The *Vishnu Purana* and the *Brahmanda Purana* say that the Nandas ruled for 100 years.[23] Alexander crossed the Hindu Kush mountain range in 327 BCE, but he then left after a brief sojourn in north-west India. Hence, no direct confrontation between the Greeks and the Nanda Empire occurred.

Chandragupta, like Mahapadma Nanda, was a Sudra. Chandragupta's mother, Mura, was propably the daughter of a Persian merchant. Reflecting the historical reality, the *Arthasastra*, unlike the *vedas*, never argue that the *vijigishu* should always come from the Kshatriya rank. Chandragupta seized Magadha around 321 BCE. By 312 BCE, he had completed the conquest of north and north-west India. If we believe the

[19] *KA*, Part III, by Kangle, p. 63.
[20] Jha, *Early India*, pp. 84–6, 90.
[21] *KA*, Part III, by Kangle, p. 11.
[22] Jha, *Early India*, p. 87.
[23] Mital, *Kautilya Arthasastra Revisited*, p. 60.

62   *Hinduism and the Ethics of Warfare in South Asia*

Mudraraksa (a fictional political drama in Sanskrit, by Vishakadatta, composed between the fourth and the seventh century CE), Chandragupta probably first acquired Punjab and then, with the help of Chanakya, moved towards the Nanda Empire. Paurava, who was ruling as a client ruler on behalf of Alexander, was killed before 318 BCE. The *Mudraraksa* tells us that Chandragupta, with the aid of some mercenaries from the north-west frontier tribes, laid siege to Kusumapura, the capital of Magadha. In the *Questions of Milinda* there is a reference to Bhaddasala, a general belonging to the Nandas, who fought against Chandragupta. Chandragupta defeated Seleucus in 305 BCE in a series of encounters along the river Indus. Megasthenes came to the Maurya court as an ambassador around 302 BCE and resided in India for four years. Around 297 BCE, Chandragupta passed away.[24]

As regards the nature of the Maurya Empire, historians are divided into two camps. While R. K. Mookerji[25] and D. N. Jha argue that it was a centralized empire, Gerard Fussman[26] and Burton Stein[27] claim that the Maurya Empire was a decentralized political entity. Some factual statements point to the fact that the Maurya Empire was a centralized bureaucratic polity. The Mauryas, like the Romans, were great road builders, and all the roads led to Pataliputra. Megasthenes noted that the thousand-mile-long royal highway connected Pataliputra to Taxila.[28] Pataliputra was connected to Nepal via Vaishali. From there a road passed through Champaran to Kapilavastu, Kalsi (DehraDun District), and Hazara up to Peshawar. Another network of roads connected Pataliputra to Sasaram, Mirzapur and central India. Yet, another road connected Pataliputra to Kalinga, Andhra and Karnataka, the southernmost limit of the empire.[29] These roads, besides facilitating trade and commerce, also functioned as military highways.

Jha claims that the Maurya economy was a sort of command economy. The Maurya polity exercised rigid control through a number of superintendents who presided over all trade and commercial activities. The metallurgy and mining industries were highly developed and were state

---

[24] Kane, *History of Dharmasastra*, vol. 1, Part 1, pp. 173–4, 184, 186, 217–18.

[25] R. K. Mookerji, *Chandragupta Maurya and His Times* (n.d.; reprint, New Delhi: Motilal Banrasidas, 1960).

[26] Gerard Fussman, 'Central and Provincial Administration in Ancient India: The Problem of the Mauryan Empire', *Indian Historical Review*, vol. 14, nos. 1–2 (1988), pp. 43–72.

[27] Burton Stein, *A History of India* (1998; reprint, New Delhi: Oxford University Press, 2004), pp. 78–83.

[28] Mital, *Kautilya Arthasastra Revisited*, p. 29.

[29] Jha, *Early India*, p. 102.

Kautilya's Kutayuddha 63

monopolies. The monopoly rights of the state over mineral resources gave it exclusive control over the manufacture of metal weaponry.[30] However, at times, mining was leased out to contractors. India produced high-quality steel, and the metal workers of Asia Minor adopted the techniques of Indian steel making.[31] Kautilya tells us about a die-striking (punch-marking) system but is unaware of casting coins in mould.[32] The Magadhan state functioned as a cash economy.[33] Money was used for trade as well as for paying the state's civilian and military officials.[34]

Megasthenes tells us that soldiers were paid and equipped by the state. Hence, it seems that the Mauryas maintained a standing army and not merely a militia.[35] On the other hand, opines P. C. Chakravarti, the existence of armed trade and craft guilds with their private militias points to the fact that the Maurya Empire was a weak state. Not only did the private militias of these armed *srenis* provide protection to these organizations from brigands and highwayman, but during emergencies the ruler also hired them to fight internal as well as external enemies. These armed guilds occasionally engaged in private warfare and, in a way, constituted semi-autonomous states within a state.[36] It seems that the Mauryan Empire was not uniformly administered and was partially centralized and partially decentralized.

Romila Thapar takes a middle position and claims that the level of control exercised by the Maurya central government over different regions varied with distance. The inner core of the Maurya Empire was the metropolitan state of Magadha, which was ruled directly by the emperor from Pataliputra. Beyond the metroplitan state was the outer core of the empire, which comprised north and central India. The outer core region was divided into several provinces ruled by viceroys appointed by the emperor at Pataliputra. Most of the viceroys were princes of the royal family. The control of the central government at Pataliputra over the outer core region was substantial, but less than its control over the metropolitan state. Beyond the outer core was the periphery, which was comprised

---

[30] Ibid., pp. 102–5.

[31] Mital, *Kautilya Arthasastra Revisited*, p. 32.

[32] Sil, *Kautilya's Arthasastra*, p. 25.

[33] D. D. Kosambi, *The Culture and Civilization of Ancient India in Historical Outline* (n.d.; reprint, New Delhi: Vikas, 2001), p. 154.

[34] Jha, *Early India*, p. 102.

[35] Biren Bonnerjea, 'Peace and War in Hindu Culture', *Primitive Man: Quarterly Journal of the Catholic Anthropological Conference*, vol. 7, no. 3 (1934), p. 36.

[36] P. C. Chakravarti, *The Art of War in Ancient India* (1941; reprint, New Delhi: Low Price Publications, 1989), pp. 6, 8.

64   *Hinduism and the Ethics of Warfare in South Asia*

of north-west India and Deccan (the region south of the Narmada River). The periphery was ruled by several hereditary vassal chiefs and tribal leaders who accepted the political suzerainty of the Mauryan emperor at Pataliputra. It goes without saying that the control exercised by the central government at Pataliputra over the distant periphery was weakest. The central government did not interfere in the internal affairs of the vassal kingdoms, but it did control the foreign and military policies of the vassal chiefs.[37] This three-tier model of Thapar seems to be the most appropriate one for explaining the structure of the Maurya Empire. It is to be noted that the *Arthasastra* also speaks of regions ruled directly by the *vijigishu*; the *janapadas* (fertile agricultural land dotted with urban centres), which were ruled by chiefs and officials appointed by the *vijigishu* and hereditary vassal chiefs; and the forest regions under indirect control of the *vijigishu*. As a basis of comparison, the Shang Empire of China seems to have been more centralized than the Mauryan Empire because the former political entity had the capacity to conscript the common people for civil engineering projects and distributed grain through a system of centrally administered state granaries.[38]

Buddhism focused mainly on *moksa*. The *arthasastra* school, asserts Sil, emerged as a reaction to Buddhism. The *arthasastra* tradition emphasizes materialism rather than morality. The *arthasastra* writers divide the goals of human life into *chatuvarga* (four categories): *dharma* (morality), *artha* (wealth), *kama* (desires) and *moksa*. And of these four, *artha* occupies the most prominent place. Kautilya himself says that material well-being is supreme, because spiritual well-being and sensual pleasures depend on material well-being. The *arthasastra* means the *sastra* (theory) of *artha*. The meaning of *artha* changes with circumstances; broadly, it refers to wealth and territory with human population. Kautilya's *Arthasastra* does not really deal with the theory of the generation of wealth but is a treatise on statecraft. Kautilya says that the source of the livelihood of men is wealth and that the means for the attainment and protection of *artha* constitutes the theory of politics. Kautilya aims to educate the prince on the acquisition of material welfare (*labha*) and its maintenance through good governance.[39] The objective of Kautilya's theory is to lay bare the study of politics, wealth and practical expediency. The subjects covered

---

[37] Romila Thapar, *The Mauryas Revisited* (1987; reprint, Calcutta: K. P. Bagchi & Company, 1993).

[38] Thomas M. Kane, *Ancient China on Postmodern War: Enduring Ideas from the Chinese Strategic Tradition* (London/New York: Routledge, 2007), p. 29.

[39] Sil, *Kautilya's Arthasastra*, pp. 20–1.

Kautilya's Kutayuddha 65

are administration, law, order and justice, finance, foreign policy, internal security and defence against external powers.[40] The *arthasastra* tradition, claims Ashok S. Chousalkar, is based on the Lokayata philosophy, which emphasized analysis of concrete facts. The Lokayatas deduced their conclusions from human behaviour and attempted an inductive investigation of the polity.[41] In the following sections, Kautilya's philosophical ideas are compared to and contrasted with both Western and Chinese philosophies.

KAUTILYA AS A REALIST PHILOSOPHER AND A THEORIST OF POWER

Realist theorists of international relations assume that the state is an unitary actor with coherent objectives and a centralized capacity to act on its decisions.[42] The Realist School argues that the behaviour of states is shaped by the power at their disposal in the fiercely competitive international environment. Actions undertaken by a polity for defensive purposes may be seen by others as posing an offensive threat.[43] The measures that one state takes to increase its security in an insecure world often decrease another state's security, even if that is not intended. One's strength may be another's weakness. Each side fears the other, but every step that one side takes to strengthen security scares the other into similar steps, and vice versa, in a continuing escalating spiral. For the polities, there is no escape from the system. This is known as a 'prisoner's dilemma', fuelled by mutual suspicion. As absolute security is difficult to achieve, constant warfare may be waged, conquests carried afar and power accumulated, all motivated by security concerns – that is, for defence.[44] The actors in the international state system pursue gain-maximizing behaviour and have difficulty effecting cooperation.[45] This is because, in the realist paradigm, the international state system is a self-help system, and today's

---

[40] Rashed Uz Zaman, 'Kautilya: The Indian Strategic Thinker and Indian Strategic Culture', *Comparative Strategy*, vol. 25, no. 3 (2006), p. 235.

[41] Ashok S. Chousalkar, *A Comparative Study of Theory of Rebellion in Kautilya and Aristotle* (New Delhi: Indological Book House, 1990), p. 65.

[42] Victoria Tin-Bor Hui, *War and State Formation in Ancient China and Early Modern Europe* (New York: Cambridge University Press, 2005), p. 15.

[43] Bruce Russett, 'Thucydides, Ancient Greece, and the Democratic Peace', *JME*, vol. 5, no. 4 (2006), p. 255.

[44] Azar Gat, *War in Human Civilization* (Oxford: Oxford University Press, 2006), pp. 98–9.

[45] Hui, *War and State Formation in Ancient China and Early Modern Europe*, p. 13.

66   *Hinduism and the Ethics of Warfare in South Asia*

friends and allies could become tomorrow's enemies.[46] In the brutish world where today's friends may be tomorrow's enemies, states are more concerned with relative gains than with absolute gains.[47] The standard realist assumption is that states are rational unitary actors calculating, under conditions of uncertainty, the costs and benefits of peace and war.[48] And going to war at any given time could be a rational and even an optimal option.[49]

The realist thinkers from Niccolo Machiavelli (1469–1527 CE) and Thomas Hobbes through Hans Morgenthau, Robert Gilpin and John Mearsheimer have observed that self-interested rulers pursue opportunistic expansion, which constitutes the driving force behind *realpolitik* competition. Victoria Tin-Bor Hui writes that classical Western thinkers like Machiavelli and Hobbes emphasized both passions and interests. My take is that both these thinkers, like Kautilya, focused more on interests than on emotions and passions. Kenneth Waltz somewhat revises the classical insights and suggests that rational states seek to maximize security rather than power, because security is the highest end, while power is a means to an end. Waltz continues that states at a minimum seek their own preservation and at a maximum drive for universal dominion[50] that will give them total security. This is exactly the point that Kautilya pushes.

The neo-realist approach assumes that states seek power. The offensive realists argue that states pursue power not only for security but also for acquiring hegemony in the inter-state arena, since only a hegemon is truly secure.[51] The defensive realists argue that states attempt to expand when expansion increases their security, and offensive realism argues that a state's capabilities shape its intentions. It will expand when it can. However, Mearsheimer, an advocate of offensive realism, accepts the idea that the fundamental objective behind state behaviour is survival.[52]

Kautilya, like the realists, believes that the world is full of disorder, anarchy and chaos. The ultimate security for the polities in such

---

[46] Russett, 'Thucydides, Ancient Greece, and the Democratic Peace', p. 260.
[47] Hui, *War and State Formation in Ancient China and Early Modern Europe*, p. 27.
[48] Russett, 'Thucydides, Ancient Greece, and the Democratic Peace', p. 255.
[49] Gat, *War in Human Civilization*, p. 100.
[50] Hui, *War and State Formation in Ancient China and Early Modern Europe*, pp. 13–14.
[51] Rajesh Rajagopalan, *Fighting like a Guerrilla: The Indian Army and Counterinsurgency* (London/New York/Delhi: Routledge, 2008), pp. 30, 74.
[52] Hui, *War and State Formation in Ancient China and Early Modern Europe*, p. 14.

an anarchic inter-state system is power. The *mandala* (circle of states' with the *vijigishu* at the centre) system is a fluid one and the relationships among the various states are always changing, thus creating danger for some and opportunities for others.[53] The international system, in Kautilya's eyes, is characterized by *matsanya* (the law of the pond, where bigger fish gobble up smaller fish). In other words, the inter-state system is characterized by chaos, and the only operating principle is 'might is right'.[54]

In contrast to the *Upanishads*, which pushes a metaphoric attitude towards violence, Kautilya presents an instrumental view of organized violence: state interests and the careful calculation of a cool strategist.[55] The *mandala* theory is essentially a doctrine of strife and struggle. Usanas notes that a king who refuses to fight is swallowed up by the earth just as a rat swallows a mouse.[56] Like the Namierites, Kautilya does not believe in any ideology behind human actions.[57] Kautilya says that the foreign policy of a *vijigishu* should be shaped by the self-interest of the state. Kautilya speaks of *karmasandhi*, that is, a treaty signed with a 'natural' enemy in order to tide over emergencies and to protect the state.[58] The implication is that such treaties are to be torn apart at the first possible opportunity. Francis X. Clooney S.J. asserts that Kautilya advocates preemptive strikes in order to protect the kingdom from external enemies.[59] Preventive war is war waged to arrest the growth of a hostile military power through bold and timely action, exploiting one's advantage while one can. By contrast, a pre-emptive strike is an attack against the enemy for the purpose of self-defence, when a massive enemy attack is almost certain to come and could not be effectively checked.

Kautilya claims that *dandaniti* is the principal instrument for acquisition of things not possessed, for protection of things one possesses and

---

[53] Zaman, 'Kautilya', pp. 236–7, 240.

[54] *KA*, Part III, by Kangle, p. 116.

[55] Laurie L. Patton, 'Telling Stories about Harm: An Overview of Early Indian Narratives', in John R. Hinnells and Richard King (eds.), *Religion and Violence in South Asia: Theory and Practice* (London/New York: Routledge, 2007), p. 24.

[56] Chakravarti, *Art of War in Ancient India*, p. 181.

[57] Chousalkar, *Theory of Rebellion in Kautilya and Aristotle*, p. 77.

[58] *KA*, Part III, by Kangle, pp. 93–4, 118.

[59] Francis X. Clooney S.J., 'Pain but Not Harm: Some Classical Resources towards a Hindu Just War Theory', in Paul Robinson (ed.), *Just War in Comparative Perspective* (Aldershot: Ashgate, 2003), p. 116.

68   *Hinduism and the Ethics of Warfare in South Asia*

for augmentation of things one would like to possess.[60] Like a true realist, Kautilya says:

Power is the possession of strength. Success is obtaining happiness. Power is threefold: the power of knowledge is the power of counsel, the power of the treasury and the army is the power of might, the power of valour is the power of energy. In the same way, success is also threefold: that attainable by the power of counsel is success by counsel, that attainable by the power of might is success by might, that attainable by the power of energy is success by energy.[61]

Roger Boesche writes that the goal of the science of politics for Kautilya, as for Hobbes, is power.[62]

In the *Shantiparva* of the *Mahabharata*, Bhisma, somewhat like a neo-realist theorist, advises Kshatriya to acquire power because a powerful person is the master of everything. Further, wealth strengthens power. Bhisma goes on to say that power is superior to *dharma* because in the final analysis, *dharma* is protected by power. This trend of thinking is further developed in the *Arthasastra*. Kautilya, like Bhisma, accepts the importance of power in public life. Taking a statist perspective, Kautilya writes that 'The king, the ministers, the kingdom, the fortified cities, the treasury, the army and the ally, are the constituent elements of the state.'[63] However, Bhisma says that if *dharma* and power are associated with truth, then this troika becomes invincible.[64] This point is not accepted by Kautilya. He separates political action from religious speculations, urging the *vijigishu* to depend on the theory of *artha* rather than on religious precepts.[65]

At times, during periods of international anarchy, cooperation among some states becomes possible. A would-be hegemon could be deterred by the formation of an anti-hegemonic coalition, and if deterrence failed, then the hegemon could actually be pushed back by a military defeat inflicted upon him by the coalition.[66] Here lies the importance of diplomacy for establishing the balance of power in the international arena. And Kautilya's *Arthasastra* gives a lot of space to the balancing behaviour of weak states as a means of survival in the anarchic world. As regards the

---

[60] Sil, *Kautilya's Arthasastra*, p. 23.
[61] *KA*, Part II, by Kangle, p. 319.
[62] Boesche, 'Kautilya's *Arthasastra*', p. 15.
[63] *KA*, Part II, by Kangle, p. 314.
[64] Chousalkar, *Theory of Rebellion in Kautilya and Aristotle*, p. 66.
[65] Boesche, 'Kautilya's *Arthasastra*', p. 15.
[66] Hui, *War and State Formation in Ancient China and Early Modern Europe*, pp. 17, 24.

Kautilya's Kutayuddha

role of allies, Kautilya's opportunism is revealed in the following words: 'The ally giving the help of money is preferable. For the use of money is made at all times, only sometimes that of troops. And with money, troops and other objects of desire are obtained.'[67] *Tasamantah* is the neighbour of the weak king whose overthrow has brought the *vijigishu* into contiguity with him. Hence, he now becomes the enemy of the *vijigishu* when formerly he was his ally, being one state away.[68]

Theodore George Tsakiris asserts that the Greek historian Thucydides is the founding father of political realism. He is principally a theorist who utilizes the empirical evidence of the Peloponnesian War to validate his own abstract conceptualizations as regards power, human nature and the dynamics of war and peace.[69] Thucydides is a narrative historian rather than a philosophical analyst like Kautilya. Still, this historian's views regarding warfare and strategy need to be assessed in relation to Kautilya's concepts. Thucydides writes that in making a case study of the Athens-Sparta conflict, he is dealing with the theme of the origins of war, a theme that is of timeless relevance. In his *History of the Peloponnesian War*, Thucydides recounts the tragedy of human action in a world of powerful forces beyond human control. For Thucydides, the major motives for going to war are land disputes, past injuries and hegemonic ambitions.[70] The fundamental drives defining the behaviour of states are ambition, fear and self-interest fuelling the state's perennial quest for power. In Thucydides' framework, states have to achieve their objectives within an antagonistic, perfidious and anarchic international system. Thucydides derives his political realism from the Greek philosopher Heracleitus (500 BCE), who claims that war is synonymous with the perpetual state of political antagonism determining the relation of states in a condition of political anarchy. Heracleitus contends that war is the father of all things, and that war is unavoidable and necessary for perpetuating the equilibrium of the international system.[71] Thucydides' history analyzes the political, social and moral-psychological dynamics that generate aggression, violence and the desire for domination and revenge. Unlike Kautilya, Thucydides assumes that the long-term security

---

[67] *KA*, Part II, by Kangle, p. 350.

[68] Ibid., p. 353.

[69] Theodore George Tsakiris, 'Thucydides and Strategy: Formations of Grand Strategy in the History of the Second Peloponnesian War (431–404 BC)', *Comparative Strategy*, vol. 25, no. 3 (2006), p. 173.

[70] Eric Robinson, 'Thucydides and Democratic Peace', *JME*, vol. 5, no. 4 (2006), p. 250.

[71] Tsakiris, 'Thucydides and Strategy', pp. 174–5.

of a state depends on moderation and the preservation of representative institutions that are particularly geared toward protecting the poor.[72] Thucydides' hero Pericles emphasizes that Athens' greatness depends on the personal courage of the citizens rather than on guile.[73] It seems that Thucydides is a supporter of heroic warfare, that is, *dharmayuddha*, which Kautilya critiques.

The classic realist thinker is Machiavelli. Hence, a detailed comparison of Kautilya and Machiavelli will be fruitful. Machiavelli was born in Florence in 1469 of an old citizen family. In 1498, he was appointed secretary and second chancellor to the Florentine Republic. In accordance with the duties of his office, he led several diplomatic missions to Louis XII, Emperor Maximilian, Julius II and others. In 1507, as chancellor of the newly appointed Nove di Milizia, he organized an infantry force that fought with the army that captured Pisa in 1509.

B. N. Mukherjee writes that Machiavelli was the Kautilya of the West.[74] For Machiavelli, power is an end in itself. Machiavelli's *The Prince* (1513), like the *Arthasastra*, investigates ways to acquire, retain and expand power. His prince prefers fear to love from his subjects. Sil claims that Machiavelli's image of the prince was modelled on the personality of Asiatic conquerors like Genghis Khan and Timur, who were regarded as the very embodiment of force and fear.[75] Machiavelli, in his *Discourses*, writes that a combination of force and fraud will overwhelm the enemy.[76]

In *The Prince*, Machiavelli writes: 'The fact is that a man who wants to act virtuously in every way necessarily comes to grief among so many who are not virtuous. Therefore if a prince wants to maintain his rule he must learn how not to be virtuous.'[77] Machiavelli elaborates: 'Everyone realizes how praiseworthy it is for a prince to honour his word and to be straightforward rather than crafty in his dealings; nonetheless contemporary experience shows that princes who have achieved great things have been those who have given their words lightly, who have known how to

---

[72] David Cohen, 'War, Moderation, and Revenge in Thucydides', *JME*, vol. 5, no. 4 (2006), p. 285.

[73] Russett, 'Thucydides, Ancient Greece, and the Democratic Peace', p. 258.

[74] B. N. Mukherjee, 'Foreword: A Note on the *Arthasastra*', in Sil, *Kautilya's Arthasastra*, p. xi.

[75] Sil, *Kautilya's Arthasastra*, p. 8.

[76] Michael I. Handel, *Masters of War: Classical Strategic Thought* (1992; reprint, London: Frank Cass, 1996), p. 123.

[77] Niccolo Machiavelli, *The Prince*, tr. with an Introduction by George Bull (1961; reprint, Harmondsworth, Middlesex: Penguin, 1981), p. 91.

Kautilya's Kutayuddha

trick men with their cunning, and who in the end, have overcome those abiding by honest principles.'[78] He sums up:

… a prudent ruler cannot, and must not, honour his word when it places him at a disadvantage and when the reasons for which he made his promise no longer exist…. Because men are wretched creatures who would not keep their word to you, you need not keep your word to them…. Those who have known best how to imitate the fox have come off best. But one must know how to colour one's actions and to be a great liar and deceiver. Men are so simple, and so much creatures of circumstances, that the deceiver will always find somebody ready to be deceived.[79]

Machiavelli notes that there are two ways of fighting: by law or by force. The first way is natural to men, and the second to beasts. But as the first way often proves inadequate, one must sometimes have recourse to the second. So a prince must understand how to make a nice use of the beast and the man.[80] These two sorts of war are somewhat equivalent to Kautilya's *dharmayuddha* and *kutayuddha*. One type of *kutayuddha* is *asurayuddha*, which, in terms of its amoral approach and lethality, is equivalent to Machiavelli's fighting like a beast. Kautilya says that the *vijigishu* should make use of both *dharmayuddha* and *asurayuddha* in accordance with the circumstances. Both Kautilya and Machiavelli believe that the end justifies the means. Both agree on the utilization of wine, women, poison and spies for the attainment of one's objectives.[81]

For Machiavelli, war is a tool of politics.[82] Machiavelli gives prime importance to armies and warfare in his paradigm of power-politics. He asserts:

A Prince, therefore, must have no other object or thought, nor acquire skill in anything, except war, its organization, and its discipline. The art of war is all that is expected of a ruler; and it is so useful that besides enabling hereditary princes to maintain their rule it frequently enables ordinary citizens to become rulers. On the other hand, we find that princes who have thought more of their pleasures than of arms have lost their states. The first way to lose your state is to neglect the art of war; the first way to win a state is to be skilled in the art of war.[83]

---

[78] Ibid., p. 99.
[79] Ibid., pp. 99–100.
[80] Ibid., p. 99.
[81] Chakravarti, *Art of War in Ancient India*, p. vii.
[82] Beatrice Heuser, *Reading Clausewitz* (London: Pimlico, 2002), p. 44.
[83] Machiavelli, *The Prince*, p. 87.

72   Hinduism and the Ethics of Warfare in South Asia

Machiavelli wants the war to be short and sharp.[84] Kautilya realizes that wars cannot always be short. Kautilya introduces the concept of *ekatra*, which means an expedition for a single specific objective. And *anekatra* refers to more than one objective, which in turn requires fighting simultaneously in various places.[85] While undertaking an expedition, Kautilya warns that the *vijigishu* should leave behind one-third to one-fourth of the troops for the purpose of protecting his base.[86]

Rather than pure force, Kautilya advises the *vijigishu* to use economic welfare in conjunction with force to maintain his power. It is to be noted that for Kautilya, *bala* (army) is less important than *kosa* (treasury). Kautilya says that an army can be raised and maintained from a well-filled treasury for maintaining *dharma*, but not vice versa.[87] In Kautilya's paradigm, *prabhavasakti* (the combined power of the army and treasury) is more important than *mantrasakti* (diplomacy) and *utsahasakti* (the personal energy and drive of the ruler).[88]

Kautilya not only attempts to conceptualize the nature of war, both within and among the states, but also tries to formulate a strategy of power. He attempts to create a systematic and universal theory of power and warfare that will be applicable in all environmental contexts. The lynchpin of Kautilya's paradigm is the assumption that human beings crave power, the most vital component for survival in the big bad cosmos. One could argue that, like the Enlightenment theorists, Kautilya is trying to formulate a theory of power/security based on universal, timeless and 'scientific' principles that will hold true for all ages.[89]

Torkel Brekke criticizes Kautilya by saying that the power and influence of the kings in the international order described by Kautilya overlap and interpenetrate in ways with internal enemies in ways that make it impossible to distinguish between external and internal affairs.[90]

---

[84] Felix Gilbert, 'Machiavelli: The Renaissance of the Art of War', in Peter Paret (ed.), *Makers of Modern Strategy from Machiavelli to the Nuclear Age* (1986; reprint, Oxford: Oxford University Press, 1990), p. 24.

[85] *KA*, Part II, by Kangle, p. 333.

[86] Chakravarti, *Art of War in Ancient India*, p. 93.

[87] G. N. Bhat, 'Means to Fill the Treasury during a Financial Crisis – Kautilya's Views', in Dr. Michael (ed.), *The Concept of Rajadharma* (New Delhi: Sundeep Prakashan, 2005), p. 148.

[88] *KA*, Part III, by Kangle, pp. 128–9.

[89] For the scientific rationalism of the Enlightenment, see Julian Reid, 'Foucault on Clausewitz: Conceptualizing the Relationship between War and Power', *Alternatives*, vol. 28, no. 1 (2003), p.11.

[90] Torkel Brekke, 'The Ethics of War and the Concept of War in India and Europe', *NUMEN*, vol. 52 (2005), p. 80.

Kautilya's Kutayuddha

Brekke, in another article, argues that Kautilya fails to distinguish between policing and war.[91] A world of self-interested actors is a world of dog-eat-dog competition, not only in interstate relations but also in state-society relations, writes Victoria Tin-Bor Hui. If a ruler betrays his allies and breaks his word in the international realm, he is also likely to subjugate his citizens in the domestic realm. The state becomes something like a predatory mafia. Victoria Tin-Bor Hui writes that a dynamic theory should view politics – both international and domestic – as a process of strategic interaction between domination seekers and targets of domination.[92]

Thucydides harps on the change in the international balance of power that creates insecurity for a state, but he also stresses the importance of domestic politics (demagogues, passions, emotions and perceptions, i.e., the role of subjective human agency) in shaping the foreign policy of a *polis*.[93] Thucydides points out that external war causes internal strife within the *polis*.[94] Machiavelli also notes the linkages between internal security and external security. He says that there are two things a prince must fear: internal subversion from his subjects, and external aggression by foreign powers. Against the latter, his defence lies in being well armed and having good allies; and if he is well armed, he will always have good allies. In addition, domestic affairs will always remain under control provided that relations with external powers are under control, and if the rebels were not disturbed by a conspiracy sponsored by a foreign power. Machiavelli notes that if the prince imposes excessive taxes on the people, his reputation will decline. This will result in his subjects turning against him, and he will be generally despised.[95]

Kautilya links up *kopa* within the state with intervention by the foreign powers. In other words, Kautilya is making a linkage between internal rebellion and the shifting power structure in the international arena. Kautilya authorizes the *vijigishu* to pursue an expansionist design as regards foreign affairs and total suppression of the civil society in order to weed out any possibility of *kopa*. The *Arthasastra* discusses *kopa* from the perspective of state security. The principal danger to the state, writes Kautilya, comes from *prakriti kopa*. This means the anger or wrath of

---

[91] Torkel Brekke, 'Wielding the Rod of Punishment – War and Violence in the Political Science of Kautilya', *JME*, vol. 3, no. 1 (2004), p. 46.
[92] Hui, *War and State Formation in Ancient China and Early Modern Europe*, pp. 2, 15.
[93] Russett, 'Thucydides, Ancient Greece, and the Democratic Peace', pp. 255, 265.
[94] Cohen, 'War, Moderation, and Revenge in Thucydides', p. 280.
[95] Machiavelli, *The Prince*, pp. 92, 103.

74   *Hinduism and the Ethics of Warfare in South Asia*

the people when they lose faith in the established government, which in turn affects the legitimacy of the government. While analyzing the factors behind *kopa*, says Chousalkar, Kautilya focuses mainly on the individual actors rather than on the social and class factors. The *Arthasastra* takes a top-down approach. Kautilya asserts that the leaders of the rebellion are not thrown up spontaneously from below; rather, they are disgruntled elites of the state like the *yuvaraj* (crown prince), the *mantri* (minister) and the *senapati* (general).[96] Ajatasatru (ruled 493–461 BCE) came to power after killing his father, Bimbisara. After Ajatasatru's death in 461 BCE, he was succeeded by five kings, all of whom came to power by killing their fathers. Kautilya's recommendations in the *Arthasastra* that a king should sow dissension among his enemies and must always guard against fratricide were probably shaped by the above-mentioned historical circumstances.

Hui criticizes Western international theories by stating that a theory should be more attentive to agency in order to explain changes in both the international and domestic realms. However, most Western international theories focus on structure rather than agency. The structuralists claim that individuals are embedded in their social environments and collectively shared systems of meanings. Structural realism claims that states make policy choices subject to the constraints they face. Hui writes that institutions are simultaneously enabling and restricting. She goes on to say that strategic mistakes made by an actor or a cluster of actors can fundamentally alter the trajectory of the whole system.[97] Machiavelli and Kautilya act as a corrective to the structuralism inherent in recent international theories. Overwhelming importance is given to the prince's and *vijigishu*'s actions and personalities in *The Prince* and in the *Arthasastra*.

Of the qualities of a successful ruler, Machiavelli writes: 'He will be despised if he has a reputation for being fickle, frivolous, effeminate, cowardly, irresolute; a prince should avoid this like the plague and strive to demonstrate in his actions grandeur, courage, sobriety, strength.'[98] Kautilya rejects astrology (meaning luck) as a way to understand fate.[99] Kautilya's philosophy calls for *paurusha* (manliness/courage) plus action and not resignation on the part of the *vijigishu*.

---

[96] Chousalkar, *Theory of Rebellion in Kautilya and Aristotle*, pp. 48, 50, 74, 76–7, 80.
[97] Hui, *War and State Formation in Ancient China and Early Modern Europe*, pp. 19–21, 23.
[98] Machiavelli, *The Prince*, p. 102.
[99] Chakravarti, *Art of War in Ancient India*, p. 95.

KAUTILYA'S *ARTHASASTRA* AND THE WESTERN POLITICAL PHILOSOPHERS AND HISTORIANS

Plato (c. 429/7–347 BCE) and Aristotle (384–322 BCE) were near-contemporaries of Kautilya.[100] So Kautilya's *Arthasastra* could be compared to and contrasted with the *Republic, Statesman* and *Laws* of Plato and the *Politics* of Aristotle. Plato entered public service in Athens when the city was under the rule of the Thirty Tyrants installed by Sparta. He withdrew to Megara after the execution of his friend cum philosopher Socrates (470–399 BCE). However, Plato returned to Athens in 387 BCE and started a garden school on the outskirts of Athens near the shrine of Academus, a local hero. In this academy, selected young men were taught Socratic philosophy and Pythagorean mathematics. On Alexander's death in 323 BCE, Plato was forced to leave Athens by the anti-Macedonian party and died in exile at Chalcis. Plato is sceptical of the common man and his virtues and values. Democracy, in Plato's eye, is nothing more than a sort of anarchy, because the common man is a bundle of unrestrained appetites, and his behaviour is dependent on the pleasure of the moment. The content of Plato's politics is autocratic, but it forces the philosopher-king to become a *politikos* for leading a life not of unmitigated luxury but of discipline and austerity, that is, a sort of military monasticism.[101]

Similarly, Kautilya advises the ruler to control his senses in order to direct the administration vigorously and to endear himself to his people. Kautilya lays down a detailed routine for the *vijigishu*: overseeing the collection of revenue, inspecting the military forces, listening to the reports of spies during the night and delegating tasks to secret agents and so on.[102] Kautilya warns that too much indulgence in *kama* (sex) by the *vijigishu* would result in disruption of governance.[103] Like Plato, Kautilya writes that common people's minds are not steady and that their behaviour is inconsistent.[104] Hence the *vijigishu*, implies Kautilya, should depend on *danda* rather than on the goodwill of the masses.

Aristotle was born at Stagira on the Chalcidic Peninsula of Thrace and was the son of the royal physician of Macedon. He entered Plato's

---

[100] Mukherjee, 'Foreword', p. x.
[101] Sil, *Kautilya's Arthasastra*, pp. 26–7, 37, 39, 45.
[102] Nirmala Kulkarni, 'Daily Routine of a King in Kautilya *Arthasastra*', in Michael (ed.), *Concept of Rajadharma*, pp. 144–5.
[103] J. S. Negi, 'Religion and Politics in the *Arthasastra* of Kautilya', in Negi, *Some Indological Studies*, vol. 1 (Allahabad: Panchananda Publications, 1966), p. 20.
[104] Sil, *Kautilya's Arthasastra*, p. 39.

76   Hinduism and the Ethics of Warfare in South Asia

academy at the age of seventeen and studied there for the next twenty years until Plato's death. He left when Plato's nephew Speusippus was elected as the head of the academy. For the next two years, Aristotle lived with Hermias, a slave turned tyrant in Asia Minor. Hermias' adopted daughter became Aristotle's wife. For next three years, Aristotle served as tutor to the young Alexander of Macedon; in 335 BCE he set up his Lyceum between Mount Lycabettus and the river Ilissus, north-east of Athens. This academy became a rival of Plato's academy.[105] For Aristotle, all sciences have a practical orientation. Each *techne* (art/science) has to perform a certain task in order to achieve a certain *telos*.[106] Kautilya says: 'Philosophy is ever thought of as the lamp of all sciences, as the means of all actions and as support of all laws and duties.'[107]

Kautilya is a supporter of the monarchical form of government and accepts, like Aristotle, that in the last instance the ruler is dependent on the suffrage of the ruled. Both the *Mahabharata* and the *Arthasastra* express a dislike of tyrants. Kautilya says that while tyrants are interested in self-aggrandizement, monarchs are more focussed on the interests of the polity. For Plato and Aristotle, power is a means to achieving a high end – the happiness of the citizens. Both Kautilya and Aristotle emphasize that moderation in the use of force ensures the stability and longevity of regimes. Kautilya warns the king to use *danda* with a sense of discrimination and by steering a middle course. The theory of the divine origin of the king in the Kautilyan tradition is slightly different from the Western theory. In the ancient Indian context, the king is divine not because he is a god in human form but because he protects the lives and properties of his subjects along with the *varna* society. As long as he is pursuing his duties, the king observes *dharma* and is a righteous king and thus a divine monarch. If he fails to discharge his duties properly, then he ceases to be divine.[108]

Kautilya's *kutayuddha* has certain commonalities with the Roman historian Tacitus' (56 CE–117 CE) description of deceptive warfare. Tacitus, in his *Annals*, speaks of poisoning among the Parthian ruling elite and the presence of treacherous subordinates.[109] The *Arthasastra* introduces the concept of *tusnimdandena*, which means getting rid of enemy leaders

---

[105] Ibid., p. 45.
[106] Tsakiris, 'Thucydides and Strategy', p. 175.
[107] *KA*, Part II, by Kangle, p. 7.
[108] Chousalkar, *Theory of Rebellion in Kautilya and Aristotle*, pp. 50–2, 60, 67–8, 79.
[109] Rhiannon Ash, 'An Exemplary Conflict: Tacitus' Parthian Battle Narrative (*Annals* 6.34–34)', *Phoenix*, vol. 53, no. ½ (1999), p. 114.

Kautilya's Kutayuddha

by assassination, poisoning and so forth.[110] Deceptive techniques were also used by the Romans. In 172 BCE, Marcius Philippus bought time for Rome, during a war with Perseus of Macedonia, by sending a deceptive embassy. And Tacitus saw merit in the Roman Emperor Tiberius' foreign policy vis-à-vis Parthia, which encouraged the various enemy factions to fight each other rather than directly waging war against them.[111]

Kautilya elaborates the various components of *kutayuddha*. *Dvaidhibhava* is dual policy. It means that maintaining peace with one party while fighting another power, and also outwardly maintaining peace with one power while secretly preparing to attack that power. *Dvaidhibhutah* is making a pact with the usual enemy in order to make war on another king. When a *kalaha* (life-and-death struggle) occurs between the enemy and a neighbouring king, the *vijigishu* sits tight, because a decline in the power of the enemy suits the *vijigishu*'s interests. Occasionally, the *vijigishu* also encourages *kalaha* between two potentially hostile states. *Yatavya* means a neighbouring prince who is afflicted with problems and hence should be attacked by the *vijigishu*.[112] Now, let us compare Kautilya to the most famous of the ultra-realist theorists of war of the Western world: Carl von Clausewitz.

CLAUSEWITZ AND KAUTILYA

On War, or *Vom Kriege*, was first published in three volumes in Berlin between 1832 and 1834. Its author, Carl Philipp Gottlieb von Clausewitz, was born on 1 June 1780, at Burg, near Magdeburg. His grandfather was a professor of theology, and he was a Lutheran pastor. Clausewitz made little reference to religion in his own writings. He did not cite faith as a motivation for war. Nor did he view Christianity as an impulse for moderation when fighting fellow Christians.[113] Clausewitz was a soldier from the age of twelve until his death in 1831. He started working on *On War* after 1815.[114] In a note written around 1818, Clausewitz comments: 'My original intention was to set down my conclusions on the principal elements of this topic in short, precise, compact statements,

---

[110] *KA*, Part II, by Kangle, p. 23.
[111] Ash, 'An Exemplary Conflict', p. 130.
[112] *KA*, Part II, by Kangle, pp. 321, 325, 334, 343.
[113] Hew Strachan, *Clausewitz's On War: A Biography* (New York: Atlantic Monthly Press, 2007), pp. ix, 32.
[114] Hugh Smith, *On Clausewitz: A Study of Military and Political Ideas* (Houndmills, Basingstoke: Palgrave, 2005), p. 3.

78   *Hinduism and the Ethics of Warfare in South Asia*

without concern for system or formal connection. The manner in which Montesquieu dealt with his subject was vaguely in my mind.'[115] In 1827, Clausewitz started to revise his work, but the task remained unfinished due to his early death.[116]

Clausewitz implies that transformation in politics results in transformation of warfare. Clausewitz's famous statement follows: 'War is nothing but the continuation of policy with other means.'[117] He clarifies: 'The political object is the goal, war is the means of reaching it, and means can never be considered in isolation from their purpose.'[118] *On War* says that 'the political aim remains the first consideration. Policy, then, will permeate all military operations, and, in so far as their violent nature will admit, it will have a continuous influence on them.'[119] Clausewitz's trinity comprises of people and their passion, the commander and his army and the nature of the government.[120] Clausewitz claims that 'the political aims are the business of government alone.'[121] Clausewitz emphasizes the supremacy of politicians over military commanders when formulating grand strategy.[122] In Kautilya's theory, the *vijigishu* completely overshadows the *senapati*.

Clausewitz, like Kautilya, sees warfare as instrumental. The conduct of war needs to reflect the fact that its objective is the establishment of peace.[123] Kautilya differs from the position of the *Bhagavad Gita*, where the purpose of war is existential. Both Clausewitz and Kautilya are realists and assume that inter-state war is necessary and inevitable in the highly competitive and harsh international arena.[124] And along with Clausewitz, Johann Jakob Otto August Ruhle von Lillienstern also argued that war fulfilled a political purpose. By 1804, Clausewitz had read Machiavelli's *Discourses* (begun in 1513). Clausewitz admired Machiavelli's emphasis on the realities of power and probably learnt from him that war

[115] Carl Von Clausewitz, *On War*, ed. and tr. by Michael Howard and Peter Paret (1984; reprint, Princeton, New Jersey: Princeton University Press, 1989), p. 63.
[116] Heuser, *Reading Clausewitz*, p. 204.
[117] Clausewitz, *On War*, ed. and tr. by Howard and Paret, p. 69.
[118] Ibid., p. 87.
[119] Ibid., p. 87.
[120] Heuser, *Reading Clausewitz*, p. 53.
[121] Clausewitz, *On War*, ed. and tr. by Howard and Paret, p. 89.
[122] Michael I. Handel, 'Clausewitz in the Age of Technology', *JSS*, vol. 9, nos. 2–3 (1986), pp. 74–5. Hew Strachan argues that Clausewitz did not write about the superiority of the politicians over the generals but emphasizes close interaction between the top civilian authority and the generals. Strachan, *Clausewitz's On War*, p. 168.
[123] Strachan, *Clausewitz's On War*, p. 91.
[124] Handel, 'Clausewitz in the Age of Technology', p. 79.

Kautilya's Kutayuddha 79

has a political purpose.[125] P. C. Chakravarti writes that Kautilya, like Clausewitz, believed that war is the continuation of politics by other means.[126]

Clausewitz writes: 'War is thus an act of force to compel our enemy to do our will.'[127] As regards the means of war, he notes:

There is only one: *combat*. However many forms combat takes, however far it may be removed from the brute discharge of hatred and enmity of a physical encounter, however many forces may intrude which themselves are not part of fighting, it is inherent in the very concept of war that everything that occurs *must originally derive from combat*.... Warfare comprises everything related to the fighting forces – everything to do with their creation, maintenance, and use.... The end for which a soldier is recruited, clothed, armed, and trained, the whole object of his sleeping, eating, drinking, and marching *is simply that he should fight at the right place and the right time*.[128]

Clausewitz dismissed Adam Heinrich Dietrich von Bulow's (1757–1807) assertion that it is always possible to avoid battle.[129] Clausewitz introduces the concept of the centre of gravity (*schwerpunkt*), which constitutes the hub of all power and movement of the enemy.[130] Clausewitz's concept of centre of gravity is taken from Newton's law of mechanics.[131] In the case of world conquerors like Alexander, Gustavus Adolphus, Charles XII and Frederick the Great (equivalent to Kautilya's *vijigishu*), the centre of gravity was their army.[132]

As regards the object of combat, Clausewitz hammers the point that 'of all the possible aims in war, the destruction of the enemy's armed forces always appear as the highest.'[133] In a note written in 1830, Clausewitz emphasized that 'victory consists not only in the occupation of the battlefield, but in the destruction of the enemy's physical and psychic forces, which is usually not attained until the enemy is pursued after a victorious battle.'[134] Clausewitz writes: 'The invention of gunpowder and the

---

[125] Strachan, *Clausewitz's On War*, pp. 83, 88.
[126] Chakravarti, *Art of War in Ancient India*, p. v.
[127] Clausewitz, *On War*, ed. and tr. by Howard and Paret, p. 75.
[128] Ibid., p. 95. Italics in original.
[129] Heuser, *Reading Clausewitz*, p. 9.
[130] Handel, *Masters of War*, p. 40.
[131] Alan Beyerchen, 'Clausewitz and the Non-Linear Nature of Warfare: Systems of Organized Complexity', in Hew Strachan and Andreas Herberg-Rothe (eds.), *Clausewitz in the Twenty-First Century* (Oxford: Oxford University Press, 2007), pp. 45, 51.
[132] Handel, *Masters of War*, 41.
[133] Clausewitz, *On War*, ed. and tr. by Howard and Paret, p. 99.
[134] Ibid., p. 71.

80 *Hinduism and the Ethics of Warfare in South Asia*

constant improvement of firearms are enough in themselves to show that the advance of civilization has done nothing practical to alter or deflect the impulse to destroy the enemy, which is central to the very idea of war.'[135] He writes that in war maximum effort must be made by simultaneous concentration of forces to obtain the first decisive victory.[136] Clausewitz claims that even when a state is on the strategic defensive, it should launch a tactical offensive.[137] Kautilya opposes the waging of a tactical offensive by the *vijigishu* when the strategic picture is becoming less favourable to him. Kautilya writes that in such a scenario tactical offensives become useless, using the expression 'entering the flame like a moth'.[138] Rather, in such circumstances, Kautilya advocates following a policy of 'wait and watch'. Both Kautilya and Clausewitz emphasize the role of reserve in the battlefield.[139]

Machiavelli emphasizes the importance of battle in warfare.[140] In Clausewitz's *On War* and also for Thucydides, bloodshed constitutes the most important characteristic of warfare. The *Arthasastra*, influenced by ancient India's military experiences, marginalizes the role of battle in warfare. Around 530 BCE, Cyrus, the Achaemenid emperor of Persia, crossed the Hindu Kush and occupied Gandhara. In 518 BCE, Darius I, the Acahemenid monarch, annexed Punjab, which became the twentieth *satrapy* (province) of his empire.[141]

The greatest battle fought in ancient India, the Battle of Hydaspes (326 BCE), influenced Kautilya's thought as regards the tactical aspects of warfare and his ideas about military organization. Initially, Paurava dispatched 2,000 cavalry and 120 chariots under his son to oppose Alexander's crossing of Jhelum. Alexander defeated this contingent, and then Paurava advanced with his main force to check Alexander.[142] In this battle, Paurava deployed 200 elephants and 30,000 infantry, 4,000 cavalry and 300 chariots.[143] Compared to the vedic and epic chariots,

---

[135] Ibid., p. 76.

[136] Ibid., p. 80.

[137] Heuser, *Reading Clausewitz*, pp. 91–3. Some scholars interpret *On War* by arguing that Clausewitz emphasizes defence rather than offence as the stronger form of war.

[138] *KA*, Part III, by Kangle, p. 264.

[139] Chakravarti, *Art of War in Ancient India*, p. vii; David Kahn, 'Clausewitz and Intelligence', *JSS*, vol. 9, nos. 2–3 (June–Sept. 1986), p. 122.

[140] Gilbert, 'Machiavelli', pp. 24–5.

[141] Jha, *Early India*, p. 83.

[142] J. R. Hamilton, 'The Cavalry Battle at the Hydaspes', *Journal of Hellenic Studies*, vol. 76 (1956), pp. 26–7.

[143] Majumdar, *Military System in Ancient India*, p. 49.

Kautilya's Kutayuddha 81

Paurava's chariots were larger. Ajatasatru introduced scythe chariots into the Magadhan army.[144] The Macedonian heavy infantry made short work of the chariots, as in Gaugemela. Paurava placed 2,000 cavalry at each of the wings. Alexander ordered Coenus with his cavalry to attack the cavalry on Paurava's right wing. As Coenus moved towards Paurava's right wing, Alexander was proceeding towards Paurava's left wing. Meanwhile, Paurava ordered the cavalry on the right wing to come to the support of his outnumbered left wing. Then Alexander ordered his horse archers to attack the Indian left wing. When the Indian cavalry concentrated on their left wing, Coenus appeared at their rear. As part of the Indian force turned around to meet Coenus, Alexander delivered his attack. As in Gaugemela, the Macedonian cavalry attacked in a wedge formation. Then the elephants advanced towards the Greek cavalry. After a furious struggle, the elephants were overwhelmed by Greek *phalangites* and 1,000 mounted archers that Alexander had bought from Central Asia.[145]

After 400 BCE, chariots were no longer used in China.[146] Despite the uselessness of the chariots in the Battle of Hydaspes, Kautilya writes about the necessity of chariots in the battle order of the *vijigishu*, and the Maurya army maintained chariots.[147] This was because disciplined infantry and good horses were not available to the Mauryas. The elephants impressed the Greeks, and the use of war elephants spread in the Western world. Pyrrhus, the king of Epirus, used elephants at Heraclea (280 BCE).[148] The Nandas maintained 80,000 cavalry, 200,000 infantry, 8,000 chariots and 6,000 elephants. Chandragupta raised the number of infantry to 600,000 and the elephant corps to 9,000, but his cavalry numbered only 30,000. In other words, the Maurya cavalry was numerically weaker than the Nanda cavalry establishment.[149] This was despite the fact that at the climactic Battle of Hydaspes, it was Alexander's cavalry that played the crucial role. Kautilya notes that good horses were available only outside India, at Kamboja (north of Gandhara,

---

[144] A. K. Srivastava, *Ancient Indian Army: Its Administration and Organization* (New Delhi: Ajanta Publications, 1985), p. 38.

[145] Hamilton, 'Cavalry Battle at the Hydaspes', pp. 27, 30–1.

[146] Stanley J. Olsen, 'The Horse in Ancient China and Its Cultural Influence in Some Other Areas', *Proceedings of the Academy of Natural Sciences of Philadelphia*, vol. 140, no. 2 (1988), p. 176.

[147] Chakravarti, *Art of War in Ancient India*, p. 25.

[148] Bimal Kanti Majumdar, *The Military System in Ancient India* (Calcutta: Firma KLM, 1960), p. 50.

[149] Bonnerjea, 'Peace and War in Hindu Culture', p. 36.

82   *Hinduism and the Ethics of Warfare in South Asia*

i.e., Afghanistan) and Vanayu (Arabia or Persia).[150] The contemporary Chinese emperors were also interested in having war horses. Around 100 BCE, the Han Emperor Wu-ti/di (140–87 BCE) directed several campaigns against Ferghana (in Russian Turkestan) to acquire horses. The horses from Ferghana were also used for breeding a better variety of horses that was required for fighting the nomadic invaders.[151] The *Mahabharata* mentions the presence of mounted archers with composite bows. Neither Paurava nor Chandragupta possessed mounted archers. In fact, Kautilya never mentions the presence of mounted archers in the *vijigishu*'s order of battle. The invading Aryans probably introduced mounted archery on the subcontinent, but this practice died out.[152]

D. D. Kosambi claims that due to a shortage of metals, most of the Indian soldiers who opposed Alexander could not afford metallic body armour. The bulk of the soldiers, in his views, were equipped with a shield, a leather cuirass and a metal helmet.[153] Herodotus tells us that the Indian bowmen in Xerxes' army used bows made of cane and bamboo.[154] The Indian bowmen at Hydaspes were foot archers and used arrows, each of whose shaft was three yards long.[155] The arrow was discharged with the pressure of the archer's left foot on the extremity of the bow, which rested on the ground, and the string was drawn far backwards. Such arrows were able to penetrate shields and breastplates.[156] Due to rainfall on the night before the battle, the ground was slippery, and the Indian archers failed to make effective use of their bows in the decisive conflict at Hydaspes.[157] Kautilya was for retaining the foot soldiers and especially the archers, but tried to raise their combat effectiveness through training.

A close reading of the *Arthasastra* challenges the observation of some modern historians that ancient India lacked a disciplined standing army. The *Arthasastra* tells us that an army is organized in squads of 10 men, companies of 100, and battalions of 1,000 each.[158] Kautilya says that the *nayaka* (warlord) with trumpets and flags should coordinate

---

[150] Mital, *Kautilya Arthasastra Revisited*, p. 25.
[151] Olsen, 'Horse in Ancient China and Its Cultural Influence', pp. 173–4, 185.
[152] Murray B. Emeneau, 'The Composite Bow in India', *Proceedings of the American Philosophical Society*, vol. 97, no. 1 (1953), p. 80.
[153] Kosambi, *Culture and Civilization of Ancient India*, p. 135.
[154] Emeneau, 'Composite Bow in India', p. 85.
[155] Majumdar, *Military System in Ancient India*, p. 50.
[156] Bonnerjea, 'Peace and War in Hindu Culture', p. 37.
[157] Majumdar, *Military System in Ancient India*, p. 50.
[158] Bonnerjea, 'Peace and War in Hindu Culture', p. 36.

Kautilya's Kutayuddha

83

the movement of the various units of the army on the battlefield.[159] For fighting *prakasya yuddha*, Kautilya urges the *vijigishu* to deploy troops in well-ordered *vyuhas*. Various types of *vyuhas* are described in the *Arthasastra*, depending on the terrain and the force structure. Each *vyuha* was comprised of five sections: a centre and two flanks that were further protected by two wings. Each section was comprised of combined battle units (infantry, cavalry, elephants and chariots).[160] At Hydaspes, Paurava came to grief for not protecting his flanks. This probably induced Kautilya to come up with wings, which would function as a flank protection force. Machiavelli writes that mercenaries and auxiliaries are useless and dangerous. He goes on to say that wise princes, therefore, have always shunned auxiliaries and made use of their own forces.[161] As regards the army, which constitutes an important part of the *danda*, Kautilya writes:

Inherited from the father and the grandfather, constant, obedient, with the soldiers' sons and wives contented, not disappointed during marches, unhindered everywhere, able to put up with troubles, that has fought many battles, skilled in the science of all types of war and weapons, not having a separate interest because of prosperity and adversity shared with the king, consisting mostly of the Kshatriyas – these are the excellences of an army.[162]

Kautilya is for recruiting troops from all four *varnas*[163] in order to prevent any one community from becoming over-powerful in the state. Machiavelli comments that natural courage is inadequate. Military success depends on order and discipline. For maintaining military discipline, Machiavelli, like the Legalists, focuses on harsh punishment.[164] Machiavelli stresses the importance of training.[165] Kautilya also emphasizes training of the men and animals in the army.[166] Even with all these improvements, Kautilya was not confident that the Mauryan military machine could successfully counter the horse archers and the *phalangites*. Hence, instead of following a battle-centric strategy, Kautilya advocated *kutayuddha*.

---

[159] Chakravarti, *Art of War in Ancient India*, p. 86.
[160] *KA*, Part III, by Kangle, p. 259.
[161] Machiavelli, *The Prince*, pp. 77, 84.
[162] *KA*, Part II, by Kangle, p. 316.
[163] *KA*, Part III, by Kangle, p. 143.
[164] Gilbert, 'Machiavelli', in Paret (ed.), *Makers of Modern Strategy*, p. 25.
[165] Machiavelli, *The Prince*, pp. 88–9.
[166] Kautilya, *The Arthasastra*, ed., rearranged, tr. and introduced by L. N. Rangarajan (New Delhi: Penguin, 1992), pp. 692–4.

84 *Hinduism and the Ethics of Warfare in South Asia*

For both Clausewitz and Jomini, deception in warfare has limited value.[167] Kautilya introduces the concept of *samdhaya yayat*, which means downright duplicity. It involves making peace and then attacking the enemy when he is least expecting such an attack.[168] Information warfare is a strong point with Kautilya. For waging information warfare, Kautilya advocates the use of various types of spies to gather knowledge about different aspects of the hostile polities. In 1620, Roger Bacon wrote that 'knowledge and human power are synonymous, since the ignorance of the cause frustrates the effect.'[169] However, Clausewitz disdains the role of intelligence (both battlefield and strategic) in warfare.[170]

Kautilya, Thucydides and Clausewitz all focus on the intangible aspects of warfare: morale and the psychology of the commander and the men under arms. Machiavelli, like Georg Heinrich von Berenhorst (1733–1814) in 1797, anticipated Clausewitz by emphasizing the role of moral and psychological factors in warfare.[171] Like Clausewitz, Berenhorst gives importance to the personality of the ruler and to chance and accidents.[172] Both Kautilya and Clausewitz give importance to the commander. Kautilya's *vijigishu* is comparable to Clausewitz's genius for war who rises above all rules.[173] Clausewitz's concept of genius for warfare is derived from Immanuel Kant's writings. The latter wrote that genius is a talent for producing for which no definite rule can be given.[174] Clausewitz's 'genius for war' is somewhat equivalent to the *utsahasakti* of Kautilya's *vijigishu*. In his 1804 notes, Clausewitz uses the word *Intelligenz* to describe the commander's rational thinking. The personality of the commander is not peripheral but central to Clausewitz's theory of warfare.[175] Clausewitz emphasizes the importance of decisiveness and daring on the part of the commander.[176] *On War* tells us: 'Strength of character does not consist solely in having powerful feelings, but in

---

[167] Handel, *Masters of War*, pp. 33, 122.

[168] *KA*, Part II, by Kangle, p. 333.

[169] Quoted in Martin Van Creveld, 'The Eternal Clausewitz', *JSS*, vol. 9, nos. 2–3 (June–Sept. 1986), endnote 12, p. 49.

[170] Kahn, 'Clausewitz and Intelligence', p. 117.

[171] Strachan, *Clausewitz's On War*, p. 83; Heuser, *Reading Clausewitz*, p. 80.

[172] Heuser, *Reading Clausewitz*, p. 9.

[173] Katherine L. Herbig, 'Chance and Uncertainty in *On War*', *JSS*, vol. 9, nos. 2–3 (June–Sept. 1986), p. 103.

[174] Heuser, *Reading Clausewitz*, p. 72.

[175] Strachan, *Clausewitz's On War*, pp. 92–3.

[176] Smith, *On Clausewitz*, p. 11.

Kautilya's Kutayuddha

maintaining one's balance in spite of them.'[177] Clausewitz speaks of 'the play of chance and probability within which the creative spirit is free to roam.'[178]

Clausewitz also speaks of *kleine krieg* (little war), which refers to the use of small detachments for skirmishing, harassing and gathering information about the movement of enemy troops.[179] In the case of a popular uprising (similar to Kautilya's *kopa*), the personalities of the leaders and public opinion constitute, for Clausewitz, the centre of gravity.[180] At times, for Clausewitz, the enemy's centre of gravity becomes the leader of a rebellious group, that is, a popular charismatic ruler.[181] Hew Strachan writes that, inspired by the uprising of nationalist guerrillas in Spain and Tyrol against the Napoleonic occupation armies, Clausewitz drew up plans for forming militias that would unite the people in arms with the 'national' army challenging the occupying force.[182] Clausewitz incorporated irregular warfare within his concept of *volkskrieg* (people's war). Irregular warfare involves popular participation. People's war also involves a wide range of popular involvement in warfare. In Clausewitz's paradigm, the militia should be used in conjunction with the regular army. Clausewitz identified several conditions necessary for generating guerrilla warfare: war on one's own territory, a large theatre of operations with rough and inaccessible terrain, and a people whose temperament is suited to irregular warfare. For Clausewitz, guerrilla warfare (he has Prussia in mind) is the weapon of last resort, to be used when everything else has failed.[183]

Clausewitz writes that there are two types of war: war designed to destroy the enemy politically and militarily, and war designed to occupy some portion of the enemy's territory. In the case of the first type of war, the victor dictates peace, and in the case of the second type of war, peace is negotiated.[184] When absolute war aimed at the complete shattering of the enemy is not possible, then war with a limited aim should be pursued. Limited war is characterized by delaying engagements, since the aim of the weak defender is to avoid decisive battles at all cost. In a limited war, the defender retreats inside his own territory and the strength of the

---

[177] Clausewitz, *On War*, ed. and tr. by Howard and Paret, p. 107.
[178] Ibid., p. 89.
[179] Smith, *On Clausewitz*, p. 10.
[180] Handel, *Masters of War*, p. 45.
[181] Heuser, *Reading Clausewitz*, p. 76.
[182] Strachan, *Clausewitz's On War*, p. 52.
[183] Smith, *On Clausewitz*, pp. 32–3.
[184] Strachan, *Clausewitz's On War*, p. 73.

86   *Hinduism and the Ethics of Warfare in South Asia*

attackers gradually decreases. The defender takes advantage of the local terrain and delays the attacker with small delaying parties until the culmination point of the attack has passed and the attacking party exhausts itself. At that critical juncture, the defender should switch to the offensive mode of warfare.[185]

Before the First World War, Hans Delbruck, a veteran of the Franco-Prussian War and an academician, argued that if Clausewitz were alive, he would have developed a system that recognized two different forms of waging war. The first is described as the strategy of annihilation, and the second is the strategy of exhaustion, which is designed to wear out the enemy so that the latter is forced to negotiate.[186] As we will see in the next section, Sun Tzu, the most famous ancient Chinese theoretician, and Kautilya are indeed followers of what Delbruck categorized as the strategy of exhaustion.

KAUTILYA'S *ARTHASASTRA* AND ANCIENT CHINESE PHILOSOPHY: A COMPARATIVE ANALYSIS

The Chinese tradition was characterized to a great extent by Legalism, which is a long-term policy for preserving and conserving the state. Legalist classics note that human beings are naturally self-seeking, so the wise ruler should use liberal rewards and stringent punishments in order to motivate the people to serve the state.[187] The *Book of Lord Shang* was composed by Shang Yang (390/59–338 BCE), the minister of Chin ruler Duke Hsiao. This political handbook of the Legalist School (*Fa-chia*) rejected the Confucian moral standard of *jen*, the Taoist natural standard of *tao* (the way) and the Moist (Mohist) religious standard of *t'ien-ming*, and stressed instead the importance of power and law in political life. Lord Shang writes that an intelligent ruler depends on force and not on virtue.[188] Shang Yang, somewhat like Machiavelli, states that virtue will not triumph over vice.[189] To achieve *shih*, Shang Yang and his Legalist successors advocate generous material rewards and harsh punishments to guide individual energies into the people's collective strength, concentrated in the ruler as *shih*.[190]

---

[185] Heuser, *Reading Clausewitz*, pp. 96, 103.
[186] Strachan, *Clausewitz's On War*, p. 17.
[187] Hui, *War and State Formation in Ancient China and Early Modern Europe*, pp. 18–19.
[188] Sil, *Kautilya's Arthasastra*, p. 9.
[189] Kane, *Ancient China on Postmodern War*, p. 64.
[190] William H. Mott IV and Jae Chang Kim, *The Philosophy of Chinese Military Culture* (Houndmills, Basingstoke: Macmillan, 2006), p. 18.

Kautilya's Kutayuddha 87

Taoism is found in Lao Tzu's teachings (sixth century BCE), *Tao-Te Ching* (*The Way and the Power*), later refined by Chuang Tzu (369–286 BCE). The Taoists observed nature to discover the way, the *tao*. People achieve happiness when they follow nature's way by acting spontaneously and trusting intuitive knowledge. The Taoist term *wu-wei* (nonaction or non-competing) does not mean doing nothing but implies refraining from activity contrary to *tao*. The ruler's *tao* is ruling, inspiring and indulgent benevolence, and the people's *tao* is comprised of following, loyalty and filial piety. The dominant pattern within the *tao* is the cycle: expansion and contraction, victory and defeat. The cyclic reversal pattern in the *tao*'s eternal motion is reflected in the eternal pairing and interplay between *yin* and *yang*. The *yang* after reaching its climax retreats in favour of the *yin* and vice versa. From the eternal pairing of opposites, the Taoists deduce that the best path to anything lies through its opposite – the indirect approach. For the Taoists, the best security for anything lies in preserving its opposite: deception.[191]

Sun Tzu's (541–481/2 BCE) thought absorbed the Taoist canon of the universal harmony of all under heaven. To avoid releasing the chaos, destruction and death that accompany war, leaders have to follow the *tao*: the universal principles of all things – the one way. Beyond its philosophical meanings, *tao* expressed the idea of path or road, not only in a physical sense but also as a moral/ethical notion of the right or the proper way. Sun Tzu urges the ruler to use economic wealth, social power and politics as alternatives to war.[192] Sun Tzu attempts to win victory through diplomatic coercion, thwarting the enemy's plan and alliances, rather than by armed combat. Even in the last resort when armed combat becomes absolutely necessary, then also the objective should still be minimum risk and exposure, limiting as far as possible the destruction to be inflicted and suffered, fighting with the aim of preservation.[193] In contrast to the Clausewitzian policy of death and destruction, Sun Tzu claims that it is better to subjugate the enemy without fighting than to destroy him.[194] Sun Tzu's emphasis on the use of force as a last resort reflects a Confucian influence.[195] According to Confucian thought, the ruler could attract support and foster stability by implementing

[191] Ibid., pp. 8, 16–17.
[192] Ibid., pp. 8–9.
[193] *Sun Tzu, Art of War*, tr. with an Historical Introduction by Ralph D. Sawyer (Boulder, Colorado: Westview, 1994), p. 129.
[194] Mott IV and Kim, *Philosophy of Chinese Military Culture*, p. 9.
[195] Handel, *Masters of War*, p. 74.

88 *Hinduism and the Ethics of Warfare in South Asia*

benevolent policies.[196] Sun Tzu and Lao Tzu warn of the danger of over-using the army by pointing out the social and economic costs of war-fare.[197] Coercive force, in Sun Tzu's paradigm, comprises a full panoply of persuasive relationships, from threats, inducements, bribes and gifts to unrestricted violence and brutal destruction. The art and science of using coercive force (equivalent to the Hindu philosophers' *dandaniti*) to persuade an enemy without fighting, instead of applying direct force to destroy and defeat the enemy, comprises the *shih* strategy.[198]

William H. Mott IV and Jae Chang Kim write that from positions of weakness, the Chinese generals developed strategies, campaign plans, operational concepts and tactics designed to win wars without the need for decisive victory in every battle. Their motto is to win without fight-ing. The two opposing concepts in Chinese strategic thought are *shih* and *li*. *Li* means self-interest or material gain. For *li* strategists every battle is decisive, but for *shih* strategists some battles are irrelevant. While *li* strategists attempt to ensure local combat superiority, *shih* strategists try to confuse the enemy by combining orthodox and unorthodox measures. The *li* strategy attempts to win by destruction, while the *shih* strategy tries to win without fighting. While the *li* strategy's objective is destruc-tion of the enemy, the *shih* strategy's aim is to subjugate the enemy. For the *shih* strategists, deception is the essence of military strategy. The *shih* strategy uses force to bring the people into ultimate harmony and accord with the ruler in *tao*. *Shih* strategy prefers to threaten, manipulate and deter the enemy. *Shih* can cause an enemy to accept compliant terms without fighting.[199]

Several generations of strategists like Tai Kung (1212?–1073 BCE), Sun Tzu, Wu Tzu (541?–482? BCE), Sun Pin/Sun Bin/Sun Tzu II (380–316 BCE), and Wei Lao Tzu (ca. 318 BCE) developed and taught *shih* as a coherent body of thought. The Legalists assume that the object of every ruler is to become a hegemon – that is, the ruler of all of China – and that the interests of the people are incidental to this process.[200] In Sun Tzu's *The Art of War*, the *shih* is the dynamic power that emerges through a combination of men's hearts, military weapons and natural conditions. The *shih* strategy includes three dimensions of warfare: the people, the context and the enemy. It somewhat differs from Clausewitz's trinity of

[196] *Art of War*, tr. by Sawyer, p. 32.
[197] Kane, *Ancient China on Postmodern War*, p. 124.
[198] Mott IV and Kim, *Philosophy of Chinese Military Culture*, p. 10.
[199] Ibid., pp. xi, 11–12, 15, 34, 43–4.
[200] Kane, *Ancient China on Postmodern War*, p. 134.

government, army and people.[201] *Shih* strategy concentrates the power of the people in the soldiers and their weapons. The enemy's power lies in the relative skill, competence and will of the opposing force. Since men and their hearts are critical to *shih* strategy, the commanders and the rulers need to know how to mobilize them. A ruler's adherence to the *tao* (the right way) brings the people into accord with the ruler in internal harmony. Without *tao*, even the best rulers and commanders could not rely on *shih*. Sun Tzu's prescription for creating *shih* is to achieve *tao*, the state in which all people are in full accord with the ruler; in such a polity the people will die for the ruler. To sum up, *shih* strategy by defeating the enemy's intent rather than using force and by building up strength by harmoniously combining the people, the ruler and the army, provides victory.[202] The five indicators of relative power in Sun Tzu's paradigm are the degree of harmony between the ruler and the people, the correctness of the season, the advantages of terrain, the skills of the military commander and the degree of military discipline.[203]

In Clausewitz's theory, the commitment of the people and their mobilization in waging war are very important.[204] *Hsing* means the employment and deployment of troops. *Hsing* is the tangible, visible and determinate shape of physical strength. *Shih* is also comprised of intangible factors like morale, opportunity, timing and psychology. These two concepts are in a way interlinked. Huai Nan Tzu (140? BCE) comes up with two kinds of military *shih*: the soldiers' morale and the generals' skill. *Chi shih* bestows intrinsic advantage and creates an army's endogenous *shih*. Exogenous *Ti-shih*, the advantage in critical terrain, expands endogenous *shih*. Sun Tzu's Confucian-Taoist premise that power resides among the people locates a state's true strength less in strong forts and powerful weaponry than in the peoples' morale and the soldiers' moral stamina.[205] Hence, Sun Tzu harps on *chi*, the spirit or motivation of the troops.[206]

In Clausewitz's paradigm, diplomacy and the conduct of warfare constitute two different watertight compartments; for Sun Tzu and Kautilya, however, these two activities fuse to comprise a continuous seamless

---

[201] Isabelle Duyvesteyn, *Clausewitz and African War: Politics and Strategy in Liberia and Somalia* (Oxon: Routledge, 2005). See especially pp. 1–2.

[202] Mott IV and Kim, *Philosophy of Chinese Military Culture*, pp. 11, 15, 18, 33.

[203] Hui, *War and State Formation in Ancient China and Early Modern Europe*, p. 19.

[204] Handel, *Masters of War*, p. 63.

[205] Mott IV and Kim, *Philosophy of Chinese Military Culture*, pp. 10–11, 26.

[206] *Art of War*, tr. by Sawyer, p. 142.

90   *Hinduism and the Ethics of Warfare in South Asia*

activity.[207] For Sun Tzu and Kautilya, unlike Clausewitz, warfare is inseparable from the broader art of statecraft. The arsenal of the *vijigishu*, in Kautilya's format, includes six types of *gunas* (policies) for dealing with external emergencies: *sandhi* (alliance), war, neutrality, marching, taking shelter and *dvaidhibhava*.[208]

Unlike Clausewitz's philosophy which is equivalent to the force-based *li* strategy, *shih* strategy considers deception a primary ingredient of military planning.[209] In fact, the roots of Clausewitzian strategy can be traced back to classical Greece. The combat philosophy of ancient Greece and its concomitant concept of valour (*andreia*) were built around the concept of fighting a *vernichtungsschlacht* (battle of annihilation). This means the immediate application of force in quest for a decisive battle that will destroy the opponent's ability to fight thereby leading to his immediate capitulation. The strike is to be directed at the opponent's centre of gravity; it must be overwhelming and should be delivered in a single blow.[210] As regards the preferred method of winning, while Clausewitz focuses on decisive battles – that is, maximum concentration of force at the decisive point of engagement – Sun Tzu emphasizes extensive use of deception, psychological warfare and non-violent methods. For Clausewitz, the centre of gravity is the enemy's army, but for Sun Tzu the centre of gravity is the enemy's will and the alliance system.[211]

Sun Tzu and Sun Tzu II are against conducting attritional campaigns even when they are bound to be successful. Sun Tzu's *The Art of War* warns against excessive dependence on violence.[212] Sun Tzu warns the rulers and statesmen not to depend solely on sheer military power or on numerical superiority.[213] Sun Tzu II writes: 'Those who enjoy militarism, however, will perish; and those who are ambitious for victory will be disgraced. War is not something to enjoy, victory is not to be an object of ambition.'[214] Both Kautilya and Sun Tzu urge subjugation rather than destruction of the enemy.[215] Sun Tzu II speaks of establishing

---

[207] Handel, *Masters of War*, p. 31.
[208] Kane, *History of Dharmasastra*, vol. 1, Part 1, p. 201.
[209] Mott IV and Kim, *Philosophy of Chinese Military Culture*, p. 41.
[210] Tsakiris, 'Thucydides and Strategy', p. 177.
[211] Handel, *Masters of War*, p. 19.
[212] Kane, *Ancient China on Postmodern War*, pp. 25, 123.
[213] Handel, *Masters of War*, p. 96.
[214] Sun Tzu II, *The Lost Art of War*, tr. with Commentary by Thomas Cleary (San Francisco: HarperCollins, 1996), p. 21.
[215] Surya P. Subedi, 'The Concept in Hinduism of "Just War"', *Journal of Conflict & Security Law*, vol. 8, no. 2 (2003), p. 353.

Kautilya's Kutayuddha

unity of command in order to avoid friction and giving independence to the commanders.[216]

Sun Tzu's famous statement is: 'Subjugating the enemy's army without fighting is the true pinnacle of excellence.'[217] He elucidates several means to achieve this object. Both Sun Tzu and the ancient Chinese historian Sima Qian advocate underhanded tactics when they can serve as a substitute for bloody battles.[218] Sun Tzu writes: 'Warfare is the Way (Tao) of deception.... Create disorder in their forces and take them.'[219] He says that the enemy must be attacked when he is unprepared.[220] Sun Tzu II, influenced by Taoism, says that an enemy ten times superior could be defeated by following several stratagems, such as 'Attack when they are unprepared, act when they least expect it.'[221] One technique of deception on the battlefield, for Sun Tzu, is tactical withdrawal. Sun Tzu says that speed is the essence of war.[222] As regards information warfare, Sun Tzu says: 'Thus it is said that one who knows the enemy and knows himself will not be endangered in a hundred engagements.'[223] Sun Tzu speaks of expendable spies who spread disinformation in foreign states. He writes that such expendable spies should be given false information for leaking to enemy agents.[224] He emphasizes the importance of paying the spies well to prevent them from deserting to the enemy.[225] Sun Tzu II says that not using secret agents results in defeat in warfare.[226] T'ai Kung discusses the possibility of undermining an enemy ruler by encouraging corruption within his state.[227] Around 236 BCE, the Qin armies followed *shih* strategy. To prevent desperate resistance, the Qin combined military campaigns with bribes, deception and good governance of the conquered territories.[228]

Kautilya advises that a king should first indulge in *mantrayuddha* (a battle of wits and diplomatic maneuvering backed by force) before resorting

---

[216] *The Lost Art of War*, tr. by Cleary, pp. 42–3.
[217] *Art of War*, tr. by Sawyer, p. 177.
[218] Kane, *Ancient China on Postmodern War*, pp. 13–14.
[219] *Art of War*, tr. by Sawyer, p. 168.
[220] Handel, *Masters of War*, p. 121.
[221] *The Lost Art of War*, tr. by Cleary, p. 29.
[222] Handel, *Masters of War*, pp. 90, 124.
[223] *Art of War*, tr. by Sawyer, p. 179.
[224] Ibid., pp. 136–7.
[225] Kane, *Ancient China on Postmodern War*, p. 147.
[226] *The Lost Art of War*, tr. by Cleary, p. 43.
[227] Kane, *Ancient China on Postmodern War*, p. 139.
[228] Mott IV and Kim, *Philosophy of Chinese Military Culture*, p. 50.

92   Hinduism and the Ethics of Warfare in South Asia

to force.[229] Kautilya introduces the concept of *yana*, which means coercive deterrence, that is, forcing a state to bow down to the *vijigishu*'s wishes through a display of military assets and valour.[230] Kautilya writes about the mission of the envoy: 'Fight with the weapon of diplomacy, assassination of the enemy's army chiefs, stirring up the circle of Kings, secret use of weapons, fire and poison ... overreaching the enemy by trickery.'[231] The secret agents are to implicate the elites of the enemy state, frame them for treason, and to encourage the officers of the enemy state to turn against the ruling authority.[232]

Kautilya writes about the various types of warfare: 'Open war is fighting at the place and time indicated; creating fright, sudden assault, striking when there is error or a calamity, giving way and striking in one place, are types of concealed warfare; that which concerns secret practices and instigations through secret agents is the mark of silent war.'[233] Silent war and concealed warfare constitute Kautilya's *kutayuddha*. Hence, for both Sun Tzu and Kautilya, unlike Clausewitz, destruction of the enemy force is a secondary objective; attacking the enemy's plans and objectives is more important.[234] For Kautilya, *Bhedopagraham copagantum* refers to the capture of the enemy king through dissension in his ranks.[235] The *Mudraraksa* notes that Kautilya won over one of the ablest Nanda ministers, a man named Raksasa, to the side of Chandragupta, thus completing the discomfiture of the Nandas.[236] Raksasa became the principal minister of Chandragupta when Kautilya retired from political life. The Raksasa episode also finds support in the *Panchatantra*, which was composed between the third and the sixth century CE. The point to be noted is that Kautilya's *kutayuddha*, which comprises winning over the enemy's commanders and councilors, was also practiced by the master during his lifetime. Sun Tzu II also speaks of capturing the enemy commanders by using unorthodox techniques.[237]

Bhedopagraham copagantum and *tusnimdandena* are techniques of conducting *kutayuddha*. Kautilya emphasizes the use of spies to gather knowledge about treasonable elements within the state, and if necessary,

---

[229] Subedi, 'Concept in Hinduism of "Just War"', p. 352.
[230] Zaman, 'Kautilya', p. 238.
[231] *KA*, Part II, by Kangle, p. 4.
[232] *KA*, Part III, by Kangle, pp. 136–7.
[233] *KA*, Part II, by Kangle, p. 342.
[234] Handel, *Masters of War*, pp. 42–3.
[235] *KA*, Part II, by Kangle, p. 337.
[236] Kosambi, *Culture and Civilization of Ancient India*, p. 142.
[237] *The Lost Art of War*, tr. by Cleary, p. 35.

the use of silent punishment against them.[238] Kautilya speaks of the *vaidehakantevasinah*, an assistant to the trader spy.[239] Kautilya is for using *bhiksuki* (mendicant women) spies also.[240] Kautilya discusses *dvahsthaparampara*, which refers to roving spies (carriers of information) disguised as acrobats, beggars, and jugglers who come periodically to houses to beg. Stationary spies deployed in enemy territory in these houses take advantage of their appearance to communicate information to them. Occasionally, the spies in these houses get orders from the secret service establishment through the above-mentioned roving spies, who claim to be relations of the servants and come to visit the latter in the houses. Another concept in the *Arthasastra* is *samjnalipibhih*, which means a code language used by spies for communication with each other as well for sending messages to their master.[241] In Kautilya's framework, an attempt should be made to win over disaffected subjects through rewards. If this attempt fails, then the leaders among them should be eliminated through unorthodox measures, and dissension should be spread deliberately within the rebel camp.[242]

T'ai Kung's *Six Secret Teachings* emphasize that the ruler should encourage industry, commerce and agriculture in order to profit the people, which will strengthen the regime. Shang Yang also says that in order to sustain warfare, a state needs to be strong, and for this, expansion of agriculture is necessary.[243] But Clausewitz is oblivious to the necessary economic muscle behind conducting warfare.

The *Arthasastra* and the *Agni Purana*, like the Legalists, emphasize regular payment of the troops to prevent any dissatisfaction among the military personnel.[244] War making requires money. Kautilya notes: 'The treasury is based upon mining, the army upon the treasury; he who has the army and treasury may conquer the whole wide earth.'[245] Kautilya provides us with a picture of an all-pervading state. The *bhaga* (royal share) comprises one-sixth of the agricultural produce and one-sixth of the animal husbandry products. The *sulka* (import and export duties) is another source of royal income. The state derives monopoly charges

---

[238] Mital, *Kautilya Arthasastra Revisited*, pp. 40–1.
[239] *KA*, Part II, by Kangle, p. 22.
[240] Srivastava, *Ancient Indian Army*, p. 101.
[241] *KA*, Part II, by Kangle, p. 25.
[242] J. S. Negi, 'Craft, Fraud and Secret Violence in the *Arthasastra* of Kautilya', in Negi, *Indological Studies*, vol. 1, pp. 37–8.
[243] Kane, *Ancient China on Postmodern War*, pp. 40, 63.
[244] Chakravarti, *Art of War in Ancient India*, p. 87.
[245] Quoted from Kosambi, *Culture and Civilization of Ancient India*, p. 154.

94   *Hinduism and the Ethics of Warfare in South Asia*

from mines, forests, minting coins and salt production. In addition, the
state owns land, factories and animals. Further, the state takes fee income
from issuing licenses to the prostitutes and liquor manufacturers.[246] To
raise revenue for the state, measures ought to be taken for the expansion of agriculture. Hence, Kautilya advocates the settling of new villages
with Sudra agriculturists.[247] Kautilya advises that the cultivators should
be given seeds, cattle and money for expanding cultivation in the waste-
land.[248] Kautilya says: 'Agriculture, cattle-rearing and trade – these constitute economics, which are beneficial, as they yield grains, cattle, money,
forest produce and labour. Through them, the king brings under his sway
his own party as well as the party of the enemies, by the use of the treasury and the army.'[249]

T'ai Kung's *Six Secret Teachings* emphasize the importance of military administration and this includes the administration of supplies.[250]
Kautilya refers to the importance of state factories that manufacture arms
and equipment for the soldiers. Kautilya emphasizes the role of logistics,
especially when defending a fort against a hostile besieging army.[251] *The
Art of War* warns commanders not to attack enemy cities except as a last
resort. The Warring States period saw the improvement of the system of
walls and towers used for defending the principal cities and sites that
dominated the major transportation routes. Mo Tzu and his followers
advised the rulers that construction of defence works would discourage
predatory rulers from practicing aggression. Mo Tzu discussed engineering and managing the civilian population during a siege.[252]

Kautilya emphasizes the importance of *puras* (fortified settlements)
and *durgas* (forts) in warfare. He says: 'For the acquisition of a fort brings
about the protection of his own land and the repulsion of enemies and
forest tribes.'[253] *Shitasatru*, in the *Arthasastra*, is an enemy with a fort,
and *kalamitra* is an enemy without a fort.[254] For Kautilya, the former
enemy is stronger than the latter. The characteristics of fortification were
walls with towers.[255] The fortifications of Patna during the Mauryan

---

[246] Mital, *Kautilya Arthasastra Revisited*, pp. 32–3.
[247] Kane, *History of Dharmasastra*, vol. 1, Part 1, p. 155.
[248] Bhat, 'Means to Fill the Treasury during a Financial Crisis', p. 149.
[249] *KA*, Part II, by Kangle, p. 9.
[250] Kane, *Ancient China on Postmodern War*, p. 38.
[251] *KA*, Part III, by Kangle, pp. 53, 128.
[252] Kane, *Ancient China on Postmodern War*, pp. 61, 149.
[253] *KA*, Part II, by Kangle, p. 353.
[254] Ibid., p. 353.
[255] Srivastava, *Ancient Indian Army*, p. 60.

Kautilya's Kutayuddha

era were made of timber and earth.[256] Kautilya warns against the use of wood in fortifications as wooden fortifications can easily be set fire by an enemy besieging force.[257] As regards siege operations, Kautilya speaks of making *surangas* (tunnels). Kane points out that there was cultural intercourse by land between Babylon and Punjab from the third millennium BCE. Construction of *surangas* against enemy forts was a technique that the Indians learnt from the Babylonians and the Egyptians before the Greeks came to India under Alexander.[258] Long before Alexander, there was contact between India and Persia. An Indian contingent comprised of infantry, chariots and cavalry accompanied Xerxes' army when it invaded Greece.[259] During the pre-Mauryan era, Indian mercenary soldiers from Punjab and the north-west frontier region accompanied Xerxes' forces and took part in the battles of Thermopylae (480 BCE) and Plataea (479 BCE).[260] Hence, it could be argued that while some Greek military traditions reached India by way of these mercenaries, some Indian military customs were also transmitted to Greece through these hired warriors.

KAUTILYA AND POST-MODERN WAR

One name for post-modern war is Fourth-Generation Warfare (hereinafter 4GW). The theorists of this sort of warfare focus on the strategic interaction between intangible elements like moral and mental dimensions, organizational culture, and so on. The new millennium is witnessing intrastate rather than interstate warfare. Domestic factors generating identity politics are the prime movers in this sort of warfare. The objectives of the insurgents are existential and not instrumental. 4GW is non-conventional and non-military in nature. This sort of warfare is characterized by very small independent groups and cells acting on mission-type orders, emphasizing maneuverability and a decreasing dependence on logistics. The goals of such warfare are psychological rather than physical. Hence, such wars are waged more on the moral and mental dimensions rather than on the physical plane. Such warfare aims not at the physical destruction of the enemy forces but at their mental and moral dislocation, with the goal of inducing paralysis and piecemeal surrender. The insurgents use all available networks – political, economic,

---

[256] Kosambi, *Culture and Civilization of Ancient India*, p. 160.
[257] *KA*, Part III, by Kangle, p. 66.
[258] Kane, *History of Dharmasastra*, vol. 1, Part 1, pp. 220–1.
[259] *KA*, Part III, by Kangle, p. 75.
[260] Majumdar, *Military System in Ancient India*, pp. 46–9.

96 *Hinduism and the Ethics of Warfare in South Asia*

social and military – in order to outwit and outmaneuver their enemies. Thus, they aim to paralyze the target state from within.[261]

Instead of calling it 4GW, one scholar terms this New War. One of the characteristics of New War is the privatization of warfare. This means that non-state and sub-state agents have seized the initiative and demilitarized warfare. The latter phrase refers to the loss of the monopoly on violence by the armed forces, the dissolution of the distinction between combatants and non-combatants and the targeting of civilian populations and the non-military infrastructure. While guerrillas have to depend on the moral and material support of the people among whom they operate, the terrorists who are conducting New War do not depend on backing from the people but conduct the war by subsisting within the general populace and simultaneously targeting them.[262]

A retired British general, Rupert Smith, argues that the globalized world is experiencing a new type of war, which he terms the 'war amongst the people'. Smith writes: 'So instead of a world in which peace is understood to be an absence of war and we move from one to the other in a linear process of peace-crisis-war; we are in a world of permanent confrontations within which nest conflicts, potential and actual, as the various opponents seek to influence each other's intentions.'[263] Smith continues: 'In fighting amongst the people the ultimate objective is to capture the will of the people.'[264] Michel Foucault accepts the assertion of Sun Tzu, Kautilya and Clausewitz that politics is the continuation of war.[265] Smith quotes Foucault: 'Power is a relationship not a possession.' In the war amongst the people, Smith continues, it is very difficult for governments with their conventional armies to exert power, to use strength and to establish a relationship of advantage.[266]

Thomas M. Kane's assertion that post-modernism includes renewed appreciation for factors that remain forever unquantifiable is acceptable. Modernism, for Kane, is the school of thought that is unwilling to accept the idea that nature sets inherent limits on what human beings can know

---

[261] Frans Osinga, 'On Boyd, Bin Laden, and Fourth Generation Warfare as String Theory', in John Andreas Olsen (ed.), *On New Wars* (Oslo: Norwegian Institute for Defence Studies, 2007), pp. 173–5, 179, 183–4, 187.

[262] Herfried Munkler, 'New Wars: Characteristics and Commonalities', in Olsen (ed.), *On New Wars*, pp. 69, 82.

[263] Rupert Smith, 'Thinking about the Utility of Force in War amongst the People', in Olsen (ed.), *On New Wars*, p. 33.

[264] Ibid., p. 34.

[265] Heuser, *Reading Clausewitz*, p. 48.

[266] Smith, 'Thinking about the Utility of Force', p. 33. The quotation is on the same page.

Kautilya's Kutayuddha

and do. Modernists always emphasize progress and are unwilling to rely on intuition, inchoate personal knowledge or allegedly innate knowledge. The post-modern military thinkers focus more on human judgement, creativity and holistic thought.[267]

The distinction between modernist and post-modernist thinking can be traced back to the Enlightenment and the Romantic movement. Enlightenment thought claims that human behaviour, like the natural sciences, can yield analytical propositions that are valid like laws. By contrast, proponents of the Romantic movement assert that human endeavours at their core are creative and beyond rational analysis. The Enlightenment saw the application of reason and the scientific method for understanding both the external world (planets, tides, geology, etc.) and the internal world of human thought and action. Enlightenment thought focuses on the scientific method and empirical study. A principal assumption of the Enlightenment thought is that human behaviour reveals broad continuities and regularities. Historical events are not unique in their essentials but rather manifestations of universal rules or tendencies. Thus, systematic knowledge of human behaviour and interactions could be envisaged. Further, the power of reason allows mankind to control its own destiny. With the Enlightenment, progress in human affairs became possible.[268]

By contrast, Counter-Enlightenment (or Romantic) thought argues that actions and motives can be known only through personal experience, since they derive from such imponderables as emotion, genius and fortune. The passions driving human beings are too powerful and human affairs too complex to be analyzed through rational theorizing. After a point, reason gives way to intuition, and empiricism to faith. Great achievements are products of inspiration and genius. War above all is a matter of passion, and its conduct cannot be made the slave of reason. Overall, the Counter-Enlightenment emphasizes an anti-materialist and anti-empiricist approach.[269]

Alan Beyerchen asserts that Clausewitz understood war as a nonlinear phenomenon, aspects of which are characterized by organized complexity. In a linear system, when the variables are plotted against each other, their relationship generates a straight line. Changes in system output are proportional to changes in input, meaning that the effects are proportional to their causes. System outputs corresponding to the

---

[267] Kane, *Ancient China on Postmodern War*, pp. 4–5, 8, 103.
[268] Smith, *On Clausewitz*, pp. ix, 53–4.
[269] Ibid., pp. 54–5.

98   *Hinduism and the Ethics of Warfare in South Asia*

sum of two inputs are equal to the sum of the outputs arising from the inputs determined discretely, meaning that the whole is exactly equal to the sum of its parts. Linearity promises prediction, and thus control, in both physical and social systems. Linear systems do not take into account feedback, trigger effects and threshold events (tipping points). By contrast, non-linear systems are characterized by random activities. In non-linear systems characterized by disorganized complexity, there are a large number of variables, and the behaviour of these variables is erratic and unknown. More important than the number of variables is the fact that a sizeable number of variables are interrelated into an organic whole. Most biological and social systems are characterized by organized complexity. Enlightenment philosophy portrays all systems as linear systems.[270]

In an essay of 1805, Clausewitz, who was influenced by Romantic thought, claimed that it is misguided and dangerous to reduce war to a formal system based on measurable quantities.[271] For Clausewitz, a theory of warfare cannot offer a set of rules and regulations.[272] Further, he states: 'In war everything is uncertain, and calculations have to be made with variable quantities.'[273] On 29 September 1806, Clausewitz introduced the concept of friction. He wrote that due to the inevitability of friction, a commander cannot adhere to military plans.[274] Clausewitz rejects calculation and probability, because in warfare, for him, chance and moral forces play very important roles. The series of consequences, writes Clausewitz, that follows from any action are endless and therefore not accessible to human reason.[275] Clausewitz writes: 'No other human activity is so continuously or universally bound up with chance. And through the element of chance, guesswork and luck come to play a great part in war.'[276] He continues: 'In short, absolute, so-called mathematical, factors never find a firm basis in military calculations. From the very start there is an interplay of probabilities, good luck and bad that weaves its way throughout the length and breadth of the tapestry. In the whole range of human activities, war most closely resembles a game of cards.'[277] He further emphasizes:

[270] Beyerchen, 'Clausewitz and the Non-Linear Nature of Warfare', pp. 47–51.
[271] Smith, *On Clausewitz*, p. 5.
[272] Heuser, *Reading Clausewitz*, p. 11.
[273] Clausewitz, *On War*, ed. and tr. by Howard and Paret, p. 136.
[274] Smith, *On Clausewitz*, pp. 6, 11.
[275] Strachan, *Clausewitz's On War*, pp. 50–1.
[276] Clausewitz, *On War*, ed. and tr. by Howard and Paret, p. 85.
[277] Ibid., p. 86.

War is the realm of uncertainty; three quarters of the factors on which action in war is based are wrapped up in a fog of greater or lesser uncertainty.... War is the realm of chance. No other human activity gives it greater scope: no other has such incessant and varied dealings with this intruder. Chance makes everything more uncertain and interferes with the whole course of events.[278]

Thomas Kane asserts that Sun Tzu's *The Art of War* contains many strands of post-modernist thinking. Sun Tzu implies that a different combination of even a small number of factors can generate a large number of outcomes and that this is simultaneously a strategist's greatest strength and his greatest weakness. Both Lao Tzu and Sun Tzu accept the idea that the interaction between opposing principles can produce so many outcomes that no mortal could appreciate the full range of options inherent in any situation. It seems that the two above-mentioned Chinese theorists are referring to warfare as a non-linear system.[279]

Machiavelli acknowledges Fortuna's power but says that if people and states become powerful, then they to a large extent cease to be helpless toys in Fortuna's hands.[280] Unlike Clausewitz, but like Antoine de Jomini (1779–1869), Kautilya to a great extent attempts to understand warfare through a set of rigid principles that would guarantee success. By contrast, Clausewitz views war largely as unmanageable, uncertain, unpredictable and messy.[281] Nevertheless, to some extent Kautilya, like Sun Tzu and Clausewitz, pushes post-modernist strands of ideas in his work.

Both Sun Tzu and Clausewitz,[282] unlike Kautilya, assume that states are the primary actors in war. In Kautilya's paradigm, however, intrastate war is more important than inter-state war. The state suffers due to *vyasanas* (calamities). *Vyasanas*, says Kautilya, are of two types: those caused by human error and those caused by divine factors. 'Divine factors' means not religious factors but those extraneous factors that are beyond the control of the human beings. Divine calamities also occur due to bad luck. Examples of divine calamities include flood, drought, and so on. Human calamities, on the other hand, occur due to the bad policies of the ruling elite.[283]

---

[278] Ibid., p. 101.
[279] Kane, *Ancient China on Postmodern War*, pp. 122–3.
[280] Gilbert, 'Machiavelli', p. 24.
[281] Michael I. Handel, 'Introduction', *JSS*, vol. 9, nos. 2–3 (June–Sept. 1986), pp. 2–3.
[282] Of course, there is no single interpretation of Clausewitz. One author claims that Clausewitz also speaks of non-state politics. Duyvesteyn, *Clausewitz and African War*, pp. 5–14.
[283] Chousalkar, *Theory of Rebellion in Kautilya and Aristotle*, p. 75.

Kautilya's prescriptions to a great extent follow what Rupert Smith characterizes as war amongst the people. Kautilya advises that it is best to wage war against an unjust king who has no public support. And it is wise to avoid war with a righteous king whose subjects will fight vigorously on his behalf. In other words, a king should march only against an enemy with disaffected subjects. Such a king's subjects, weary of the unjust ruler, will not help their ruler and might even join in the war against him.[284] In case of divine calamities, Kautilya harps on the initiation of relief measures by state officials in order to regain the goodwill of the populace.[285] So Kautilya is implying that, morally and practically, it is easier to conquer an internally divided kingdom that is rocked by *kopa*. As part of the *kutayuddha*, Kautilya notes that special cash payments and prizes should be announced encouraging soldiers to kill the opposing side's commander-in-chief and king.[286] Kautilya is aiming to eliminate the enemy leadership/brains by deploying small cells rather than by a mass deployment of force. Kautilya also hints at 'biological warfare' when he writes that the enemy's food supplies and wells should be poisoned by secret agents.[287] In order to temporarily obscure the vision of the enemy, Kautilya says, 'The leaves of *putikaranja*, yellow orpiment [ointment], red arsenic, *gunja* seeds and stalks of red cotton plant, made into a dough with the sap of *asphota*, *kaca* and cow dung, make a blinding smoke.'[288]

Rupert Smith puts a premium on the role of information in successfully fighting the war amongst the people. He argues that we need information in order to know what the opponent is thinking, and we cannot change his intentions until we understand the mind of the formless, shapeless enemy.[289] Kautilya's *vijigishu* sought power in order to control not only the outward behaviour but also the thoughts of one's allies and enemies.[290] Kautilya highlights the role of secret agents, whose duty is to find out what the common people are thinking about the monarch. Besides reporting seditious activities among the people to the higher authorities, at times the secret agents are to dissuade the people from entertaining

---

[284] Manoj Kumar Sinha, 'Hinduism and International Humanitarian Law', *International Review of the Red Cross*, vol. 87, no. 858 (2005), p. 289.

[285] *KA*, Part III, by Kangle, p. 234.

[286] Srivastava, *Ancient Indian Army*, p. 108.

[287] *KA*, Part III, by Kangle, p. 263.

[288] Ibid., p. 495.

[289] Smith, 'Thinking about the Utility of Force', p. 40.

[290] Boesche, 'Kautilya's *Arthasastra*', p. 15.

Kautilya's Kutayuddha

feelings of disaffection toward the king.[291] In a way, the Kautilyan state is the precursor of Foucault's panopticon.

ETHICS IN KAUTILYAN PHILOSOPHY

Both Machiavelli and Clausewitz consider war to be outside moral categories. Military ethics, writes Hew Strachan, has no important role in their framework for studying warfare.[292] For Clausewitz, war is anything but humane. He is concerned with efficiency in military affairs and not ethics.[293] D. D. Kosambi claims that not one iota of morality or altruism is present in Kautilya's *Arthasastra*.[294] The name Kautilya is derived from the Sanskrit word *kutila*, meaning wicked, shrewd or astute.[295] *Mudraraksa* refers to Kautilya as *kutilamati*, that is, one with a crooked intellect.[296] It means evil genius. As regards the role of ethics in the *Arthasastra*, B. N. Mukherjee asserts: 'The main objective of this treatise was to provide the king with the ideas and methods to rule and expand his territory without caring much for moral ethics.'[297] However, we will see that there are elements of ethics in the thought of these realist thinkers.

Machiavelli claims that one of the most powerful safeguards against conspiracies a prince can have is to avoid being hated by the populace. This is because the conspirator always thinks that by killing the prince he will satisfy the people; but if he thinks that he will outrage the people, he will never have the courage to go ahead with his enterprise, because there are countless obstacles in the path of a conspirator. Good governance is an important facet for Machiavelli. He says that a prince must want to have a reputation for compassion rather than for cruelty. Nonetheless, he must be careful that he does not make bad use of compassion. So a prince must not worry if he incurs reproach for his cruelty so long as he keeps his subjects united and loyal. By making an example or two, he will prove more compassionate than those who, being too compassionate, allow disorder, which leads to murder and rapine.[298] He writes: 'The prince must nonetheless make himself feared in such a way, that if he is

---

[291] *KA*, Part III, by Kangle, p. 116.
[292] Strachan, *Clausewitz's On War*, pp. 88–9.
[293] Smith, *On Clausewitz*, p. 46.
[294] Kosambi, *Culture and Civilization of Ancient India*, p. 142.
[295] Sil, *Kautilya's Arthasastra*, p. 18.
[296] Kane, *History of Dharmasastra*, vol. 1, Part 1, p. 166.
[297] Mukherjee, 'Foreword', in Sil, *Kautilya's Arthasastra*, p. x.
[298] Machiavelli, *The Prince*, pp. 95, 103.

Hinduism and the Ethics of Warfare in South Asia

not loved, at least he escapes being hated. For fear is quite compatible with an absence of hatred; and the prince can always avoid hatred if he abstains from the property of his subjects and citizens and from their women.'[299] Machiavelli continues that his behaviour must be tempered by humanity and prudence so that over-confidence does not make him rash or excessive distrust make him unbearable.[300]

Even Clausewitz warns the militarists: 'Since war is not an act of senseless passion but is controlled by its political object, the value of this object must determine the sacrifices to be made for it in *magnitude* and also in *duration*. Once the expenditure of effort exceeds the value of the political object, the object must be renounced and peace must follow.'[301] Clausewitz did not allow for murder or torture of prisoners of war.[302] And Clausewitz never thinks of deliberately targeting the enemy civilian population as a legitimate war aim.[303] Traditional Taoism, writes Thomas Cleary, condemns militarism as both immoral and inefficient. However, defensive, protective, peacekeeping and punitive operations are considered rational and natural. Sun Tzu II also justifies judicious use of arms for pacification and the maintenance of law and order.[304]

Strands of ethics are present in Kautilyan philosophy, but they are related to the realist stance taken by Kautilya. In the interests of the state, officials and rulers might sometimes set aside religious considerations, but in ordinary times governance should be based on a balanced combination of *dharma* and *artha*.[305] Kautilya warns that during emergencies, the state might resort to extra taxation, but these measures should not be used frequently. The *Arthasastra* tells us that excessive taxation in the long run destroys the economic potential of the kingdom,[306] and implies that such a situation might give rise to *kopa*. *Danda*, which is the legitimate coercive apparatus of the state, for Kautilya, can be used for harassing, plundering and even killing the enemies of the state[307] but not ordinary peace-loving subjects. Kautilya emphasizes good governance especially with regard to the moderate use of force to prevent *kopa*. He continues: 'For the king,

---

[299] Ibid., p. 97.
[300] Ibid., p. 96.
[301] Clausewitz, *On War*, ed. and tr. by Howard and Paret, p. 92. Italics in original.
[302] Paul Cornish, 'Clausewitz and the Ethics of Armed Force: Five Propositions', *JME*, vol. 2, no. 3 (2003), p. 215.
[303] Heuser, *Reading Clausewitz*, p. 50.
[304] *The Lost Art of War*, tr. by Cleary, p. 59.
[305] Negi, 'Religion and Politics in the *Arthasastra* of Kautilya', p. 23.
[306] Mital, *Kautilya Arthasastra Revisited*, p. 41.
[307] Sil, *Kautilya's Arthasastra*, p. 23.

severe with the Rod, becomes a source of terror to beings. The king, mild with the Rod, is despised. The king, just with the Rod, is honoured. For the Rod, used after full consideration, endows the subjects with spiritual good, material well-being and pleasures of the senses.'[308]

Kautilya warns the *vijigishu* that an unjust use of power over his subjects results in *kopa*. The *sastras* have nothing against regicide if the ruler is unjust and fails to protect his subjects properly or oppresses them unnecessarily. Too much coercion by the ruler might result in the disaffected subjects joining hands with the foreign enemies of the state. Hence, the threat of a revolt by the people functions as a check upon the misuse of power by the ruler. In the final analysis, writes Kautilya, internal security depends on the contentment of the subjects.[309]

In Kautilya's paradigm, the objectives of the *vijigishu* are *labha* (economic improvement) and *palana* (protection) of his subjects. Kautilya tells that *raksha* (security) of the subjects is one of the principal duty of the ruler.[310] Though Kautilya was aware of India's neighbouring countries, he did not advocate that the *vijigishu* expand his realm beyond the subcontinent. In fact, his *mandala* doctrine refers to the circle of states within India, which ultimately should be brought under the control of a single ruler – *eka vijigishu*. P. V. Kane writes that Kautilya had seen at first hand the devastation caused by foreign rule. Hence, his ambition was that the subcontinent should be united under the rule of a strong but benevolent *chakravartin*.[311] The objective of Kautilya's *vijigishu* is to establish an empire encompassing all the regions between the Himalayas and the sea, but not the region outside the Jambudipa (the traditional name of the subcontinent). The expansion of the empire beyond the subcontinent is seen as undesirable, impracticable and unjust.[312] Hence, Kautilya is no mad militarist advocating world conquest.

Like Kautilya, Sun Tzu implies that a victorious society should learn to live with the erstwhile enemy in a stable controlled insecurity.[313] Kautilya tells the *vijigishu* that even in conquered territories, he should maintain the existing social order.[314] In order to co-opt the people of the newly gained territories and to avoid causing any psychological shock, Kautilya

---

[308] *KA*, Part II, by Kangle, p. 10.
[309] *KA*, Part III, by Kangle, p. 120.
[310] Ibid., pp. 2, 117.
[311] Kane, *History of Dharmasastra*, vol. 1, Part 1, p. 223.
[312] *KA*, Part III, by Kangle, pp. 2–3.
[313] Mott IV and Kim, *Philosophy of Chinese Military Culture*, p. 9.
[314] *KA*, Part III, by Kangle, p. 93.

104   *Hinduism and the Ethics of Warfare in South Asia*

urges the *vijigishu* to adopt the dress, language and customs of the people of the conquered region. However, Kautilya is not advocating absorption in toto. He warns the *vijigishu* that unrighteous customs should not be followed but abolished.[315] There are ethical limits in Kautilya's philosophy regarding the conduct of war that prevent it from progressing towards the concept of Total War. Kautilya is against harming noncombatants in enemy territory. Kautilya writes that after conquering the enemy king, the victor should release the prisoners and give help to the helpless and the sick.[316]

CONCLUSION

Neither Kautilya nor Thucydides and not even Clausewitz emphasizes the importance of the dialectic between technology and the conduct of warfare. Thus we find Kautilya advocating the use of war chariots long after they have become outdated. Sun Tzu, Kautilya and Clausewitz neglect the role of sea power. Clausewitz was an army officer, and his country, Prussia, was a state facing grave threat along its land borders. Moreover, Prussia had no colonies.[317] Hence, Clausewitz did not concern himself with the issue of maritime power. Both Sun Tzu and Kautilya, operating in the context of continental agrarian-bureaucratic empires, failed to envisage the importance of sea power. Unlike Thucydides and Kautilya, Clausewitz ignores the origins of war and the interrelationship between warfare and economics. The post-modernist trend is most apparent in Clausewitz's ideas, to a lesser extent in Sun Tzu and in Kautilya's framework. By contrast, the linkage between internal security and external security – that is, between conventional and non-conventional/irregular warfare – is strongest in the *Arthasastra*, is comparatively weak in *The Art of War*, and is extremely limited in *On War*.

Kautilya, Sun Tzu and Clausewitz are strategists of power. Power-politics determine everything in Kautilya's paradigm. For Kautilya, the security of a state ultimately depends on the acquisition of power. Kautilya believes in the rational actor analysis when trying to formulate inter-state behaviour. Like Sun Tzu, but unlike Clausewitz, Kautilya advocates following a multidimensional grand strategy rather than a purely military strategy for overwhelming an enemy. The *Arthasastra* opens a new dimension by

---

[315] Negi, 'Religion and Politics in the *Arthasastra* of Kautilya', p. 17.
[316] Sinha, 'Hinduism and International Humanitarian Law', p. 293.
[317] Smith, *On Clausewitz*, p. 48.

introducing biological warfare. Kautilya's *chara* is geared more to collecting strategic information than to gathering battlefield intelligence. One of the cardinal points of Kautilya's philosophy is that regular and irregular military operations should be conducted simultaneously. When undertaking invasion of an internally divided kingdom, the conqueror should encourage internal rebellion in the enemy kingdom. At the beginning of new millennium, as the power of states is waning and intra-state violence and peace-keeping missions are becoming more important, Kautilya's *kopa*, with its foreign interconnections and peace-war amalgam, holds all the more attraction for theorists of state behaviour.

4

Dharmayuddha and *Kutayuddha* from the Common Era to the Advent of the Turks

The dominant view among scholars is that the post-Mauryan polities in India until the advent of the Turks were segmentary states. Being weak entities, these polities were unable to harness resources and develop the administrative tentacles needed for maintaining standing professional armies. Further, the geographic isolation of India resulted in stagnation of the tactics and techniques of warfare.[1] Early medieval India seems to have had no military theory worth studying. By contrast, this chapter, on the basis of a transcontinental cross-cultural comparative analysis, argues that South Asia's military system underwent innovation and that the *acharyas* generated sophisticated theories in tune with political and ecological conditions. We will deal with the various theories in a chronological manner. The first part deals with political conditions after the collapse of the Mauryan Empire. The second part deals with Manu, who operated at the beginning of the Common Era. The third part narrates the steppe nomadic intrusion and the military response (on the planes of both theory and practice) of Hindu India. The fourth part deals with Bana, who describes the political and military scenarios during late antiquity. The fifth part focuses on Kamandaka, who charts the political and military landscape towards the end of the early medieval era. All of these theorists were Brahmins of north India, and they composed their works for the monarchs who tried to carve out a pan-Indian empire from their bases in north India. The sixth section deals with three 'folk tale variety' works whose readership was the provincial/regional elite. The last section

[1] Pradeep P. Barua, *The State at War in South Asia* (Lincoln/London: University of Nebraska Press, 2005), pp. 15–22.

106

From the Common Era to the Advent of the Turks   107

deals with a low-caste Tamil military theorist who depicted the political and military conditions of peninsular India.

Christopher C. Rand asserts that the ancient Chinese philosophy of war concerned itself with the relationship between martiality and civility during periods of internal and external violence. There was an ongoing debate about whether violent means (*wu*), ranging from a show of force to peremptory attack, or non-violent means (*wen*) – including peaceful moral example, intentional yielding and ethical suasion – or a combination of both was proper for dealing with chaos (*luan*). Ethical suasion included clever deception, false argumentation, and so on – that is, methods that avoided battle.[2] From 400 CE onwards, in Western Europe, the church was regarded as the arbiter of moral behaviour and developed the Christian just war doctrine. The just war concept emerged in Christianity from the fourth century onwards when the Christians started to assume positions of leadership in the temporal sphere. The just war doctrine evolved to address the issues of defence of the homeland from attack, repression of criminality and protection of the innocent.[3] In India, it was mainly the brahmanical elite who tried to resolve the tension between *dharmayuddha* and *kutayuddha*. We will see that the *acharyas* not only evolved a grand strategy, like the Chinese military commentators, but also came up with thoughts on military tactics, like the ancient and medieval Western European theorists.

R. Brian Ferguson asserts that the realist conception of the state as a unitary independent actor following a rational policy may not always be adequate. A polity may be seen as a potentially divided congeries of people dialectically interacting with the larger social system. Ferguson makes a division between territorial conquest and hegemony. In the case of territorial conquest, the defeated rulers were uprooted and imperial garrisons were installed. In the case of hegemony, the local rulers, after being defeated, were left in place. A hegemonic polity fails to stop the local strongmen from waging war. Ferguson warns that such a neat division between territorial and hegemonic political systems did not operate in practice. In polycentric states, the clear division between hegemonic and territorial states was absent. Even within territorially consolidated states, a weakening of the centre resulted in

---

[2] Christopher C. Rand, 'Li Ch'uan and Chinese Military Thought', *Harvard Journal of Asiatic Studies*, vol. 39, no. 1 (1979), pp. 107–8.

[3] Gregory M. Reichberg, 'Norms of War in Roman Catholic Christianity', in Vesselin Popovski, Gregory M. Reichberg and Nicholas Turner (eds.), *World Religions and Norms of War* (Tokyo/New York: United Nations University Press, 2009), pp. 143–4.

Hinduism and the Ethics of Warfare in South Asia

increasing local autonomy.[4] This model can be applied when studying the various polities of the subcontinent between the fall of the Maurya Empire and the advent of the Turks. The concept of a strong state in late ancient and early medieval Western Europe has probably been overemphasized.[5]

POLITICAL CONDITIONS ON THE INDIAN SUBCONTINENT AROUND THE COMMON ERA

Shailendra Bhandare, on the basis of numismatic evidence, asserts that there was no Sunga or Kanva empire. What happened in post-Mauryan India was imperial fragmentation and the rise of several feudatories.[6] The Greeks from Bactria, known as Bactrian Greeks, established a short-lived Indo-Bactrian Empire in Punjab that continued until 130 BCE, when it was destroyed by the Sakas. By 80 BCE, the Saka Empire in India had spread across Punjab, Uttar Pradesh and West India. The Sakas in turn were pushed into Saurashtra (Gujarat) by the Parthians, who ruled parts of west and north-west India during the first century CE. Around 120 CE, the Parthians were eclipsed by the Kushanas.[7] The Kushana Emperor Kanishka I (78–102 CE) ruled large parts of west and north India. In 226 CE, the Sassanians of Persia destroyed the Kushanas.[8] In central and west India, the dominant power was the Satavahanas. However, none of these polities were pan-Indian entities like the Maurya Empire.[9]

Romila Thapar claims that after the breakup of the Maurya Empire, the monarchical system, which increasingly leaned on religious orthodoxy, tended to blur the concept of state; instead, loyalty was directed to the social order. The interdependence of caste and politics had gradually led to caste being accorded higher status than political institutions. Social

---

[4] R. Brian Ferguson, 'A Paradigm for the Study of War and Society', in Kurt Raaflaub and Nathan Rosenstein (eds.), *War and Society in the Ancient and Medieval Worlds: Asia, the Mediterranean, Europe, and Mesoamerica* (Cambridge, Massachusetts: Centre for Hellenic Studies, distributed by Harvard University Press, 1999), pp. 404–18.

[5] John France, 'Recent Writing on Medieval Warfare: From the Fall of Rome to c. 1300', *Journal of Military History*, vol. 65, no. 2 (2001), p. 442.

[6] Shailendra Bhandare, 'Numismatics and History: The Maurya-Gupta Interlude in the Gangetic Plain', in Patrick Olivelle (ed.), *Between the Empires: Society in India 300 BCE to 400 CE* (2006; reprint, New York: Oxford University Press, 2007), pp. 96–7.

[7] D. N. Jha, *Early India: A Concise History* (New Delhi: Manohar, 2004), pp. 117–23.

[8] Romila Thapar, *The Penguin History of Early India from the Origins to AD 1300* (2002; reprint, New Delhi: Penguin, 2003), p. 223.

[9] Jha, *Early India*, pp. 126–7.

From the Common Era to the Advent of the Turks   109

and ritual obligations in accordance with *varna* took precedence over the state. Based on Thapar's observation, it seems that the Indian armies of the post-Mauryan era were no more formal institutions standing in a defined relationship to the institutions of civil administration and organized religion. The Bactrian and Parthian rulers were considered *mlechchas* by the Brahmin intellectuals because these foreigners patronized Buddhism rather than Hinduism.[10] Mahayana Buddhism spread rapidly during the first three centuries CE.[11] Some Greek rulers however accepted Vaishnavism and Saivasim in order to legitimize their rule among the eyes of the common people of the subcontinent.

MANU'S *DHARMAYUDDHA*

The *sutra* literature emerged between 700 BCE and 300 CE. The *dharmasutras* are concerned with society and deal with the social usages and customs of everyday life. Though the *sutra* literature deals mainly with religious matters, it also discusses the duties of the king, civil and criminal law[12] and, in the case of the *Manava-Dharmasastra* (hereafter *MD*) of Manu, even military law. The term *Manusmriti* was first used in 1503 CE. Hence, it is better to refer to Manu's work as *MD*. Compared to previous *dharmasastra* works, Manu gives much more importance and space to *rajadharma* in his compendium of laws.[13]

P. V. Kane asserts that before the fourth century BCE, there was a work on *dharmasastra* composed by or attributed to Svayambhuva Manu. There was also a work on *rajadharma* by Pracetasa Manu. The *Mahabharata* and the *Arthasastra* refer to these works. The abovementioned two works constitute the kernel of the *MD*, which was recast by Bhrgu between the second century BCE and the second century CE.[14] A. Berriedale Keith also accepts this dating.[15] Michael Witzel claims that

[10] Thapar, *Penguin History of Early India*, pp. 207, 217.
[11] K. M. Shrimali, 'Religions in Complex Societies: The Myth of the "Dark Age"', in Irfan Habib (ed.), *Religion in Indian History* (New Delhi: Tulika, 2007), p. 52.
[12] Ramashankar Tripathi, *History of Ancient India* (1942; reprint, New Delhi: Motilal Banarasidas, 1999), pp. 56, 59, 61.
[13] *Manu's Code of Law, A Critical Edition and Translation of the Manava-Dharmasastra*, by Patrick Olivelle, with the editorial assistance of Suman Olivelle (2005; reprint, New Delhi: Oxford University Press, 2006) (hereinafter *MD*, by Olivelle), pp. 13, 18.
[14] P. V. Kane, *History of Dharmasastra (Ancient and Medieval Religious and Civil Law in India)*, vol. 1, Part 1 (Pune: Bhandarkar Oriental Research Institute, 1968), pp. 335, 344.
[15] A. Berriedale Keith, *A History of Sanskrit Literature* (1920; reprint, New Delhi: Oxford University Press, 1973), p. 441.

110 *Hinduism and the Ethics of Warfare in South Asia*

the *MD* was first collected under the Brahmin ruler Pushyamitra Sunga around 150 BCE.[16]

Patrick Olivelle asserts that the *MD* was composed by a single individual or perhaps by a committee of scholars under the chairmanship of a strong personality. However, Manu is not the real name of that gifted person. His original name is forever lost in the mist of history. For this reason, we will continue to call the author Manu. He was probably a learned Brahmin from north India. Olivelle rejects the view that *MD* was the product of gradual accretions by countless people over several centuries, because the work reflects a coherent structure and style that could come only from the pen of a particular individual. Olivelle goes on to say that the code was initially written down.[17] While Tripathi, Doniger and Smith accept the idea that Manu's *MD* was composed around the beginning of the Christian era,[18] Olivelle asserts that the text was composed and written down between the first century BCE and the second century CE.[19] Manu's text was a product of the brahmanical response to the rise of Buddhism and Jainism. Doniger and Smith claim that Chapters 8 and 9 are later additions.[20] For our part, we will be concerned mainly with Chapter 7.

The brahmanical reaction constitutes the context in which Manu's *MD* was generated. One aspect of the brahmanical reaction on the political plane was that while both the Nanda and Maurya dynasties were established by the Sudras, the Brahmins established the two succeeding Sunga and Kanva dynasties. After the death of Asoka in 232 BCE, the Maurya Empire started to decline. Brihadratha, the last Maurya emperor, was executed by his Brahmin general Pushyamitra Sunga, who subsequently established the Sunga Dynasty around 187 BCE. The Sungas fought against the Bactrian Greeks in north-west India. A Greek invasion led by the Bactrian King Demetrios around 190 BCE was repulsed by the Sunga prince Vasumitra. In 75 BCE, a Brahmin *amatya* (bureaucrat) of the last Sunga ruler deposed his master and established the Kanva Dynasty, which continued to function until 28 BCE.[21]

---

[16] Michael Witzel, 'Brahmanical Reactions to Foreign Influences and to Social and Religious Change', in Olivelle (ed.), *Between the Empires*, p. 482.

[17] *MD*, by Olivelle, pp. 5, 7, 19–20.

[18] Tripathi, *History of Ancient India*, p. 73; *The Laws of Manu*, with an Introduction and Notes, tr. by Wendy Doniger with Brian K. Smith (New Delhi: Penguin, 1991), Introduction, p. xvii.

[19] *MD*, by Olivelle, pp. 21–2.

[20] *Laws of Manu*, p. lxi.

[21] Bimal Kanti Majumdar, *The Military System in Ancient India* (Calcutta: Firma KLM, 1960), p. 76.

From the Common Era to the Advent of the Turks 111

Manu is trying to ward off the threat to the dominance of the Kshatriyas and the Brahmins posed by the Sudras. However, for the purpose of maintaining internal stability, Manu (like a modern counterinsurgency theorist) focuses not only on the use of force but also on political legitimacy. Manu's policy was that the Brahmins should legitimize Kshatriya kingship and in return should receive the lion's share of material and non-material rewards from the ruling regime. The rulers were dependent on the Brahmins both for legitimacy and for the practical purpose of running the administration. In Manu's framework, though kingship is a divine creation, the king holds a sacred position just below the Brahmin. This is a challenge to the Buddhist doctrine of monarchy as a social contract, where the king is merely receiving the highest wages for performing certain duties towards the society.[22] Manu implies that the Brahmins are above the law. The *MD* advocates that within his realm, the monarch should act in accordance with the rules. Against his enemies, he should impose harsh punishments; towards his friends and loved ones, he should behave without guile; and to the Brahmins, he should show compassion.[23]

Manu uses the concept of *dharma* both in the general sense of righteousness and in the particular sense of social conduct and legal rules. Manu accepts the laws of *karma*. Unlike Kautilya, Manu over-emphasizes the role of *dharma* in statecraft. Kautilya advocates the idea that the king should pursue *artha*, *kama* and *dharma* in a balanced manner and that these three are interdependent. However, Manu ordains that if *artha* and *kama* go against *dharma*, then the first two ought to be abandoned. In Manu's paradigm, the *dharma* of the Kshatriya is protection of the people, which in turn requires taxation of the *prajas* (subjects) of the *rashtra* (state).[24]

Manu emphasizes that the highest and ultimate source of all learning, which guides the ruler in governance, remains the *vedas*. The *MD* notes that the ruler should learn the timeless science of government and logical reasoning from the *vedas*. Hence, Manu advises the ruler to take special care to sustain the Brahmins engaged in vedic studies. The *MD* says that the monarch should provide the Brahmins with means of subsistence consistent with the *sastras* and protect them in every way like a father. When the Brahmins practice the *sastras* every day under the protection

---

[22] Keith, *History of Sanskrit Literature*, pp. 443–4.
[23] *MD*, by Olivelle, p. 155.
[24] D. Devahuti, *Harsha: A Political Study* (Oxford: Clarendon Press, 1970), pp. 119, 121, 123.

of the king, it augments the king's life span, wealth, and realm. The *MD* further states that even at the point of death, the ruler shall never extract any tax from the Brahmins.[25]

Manu defines the polity as possessing the following five elements: officials, realm, forts, treasury, and army. Manu advocates the use of a moderate amount of force on the part of the ruler for maintaining law and order in the realm and for maintaining the *chaturvarna* system (fourfold caste system).[26] The *chaturvarna* system was the ideal, according to the orthodox Brahmin thinkers. In reality, during Manu's time, there were sixty mixed castes.[27] Manu emphasizes the welfare of the subjects. He tells us that the king should employ trusted officials to collect annual taxes, strictly follow brahmanical laws in his dealings with the population, and behave like a father towards his people. Manu warns against the dangers of over-taxation of the subjects in order to prevent any grievances among the populace and to preserve the economic prosperity of the realm in the long run. Manu points out the danger of bad governance. When a king in his folly oppresses his own realm indiscriminately, he is soon deprived of his kingdom and his life, along with his relatives. When his realm is well managed, the king prospers with ease. Manu says that punishment can be administered in a just manner only by a ruler who is honest and true to his word, who acts in conformity with the *sastras* and who has good assistants.[28]

Manu notes the importance of a hierarchical state bureaucracy for surveillance of the people as part of good governance. Manu, like Asoka, was aware that state officials occasionally oppress their subjects, which in turn alienates the latter and results in rebellion against the monarch. To prevent oppression of his subjects by corrupt bureaucrats, Asoka appointed a special class of officers known as *rajukas/dhamma mahamattas* to overlook the activities of the bureaucrats. The *MD* also speaks about the necessity of having a special class of officers to supervise the day-to-day activities of the officials.[29]

As regards *raksha* of the King's subjects, Manu notes that it is the duty of the ruler to maintain internal security in his realm. For a Kshatriya

---

[25] *MD*, by Olivelle, pp. 156, 161. Instead of 'law', as translated by Patrick Olivelle, I would translate it as *dharma*. For the Sanskrit text, see *MD*, by Olivelle, p. 636.

[26] Ibid., pp. 154–5, 162.

[27] Shrimali, 'Religions in Complex Societies', p. 49.

[28] *MD*, by Olivelle, pp. 155, 158, 160–1.

[29] Ibid., pp. 160–1.

From the Common Era to the Advent of the Turks 113

ruler, the protection of his subjects is the highest law. If he fails to do that, he will lose legitimacy among his subjects. At the same time, Manu also warns the ruler that despite good governance, *kopa* may be instigated by evil-minded people. And the king should be prepared to strike at the evil-mongers silently.[30]

Manu, somewhat like Kautilya, emphasizes the *utsahasakti* (personal dynamism) of the ruler for maintaining internal and external security. Manu enumerates the following duties of the king during battle: he should organize the troops in battle formation; he should rouse their fighting spirit and inspect them carefully; and he should monitor their behaviour even when they were engaged in combat with enemy troops. When considering external security, Manu accepts the *mandala* doctrine of Kautilya. The ruler, emphasizes Manu, should give attention to maintaining a stable *mandala*. Manu accepts the traditional doctrine of the *mandala* as comprised of twelve states.[31] Pusyamitra (150 BCE) reigned from Vidisa. The Sungas fought with the central Indian kingdom of Vidarbha (Berar, Nagpur) and the ruler of Kalinga. The Satavahanas (Andhra Dynasty) had their capital at Paithan (Pratisthana). The Satavahana King Simuka fought the Sungas as well as the Sakas in Sind. The Bactrian Greeks raided north-west India, and their raids penetrated into Ayodhya, Ujjain and even Pataliputra. Probably, the chaotic post-Mauryan political scenario encouraged the *mitra-amitra-mitra* scheme in the *MD*.[32]

Manu was certainly no pacifist. Manu accepts that though he may dislike waging war, a monarch cannot totally ignore the issue. In fact, Manu says '*yodha dharma sanatanah*', meaning war is the eternal law of the king.[33] As regards the duties of a just king, he, like Kautilya, offers the following advice. The king should try to expand his influence or at best maintain his kingdom. He should keep his military force in constant readiness, constantly display his might, and constantly probe his enemy's weaknesses. Manu suggests the use of military force as part of coercive diplomacy or as a technique to deter a potential enemy state. The *MD* accepts the fact that the whole world stands in awe of the man who keeps his military force in constant readiness and that it

---

[30] Ibid., pp. 161–2.
[31] Ibid., pp. 162, 164.
[32] Witzel, 'Brahmanical Reactions to Foreign Influences and to Social and Religious Change', pp. 458–9.
[33] Quoted from P. C. Chakravarti, *The Art of War in Ancient India* (1941; reprint, Delhi: Low Price Publications, 1989), p. 181.

114   *Hinduism and the Ethics of Warfare in South Asia*

is ultimately with military force, therefore, that the king should subdue others.[34]

However, the use of *bala* remains the last and the ultimate option. Manu says that initially the policy of *sama*, *dana* and *bheda* should be pursued. When they fail, the last resort is to declare war.[35] Manu, like the ancient Chinese political and military theorists, is aware of the dangers of warfare for the king and the polity.[36] Manu notes that victory and defeat in battle are often uncertain. The king, according to Manu, should go to war only when he is certain of victory. He should declare war and launch the expedition when a calamity has struck the enemy. The *MD* continues that if the ruler believes that his subjects are exceedingly content and that he himself is overwhelmingly powerful, then he should consider waging war. If he believes that his own army is in high spirits and the opposite is true of his adversary, then he should march into battle. If the military balance shifts unfavorably, then, the *MD* suggests, the ruler should follow an appeasement policy.[37]

At the strategic level, Manu notes the importance of forming coalitions with allies for a common objective. Unlike Kautilya, who gives more importance to unilateral action by the *vijigishu*, Manu focuses more on coalition warfare under the leadership of the just ruler. However, the ruler should display flexibility towards coalition politics as the alliance must suit his long-term purposes.[38] Like Sun Tzu, Manu emphasizes overcoming the enemy's intention and will by disrupting the enemy alliance through coercive diplomacy rather than destroying the hostile army in battle.[39] Manu says that diplomatic agents should use bribery and force, with the army standing in the background, to tear apart the enemy alliance.[40]

The *MD* notes the importance of logistics in warfare. The king should first make the necessary arrangements to gather provisions for the

---

[34] *MD*, by Olivelle, p. 159.

[35] Ibid., pp. 160, 162.

[36] The rulers and the bureaucrats of ancient China, steeped in Confucianism, believed in the myth of the supremacy and attraction of Chinese culture based upon virtue and grandiose material achievement. Diplomacy, gifts (somewhat equivalent to *sama*) and a divide-and-rule policy (equivalent to the *acharyas' bheda*), assumed the Chinese philosophers, would overwhelm the enemy. Sun Tzu states that warfare is a matter of life and death for the polity. Sun Tzu, *Art of War*, tr. with an Historical Introduction by Ralph D. Sawyer (Boulder/San Francisco: Westview, 1994), pp. 32, 128.

[37] *MD*, by Olivelle, pp. 163–4.

[38] Ibid., p. 163.

[39] *Art of War*, tr. by Sawyer, p. 129.

[40] *MD*, by Olivelle, p. 157.

From the Common Era to the Advent of the Turks   115

expedition in his home territory. Then he should secure a base of military operations, deploy spies, secure the roads, inspect the divisions of his army, and only then march in battle formation. The superintendents of the villages shall collect food, drink, firewood and so forth from the villagers in order to supply the king's army.[41] Flavius Vegetius Renatus, the later Roman Empire's military theorist, warns that a scarcity of provisions ruins large armies. So the greatest care should be taken to fill up the magazines.[42] Vegetius notes: 'Famine makes greater havoc in an army than the enemy, and is more terrible than the sword.... The main and principal point in war is to secure plenty of provisions and to weaken or destroy the enemy by famine.'[43] The *MD* speaks of *sastrasalas* (magazines filled with weapons and provisions for use by the army) that are run by the state.[44]

When campaigning, the *MD*, like *The Art of War*, notes the importance of weather and terrain.[45] The scorching heat of the summer and the rainy season are to be avoided. The king is advised to start a military expedition during November–December, or in the months of February–April, depending on his force structure. He should deploy chariots and horses and infantry equipped with swords and shields when campaigning on level ground, boats and elephants in marshy lands, and archers in areas covered with trees and shrubs.[46] As a point of comparison, the campaign season for the army of the early Roman Republic opened in March and closed in October.[47]

Manu for the first time talked about amphibious warfare. Two coins belonging to the Satavahana rulers Pulamayi and Yajnasri bear the figure of a two-masted sailing ship. One can infer that the Satavahanas maintained a coastal or riverine navy.[48] Kalidasa, a poet of the fourth and fifth century CE, in his *Raghuvamsa*, notes that the Gauda (Bengal) kings maintained a riverine navy that controlled the river Ganga. However,

---

[41] Ibid., pp. 160, 164.
[42] *The Art of War in World History from Antiquity to the Nuclear Age*, ed. by Gerard Chaliand (Berkeley/Los Angeles: University of California Press, 1994), p. 201.
[43] Ibid., p. 202.
[44] U. P. Thapliyal, 'Military Organization in the Ancient Period', in S. N. Prasad (ed.), *Historical Perspectives of Warfare in India: Some Morale and Material Determinants* (New Delhi: Centre for Studies in Civilizations, 2002), p. 83.
[45] *Art of War*, tr. by Sawyer, pp. 213–24.
[46] *MD*, by Olivelle, p. 164.
[47] Lawrence Keppie, *The Making of the Roman Army: From Republic to Empire* (1984; reprint, London: Routledge, 1998), p. 51.
[48] Majumdar, *Military System in Ancient India*, p. 91.

116   *Hinduism and the Ethics of Warfare in South Asia*

Raghu, the hero of *Raghuvamsa*, crossed the rivers with the help of elephants.[49]

Elephants were used in warfare both inside and outside South Asia during early and late antiquity. Seleucus, the ex-general of Alexander and ruler of Syria, invaded India around 305/301 BCE in an attempt to reconquer Alexander's Indian provinces, which were then under the control of the Maurya Empire. However, Seleucus was defeated at a battle fought near the river Indus. While Seleucus had to surrender north-west India and Afghanistan to Chandragupta Maurya, the Maurya monarch gave the former 500 elephants in return. Seleucus took them back to Syria. Some of them survived and were used to great effect in battles against Demetrius and Alexander's ex-general Ptolemy. In a challenge-response dynamic, the Ptolemids also started using elephants in battle.[50] The Ptolemids of Egypt acquired elephants from the Upper Nile and the Red Sea coast.[51] Antiochus III of Syria invaded north-west India around 206 BCE. He received 150 elephants from an Indian ruler named Subhagsena and went back.[52] In 191 BCE, Antiochus of Asia Minor deployed elephants against the Roman army.[53] At Heraclea, King Pyrrhus of Epirus used elephants to frighten the Roman cavalry and then smash the Roman legions. In 289 BCE, King Pyrrhus deployed elephants against the Carthaginians. The Carthaginians were probably influenced by the Ptolemids in the use of war elephants. The Carthaginians first used elephants against the Romans in 262 BCE at Agrigentum.[54] Hannibal marched towards Italy from Spain in 218 BCE with eighty elephants.[55] In 197 BCE, at Cynoscephalae, the Roman commander Flamininus used elephants to smash the left wing of the Macedonian army of Philip.[56] Elephants were also used for warfare in South China. In 506 BCE, the

---

[49] *Mahakabi Kalidas Birachitam Raghuvamsam, Pratham Sarga to Chaturdash Sarga,* Mallinath krita Tikapetam, Gurunath Vidhyanithi Bhattacharyamanudithancha, edited by Ashok Kumar Bandopadhyay (Kolkata: Sanskrit Pustak Bhandar, 1411) [in Bengali, all translations by the author], Abataranika, *Chaturtha Sarga,* 36–8, p. 75.

[50] B. Bar-Kochva, *The Seleucid Army: Organization and Tactics in the Great Campaigns* (1976; reprint, Cambridge: Cambridge University Press, 1979), pp. 75–83.

[51] Richard Glover, 'The Elephant in Ancient War', *Classical Journal,* vol. 39, no. 5 (1944), p. 267.

[52] Majumdar, *Military System in Ancient India,* p. 77.

[53] Keppie, *Making of the Roman Army,* p. 43.

[54] Richard A. Gabriel, *The Great Armies of Antiquity* (Westport, Connecticut and London: Praeger, 2002), pp. 203, 234.

[55] Daneta Billau and Donald A. Graczyk, 'Hannibal: The Father of Strategy Reconsidered', *Comparative Strategy,* vol. 22, no. 4 (2003), p. 336.

[56] Keppie, *Making of the Roman Army,* pp. 41–3.

From the Common Era to the Advent of the Turks   117

Ch'u used elephants against Wu.[57] Unlike Kamandaka, Manu did not emphasize the role of elephants on the battlefield. At the tactical level, Manu notes that in the absence of a strong cavalry, a ruler should not undertake aggressive campaigns but rather follow an appeasement policy towards the enemy. The *MD* notes that at the flanks, special units of reliable soldiers are to be deployed to avoid encirclement by hostile units.[58]

Manu offers a strong critique of Kautilya's *kutayuddha* on the tactical and strategic planes. The *MD* notes that the king should always act without guile. However, being prudent does not mean being inefficient. Manu emphasizes constant vigilance on the part of the ruler to guard against fraud by the enemy. The ruler must not let the enemy discover any weakness of his, the *MD* continues, but should instead discover the weakness of the enemy.[59]

Unlike Kautilya, who asserts that all alliances and treaties are pieces of paper that are to be torn up if necessary, Manu emphasizes the importance of good faith towards one's allies. The *MD* says that when the ruler has become extremely vulnerable to his enemy's forces, he should quickly seek asylum with a strong and righteous king. Should that king keep both his own subjects and the forces of his enemy in check, he should serve him obediently with all his strength. Even in that case, however, if he notices a liability resulting from his asylum, he should resort to the just war without hesitation.[60]

Manu elaborates the normative model for fighting *prakasayuddha*, which is a constituent of *dharmayuddha*:

When challenged by rivals – whether they are stronger, weaker, or of equal strength ... a king must never back away from battle, recalling the Law of Kshatriyas. Refusal to turn back in battle, protecting the subjects, and obedient service to Brahmins – for kings, these are the best means of securing happiness. When kings fight each other in battles with all their strength, seeking to kill each other and refusing to turn back, they go to heaven. When he is engaged in battle, he must never slay his enemies with weapons that are treacherous, barbed, or laced with poison, or whose tips are ablaze with fire. He must never slay a man standing on the ground, an effeminate man, a man with joined palms, a man with loose hair, a seated man, a man declaring 'I am yours', ... a man without his armour ... a man without his weapons, a non-combatant, a man engaging

---

[57] Edward H. Schafer, 'War Elephants in Ancient and Medieval China', *Oriens*, vol. 10, no. 2 (1957), p. 290.
[58] *MD*, by Olivelle, p. 164.
[59] Ibid., pp. 159–60.
[60] Ibid., p. 163.

118   Hinduism and the Ethics of Warfare in South Asia

someone else, a man with damaged weapons, a man in distress, a badly wounded man, a frightened man, or a man who has turned tail.... When a man is killed in battle by the enemy as he turns tail frightened, he takes upon himself all the evil deeds committed by his master.[61]

Like the *Arthasastra*, rather than battle, the *MD* advocates fortress warfare. In Western Europe, the Franks also pursued a defensive strategy based on a network of forts in order to defeat the principal military threat posed by the Vikings.[62] The *MD* notes that when a king launches a military expedition against the realm of an enemy, he should advance towards the enemy's fort. As regards the construction of forts, Manu notes that a fortress can be secured by a desert, or with an earthen rampart, or may be surrounded by water. In addition, forts can be protected by a forest, or located at the top of a hill. In Manu's paradigm, the *giridurga* (hill fort) is the best. The best way to defend a fort is by stationing archers in the ramparts, and the fort should be well stocked with weapons, money, grain, artisans, machines, fodder, and water in order to withstand a long siege.[63]

In the alluvial zones, the forts were constructed with bricks, and in the rocky places with stones. Jean Deloche opines that the indigenous tradition emphasized a massive structure – a system of protection based on accumulation and enormity of obstacles to assailants – and thought that such entrenchments guaranteed security. Fortifications constructed in accordance with indigenous styles have massive and compact earthen walls, with a baked brick or stone facing, surrounded by wide and deep ditches. These ramparts are in some cases reinforced at regular intervals by solid towers. The gateways are elaborate and the openings strengthened with powerful towers, with an open courtyard.[64]

The Greek and Kushana styles were different. The Kushanas introduced Central Asian traditions of fortifications on the subcontinent. The chief features were curtain walls pierced with long loopholes and hollow semicircular towers. In the Greco-Buddhist representations, the curtain walls are pierced by triangular loopholes, and the parapets are made of merlons. The little projecting towers are either rectangular or semicircular

---

[61] Ibid., p. 159. My translation is slightly different from that of Olivelle.

[62] Bernard S. Bachrach and Rutheford Aris, 'Military Technology and Garrison Organization: Some Observations on Anglo-Saxon Military Thinking in Light of the Burghal Hidage', *Technology and Culture*, vol. 31, no. 1 (1990), p. 5.

[63] *MD*, by Olivelle, pp. 157–8, 164.

[64] Jean Deloche, *Studies on Fortification in India* (Pondicherry: Institut Francais De Pondichery and Ecole Francaise D'Extreme Orient, 2007), pp. 37–8.

From the Common Era to the Advent of the Turks 119

and hollow with openings in the upper part for use by archers.[65] Some examples will suffice.

Ahichatra, the ancient capital of the Pancalas in the Bareilly district of Uttar Pradesh, is located in a flat region. Initially built of mud around 100 BCE, the rampart was raised with a brick wall protected by a mud cover. The towers are rectangular in shape.[66] The rampart was constructed by digging out mud from the ditch and heaping it onto the banks.[67] At Rajgir, the rampart was built with massive undressed stones carefully fitted and bonded together with a core composed of smaller blocks without mortar. The inside of the wall is provided with stairs or ramps for giving access to the top and is flanked by rectangular towers. This rampart was built before the fifth century BCE. Between the fifth century BCE and the first century CE, a new town to the north was surrounded by a thick rampart in the shape of an irregular pentagon and strengthened by a ditch. This earthen rampart is revetted with bricks. Kausambi is situated on the left bank of the Jamuna River in Uttar Pradesh. It was inhabited between the first millennium BCE and the sixth century CE. The rampart is quadrilateral in shape.[68]

Srikap, in Pakistan's Punjab, was founded by the Indo-Greeks during the second century BCE. The wall is composed of rubble in mud revetted with hard limestone. The wall is strengthened at irregular intervals by solid rectangular towers, 7.7 meters wide and projecting 8.3 meters but with towers at the corners, pentagonal in shape, 15 meters wide and projecting 20 meters on the outside. Several types of fortifications are depicted in bas reliefs – rectangular towers, towers topped with hemispherical domes and towers with loopholes above the curtain walls – in Amaravati during the second century CE. A relief at the south gate of Sanchi Stupa shows the siege of the Kusinara fort. The walls have specially built constructions that functioned as shooting posts for the archers. This development in fortification style is known as *Indrakosa*. Mathura, in Uttar Pradesh, is situated on the bank of the Jamuna. During the fourth century BCE, the place was fortified by a massive mud wall. Between the first and third centuries CE, under the Kushanas, on the northern side a new inner enclosure made of mud and strengthened by a brick wall, circular in shape, was built with semicircular towers. During the second

---

[65] Deloche, *Studies on Fortification in India*, pp. 36–7.
[66] Ibid., pp. 39–40.
[67] Udai Narain Roy, 'Fortifications of Cities in Ancient India', *Indian Historical Quarterly*, vol. 30, no. 3 (1954), p. 238.
[68] Deloche, *Studies on Fortification in India*, pp. 40–2.

120 Hinduism and the Ethics of Warfare in South Asia

century CE, in the types of fortifications depicted in the bas reliefs about Mathura, we find quadrangular towers and rectangular merlons, as well as a hollow spherical tower. Architectural remains of this type are found in Mathura (one of the capitals of the Kushanas during the beginning of the Common Era) and are also depicted in Gandhara art.[69]

During the Second Punic War, Rome was surrounded by a wall that exceeded five miles in circumference.[70] The wall around Rome, constructed by Greek engineers out of volcanic stone, was twelve feet thick and twety-four feet high.[71] During the later Roman Empire, the cities of Gaul were surrounded by massive walls about ten meters in height and four meters in thickness at the base, with stone foundations four to five meters below ground level. The walls were further strengthened by construction of massive projecting semi-circular towers which were placed at intervals of about twenty-five meters. The garrison fought with archers and light artillery. In addition to wet ditches outside the walls, the forts were strengthened by the construction of citadels.[72]

Due to the strength inherent in a fort, Manu, instead of a costly frontal assault, points to the various *upayas* that could be followed by an invading army laying siege to a fort. After laying siege to the enemy fort, the king should plunder the enemy realm and ruin the latter's supplies of fodder, food and water by demolishing the reservoirs, ramparts and moats. In addition, surprise assaults should be launched against the enemy, particularly at night. Further, sedition should be fomented in the enemy party to encourage desertion.[73]

As regards the distribution of war booty, Manu comes up with several laws. Whatever a soldier wins – chariot, horse, elephant, money, grain, livestock, women or base metal – all that belongs to him. A preemptive share, however, should be given to the king in accordance with the vedic scripture. Ultimately, Manu advocates establishing a 'just peace'. The *MD* says that after the victory, the victor should grant exemptions and issue proclamations of amnesty.[74]

In Manu's text, political power is considered inferior to priestly ideals and rituals. However, Manu never says that the Brahmins should

---

[69] Ibid., pp. 32–3, 37, 41, 43, 80.

[70] Billau and Graczyk, 'Hannibal', p. 337.

[71] Gabriel, *Great Armies of Antiquity*, p. 227.

[72] Bernard S. Bachrach, 'Early Medieval Europe', in Raaflaub and Rosenstein (eds.), *War and Society in the Ancient and Medieval Worlds*, p. 277.

[73] *MD*, by Olivelle, p. 164.

[74] Ibid., pp. 159, 164.

From the Common Era to the Advent of the Turks 121

interfere in temporal affairs directly. Though Manu constructs a normative model for *dharmayuddha* during a battle, for siege warfare Manu incorporates at least two elements of *kutayuddha*: pillaging enemy country surrounding the fort, and launching surprise night attacks. Overall, Manu succeeds in propounding a theory for maintaining internal order but fails to address the problem of external invasion as posed by the 'mlechchas'. Manu's normative model of conducting *dharmayuddha* reduced the combat effectiveness of the Hindu armies. Archaeological references note the legacy of *MD*. An inscription of the Valabhi King Dharasena, dated 571 CE, says that the rules made by Manu were obeyed by this king.[75]

THE STEPPE NOMADS AND THE CHANGING CHARACTER OF WARFARE

Despite the uselessness of the chariots in the Battle of Hydaspes, Manu continues to emphasize their importance in warfare. To be fair to Manu, he realized the importance of horses in warfare. Due to the intervention of the Central Asian steppe nomads, the importance of war horses rose in the subcontinent. Between the fifth and seventh centuries BCE, the bit, bridle, headstall and reins, together with the form of the S-shaped cheek bars and saddles, were developed by the steppe nomads.[76]

The classical Greeks encountered the Scythian mounted archers, who were equipped with compound bows and dressed in breeches, high shoes and riding caftans with long sleeves. The Sarmatians in the age of Roman Emperor Trajan (98–117 CE) were equipped with the same compound bow. The horsemen of classical Greece were equipped with swords and shields.[77] Around 150 BCE, the Roman cavalry adopted the Greek lance and shield. The Roman cavalryman was protected by a leather cuirass and carried a short thrusting spear.[78] In the coins of the Greek, Scythian and Parthian invaders of India, the cavaliers were shown clad in chain mail armour. The Scythians introduced into India the heavy cavalry: cavaliers equipped with bows and lances and

---

[75] Kane, *History of Dharmasastra*, vol. 1, Part I, p. 328.

[76] Chauncey S. Goodrich, 'Riding Astride and the Saddle in Ancient China', *Harvard Journal of Asiatic Studies*, vol. 44, no. 2 (1984), pp. 294–5.

[77] M. Rostovtzeff, 'The Parthian Shot', *American Journal of Archaeology*, vol. 47, no. 2 (1943), pp. 176–7.

[78] John W. Eadie, 'The Development of Roman Mailed Cavalry', *Journal of Roman Studies*, vol. 57, no. ½ (1967), p. 163.

122 Hinduism and the Ethics of Warfare in South Asia

protected by heavy armour.[79] The Indo-Scythian coins show a king named Azes mounted on horseback and holding a spear.[80] After 150 CE, the Huns started moving into northern Turkestan. The Huns occupied Bactria around 350 CE. The Huns (also known as the White Hunas or Ephthalites) established their base at Herat in Afghanistan and started attacking Persia and India. The defeat of the Persian Emperor Firoz in 480 CE resulted in the breakup of the Sassanian realm.[81] Between 420 and 550 CE, the Huns attacked India.[82] The Huns captured Gandhara in 454 CE and moved into west Punjab.[83]

The Gupta Empire lasted from 320 CE until 550 CE. The Gupta Empire was founded by Chandragupta I Samudragupta (ruler from 335 to 375 CE), who made a raid into south India but did not annex those regions. This was probably due to the huge distance and bad communications with the central part of north India (the core of his empire), which made direct administration of peninsular India difficult if not impossible. Secondly, in accordance with *dharmayuddha*, Samudragupta probably invaded south India for the purpose of getting glory and performing *asvamedha* sacrifice.[84] The Gupta Empire's direct administration extended over north, central and west India. The principal threat faced by the Gupta Empire was nomadic invasion by the Sakas and the Huns. R. K. Mookerji asserts that Chandragupta II Vikramaditya (ruler from 380 to 414 CE) crossed the Indus and its five mouths (the Jhelum, Chenab, Ravi, Beas and Sutlej rivers) and invaded Vahlika (Balkh/Bactria).[85] This expedition was probably a preemptive attempt by Chandragupta Vikramaditya to protect the north-west frontier passes through which the steppe nomads traditionally invaded India.

The Huns attacked India during the reign of Gupta Emperor Kumaragupta (ruler from 414 to 455 CE).[86] Skandagupta (Gupta emperor

---

[79] Majumdar, *Military System in Ancient India*, pp. 79, 90.

[80] Bhandare, 'Numismatics and History', p. 74.

[81] Ashvini Agrawal, *Rise and Fall of the Imperial Guptas* (New Delhi: Motilal Banarasidas, 1989), pp. 165, 212–13, 240.

[82] *The Harshacarita of Banabhatta with Exclusive Notes (Uchchhvasas I–VIII)*, ed. with an Introduction and Notes by P. V. Kane (New Delhi: Motilal Banarasidas, 1965), *Uchchhvasa* IV, p. 4.

[83] Major-General Gurcharn Singh Sandhu, *A Military History of Ancient India* (New Delhi: Vision Books, 2000), p. 370.

[84] J. Sundaram, 'Warfare in South India – The Background', in Prasad (ed.), *Historical Perspectives of Warfare in India*, p. 174.

[85] R. K. Mookerji, *The Gupta Empire* (1973; reprint, New Delhi: Motilal Banarasidas, 1997), p. 68; *Harshacarita*, by Kane, *Uchchhvasa* IV, p. 30.

[86] Agrawal, *Rise and Fall of the Imperial Guptas*, p. 213.

From the Common Era to the Advent of the Turks   123

455–67 CE) was able to defeat the Huns, who were called Hunas by the Sanskrit scholars. Skanda was also able to defeat the Sakas in Gujarat.[87] The Hun chief Toramana moved into the Salt Range of the Jhelum district.[88] Only in 510 CE, under the Gupta Emperor Bhanugupta, was Toramana able to defeat the Gupta General Goparaja at the Battle of Eran fought at Malwa.[89]

How can the Gupta success against the Huns until 510 CE be explained? The Gupta army recruited from the traditional four sources: *maula* (families who supplied soldiers through several generations), *bhrta* (mercenaries), *mitra* (troops of the allies) and *sreni* (troops maintained by the various guilds).[90] The Mandasore Inscription of Kumaragupta and Bandhuvarman records that members of the silk weaver's guild were expert in archery. Many Brahmins joined the army. Kumaragupta had a Brahmin general named Prthivisena.[91]

Kalidasa's *Raghuvamsa* gives a generalized picture of force structures and combat between Raghu and the *yavanas* of north-west India. Kalidasa's description of Raghu's conquest shows that the author was intimately acquainted with the pearl fisheries of Tamraparni, the deodars of the Himalayas, the betel nuts and coco palms of Kalinga and the sand of Sind. In his works, Kalidasa accepts the brahmanical system and the *asvamedha yagna* by the victorious sovereign. According to Keith, Kalidasa lived in the fifth century CE.[92] Kalidasa writes that the Hindu soldiers generally fought with lances, battle axes, spears, and so on.[93] Kalidasa says that the *yavanas* mainly depended on mounted archers. The principal advantage of possessing a horse in the battlefield, he says, is that it confers speed to the cavalier. The mobile cavalry of the *yavanas/Turangas* created terror among the *samantarajas*. Hence, Raghu also deployed many mounted archers. When the mounted archers launched their barrage of arrows, the sky became dark. Though the *yavanas* were encased in armour, they still fell victim to the barrage of arrows. When the mounted archers dislocated the *yavana* formation, Raghu's heavy cavalry, equipped with *bhallas* (heavy spears), charged the *yavanas*. Raghu with his victorious cavalry

---

[87] Mookerji, *Gupta Empire*, pp. 92–3.
[88] Agrawal, *Rise and Fall of the Imperial Guptas*, p. 242.
[89] Mookerji, *Gupta Empire*, p. 120.
[90] Ibid., p. 100; Majumdar, *Military System in Ancient India*, p. 88.
[91] Chakravarti, *Art of War in Ancient India*, pp. 6, 79.
[92] Keith, *History of Sanskrit Literature*, pp. 80, 82.
[93] Majumdar, *Military System in Ancient India*, p. 89.

Hinduism and the Ethics of Warfare in South Asia

army advanced to Kashmir and the river Sindhu. Raghu acquired many good horses as tribute from the country of Kamboja.[94] Raghu also fought the Persians, who are described as bearded men equipped with bows. The *Raghuvamsa* continues that the Kalinga army, comprised of elephants and foot archers, was defeated. Then Raghu went to Kamarup and acquired elephants.[95] Like the epics and the *Bhagavad Gita*, the *Raghuvamsa* states that those soldiers who died on the battlefield ascended to heaven.[96]

Ashvini Agrawal asserts that under Chandragupta Vikramaditya, the Gupta army became cavalry-centric.[97] Such a transition probably occurred in the armies of the other great powers of Eurasia as well. During the early days of the Roman Empire, the ratio of cavalry to infantry was 1:12, but in the late fourth century, the ratio became 1:3.[98] The *Raghuvamsa* portrays the presence of heavy cavalry (cavaliers armed with *bhallas* and bows and protected by armour) in the Gupta army.[99] In Kashmir, some brick tiles that can be dated to the third century CE show horsemen in armour riding accoutred horses at full gallop and drawing their bows. The quivers are attached to the saddles. The coins of the Pahlava rulers of north-west India also depict mounted archers.[100]

Under the influence of the Sakas, Parthians and Kushanas, the Guptas took up mounted horse archery. Several Gupta emperors are depicted on their coins on horseback equipped with the nomadic bows. The horses were richly caparisoned, and these coins were issued from the reign of Chandragupta Vikramaditya onwards. Murray B. Emeneau claims that the Guptas used the Scythian/Sassanian-type curved bows. These bows were introduced onto the subcontinent by the Saka, Parthian and Kushana invaders.[101] The Sanchi sculptures (some of which can be dated to the end of the first century BCE) show composite bows.[102] The

---

[94] *Mahakabi Kalidasa Birachitam, Raghuvamsam, Chaturtha Sarga*, 62, 64, 67, 70–1, *Sastha Sarga*, 33, *Nabam Sarga*, 56, pp. 79–81, 107, 163.

[95] Keith, *History of Sanskrit Literature*, pp. 93–4.

[96] U. P. Thapliyal, 'Early Indian Heraldry and Ceremonials', in Prasad (ed.), *Historical Perspectives of Warfare in India*, p. 140.

[97] Agrawal, *Rise and Fall of the Imperial Guptas*, p. 166.

[98] Gabriel, *Great Armies of Antiquity*, p. 254.

[99] Majumdar, *Military System in Ancient India*, p. 90.

[100] U. P. Thapliyal, 'Weapons, Fortifications and Military Training in Ancient India', in Prasad (ed.), *Historical Perspectives of Warfare in Ancient India*, p. 108.

[101] Majumdar, *Military System in Ancient India*, p. 85; Agrawal, *Rise and Fall of the Imperial Guptas*, p. 22; Murray B. Emeneau, 'The Composite Bow in India', *Proceedings of the American Philosophical Society*, vol. 97, no. 1 (1953), pp. 85–6.

[102] Emeneau, 'Composite Bow in India', p. 83.

From the Common Era to the Advent of the Turks   125

composite bow was constructed by joining two curved pieces of wood with an iron plate.[103]

Gurcharn Sandhu asserts that the superiority of the Gupta heavy cavalry over the Huns was due to the introduction of loop stirrups by the former. He says that the reliefs and sculptures of Barhut and Sanchi show the use of the loop stirrup by the Hindus. The Huns rode without stirrups; hence the rider had an unsteady seat, and the mount could function only as a precarious weapon platform. Due to the use of the loop stirrup, the Gupta cavaliers were able to press a charge and engage in close-quarter combat. By contrast, the Hun cavaliers, without stirrups, could easily be pulled down from their horses in close-quarter combat. For implementing a cavalry charge and close-quarter combat, the Guptas introduced heavy cavalry, which meant that the riders wore knee-length chain mail, and the horses were also covered with plate armour. The Gupta heavy cavalry, equipped with lances, was able to deliver a compact close-order charge. In addition, the Guptas also had light cavalry. The riders belonging to the light cavalry wore only a padded jacket and were equipped with bows and arrows.[104]

According to Robin D. S. Yates, stirrups were introduced on the Eurasian steppes between 200 BCE and 300 CE.[105] In Denis Sinor's view, the earliest known representations of the stirrup come from Korea and Japan and can be dated to the fourth and fifth century CE. He argues that the Huns (370–450 CE) did not use stirrups, but their use was known to the Avars (the Juan-Juan of the inner Asian steppes) during the sixth century CE. From the Avars, the Byzantines learnt the use of stirrups. Even in the early seventh century CE, stirrups were not used in Iran.[106] By contrast, John W. Eadie claims that stirrups were known in south Russia during the first century CE.[107]

Mounted archery vanished from the Hindu armies after the demise of the Guptas. One factor was that the ecology of India was not suitable for breeding good horses. Rudi Paul Lindner forcefully argues that the lack of adequate grassland in central and west Europe prevented the Huns from attacking the Western Roman Empire with large numbers of mounted

---

[103] Thapliyal, 'Weapons, Fortifications and Military Training in Ancient India', p. 106.

[104] Sandhu, *Military History of Ancient India*, p. 372.

[105] Robin D. S. Yates, 'Early China', in Raaflaub and Rosenstein (eds.), *War and Society in the Ancient and Medieval Worlds*, p. 39.

[106] Denis Sinor, 'The Inner Asian Warriors', *Journal of the American Oriental Society*, vol. 101, no. 2 (1981), pp. 137–8.

[107] Eadie, 'Development of Roman Cavalry', p. 163.

126 *Hinduism and the Ethics of Warfare in South Asia*

archers. West of the Carpathian Mountains, the grassland of Hungary could at best support only 15,000 horsemen. Each mounted archer, for full efficiency, needed to be accompanied by ten to eighteen horses, and each steppe horse required twenty-five acres of pasture annually. Due to the small number of horse archers that Attila could mobilize against the Western Roman Empire, the Hun leader could launch only plundering raids and could not employ the large mobile force needed for complete destruction of the Roman armies. Hence, the ecology of Western Europe limited the effectiveness of the Hunnic cavalry army.[108] This also applies to the case of the subcontinent. South Asia east of Indus lacks grasslands, and the densely populated, paddy-cultivated river valleys were not suitable for breeding horses.

Secondly, mounted archery could only be performed creditably by the steppe nomads. The steppe nomads from their childhood learnt the art of riding and shooting from horseback for the purpose of hunting. Between 520 and 535 CE Toramana's son Mihirakula was engaged in attacking Kashmir. Interestingly, besides keeping cavalry, Mihirakula also maintained a large number of elephants in his army. The Huns were becoming partly Indianized. Ecological factors partially explain this transition. In 532 CE, Mihirakula's Indianized force was defeated in central India by a chief named Yasodharman.[109] The latter was a feudatory who had become independent of the disintegrating Gupta Empire. After the demise of the Guptas, King Harsa of Kanauj tried to resurrect a north Indian empire; our main source for this is Banabhatta.

BANABHATTA'S *HARSACHARITA*

Harsacharita is an historical romantic fiction in *akhyayika* form composed by Bana in eight *uchchhvasas*. Bana was patronized by King Harsavardhana (604/6–47/48 CE) of Thaneswar and Kanauj. Bana was the first poet to write the story of his patron in Sanskrit prose. The *Harsacharita* furnishes us with some historical details. However, Bana did not write as an historian but as an epic bard decorating his tale with fancy, fantasy and bits and pieces of romance and adventure. The *akhyayika* is an historical tale rooted in authentic tradition, and the outlines of the story are more or less factually correct. The *Harsacharita* is a sort of

---

[108] Rudi Paul Lindner, 'Nomadism, Horses and Huns', *Past and Present*, no. 92 (Aug. 1981), pp. 3–19.

[109] Agrawal, *Rise and Fall of the Imperial Guptas*, pp. 243–4, 246.

From the Common Era to the Advent of the Turks 127

epic in prose, in the romantic tradition of wandering minstrels and bards. Bana created a new genre of prose romances by writing an historical tale, the biography of his patron king, under the title *Harsacharita*. At times, Bana becomes dramatic. Bana is a master of the *puranic*-historical tradition. Overall, Bana utilizes all the rhetorical devices of *kavya* (poetry) in the writing of prose. Bana is a powerful prose writer. His work is characterized by his power of observing men and circumstances.[110] To sum up, despite being more a literary work than a history in the strict sense of the term, the *Harsacharita* contains a mass of information about ancient Indian society and military organization.

In the first two chapters of *Harsacharita*, Bana gives some detail about his personal life and his interview with Harsa. The story of Harsa proper begins in the third chapter. Bana gives his autobiographical account in *Kadambari*, which is a romantic novel.[111] A Brahmin named Kubera received high honours from a Gupta emperor. One of the four sons of Kubera, named Pashupata, was the great grandfather of Harsa. Pashupata's son Arhapati had eleven sons, and one of them, named Chitravanu, was the father of Bana. His mother was Rajadevi.[112] Bana grew up in an intellectually rich domestic atmosphere absorbing the knowledge of all *sastras*. When Bana was fourteen, he lost his father; his mother had died earlier. Bana developed a wanderlust in his heart. So he left his home for a tour of north India. While touring north India, Bana became friendly with Krishna (not to be confused with the Hindu god Lord Krishna), the cousin of Harsa. One day in summer when Bana was sitting in his house after the midday meal, a messenger brought news from Krishna. The message was that Harsa would like to meet Bana. The meeting took place at the town of Manitara on the bank of the river Ajiravati. Harsa himself was also a poet as well as a dramatist and a lover of the arts.[113] Bana died leaving his romance *Kadambari* unfinished. The work was completed by Bana's son named Bhusanabana or Pulinda. Bana was a contemporary of the poet Kalidasa.[114] Bana's writings belong to a genre that marks a complete break with the genre

---

[110] *The Harsacharita by Banabhatta*, tr. by E. P. Cowell and P. W. Thomas, ed. by R. P. Shastri (New Delhi: Global Vision, 2004), pp. v, viii, x–xi, xii.

[111] *Harsacharita*, tr. by Cowell and Thomas, pp. v, viii, x.

[112] *Harsacharita*, tr. by Cowell and Thomas, p. ix; *Harshacarita*, ed. by Kane, Introduction, p. ii.

[113] *Harsacharita*, tr. by Cowell and Thomas, pp. ix–x; *Harshacarita*, ed. by Kane, Introduction, p. iii.

[114] *Harshacarita*, ed. by Kane, Introduction, pp. iv, x.

128   *Hinduism and the Ethics of Warfare in South Asia*

represented by Kautilya and Manu. Unlike Kautilya and Manu, Bana refers to historical events and historical persons in his work. Further, Bana, unlike Kautilya and Manu, gives lot of details regarding himself and his family.

From *Harsacharita*, we get some glimpses of Bana's attitude towards warfare, and he also describes the techniques of warfare. Bana, like Kautilya, writes that the *mandala* is comprised of friends, neutrals and enemies. The *Harsacharita* implies that Harsa's realm, unlike the Maurya Empire, was a weak state. Harsa, unlike the Mauryas, seems to have lacked a standing army administered by a centralized bureaucracy. Bana says that the king must possess a *vahini* (army).[115] Bana describes Harsa's camp as filled with conquered vassal chiefs, and the royal army was accompanied by contingents provided by tributary chieftains.[116] This was not a unique South Asian development.

The Roman Empire's army was a standing professional force whose soldiers normally served for twenty-five years.[117] The regular army was supplemented by irregular levies. The standing professional legionary army vanished slowly but steadily during the later Roman Empire. About 25 percent of the army of the later Roman Empire was comprised of 'barbarian personnel,' that is men from Germanic and other tribes outside the borders of the empire.[118] Western Europe during late Roman Empire was becoming feudal. The Franks and the Germans were settled within the boundaries of the empire and were granted land in lieu of military service. The inheritance of the land became hereditary, and in return the sons of the original grantees had to serve the empire militarily. Besides these military settlers (*laeti*), many Celt and German tribes served in the Roman army as *foderati* (mercenary allies) and *auxilia*. In 405 CE, a Gothic king named Radagasius invaded Italy. After his defeat, about 12,000 of his followers were incorporated into the Roman army.[119] Justinian (527–65 CE), the Byzantine emperor, used 'barbarian' tribal contingents (*foderati*), who served under their own chiefs.[120] In addition,

---

[115] *Harshacarita*, ed. by Kane, *Uchchhvasa* IV, p. 9.

[116] *Harsacharita*, tr. by Cowell and Thomas, pp. 55, 62, 298.

[117] Brian Campbell, 'The Roman Empire', in Raaflaub and Rosenstein (eds.), *War and Society in the Ancient and Medieval Worlds*, p. 219.

[118] Wolfgang Liebeschuetz, 'The End of the Roman Army in the Western Empire', in John Rich and Graham Shipley (eds.), *War and Society in the Roman World* (1993; reprint, London/New York: Routledge, 1995), p. 266.

[119] Peter Heather, 'The Huns and the End of the Roman Empire in Western Europe', *English Historical Review*, vol. 110, no. 435 (1995), p. 12.

[120] Gabriel, *Great Armies of Antiquity*, pp. 261, 278.

From the Common Era to the Advent of the Turks   129

large landowners maintained armed retainers for local defence and protection of their castles.[121]

It seems that in South Asia, defeated rulers, in accordance with the concept of *dharmayuddha*, were reinstated in their kingdoms as vassal chiefs who were bound to obey the political suzerainty of the emperor. *Dharmayuddha* demands that the realm of the defeated ruler not be annexed by the victorious ruler; rather, the kingdom should be returned to the defeated ruler after the latter has accepted tributary status and provided booty and tribute to the victor. Also, it was obligatory for the tributary ruler to provide his political suzerain with a loyal contingent during a campaign.[122] Kalidasa, in *Raghuvamsa*, says that the monarch Raghu, who was following the code of *dharmayuddha,* defeated and captured Mahendranath, the ruler of Kalinga. When Mahendranath accepted the suzerainty of Raghu, the latter released the former and returned his kingdom without annexing it.[123] By waging *dharmayuddha*, says Bana, the just ruler should become the sovereign of the earth bound by four oceans.[124] Kalidasa says that *dharmayuddha*, which involves symmetrical warfare (i.e., cavalry fighting cavalry, infantry fighting infantry, etc.), can be waged against the monarchs within India but not against the *yavanas*. In fact, the *Raghuvamsa* does not mention the presence of chariots or elephants in Raghu's force structure as deployed against the *yavanas* of north-west India. So Kalidasa's implication in the *Raghuvamsa* is that against foreign invaders, the model of *dharmayuddha* is not applicable. Against the non-Aryan *yavana*s, *kutayuddha* involving guile and deceit could be waged even by a *dharmik* (law-abiding) king. The *Raghuvamsa* says that even a *dharmik* king like Raghu maintained spies.[125]

Bana writes that Harsa's ancestors ruled from Thaneswar (Haryana), while Hiuen Tsang, who was in India from 629 to 645 CE, states that Harsa's capital was Kanyakubja. Hiuen Tsang visited Harsa in 643 CE. Probably, after the death of Grahavarman, Harsa absorbed his brother-in-law's kingdom and made Kanyakubja his capital as it was more centrally located than to Thaneswar.[126] Chapter 4 of *Harsacharita* begins with the story of Prabhakarvardhana (ruler from 580 to 606 CE), who is described

---

[121] Bachrach, 'Early Medieval Europe', pp. 284, 286.
[122] *Harshacharita*, ed. by Kane, *Uchchhvasa* IV, p. 8.
[123] *Mahakabi Kalidas Birachitam, Raghuvamsam, Chaturtha Sarga*, 43, p. 76.
[124] *Harshacarita*, ed. by Kane, *Uchchhvasa* IV, p. 43.
[125] *Mahakabi Kalidasa Birachitam, Raghuvamsam, Saptam Sarga*, 37, *Chaturdash Sarga*, 31, pp. 126, 245.
[126] *Harshacarita*, ed. by Kane, Introduction, pp. vi, xxx.

130 *Hinduism and the Ethics of Warfare in South Asia*

as a terror of the Huns. Prabhakarvardhana's queen, Yasomati, gave birth to two sons – Rajyavardhana, the elder one, and Harsa – and a girl named Rajyasri. Rajyasri was married to Grahavarman of the Maukhari family and left for her husband's place at Kanyakubja. Chapter 5 narrates the death of Prabhakargupta at the time when Rajyavardhana and Harsa were engaged in fighting the Huns. Rajyavardhana was treacherously murdered by Sasanka, the king of Gauda. After Rajyavardhana defeated the ruler of Malwa (either in central Punjab or in central India), Sasanka invited the former for a peace parley. And when Rajyavardhana went to the camp of Sasanka alone, the latter captured and executed him.[127] This was an instance of *kutayuddha* by Sasanka.

Chapter 7 gives an account of Harsa's military expedition. Harsa crowned himself king and set out with a huge army. From the account of a Chinese traveller, we know that Harsa moved against the Gauda king with 5,000 elephants, 29,000 cavalry and 50,000 infantry.[128] As Harsa was advancing towards Gauda, Bhandin (his cavalry commander) joined him with loot secured from the defeated ruler of Malwa. Harsa put Bhandin in charge of the invading force and, along with a small contingent, went to the Vindhya Mountains to search for his sister Rajyasri.[129]

Bana, however, does not give the full story of Harsa's career. Since Harsa was Bana's patron, Bana avoids Harsa's defeat on the banks of the river Narmada or in the Vindhya Mountains at the hands of the Chalukya ruler Pulakesi II of Vatapi (ruler between 610 and 642 CE).[130] The battle with Pulakesi II was fought sometime between 630 and 633 CE.[131] Pulakesi's army was comprised of cavalry and elephants. The cavaliers in his army fought with swords.[132] Harsa also met with other defeats in his career. In 618 CE, Harsa moved against Sind, but the expedition was unsuccessful. Around 628–30 CE, Harsa advanced against Dadda II, the Gurjara ruler of Broach. That campaign was unsuccessful, and Harsa also failed against Dhruvasena Baladitya, the ruler of northern Gujarat.[133]

The early Christian just war tradition held that the use of armed forces for restoring a situation that had been violated by prior wrongdoing is

---

[127] *Harsacharita*, tr. by Cowell and Thomas, pp. vi, 226.
[128] Sandhu, *Military History of Ancient India*, p. 350.
[129] *Harsacharita*, tr. by Cowell and Thomas, p. vii.
[130] Majumdar, *Military System in Ancient India*, p. 95.
[131] Sandhu, *Military History of Ancient India*, pp. 352–3.
[132] J. Sundaram, 'Chola and Other Armies – Organization', in Prasad (ed.), *Historical Perspectives of Warfare in India*, p. 184.
[133] Sandhu, *Military History of Ancient India*, p. 350.

From the Common Era to the Advent of the Turks   131

a just use of force.[134] The *Harsacharita* implies that avenging a wrong done to one's family is justification enough for starting a righteous war. However, it should involve an open challenge to battle. The news of Rajyavardhana's treacherous murder was brought to Harsa by Kuntala, a cavalry officer who was a favourite of Rajyavardhana.[135] Harsa resolved to avenge the death of his brother. Harsa took a vow to destroy Sasanka and through Avanti (the minister for foreign affairs) send a proclamation to all the tributary chiefs that they should either ally themselves with Harsa or be prepared for war with him. Harsa's commander-in-chief, Simhananda (who also served as commander-in-chief under Prabhakarvardhana), supported his decision, and the commander-in-chief of the elephant forces, named Skandagupta (not to be confused with the Gupta emperor who had defeated the Huns), warned Harsa to steer clear of treachery and political intrigue.[136] Bana says that great persons even in dreams do not want to employ deceitful tricks. This assertion of Bana is somewhat similar to Saint Augustine's (Bishop of Hippo in North Africa during the fifth century CE) claim 'the wise man will wage only just wars.' But Bana, speaking through the commander-in-chief of the elephant forces, warns Harsa to guard against the *kutayuddha* that might be waged against him by his enemies.[137]

Bana offers a critique of various forms of *kutayuddha*. Bana writes that Pusyamitra, despite being a Brahmin, behaved like a base-born when he executed his royal master, the Maurya Emperor Brihadratha, when the latter was inspecting the army in the parade ground.[138] So, a military coup is considered by Bana as a sort of *kutayuddha*. It is to be noted that even Kautilya, the greatest advocate of *kutayuddha*, is against the tradition of *mantris* and *senapatis* capturing power by executing their royal masters.

Bana is ambiguous about whether a commando strike for a good cause is justified. Bana gives the example of the Gupta Emperor Ramgupta's army, which was surrounded in a pass at the border between Malwa and Gujarat. The Saka ruler proclaimed that he would allow the Gupta

---

[134] Reichberg, 'Norms of War in Roman Catholic Christianity', in Popovski, Reichberg and Turner (eds.), *World Religions and Norms of War*, p. 145.

[135] *Harshacarita*, ed. by Kane, Appendix A, p. 257.

[136] *Harshacarita*, tr. by Cowell and Thomas, pp. 229–30, 240; *Harshacarita*, ed. by Kane, Appendix A, p. 257.

[137] *Harshacharita*, ed. by Kane, *Uchchhvasa* IV, verse 1, p. 1. For the quotation from Augustine, see Gregory M. Reichberg, Henrik Syse and Endre Begby (eds.), *The Ethics of War: Classic and Contemporary Readings* (Oxford: Blackwell, 2006), p. 72.

[138] *Harshacarita*, tr. by Cowell and Thomas, p. 244.

132   Hinduism and the Ethics of Warfare in South Asia

army to exit the pass unmolested provided Ramgupta surrendered his chief queen, Dhruvadevi, to him. In desperation, Ramgupta agreed. The Saka ruler was told that Dhruvadevi would visit his camp along with his female retainers. Ramgupta's younger brother, Chandragupta, and some of his armed retainers were dressed as women and carried in *doolies* towards the Saka camp. The Saka guards allowed them to enter the Saka ruler's private apartment. Then Chandragupta, dressed as Dhruvadevi, killed the Saka ruler, and Chandragupta's retainers attacked the Saka guards. In the ensuing pandemonium, Chandragupta and his retainers were able to escape and return to the Gupta camp. The Sakas were demoralized, and the Gupta army was able to exit the pass safely. After this incident, Ramgupta's prestige nose-dived and he was assassinated, probably by Chandragupta, who later became the Gupta Emperor Chandragupta Vikramaditya. Interestingly, Dhruvadevi became Chandragupta's queen. Vishakadatta, the author of the political drama *Mudraraksa*, describes Ramgupta as *kliba* (impotent/unmanly) for failing to protect his empire and his wife.[139] Replacement of a *kliba* king who has failed to display *paurusha* was not considered *kutayuddha*. Even Manu says that a king who fails to protect his subjects is not worthy to remain a ruler.

Bana mentions that Harsa's army marched when the astrologers accompanying the force decided that the hour of marching had arrived. This is in accordance with the tenets of *dharmayuddha*. Bana writes that occasionally the army marched at night with the aid of torches.[140] It is to be noted that marching and fighting at night violates the code of *dharmayuddha*.

The *Harsacharita* portrays the force structure of Harsa. Bana does not mention the presence of war chariots in Harsa's army. Harsa's army, like the Gupta army, was comprised of infantry, cavalry and elephants.[141] Bana emphasizes the importance of elephants in the royal army. Harsa obtained elephants as tribute and presents from vassal chieftains. Some elephants were also obtained by the forest rangers from the jungles. Finally, some elephants were taken by force from defeated hostile powers. Bana tells us that the elephants ate trees along with mangoes and sugarcane.[142] Each elephant consumed about 600 pounds of green fodder

---

[139] Ibid., p. 246; Mookerji, *Gupta Empire*, p. 64.
[140] *Harsacharita*, tr. by Cowell and Thomas, pp. 249, 252.
[141] Majumdar, *Military System in Ancient India*, p. 95.
[142] *Harsacharita*, tr. by Cowell and Thomas, pp. 60, 68–9.

From the Common Era to the Advent of the Turks   133

per day.[143] We can speculate that the demands of feeding a large number of war elephants gave rise to a nascent bureaucracy in Harsa's empire.

Bana writes that Prabhakarvardhana and Rajyavardhana defeated the ruler of Malwa and captured elephants belonging to the defeated ruler. Malwa, in central India, was a source of elephants. Bana says that the forest-covered Vindhya Mountains in central India were full of elephants. The newly captured elephants were trained for battle; the *Harsacharita* says that the elephants were used to smash hostile armies. Bana describes the iron-plated *howdah* on the back of the elephant; through loopholes in the *howdah*, the archers shot arrows at enemy soldiers. The back of the elephant provided the archers in the *howdah* the advantages of mobility and height. The *howdah* was plated with iron for protection of the archers inside it from enemy arrows and spears. Harsa rode a female elephant while reviewing his army.[144] So the elephant also served as a royal command vehicle. The elephant was controlled by the *mahout* with the help of an *ankush*.[145] When the elephant became uncontrollable during battle, the *mahout* pierced the elephant's brain with it.

War elephants were used in early medieval China. In December 554 CE, at the Battle of Chiang-ling, armoured elephants carrying towers and guided by Malayan trainers were sent against the army of Western Wei by the Liang defenders. The elephants were turned back by a flight of arrows. The Southern Han used elephants with towers. Each tower carried ten men. The elephant unit was effective during the Han invasion of Ch'u in 948 CE. However, in 971 CE, Sung soldiers equipped with crossbows decimated the elephant corps of the Southern Han.[146]

Bana, to a greater extent than Manu, emphasizes the importance of war horses. This was due to the Hunnic interlude that has been discussed earlier. Each elephant consumed a huge amount of green fodder per day.[147] So elephants could not be used for fighting in the drier regions or in the semi-arid regions. Bana writes that Harsa's stables were filled with horses from Kamboja, Sind and Persia. The *Harsacharita*, like the *Raghuvamsa*, imply that Kamboja horses were the best.[148] The *Raghuvamsa* says that Persian horses were also good.[149] Like India, another agrarian bureaucratic polity,

[143] Glover, 'Elephant in Ancient War', p. 257.
[144] *Harsacharita*, tr. by Cowell and Thomas, pp. 70–1,130, 241, 257, 284–5, 304.
[145] *Mahakabi Kalidas Birachitam, Raghuvamsam, Chaturtha Sarga*, 39, p. 75.
[146] Schafer, 'War Elephants in Ancient and Medieval China', pp. 290–1.
[147] Glover, 'The Elephant in Ancient War', p. 257.
[148] *Harsacharita*, tr. by Cowell and Thomas, pp. 65, 257.
[149] *Mahakabi Kalidasa Birachitam, Raghuvamsam, Pancham Sarga*, 73, p. 99.

134 Hinduism and the Ethics of Warfare in South Asia

China also realized the importance of war horses. Between the third century BCE and the eighth century CE, the agrarian bureaucratic empires of China failed to breed good war horses and attempted to acquire the best quality horses from the Central Asian steppe nomads, either through launching campaigns or through trade. The Chinese offered the nomads silk in return for horses.[150] The horses were fed, *Harsacharita* informs us, with *durva* grass. Bana writes that Prabhakarvardhana defeated the ruler of Gandhara.[151] Prabhakarvardhana probably obtained horses from Gandhara as tribute from the defeated ruler.

From the *Harsacharita* it is clear that saddles were used by the cavaliers.[152] The saddle was used by the Roman cavalry from the late first century CE onwards.[153] Bana says that the cavalier had footrests as well as a cloth cushion attached with girths on both sides of the horse. The cavaliers were equipped with scimitars for close-quarter combat.[154] Richard Gabriel comments that the horseshoe was invented by the Celts and adopted by the Roman cavalry during the late first century CE. The Gothic heavy cavalry, equipped with lance and sword, used the saddle but not the stirrup.[155] Bana says that the leather quiver was made of bearskin. We are not sure whether Bana is saying that mounted archers equipped with compound/composite bows were present in Harsa's army. Bana describes the cavaliers as dressed in tunics, waistband and trousers.[156] At that time, the Indians knew how to make garments from flax, linen, cotton and silk.[157]

Raiding and counter-raiding by small groups, both within the Merovingian kingdom and between kingdoms, dominated the post-Roman military landscape of Western Europe. The limited and localized nature of military affairs was punctuated occasionally by raids undertaken by enemies living beyond the frontiers of the highly fragmented *regnum Francorum*. Bernard S. Bachrach asserts that post-Roman Western Europe experienced mainly siege warfare. Owing to the centrality of sieges, mounted horsemen rather than infantry played the decisive role in warfare. The Carolingian horsemen frequently dismounted from

---

[150] H. G. Creel, 'The Role of the Horse in Chinese History', *American Historical Review*, vol. 70, no. 3 (1965), pp. 648–67.
[151] *Harsacharita*, tr. by Cowell and Thomas, pp. 66, 96–7, 130.
[152] Ibid., p. 172.
[153] Gabriel, *Great Armies of Antiquity*, p. 252.
[154] *Harsacharita*, tr. by Cowell and Thomas, p. 255.
[155] Gabriel, *Great Armies of Antiquity*, pp. 252, 274.
[156] *Harsacharita*, tr. by Cowell and Thomas, pp. 256, 292–3.
[157] *Harshacarita*, ed. by Kane, *Uchchhvasa* IV, p. 55.

From the Common Era to the Advent of the Turks   135

their horses and fought on foot. Overall, the medieval Western European commanders avoided a battle-centric strategy.[158]

Bana writes about a special corps of infantry wearing turbans on their heads and equipped with sharp swords and daggers for close-quarter combat. They were adept at launching commando-style night attacks. Here, Bana is referring to *kutayuddha*. The *Harsacharita* tells us that the handle of the sword was made of horn and wrapped in a black antelope skin.[159] The Chinese infantry from the fourth century BCE used long swords.[160] Some infantry, Bana tells us, also wore body armour.[161] The foot soldiers of Japan until 500 CE wore iron cuirass with helmets. After 500 CE, the Japanese adopted lamellar armour from the Koreans.[162]

Harsa's army was anything but a lean and agile striking force. The *Harsacharita* portrays a royal army accompanied by nobles' wives, grooms, camp followers and other paraphernalia.[163] The later Roman Empire's military theorist Vegetius emphasizes the importance of surprising the enemy whenever and wherever possible.[164] A select corps of Harsa's army functioned as a rapid strike force for surprising the enemy. When the king of Malwa (probably Devagupta, the ruler of central Punjab or central India) assassinated Grahavarman and imprisoned Rajyasri, Rajyavardhana, accompanied by Bhandin and a force of 10,000 cavalry, went to attack the king of Malwa. The main body of the army, comprised of elephants and contingents of the allied chiefs, followed behind.[165]

Each combatant soldier required 3,500 calories every day. Under Marius (90 BCE), each Roman legionary carried fourteen days' rations, and each legion (4,800 men) had a standard complement of 400 mules for carrying baggage.[166] Among the Hindu theorists, Bana was the first to note the importance of camels for logistical purposes.[167] Camels were required when an army operated in the semi-arid or dry regions like Rajasthan, Sind and Afghanistan. During the seventh and eighth centuries CE, the use

---

[158] Bachrach, 'Early Medieval Europe', pp. 280, 289, 292–3, 295.
[159] *Harsacharita*, tr. by Cowell and Thomas, pp. 118–19, 292.
[160] Yates, 'China', p. 28.
[161] *Harsacharita*, tr. by Cowell and Thomas, pp. 122, 169.
[162] W. Wayne Farris, 'Japan to 1300', in Raaflaub & Rosenstein (eds.), *War and Society in the Ancient and Medieval Worlds*, p. 50.
[163] *Harsacharita*, tr. by Cowell and Thomas, pp. 253, 262.
[164] Bernard S. Bachrach, 'The Practical Use of Vegetius' *De Re Militari* during the Early Middle Ages', *Historian*, vol. 48, no. 2 (1985), p. 247.
[165] *Harsacharita*, tr. by Cowell and Thomas, pp. 221–2.
[166] Gabriel, *Great Armies of Antiquity*, pp. 41, 238–9.
[167] *Harsacharita*, tr. by Cowell and Thomas, p. 61.

of camels for commissariat purpose became common among the armies operating in the desert of Rajasthan.[168] Oxen, mules, carts, elephants and porters were used for carrying baggage. The commissariat officials stored food in advance in the villages and the towns through which the royal army passed. Bana says that the villagers had to provide oxen and grain for the royal army. Manu also hints that the superintendents of the villages were in charge of collecting supplies for the royal army. The villagers demanded protection of their crops from the soldiers, who spread like locusts over the region through which Harsa's army passed. Blacksmiths accompanied the army for the purpose mending and preparing weapons.[169] Kautilya speaks of a superintendent of armoury who employed full-time artisans. These artisans were paid from the royal treasury; their job was to prepare and mend the weapons of the royal army.[170] Kalidasa, in *Raghuvamsa*, says that the soldiers were supplied with armour and helmets by the ruler.[171]

Until the 1905 Russo-Japanese War, more soldiers had been killed by disease than by enemy weapons.[172] The *Harsacharita* gives us some scattered bits of information about the medical service. Bana writes that the arrow wounds of the Huns were dangerous, and those wounded by the Huns' arrows had long white bandages on their wounds.[173] The ancient Sumerian and Egyptian medical texts discuss the treatment of broken bones. The Egyptians knew about the technique of applying splints to broken bones, and amputation was practiced by the Romans. Each Roman legion had a corps of medical orderlies, and most of the doctors were Greeks.[174] Harsa's army also had elephant doctors for tending the huge pachyderms. For distribution of war booty, Harsa appointed imperial overseers.[175]

Harsa was a Kshatriya.[176] Bana maintains that the duty of a ruler is to take special care of the Brahmins.[177] Here, Bana is following Manu's line.

---

[168] Majumdar, *Military System in Ancient India*, p. 88.

[169] *Harsacharita*, tr. by Cowell and Thomas, pp. 241, 253–5, 262–4, 287.

[170] B. P. Sinha, 'Art of War in Ancient India (600 BC–300 AD)', in Guy S. Metraux and Francois Crouzet (eds.), *Studies in the Cultural History of India* (Agra: Shiva Lal Agarwal & Co., 1965), p. 160.

[171] Majumdar, *Military System in Ancient India*, p. 89.

[172] Gabriel, *Great Armies of Antiquity*, p. 37.

[173] *Harsacharita*, tr. by Cowell and Thomas, p. 211.

[174] Gabriel, *Great Armies of Antiquity*, pp. 35–6, 242–3.

[175] *Harsacharita*, tr. by Cowell and Thomas, pp. 240, 285.

[176] *Harshacarita*, ed. by Kane, Introduction, p. xxx.

[177] *Harshacarita*, ed. by Kane, *Uchchhvasa* IV, verse 2, p. 1.

From the Common Era to the Advent of the Turks   137

Unlike Manu, Bana emphasizes the cavalry and introduces the elephant as the elite corps in the king's arsenal. Bana, unlike Manu, did not accept the normative model of *dharmayuddha* because, due to the invasion of the steppe nomads, such a model was no longer operable. After the death of Harsa, the principal source for understanding the norms and techniques of warfare in north India is Kamandaka's *Nitisara*.

KAMANDAKA'S *NITISARA*

P. V. Kane writes that Kamandaka lived around the third century CE.[178] The *Nitisara* of Kamandaka, also known as *Kamandakiya-Nitisara*, is mostly based on Kautilya's *Arthasastra* and is believed to be a recension of *Sukra-Nitisara*. Kamandaka's *Nitisara* was composed, in the view of G. P. Singh, around 400 CE, during the reign of the Gupta Emperor Chandragupta II. The *Sukra-Nitisara* was probably composed around the fourth century BCE.[179] D. Devahuti claims that Kamandaka was a contemporary of Varahamihira, the astronomer and mathematician who lived around 550 CE, and says that the *Kamandaka Nitisara* was composed between 450 and 550 CE.[180] However, P. C. Chakravarti assigns the eighth century CE as the date for Kamandaka's *Nitisara*.[181] Keith claims that the *Nitisara* written in verse was composed around 800 CE.[182] Most recently, Upinder Singh has claimed that Kamandaka's *Nitisara* was composed between 500 and 700 CE.[183] We can assume that Kamandaka's *Nitisara* belongs to the post-Harsa and pre-Islamic Turkish period.

Kamandaka states that he considers Vishnugupta/Kautilya as his guru. Like Kautilya, Kamandaka also propounds Lokayata philosophy; ascetic principles and practices are marginalized in his work.[184] The *Brihaspati Sutra*, a work just anterior to Kamandaka's *Nitisara*, also falls within the genre of *arthasastra* literature. While the *Brihaspati Sutra* overtly stresses the acquisition of financial assets by the king as a way to maintain strong rule,[185] Kamandaka, like Kautilya, includes politics

---

[178] Kane, *History of Dharmasastra*, vol. 1, Part 1, pp. 164, 170.
[179] G. P. Singh, *Political Thought in Ancient India* (1993; reprint, New Delhi: D. K. Printworld, 2005), p. 10.
[180] Devahuti, *Harsha*, pp. 132–3.
[181] Chakravarti, *Art of War in Ancient India*, p. viii.
[182] Keith, *History of Sanskrit Literature*, p. 463.
[183] Upinder Singh, 'Politics, Violence, and War in Kamandaka's *Nitisara*', *IESHR*, vol. 47, no. 1 (2010), p. 32.
[184] Keith, *History of Sanskrit Literature*, p. 463.
[185] Devahuti, *Harsha*, p. 121.

138 *Hinduism and the Ethics of Warfare in South Asia*

and diplomacy along with wealth as ways to maintain strong rule by the *vijigishu*. Kamandaka believes that a just ruler's power depends on the following trinity: the people, good governance and the army (for conducting *dharmayuddha*).

Kamandaka, like Kautilya, accepts the *saptanga* (seven elements) theory of the state.[186] Kamandaka frequently uses animal imagery to explain the various strategic scenarios. Like the *Arthasastra*, the *Nitisara* emphasizes the importance of daily exercise and drill for the troops. Both Kautilya and Kamandaka refer to six types of troops: hereditary troops, mercenaries, gild levies, soldiers supplied by the feudatory chiefs and the allies, contingents from the forest tribes and troops captured and won over from the enemy. Both authors refer to the existence of trading and craft guilds with their private soldiery, who were hired by the rulers during emergencies in order to meet internal as well as external threats. As regards the composition of the army, Kamandaka claims that mercenaries are more loyal than the *sreni bala* because the former are dependent on the king for wages. Kautilya and Kamandaka refer to the existence of predatory forest chieftains.[187]

In Western Europe during the fifth and the sixth centuries CE, the military officers became landlords and turned farmers and peasants of the land under their control into their own armed retainers. The retainers were bound by personal ties to their leaders. The net result was the growth of semi-private armies that engaged in brigandage. Many 'barbarian' chieftains also became landlords and pursued the same policy. The landlords' power increased as they expanded their estates, which in turn brought more dependants into the fold. The estates of the landlords were further fortified by the construction of castles.[188] The Carolingian armies were comprised of war bands of nobles who engaged in raiding for pillage and plundering.[189]

A somewhat similar scenario unfolded in north India after the collapse of Harsa's empire. Comparing internal and external dangers, the internal threat is considered more dangerous. Hence, before starting an invasion of a foreign kingdom, asserts Kamandaka, the causes of internal disturbance should be properly remedied by the ruler through conciliation, rewards,

---

[186] *The Nitisara by Kamandaki*, ed. by Rajendra Lala Mitra, revised with English translation by Sisir Kumar Mitra (1849; reprint, Calcutta: The Asiatic Society, 1982), pp. i, iii.
[187] Chakravarti, *Art of War in Ancient India*, pp. 3, 6–8, 9, 86.
[188] Dick Whittaker, 'Landlords and Warlords in the Later Roman Empire', in Rich and Shipley (eds.), *War and Society in the Roman World*, pp. 281–3, 292–3.
[189] France, 'Recent Writings on Medieval Warfare', p. 449.

From the Common Era to the Advent of the Turks   139

and so on, and by looking after the subjects' welfare. Kamandaka warns the monarch that a powerful ruler, apparently invincible, may easily be subjugated by his enemies if he lacks self-restraint. But a comparatively weak ruler who practices self-restraint towards his subjects, as prescribed in the *sastras*, never suffers defeat.[190] Like Manu, Kalidasa says that a just ruler should rule in accordance with the *sastras*. Kalidasa notes that the real father of the *prajas* is their just king who nurtures and sustains his subjects. Kalidasa adds that it is the duty of a just ruler to educate his subjects.[191] This sort of thinking further evolved into paternal despotism in Kamandaka's theory.

In verse 20, *sarga* 4, Kamandaka elaborates the concept of paternal despotism. Kautilya also expounds the concept of paternal despotism when he says: '*sarvatra copahatan pitevanugrhniyat*'.[192] As regards ensuring internal security, Kamandaka writes that an essential duty of the king is to protect the subjects of his dominion, particularly their gainful occupations (agriculture, cattle rearing, trade), which flourish only under royal protection. Disruption of economic vocations causes the most distress among the people. Kamandaka asserts that a just king should by all means protect his subjects, who in turn contribute to his *kosa* (royal treasury) by contributions in cash and in kind as part of the *bhaga*. He continues that a king, who governs justly, conforming to the vedic laws, acquires merits of *Trivarga* for himself as well as for his subjects.[193]

Concerning the various types of insurgency in the kingdom, the *Nitisara* goes on to say that disaffection among the priests, ministers, princes, members of the royal family, commanders and chiefs of the army contingents stationed within the capital generates internal disturbance. Disaffection among provincial governors, wardens of the marches, military governors of the frontier regions, and chiefs of forest tribes also leads to large-scale disturbance. By conciliation and other relevant means (reward and punishment), as well as by creating disunion and dissension among the disaffected parties, insurgent leaders should be appeased or subjugated.[194]

For maintaining internal order, Kamandaka urges the king to act, if necessary, like Yama, the God of Death. Kamandaka notes that those

---

[190] *Nitisara*, by Mitra, pp. 33, 332.
[191] *Mahakabi Kalidas Birachitam, Raghuvamsam, Pratham Sarga*, 24, *Nabam Sarga*, 2, pp. 25, 153.
[192] Kane, *History of Dharmasastra*, vol. 1, Part 1, p. 250.
[193] *Nitisara*, ed. by Mitra, pp. 7–8.
[194] Ibid., p. 332.

140 *Hinduism and the Ethics of Warfare in South Asia*

powerful men who obstruct the growth of prosperity (of the state) should be wiped out using secret methods of assassination (*upangsudanda*).[195] In *sarga* 16, verse 21, Kamandaka, like Kautilya, points out the linkage between internal disturbance and external danger.

Kamandaka elaborates on the origins of war. Economic gain is one of the motives for warfare. The *Nitisara* says that despite *vyaya* (economic expenditure) in the short run, an expedition likely to produce decisive gains and benefits in the long run may be undertaken. But an expedition likely to involve the destruction of *ksaya* (men and animals) must never be attempted.[196]

Plato and Aristotle accept the idea that war is a necessary evil, and they condemn those *polis* whose only purpose is war. Kamandaka's view is similar, and he also criticizes the *ativigrahis* (aggressive warlords) who practice militarism. The *Nitisara* recommends avoiding the use of the *chaturanga bala*; it is better to fight with the treasury and wise counsel, that is, through the techniques of *sama* and *dana*. Hence, it would be wise to conquer (or win over) the enemy by the duly deliberated expedients of *sama* or by conciliation and *dana* (*kosa*).[197] Kamandaka regards war as the last option because the result of war is always uncertain. Similarly, Procopius (500–565 CE?), the Byzantine historian, thought that Fortune plays an important role in the conduct of warfare.[198] Kamandaka's argument that organized violence should be used to keep the peace and that war is not something that a wise ruler engages in gladly, but only out of necessity, is somewhat akin to Saint Augustine's (354–430 CE) view.[199]

Kamandaka says that war should be started only after taking into consideration all the possible factors as it is a very serious business. Kamandaka notes that a battle-centric strategy should be pursued when the *vijigishu* is confident of his superior strength. Otherwise, it is better to wage *kutayuddha*. Kamandaka writes that the intelligent ruler should plan his *vyuha* of the army considering the suitability of time and place. The composite *vyuha*, in which the different wings of the army (infantry, cavalry and elephants) charge simultaneously but separately, is called *Asamhatavyuha*.[200] Maurikos (539–602 CE), the Cappadocian general who became the Byzantine emperor in 582 CE

[195] Ibid., p. 368.
[196] Ibid., p. 333.
[197] Ibid., p. 365.
[198] *The Art of War in World History from Antiquity to the Nuclear Age*, p. 347.
[199] Reichberg, Syse and Begby (eds.), *The Ethics of War*, p. 71.
[200] *Nitisara*, ed. by Mitra, pp. 405, 429.

From the Common Era to the Advent of the Turks 141

composed the *Strategikon* around 600 CE. He notes: 'Warfare is like hunting.... To try simply to overpower the enemy in the open, hand to hand and face to face, even though you might appear to win, is an enterprise which is very risky and can result in serious harm. Apart from extreme emergency, it is ridiculous to try to gain a victory which is so costly and brings only empty glory.'[201] Kamandaka, citing the just war criteria, criticizes the linkage between military training and hunting, saying that it is unethical to kill innocent animals in a hunting exercise geared to improving military skill. Kamandaka, following Manu's normative model of *dharmayuddha*, writes that enemy soldiers who have turned their backs or have despaired of life or have lost their mobility (besieged from all sides) should not be struck down as they have practically surrendered.[202]

Kamandaka, like Bana, notes that the *vijigishu* should take steps to protect himself from *kutayuddha* being waged by his opponents. The *Nitisara* reminds one that a portion of the army, ready with weapons and led by a commander, should move around the camp area during the night, lest the enemy attempt a surprise attack. However, Kamandaka, unlike Manu and Bana, later notes that if necessary, the *vijigishu* must wage *kutayuddha* also. Kamandaka justifies the necessity of waging *kutayuddha* under certain circumstances. Kamandaka is urging *kutayuddha* as a means of limiting the impact of warfare. In Kamandaka's paradigm, the impact of regular warfare (which comprised *dharmayuddha*) on society is much greater than the impact of *kutayuddha* (comprising irregular warfare) on the social fabric. Kamandaka asserts that ultimately there is nothing unfair in war.[203]

Kamandaka, like Kautilya, argues that it is quite ethical for the *dutas* to function as spies in foreign kingdoms. They are to gain strategic intelligence. Kamandaka, like Kautilya, notes the importance of battlefield intelligence for winning a war.[204] As regards the various *upayas* of *kutayuddha*, Kamandaka elaborates: 'Enticing away the subjects of the enemy out of their fortifications and ... cities and markets, villages and pastures [through secret agents] the cool headed *vijigishu* should plunder and destroy the dominion of the enemy.... The enemy deeply addicted to hunting may be assailed upon within the forest by secret means.'[205] The

---

[201] *The Art of War in World History from Antiquity to the Nuclear Age*, p. 349.
[202] *Nitisara*, ed. by Mitra, p. 411.
[203] Ibid., pp. 355, 412.
[204] Ibid., p. 411.
[205] Ibid., p. 408.

142   *Hinduism and the Ethics of Warfare in South Asia*

technique of *kutayuddha*, which Bana decries, is adopted by Kamandaka. In *sarga* 19, verse 62, Kamandaka advocates harming even the civilian economy of the enemy kingdom as part of *kutayuddha*.

Instead of a battle-centric strategy, Kamandaka puts forward a strategy for subduing the enemy by harassment. Kamandaka advises the *vijigishu* that an attritional campaign would dissipate his manpower and financial resources. He writes that when the enemy forces are found to be unprepared (or resting in camps) and/or in unfavourable places or situations, the *vijigishu* should annihilate them by surprise attack. Even if they are in their own country, steps should be taken to plunder their realm.[206] Kamandaka continues:

When the *vijigishu* is able to alienate the … border tribes … of the enemy through bribes and harassments, the elements of state … of the enemy are also harassed, he should charge with his own heroic soldiers and annihilate the enemy. With the demonstration of a frontal attack [as a ruse] and making the enemy firmly believe that [thus keeping the enemy forces engaged in that direction], the *vijigishu* should employ his heroic band of soldiers to charge swiftly [to surprise] the enemy forces from the rear. In the same way making the enemy concerned about his rear [i.e., making the ruse of a rear attack and keeping the enemy engaged in that direction] the enemy may be assailed by frontal attack with the best of soldiers. Similar methods of *kutayuddha* may be adopted on either flank (right or left).[207]

Kamandaka's concept of *prakasayuddha*, which is originally part of *dharmayuddha*, also contains certain elements of *kutayuddha*. If the intention is noble, then elements of *kutayuddha* can be implemented at the tactical level. Saint Augustine noted that 'the just war is waged by someone who has the right to do so because not all men have that right. Once an individual has undertaken this kind of war, it does not matter at all, as far as justice is concerned, whether he wins victory in open combat or through ruses.'[208] The *Nitisara* says that the army deployed for battle should be comprised of the following divisions: centre, flanks with *koti* (elite) units at the outer flank, and a reserve. As regards the conduct of *prakasayuddha*, Kamandaka writes of charging the outer flanks and the rear of the enemy force with special units. The ruler must concentrate superior forces at the point of attack.[209] Vegetius advocates using a

---

[206] Ibid., pp. 405–6.
[207] Ibid., p. 406.
[208] Reichberg, Syse and Begby (eds.), *The Ethics of War*, p. 83.
[209] *Nitisara*, ed. by Mitra, p. 442.

From the Common Era to the Advent of the Turks   143

tactical reserve.[210] The *Nitisara* advocates keeping *koti* units as a tactical reserve for conducting flank attacks on the enemy.[211] So, according to Kamandaka's battle-winning tactics, the special units of the wings should first encircle and overwhelm the enemy flanks. Meanwhile, the *ura* should check the enemy centre. Finally, the reserve units should envelop and overwhelm the encircled enemy army.[212]

One strand of ancient Chinese military philosophy emphasizes the role of the sage general. The ideal commander is portrayed as possessing supranormal intuitive power.[213] Leadership is important in Kamandaka's scheme. Kamandaka says that when, as a result of nocturnal encounters, enemy troops feel exhausted because they have been kept awake at night and then fall asleep or feel sleepy during the day, the *vijigishu* should suddenly fall upon them and annihilate them. The enemy troops, wounded or exhausted (in serious combat) during the first half of the day, should be attacked and annihilated during the second half (i.e., before they can recuperate). Kamandaka continues that to fool the enemy, an expert warrior may be set up as a dummy of the king; his own forces may thereby be inspired to feel the royal presence, and the enemy's attention is diverted. War depends upon the integrity of the *vijigishu*, and without him the army is annihilated.[214] The *vijigishu* is supposed to take care of the food supply, and the army should not be dispatched into an area where food cannot be obtained by foraging.[215]

At the tactical level, Kamandaka over-emphasizes the importance of elephants in battle (his *prakasayuddha*), which are to be used as battering rams like modern-day tanks. Kamandaka goes on to say that tuskers should be used not only to destroy the hostile infantry but also to defeat the enemy force's elephants.[216] The premier power of Deccan, the Satavahanas, who fought the Sakas in Maharashtra during the first century CE, maintained only 2,000 cavalry. This was because good mounts were not available in Deccan, and the terrain was unsuitable for a large-scale

---

[210] Bachrach, 'The Practical Use of Vegetius' *De Re Militari* during the Early Middle Ages', p. 247.

[211] *Nitisara*, ed. by Mitra, p. 441.

[212] U. P. Thapliyal, 'War in Ancient India – Concepts', in Prasad (ed.), *Historical Perspectives of Warfare in India*, p. 59.

[213] Rand, 'Li Ch'uan and Chinese Military Thought', p. 110.

[214] *Nitisara*, ed. by Mitra, pp. 409, 427. My translation differs from that of the editor of this edition of *Nitisara*.

[215] Thapliyal, 'Military Organization in the Ancient Period', p. 76.

[216] *Nitisara*, ed. by Mitra, pp. 442–3.

144   *Hinduism and the Ethics of Warfare in South Asia*

cavalry charge. Moreover, the hilly terrain of central India and the Vindhya Mountains, covered with extensive forest, did not favour operations by a large group of cavalry. The victories of the Rashtrakutas over the Palas and the Pratiharas during the eighth and ninth centuries CE strengthened the model of an army based on elephants and infantry.[217] The principal source of elephants was the mountainous, forested region at the southern extremity of the Western Ghats.[218]

Thus, Kamandaka, unlike Manu, is willing to consider night attack, deceit and ambush as part of the repertorie of a modified form of *dharmayuddha* that includes elements of *kutayuddha*. To sum up, there is tension in the *Nitisara* as regards the proper ethical limits when conducting warfare. Kamandaka accepts the necessity of flank attacks as part of *kutayuddha* but, like Manu, notes that it is unethical to destroy retreating enemy soldiers. In *sarga* 12, verse 6, it seems as if Kamandaka is opposed to surprise attack. However, in *sarga* 19, verse 55, Kamandaka, like Kautilya, advocates surprise attack. Overall, while Kautilya is totally for *kutayuddha*, Kamandaka is only half-heartedly pushing the concept of *kutayuddha*.

KATHASARITSAGARA, PANCHATANTRA AND THE *HITOPADESA*

Upinder Singh writes that treatises like Kamandaka's *Nitisara* not only reflected contemporary political reality but also shaped the political discourse. The ideas of political theorists were absorbed and expressed in poetry, drama, didactic stories, and so on and reached a wider audience.[219] Didactic fables like *Panchatantra* and *Hitopadesa* are collections of stories of birds and beasts who appear to possess human feelings and emotions. The animals appear in the role of wise politicians and advocates of *niti* (policy). They aim to educate the sons of Kshatriyas in politics and practical wisdom in a way that allows them to learn with pleasure.[220] By contrast, the *Kathasaritsagara* is a collection of stories focusing on man-woman relationships, with politics and the state appearing at the background. R. C. Majumdar opines that the *Kathasaritsagara* was composed

---

[217] Sandhu, *Military History of Ancient India*, pp. 309, 373, 486.
[218] Sundaram, 'Warfare in South India', p. 171.
[219] Singh, 'Politics, Violence and War in Kamandaka's *Nitisara*', p. 33.
[220] W. Prahlada Naidu, 'Narayana Pandita's *Hitopadesa* and Ethics', in K. B. Archak (ed.), *Ethics for Modern Man in Sanskrit Literature* (New Delhi: Sundeep Prakashan, 2007), pp. 150–1.

From the Common Era to the Advent of the Turks   145

around 500 CE.[221] Keith claims that Somadeva, a Brahmin of Kashmir, lived in the eleventh century CE.[222] My take is that Somadeva lived before the onset of the Turkish invasions of the tenth century onwards, because the *Kathasaritsagara* does not mention the presence of the *Turuskas*. The literal meaning of *Kathasaritsagara* is 'ocean of stories'. The book is a collection of short stories. The stories may be fictional, but they reflect certain social practices and morals of the contemporary age. The structure of the *Kathasaritsagara* is a person telling a story; after hearing it, another person tells another story, and this process continues. The structure is somewhat similar to the thousand and one stories of the *Arabian Nights*, where the princess tells one story and that leads to another story and so on.

Somadeva, like Kautilya and Bana, criticizes coups, even those against inefficient rulers. One story develops the theme of the principal minister (named Shatkal) of a king planning to execute the reigning monarch and raise a puppet ruler. The king is advised to get rid of the treacherous powerful minister by secret assassination. This is an example of silent war, which is part of *kutayuddha*. Somadeva elaborates the duties of a loyal minister. When the king is energetic and following an active policy, the minister should be docile and implement the King's policy. However, when a monarch is interested in the pleasures of the flesh, alcohol and hunting, the minister should take a proactive role in running the affairs of the state. In the case of an inactive monarch, if the minister also remains inactive, then such a state is doomed. One story of Somadeva's reflects the idea that during the reign of an inefficient king, the loyal minister should try to expand the kingdom by using *buddhi* rather than brute force. Diplomacy should be used for strengthening the position of the state that is surrounded by enemies, both in front and to the rear. The powerful kingdom to the rear should be won over by matrimonial alliance and thus neutralized. Then an expansionist policy should be followed vis-à-vis the polity in the front. However, Somadeva concedes that such a strategy is risky and might destroy the state. Somadeva advises that when an able ruler of a small kingdom is threatened by a powerful neighbour, instead of experiencing total destruction, the former ruler should make peace by paying tribute to the powerful neighbour. However, the

---

[221] Somadeva Bhatta, *Kathasaritsagara*, tr. from Sanskrit into Bengali by Hirendralal Biswas, Introduction by R. C. Majumdar, 5 vols. (1975; reprint, Kolkata: Academic Publishers, 1983), vol. 1, *Mukhbanda*. All translation from this Bengali edition is by the author.
[222] Keith, *History of Sanskrit Literature*, pp. 246, 281.

146   *Hinduism and the Ethics of Warfare in South Asia*

able tributary prince should wait for the right opportunity to regain his independence.[223]

When the powerful invader is not merely interested in making the neighbouring ruler a tributary prince but intends to destroy and absorb the kingdom, then the intended victim should follow *kutayuddha*. Somadeva asserts that *kutayuddha* in self-defence becomes *dharmayuddha*. Somadeva narrates a story: once upon a time, when Punyasena was ruling over Ujjain, it was invaded by a strong ruler. Punyasena realized that the invader could not be defeated in *prakasayuddha*. So Punyasena, in self-defence, decided to follow *kutayuddha*. The ministers of Punyasena spread the news that Punyasena had died, and a dead body was presented for public display as proof. The ministers of Punyasena invited the invader to become king of Ujjain. The invader got overconfident and careless and, without taking proper precautions, moved into Ujjain. Suddenly Punyasena's soldiers, who had prepared an ambush, fell upon the advance guard of the invader and destroyed it, and a select group of warriors also fell upon the invader and executed him. Punyasena came out from his hiding place and became the ruler again.[224]

Somadeva, in another story, argues that a just king should wage *dharmayuddha*. After defeating his opponents, the victorious just ruler should win their affection by showing kindness and respect to his fallen enemies. The defeated ruler should be reinstated in his kingdom and should remain a loyal tributary to the victorious just ruler. However, if the defeated ruler turns out to be a treacherous tributary, then it is ethical for the just ruler to execute him and annex his kingdom. In one story, told by one minister Yogendhanarayan, Somadeva writes that a king should get glory and exhibit *paurusha* by waging *dharmayuddha* against the kingdoms located in the eastern part of the subcontinent. The eastern part of the subcontinent is considered fertile because of the bumper crops grown in the river valleys. The king is warned not to attack north-west India as that region is dominated by the *mlechchas*.[225] The *mlechchas* did not obey the normative model of *dharmayuddha* as laid down by Manu. Only the members of a single ethno-cultural group, imbued with a particular philosophy, could accept the cultural norms introduced by the proponents of that philosophy. Moreover, the Hindu kings' elephant-centric armies could not compete with the military effectiveness of the composite

---

[223] *Kathasaritsagara*, tr. by Biswas, vol. 1, pp. 22, 101–2, 104.
[224] Ibid., p. 107.
[225] Ibid., pp. 130, 156, 169.

From the Common Era to the Advent of the Turks   147

bow–equipped, cavalry-centric armies of the Central Asian steppe invaders who had occupied north-west India.

One story discussing the origins of Pataliputra city, recounts that a Brahmin ruler decided to kill his son in order to retain the throne. The father hired *guptaghataks* (secret assassins) to murder his son. The *guptaghataks* hid in a temple and planned to kill the intended victim when he came to worship the deity. The intended victim discovered the *guptaghataks* and bought them off. Next, he killed his father with the help of the ministers. This story reflects a sort of *kutayuddha* carried on by the *guptaghataks*. In the same story, the intended victim who later becomes the hero claims that many Brahmins, like prostitutes, were running after money and could not be relied upon. The same story narrates the Kings' use of *guptachars* (secret agents) who functioned as the eyes and ears of the monarch.[226]

Bana writes that a ruler named Vatsapati, while on a trip to the elephant forest, was imprisoned by an enemy ruler (Mahasena) and his soldiers, who issued from the belly of an artificial elephant. Bana says that this sort of commando strike is unfair.[227] This story reminds one of the Trojan horse. A similar story is recounted by Somadeva. Chandamahasena, the ruler of Ujjain, after consulting with his ministers, created a mechanical elephant and inside it put some of his crack warriors. Then, with the mechanical elephant, Chandamahasena moved towards the Vindhya Mountain. Vatsaraj, the ruler of Kausambi, was hunting more or less alone on the Vindhya Mountain. Suddenly, he saw the mechanical elephant and advanced towards it. It is to be noted that the Vindhya Mountain was famous for its elephant herds. The warriors of Chandamahasena suddenly jumped out of the mechanical elephant and surrounded Vatsaraj. When the news of Vatsaraj's capture reached Kausambi, Rumnat, the person in charge of policy making in that kingdom in the absence of the king, argued that a frontal attack on Ujjain would only harm the security of Vatsaraj. Rather, Ujjain needed to be attacked by means of *kuta*, depending on brain power rather than muscle power. The point to be noted is that both Bana and Somadeva repeat the story. Therefore, such a *kutayuddha* technique (a sort of 'Trojan horse' motif) was apparently used by the monarchs of that time. Secondly, the construction of a movable elephant shows the existence of a high degree of mechanical skill among the Hindus of north India. Thirdly, the argument put forward

---

[226] Ibid., pp. 12–15.
[227] *Harsacharita*, tr. by Cowell and Thomas, p. 244.

148   *Hinduism and the Ethics of Warfare in South Asia*

is that *dharmayuddha* could not succeed against *kutayuddha*. Crooked techniques need to be used, even by a just ruler, to check *kutayuddha* by an opponent. However, Somadeva is ambiguous about whether the use of *kutayuddha* in response to the unrighteous techniques of an unjust ruler, resulting in an upward spiral of violence, is morally correct or not.[228]

A particular story elaborates on the various techniques of *kutayuddha* that were used in the event of inter-state war. Before attacking a kingdom, spies were sent by the invader to ascertain the strength of the king and his domain. The spies practiced a sort of biological warfare by spreading poison among the animals and agricultural fields of the kingdom. The objective was to ruin the economic infrastructure of the kingdom in the long run. In the short run, to blunt the military effectiveness of the kingdom's army, the invader sent *vishyakanyas* (female assassins) to poison and murder the military leaders and to demoralize the army. Thus, we find that Somadeva is aware of the techniques of *kutayuddha* elaborated on by Kautilya. Somadeva asserts that ultimately *kutayuddha* backfires on its practitioners; it is always good, if possible, to wage *dharmayuddha*.[229]

One story tells us that many Brahmins acquired training in weapons and developed their physiques through wrestling. Obviously, such Brahmins joined the army. Another story of Somadeva's tells that a monarch should be well versed in *dhanurveda* (the science of archery) and that with a bow one can get rid of fifty foot soldiers. We see that both Manu and Somadeva give great importance to foot archers. Somadeva like Sun Tzu shows awareness of the linkage between the terrain and the army's force structure. One of his stories says that elephants should be used for conquering the region south of Vindhya Mountain and cavalry for fighting in Sind, especially against the *mlechchas*. Elephants are to be acquired by capturing them from the Vindhya Mountain or taken as tribute from the ruler of Kamrup (Assam). In one story, the protagonist states that good horses are like gods. Somadeva tells us that kings frequently fought each other to protect grasslands that were suitable for feeding horses.[230]

The original *Panchatantra*, composed in Sanskrit, is lost. The Pahlavi version of the *Panchatantra* was composed before 570 CE but is now lost. The *Panchatantra* was translated into Arabic, and this version

---

[228] *Kathasaritsagara*, tr. by Biswas, vol. 1, pp. 74–5.
[229] Ibid., pp. 153–4.
[230] Ibid., pp. 58, 86, 108, 133, 155–6.

From the Common Era to the Advent of the Turks   149

has survived. The present translations of the *Panchatantra* are reconstructed from the Arabic and Syrian versions. Within South Asia, the *Panchatantra* was also translated into the Newari language of Nepal. Keith claims that the *Panchatantra* was composed before 450 CE and had been translated into Chinese by the last decade of the fifth century CE.[231] The *Panchatantra* is a *niti-shastra*, or textbook on *niti*. *Niti* means 'the wise conduct of life'. Several stanzas in the *Panchatantra* emphasize security. The *Panchatantra* takes a realist attitude, implying that the world is full of evil men who cannot be reformed. In such a scenario, gaining security requires the exercise of intelligence. Readers are warned of deception at various levels of society. The past, for *Panchatantra*, offers material for gaining wisdom in order to understand the present and the future.[232]

The *Panchatantra* describes the internal and external threats that a ruler has to face. It warns the ruler that he should never delegate all power to a single person, even though the latter may be very efficient. Sole command might encourage the efficient subordinate to overthrow the monarch.[233] The *Panchatantra* claims that wars are fought for both tangible and intangible objects. Warriors fight when their honour is insulted. As regards the tangible objectives of war, the *Panchatantra* says:

> Land and friends and gold at most
> Have been won when battle ceases.[234]

The *Panchatantra* stresses winning and retaining loyal allies. Like the *MD*, it notes that a fort filled with archers is more effective in stopping an invasion than innumerable elephants and horses. The *Panchatantra* gives a vivid description of fortification comprised of gates fitted with bolts, bars, and *yantras*. Moats and walls provided additional protection.[235] We are not sure whether ancient and early medieval Indians, like the Greeks and the Romans, possessed artillery machines like catapults for shooting arrows, *ballista* for throwing stones and *scorpio* for discharging javelins. Dionysius the Elder, the tyrant of Syracuse around 400 BCE, constructed catapults with the help of engineers brought from all over the Mediterranean world. According to one view, towers with battlements

---

[231] Keith, *History of Sanskrit Literature*, pp. 246, 262, 283.
[232] *The Panchatantra*, tr. from the Sanskrit by Arthur W. Ryder (1949; reprint, Mumbai: Jaico, 2003), Introduction, pp. 4–5, 8.
[233] *The Panchatantra*, Book 1, p. 85.
[234] Ibid., p. 70.
[235] *The Panchatantra*, Introduction, p. 7; Book 1, pp. 17, 70.

150 *Hinduism and the Ethics of Warfare in South Asia*

for shooting arrows and stones were invented around 750 BCE in the Near East.[236]

Like the *Bhagavad Gita*, the following verse from the *Panchatantra* demands that soldiers die willingly in battle:

> One who finds in battle, peace
> Free from questionings,
> ....
> Is beloved of kings.[237]

The *Panchatantra* is aware of the importance of careful planning, military training and intelligence on the part of the military leader for enhancing the military effectiveness of the force at his disposal. It is no use blaming defeat and disaster on fate. Here, the *Panchatantra* differs from Kamandaka's *Nitisara*, which states that the result of war is always uncertain. Rather than having soldiers rush madly to defeat their enemies, pre-battle evaluation of the enemy and training of the soldiers, comments the *Panchatantra*, are necessary. And a weaker power, warns the *Panchatantra*, should never resort to war against a stronger power.[238]

One stanza notes:

> In case of horse or book or sword,
> Of woman, man or lute or word,
> The use or uselessness depends
> On qualities the user lends.[239]

Another verse tells us:

> Intelligence is power. But where
> Could power and folly make a pair?
> The rabbit played upon his pride
> To fool him; and the lion died.[240]

The *Panchatantra* advises that before battle, the army should be deployed in proper *vyuha*, and the conch should be used for signaling the various detachments of the army in the midst of battle.[241] Bana writes that the

---

[236] Leigh Alexander, 'The Origin of Greek and Roman Artillery', *Classical Journal*, vol. 41, no. 5 (1946), pp. 208–12.
[237] *The Panchatantra*, Book 1, p. 28.
[238] Ibid., pp. 71–2.
[239] Ibid., p. 36.
[240] Ibid., p. 66.
[241] Ibid., p. 82.

From the Common Era to the Advent of the Turks 151

sound of the conch shell and drums were used as a device for signaling the various detachments of the army.[242]

The *Hitopadesa* (the east Indian derivative of the *Panchatantra*) is a collection of animal and human fables in prose, illustrated with numerous maxims and sayings in verse, both intended to impart instruction in worldly wisdom and the conduct of political affairs.[243] Its author, named Narayana, lived in the court of a monarch named Dvalachandra.[244] Narayana, the court poet, was a devotee of the god Shiva. He was a philosopher and probably composed his work between 800 and 950 CE. The *Hitopadesa* contains quotations from the *Nitisara*. Most of the stories aim to teach by example and are satirical. So the structure of *Hitopadesa* is similar to that of the *Panchatantra*, which Narayana acknowledges. The *Hitopadesa* deals with certain aspects of *niti*, that is, political theory in its various aspects, including politics, diplomacy, and problems of war and peace.[245]

The *Hitopadesa* asserts that during *vigraha*, proper strategy leads to victory. For proper strategy, the king needs to hear the advice of wise ministers. For giving the right advice, the ministers require information about hostile polities.[246] Before starting a war, it is necessary to send spies in order to ascertain the strength of the enemy force. As the *Hitopadesa* advises: 'Sir, let a spy go there first. Then we will get to know their organization and their strengths and weaknesses.'[247] Once war is inevitable, the *Hitopadesa* agrees with Kautilya and Kamandaka that it is better to defeat the enemy by treacherous diplomacy than by outright combat because of the unpredictability inherent in battle. Here, the *Hitopadesa*, unlike the *Panchatantra*, accepts Kamandaka's advice that the result of war is *anitya*.[248]

As regards *vigraha*, the *Hitopadesa* tells us that treacherous conduct by allies leads to defeat.[249] Boldness in combat is regarded as essential. As one stanza puts it:

> At other times it does behove
> For menfolk to forbearing be,

---

[242] *Harsacharita*, tr. by Cowell and Thomas, pp. 172, 223; *Harshacarita*, ed. by Kane, *Uchchhvasa* IV, p. 42.

[243] Narayana, *The Hitopadesa*, tr. from the Sanskrit with an Introduction by A. N. D. Haksar (New Delhi: Penguin, 1998), Introduction, p. ix.

[244] Keith, *History of Sanskrit Literature*, p. 263.

[245] Narayana, *The Hitopadesa*, pp. x–xiii.

[246] Naidu, 'Narayana Pandita's *Hitopadesa* and Ethics', p. 160.

[247] Narayana, *The Hitopadesa*, pp. 151–2.

[248] Ibid., p. 153.

[249] Ibid., p. 137.

Hinduism and the Ethics of Warfare in South Asia

> And for maidens so to move
> As befits their modesty.
> Except in combat and in love,
> Brave should one, and bold the other, prove.[250]

Like the *MD* and the *Panchatantra*, the *Hitopadesa* emphasizes the effectiveness of fortress defence rather than open battle. According to the *Hitopadesa*, forts defended by battlements and a garrison comprised of archers constitute an effective defence.

As regards the construction of different types of forts, the *Hitopadesa* goes on to say that a fort surrounded by a lake is most defensible. Eastern India in general and Bengal in particular are full of rivers, streams and marshes. So the *Hitopadesa* emphasizes what Kautilya describes as *jaladurga* (water forts). The *Hitopadesa* elaborates on the importance of forts functioning as bases for the defending force. Food and war materials can be stored in forts. In addition, forts are essential for housing reinforcements as well as for providing rest and recuperation for exhausted soldiers.[251]

TAMIL MILITARY THEORY OF SOUTH INDIA

All of the above-mentioned literary pieces composed in Sanskrit describe the political and military culture of north and central India. In order to get a pan-Indian view, it is essential to have an overview of the works on statecraft composed in the Dravidian south. Tamil literature is one of the oldest literatures. According to some scholars, Tamil is one of the oldest living languages of the world, with an unbroken literary history of over two millennia. Originally, Tamil literature belonged to the Dravidian stock of people living in southern part of the subcontinent. Saint Valluvar's *Kural*, or *Tirukkural*, is one of the great classics of Tamil literature. The word *Tiru* is somewhat similar to Sanskrit *Sri* and means 'sacred'. *Sri* is added to one's name as mark of respect. *Kural* means something that is short, concise and abridged.[252] The *Kural* is a compendium of moral rules. The date of *Tirukkural* is still debated. The work belongs to the post-Sangam era.[253] The latest assessment is that it was

---

[250] Ibid., p. 140.
[251] Ibid., pp. 156–7.
[252] *Tiruvalluvar, The Kural*, tr. from the Tamil with an Introduction by P. S. Sundaram (New Delhi: Penguin, 1990), Introduction, p. 7.
[253] P. Sensarma, *Military Thoughts of Tiru Valluvar* (Calcutta: Noya Prakash, 1981), pp. 2, 5.

From the Common Era to the Advent of the Turks 153

composed around the seventh century CE. *Kurals* are couplets by the saint poet Valluvar. Valluvar deals with *aram* (virtue), *porul* (polity) and *inpam* (love, pleasure and happiness). To an extent, *aram* is equivalent to Sanskrit *dharma, porul* to Sanskrit *artha* and *inpam* to Sanskrit *kama*.[254] Of 1,330 *kurals* of Valluvar, 700 are on *porul*, 380 deal with *aram* and 250 with *inpam*. In the 700 *kurals* dealing with *porul*, Valluvar discusses various aspects of statecraft and warfare.[255] P. S. Sundaram rightly says that the *Kural* is the work not of a mystic but of a down-to-earth man of the world. The author of the *Kural*, continues Sundaram, is a statesman and not a politician, a realist and not a cynic.[256] Ranganayaki Mohapatra asserts that the *Kural* represents a fusion of Dravidian and non-Dravidian values.[257]

Unlike Manu, Valluvar does not give any importance to the castes or lineages of the rulers and ministers. This is despite the fact that the caste system had percolated into south India by the second century CE.[258] The *Kural* says:

> Call them Brahmins who are virtuous
> And kind to all that live.[259]

This is probably because Valluvar belonged to a low caste. Valluvan is the caste name of the drummers in the villages, and the profession of drummer was considered very low in pre-modern India.[260] The term 'valluvan' was also associated with the weavers caste. According to one theory, Valluvar was the illegitimate son of a Brahmin father and a *harijan* mother. His birthplace was probably Mylapore in Madras. According to another version, Valluvar was from Kanyakumari in the extreme south of Tamil Nadu; he was a chieftain ruler named Valluvanadu. Like Mahavira and Gautam Buddha, he left the royal household and became a wandering spiritual monk. He probably died at Mylapore.[261]

P. Sensarma writes that Valluvar assumed that a man can think of God only when his life in the world is peaceful and is protected by a

---

[254] Ranganayaki Mahapatra, '*Tirukkural* and the Indian Ethical Literary Tradition', in Mahapatra, P. Bhanumathi and Sukla Chakrabarti (eds.), *Studies in Tirukkural* (Calcutta: Calcutta University, 1996), p. 20.

[255] Sensarma, *Military Thoughts of Tiru Valluvar*, p. 3.

[256] *Tiruvalluvar, The Kural*, tr. by Sundaram, Introduction, p. 11.

[257] Mahapatra, '*Tirukkural* and the Indian Ethical Literary Tradition', p. 3.

[258] Sensarma, *Military Thoughts of Tiru Valluvar*, p. 11.

[259] *Tiruvalluvar, The Kural*, tr. by Sundaram, p. 21.

[260] Sensarma, *Military Thoughts of Tiru Valluvar*, p. 4.

[261] *Tiruvalluvar, The Kural*, tr. by Sundaram, Introduction, p. 8.

154   *Hinduism and the Ethics of Warfare in South Asia*

benign ruler.[262] In Valluvar's paradigm, *porul* leads to *inpam*. Kautilya also says that *dharma* can only flourish only if one has *artha* and *kama*. Like Manu, Valluvar says that protection of his subjects is one of the primary duties of the monarch. The *Kural* elaborates:

> He who is a just protector
> Will be deemed the Lord's deputy.[263]

Valluvar warns the ruler:

> Groupism, internal dissensions and seditious chiefs
> Are absent in an ideal land.[264]

The *Kural*, like the *MD*, is against illegal heavy taxation of the subjects.[265] In order to avoid internal rebellion, Valluvar emphasizes good governance and criticizes nepotism as evil and unwise. Further, Valluvar is against micromanagement of subordinates' activities by the ruler.[266] In a way, Valluvar is promoting what the Germans called *auftragstaktik*.

In contrast to Kautilya and Kamandaka's *saptanga* theory of the state, Valluvar claims that the state is comprised of six elements: *patai* (army), *kuti* (subjects), *kul* (treasure), *amaiccu* (ministers), *natpu* (allies) and *aran* (forts). Valluvar is against giving undue importance to the ruler by accepting him as one of the constituent element of the polity. Unlike Kautilya and Kamandaka, Valluvar asserts that the army is the most important element within the state.[267]

According to Nathan Rosenstein, the army played a vital role in fostering and strengthening a common civic identity among the Romans. Military service entailed a direct interaction between the citizen and the state. Rosenstein claims that the ideology of republican Rome stressed the possession of *virtus* (manly excellence) displayed in the pursuit and acquisition of *gloria* and *fama* (glory and renown) won through service to the *res publica* (Rome's public affairs). War constituted by far Rome's most important public business by far, and war afforded the greatest scope for accumulating *gloria* and *fama*. These, along with *virtus*, demonstrated a man's fitness for leadership and paved the way to high public office.[268] In

---

[262] Sensarma, *Military Thoughts of Tiru Valluvar*, p. 3.
[263] *Tiruvalluvar, The Kural*, tr. by Sundaram, p. 59.
[264] Ibid., p. 94.
[265] P. Bhanumathi, 'Kingship in *Tirukural* and *Sukraniti*', in Mahapatra, Bhanumathi and Chakrabarti (eds.), *Studies in Tirukkural*, p. 35.
[266] *Tiruvalluvar, The Kural*, tr. by Sundaram, Introduction, p. 12.
[267] Sensarma, *Military Thoughts of Tiru Valluvar*, p. 8.
[268] Nathan Rosenstein, 'Republican Rome', in Raaflaub and Rosenstein (eds.), *War and Society in the Ancient and Medieval Worlds*, pp. 200, 205.

From the Common Era to the Advent of the Turks   155

Achaemenid Persia, the chief proof of *andragathie* (manliness) was prowess in fighting and having many sons.[269] Valluvar says that dying in battle is the best possible death for a soldier.[270] Here, the *Tirukkural* takes the same line as the *Bhagavad Gita*.

Before using the army, Valluvar, like Sun Tzu, stresses strategic planning. The *Kural* notes that an ill-planned scheme will be unsuccessful.[271] Valluvar, somewhat like Sun Tzu, points out that knowing the enemy and knowing oneself are essential for victory.[272] The *Kural* claims that proper assessment of the enemy's strengths and weaknesses is the path to victory.[273] Like Sun Tzu, Valluvar emphasizes the importance of striking at the right time and seizing the right opportunity.[274] In order to achieve this, notes the *Kural*, patience is necessary.[275]

Conducting warfare requires money and the establishment of an administrative infrastructure. During the Roman Empire, the individual legions and auxiliary regiments remained permanently in commission, with particular names, numerals and titles. Many soldiers served all of their lives. To give an example, Legion II was probably formed in 43 CE. Its emblem was a Capricorn and its title Augusta. Legion III was given the title Cyrenaica by Augustus for service in that province. In 13 CE, Emperor Augustus ordered that terms of military service in the legions be fixed at sixteen years, followed by four years of service in reserve. Upon retirement, the soldiers were rewarded with a grant of gratuity. Augustus established a military treasury for paying gratuities to the soldiers. The revenues for the military treasury came from two taxes imposed on the Roman citizens: a 5 percent tax on inheritance and a 1 percent tax on auction sales. To prevent any divided loyalty, the wages of the soldiers were paid by the imperial treasury.[276] All this generated regimental/legionary cohesion and gave the army a strong formal institutional ethos and infrastructure.

The Tamil word *kul* is equivalent to the Sanskrit word *kosa*. Valluvar says that the monarch should generate wealth through customs, taxes and tribute from defeated enemies. Valluvar hints at economic warfare

---

[269] Pierre Briant, 'The Achaemenid Empire', in Raaflaub and Rosenstein (eds.), *War and Society in the Ancient and Medieval Worlds*, p. 109.
[270] Sensarma, *Military Thoughts of Tiru Valluvar*, p. 13.
[271] Tiruvalluvar, *The Kural*, tr. by Sundaram, p. 67.
[272] *Art of War*, tr. by Sawyer, p. 179.
[273] Tiruvalluvar, *The Kural*, tr. by Sundaram, p. 68.
[274] *Art of War*, tr. by Sawyer, pp. 183–4.
[275] Tiruvalluvar, *The Kural*, tr. by Sundaram, p. 69.
[276] Keppie, *Making of the Roman Army*, pp. 55, 76, 146–8, 205–6.

156 *Hinduism and the Ethics of Warfare in South Asia*

against the enemy but does not elaborate the point. Valluvar claims that an army must have a grand, imposing look. The enemy should be cowed by exhibiting the grandeur of the army. The army's imposing look is the product of numerical superiority as well as its smart appearance. One could speculate that a large number of well-dressed soldiers not only instills a sense of confidence among the military personnel but also tends to demoralize the enemy.[277] The Romans also emphasized public display of soldiers along with their polished arms and armour. Not only did these exercises encourage recruitment and maintain unit morale, the public was also intimidated by such sights. On the battlefield, the flashing of metal and colour and the sound of clanking arms created an imposing and intimidating impression that gave one's own side encouragement and struck fear into the hearts and minds of the enemy. The psychological impact of such public display on the adversary was enormous.[278]

Valluvar, like Kamandaka, states that numerical superiority means nothing in warfare without an able commander.[279] The *Kural* emphasizes that even a numerically superior force comprised of trained soldiers will melt away without proper leadership.[280] Valluvar is also an admirer of energy and action (somewhat similar to Kautilya's *utsahasakti*) on the part of the monarch.[281] The *Kural* notes that a successful king must display courage, liberality, wisdom and energy.[282] Valluvar emphasizes the importance of sound administration for sustaining the army.[283] The *Kural* points out that to eliminate desertion and disaffection among the soldiers, a proper administrative fabric that takes care of the soldiers' creature comforts under a generous ruler is necessary.[284]

Let us have a look at the military landscape that provided the background for Valluvar's theorizing. J. Sundaram asserts that the Chola army was organized in regiments. The name of one such regiment was Rajaraja-*terinda-vil*. 'Rajaraja' refers to the monarch who raised the unit, and the term *terinda* refers to the high level of training and fitness of the personnel of the unit. It means that this was an elite unit. And *vil* means

---

[277] Sensarma, *Military Thoughts of Tiru Valluvar*, pp. 15, 20–1, 23.

[278] Kate Gulliver, 'Display in Roman Warfare: The Appearance of Armies and Individuals on the Battlefield', *War in History*, vol. 14, no. 1 (2007), pp. 1–21.

[279] Sensarma, *Military Thoughts of Tiru Valluvar*, p. 15.

[280] *Tiruvalluvar, The Kural*, tr. by Sundaram, p. 97.

[281] Ibid., Introduction, p. 12.

[282] Ibid., p. 59.

[283] Sensarma, *Military Thoughts of Tiru Valluvar*, p. 17.

[284] *Tiruvalluvar, The Kural*, tr. by Sundaram, p. 97.

From the Common Era to the Advent of the Turks   157

that it is a corps of archers. While the *valavans* were in charge of training the troops, the unit was lead into battle by an officer called a *nayakan*. The *senamukham* was the headquarters for training the troops. There were *bazaars* and merchants for supplying the troops. Chalukyan troops between the sixth and eighth centuries CE were led into battle by the king or his sons or by the favoured princes of collateral branches.[285] Many Brahmins served as generals in the armies of the Cholas and Chalukyas during the tenth and eleventh centuries CE.[286]

Besides the army, Valluvar states that forts are necessary for both offensive and defensive warfare. Valluvar writes that a fort should be surrounded by a high and massive wall. The fort, according to him, should have large space inside, but the approaches from the outside should be narrow. He, like Manu and Narayana, further emphasizes that foodstuffs and other supplies should be stored within the fort.[287] The *Harsacharita* says that forts were surrounded by water-filled moats, which in turn were protected by rock walls.[288] Kautilya recommends that a fort be protected by three parallel ditches: one filled with water, another with mud; the third ditch should be dry.[289] Valluvar continues that a properly stocked fort with a well-motivated garrison can withstand a long siege.[290]

Except in north-west India, fortifications on the subcontinent during the Common Era were characterized by the presence of massive ramparts flanked by solid quadrangular towers.[291] Towards the end of the Maurya period, the Andhras in Deccan had towns protected by walls.[292] At Banavasi, situated on the left bank of the Varada River, a tributary of the Tungabhadra, the rampart, oval in shape and covering an area of forty-two hectares, was pierced by two openings. It was a brick structure on a rubble foundation and surrounded by a deep moat constructed during the Satavahana period (first century BCE–second century CE). At Satanikota, situated on the right bank of the Tungabhadra River in Andhra Pradesh, the fortifications were constructed between the first century BCE and the third century CE. The wall, about 3.2 meters in width and built of stone slabs laid in mud mortar, was provided

---

[285] Sundaram, 'Chola and Other Armies – Organization', pp. 185, 189, 197, 201.
[286] Chakravarti, *Art of War in Ancient India*, p. 80.
[287] Sensarma, *Military Thoughts of Tiru Valluvar*, pp. 40–1.
[288] *Harsacharita*, tr. by Cowell and Thomas, p. 77.
[289] Sinha, 'Art of War in Ancient India', in Metraux and Crouzet (eds.), *Cultural History of India*, p. 151.
[290] *Tiruvalluvar, The Kural*, by Sundaram, p. 95.
[291] Deloche, *Studies on Fortification in India*, p. 26.
[292] Majumdar, *Military System in Ancient India*, p. 78.

158   *Hinduism and the Ethics of Warfare in South Asia*

with a 1.45-meter baked brick facing. The wall was skirted by a rock-cut ditch about 3.20 meters deep and 4.25 meters wide. The citadel at Nagarjunakonda, on the right bank of Krishna River in Andhra Pradesh, covered an area of fifty hectares and was probably constructed during the third and fourth centuries CE. The rampart, made of mud, was twenty-four meters wide at the base and was later strengthened by a revetment of baked brick built on the bare rock surface. The citadel was surrounded by a ditch.[293] As a point of comparison, during the ninth century CE fortifications in England were comprised of an eight foot-thick wall, a rampart of about nine feet from the base of the ditch that fronted it to its earth-covered top, and a wooden palisade atop the earth. The stone-and-wood rampart was about six feet in height.[294]

CONCLUSION

Rather than technical aspects, which are over-dominant in classical Western military tracts, the ancient Hindu philosophy of warfare focused on the moral objectives and cosmic significance of *vigraha*. As in the case of ancient Chinese military philosophy, which witnessed the continuous tussle of *wen-wu*, in Hindu philosophy one witnesses a continuous tension between *dharmayuddha* and *kutayuddha*. There are both similarities and dissimilarities between the just war tradition of Saint Augustine and the Hindu *acharyas'* concept of *dharmayuddha*. Both Augustine and the *acharyas* believed that preventing war through persuasion and regarding war as a last option are more glorious than slaying human beings with swords on the battlefield. Augustine and the *acharyas* accepted the idea that the use of coercive force constitutes an essential component of the political authority of the ruler. In Saint Augustine's framework, in the Christian just war tradition, a just war could be initiated by a legitimate ruler or by the command of God.[295] In the Hindu *dharmayuddha* corpus of thinking, a just war is initiated for a just reason by a just ruler, but never by God. Occasionally, *dharmayuddha* was conducted for the purpose of maintaining the *chaturvarga* system. For the traditional Hindu ideologues, the *chaturvarga* system was an ideal, but in practice the presence of numerous mixed castes and the Brahmins in the army give the lie to the idea of a strictly enforced fourfold social system.

---

[293] Deloche, *Studies on Fortification in India*, pp. 39, 41, 43.
[294] Bachrach and Aris, 'Military Technology and Garrison Organization', pp. 3–4.
[295] Reichberg, Syse and Begby (eds.), *The Ethics of War*, pp. 73, 80–1.

From the Common Era to the Advent of the Turks 159

Compared to the Roman Empire, the Indian polities, like the Chinese empires, were less militaristic. The Roman political system was not only competitive but also militaristic. For instance, a tribune had to serve at least five years in the army as a qualification for office.[296] In India, an *amatya* didn't require experience of military service as a qualification for reaching the top stratum of the state. The Gupta Empire was to a great extent a territorial empire and to a lesser extent a hegemonic empire. The rest of the big polities like the Sungas, Kanvas, Satavahanas, Harsa's empire, Rashtrakutas, and so on were mainly hegemonic empires containing numerous semi-autonomous tribes and agrarian communities. To a great extent, the concept of *dharmayuddha* gave rise to hegemonic empires. However, the rules of *dharmayuddha* were not always accepted on the battlefield. Despite Manu's injunctions, incendiary arrows (arrowheads smeared with oil and set alight before firing) were used occasionally.[297] Manu's and Kamandaka's emphasis on the use of troops in close-quarter battle formation gives the lie to the assertion of several historians that ancient Indian warfare was merely ritualized combat between undisciplined militias.

Both Manu and Kalidasa speak of the riverine navies of the polities in east India, but neither mentions the existence of a seagoing or oceangoing navy. The Indo-Greeks introduced geometrical plans for constructing forts, but the indigenous system did not absorb these elements completely. Even the Central Asian influence, which involved constructing circular and hollow towers, was partially rejected by the Hindu military architects. According to an age-old tradition, the Hindu fort architects continued to emphasize the construction of solid, massive structures. Both Manu and Valluvar, like Kautilya, emphasize a fortress-oriented strategy based on positional warfare. It seems that both the medieval Western European military commanders and the *acharyas* like Sun Tzu were against a battle-centric strategy.

Sreni troops were used both by the Guptas in north India and by the Cholas in south India.[298] The *acharyas* also advocated the use of defeated enemy troops. The Roman Empire, like the Hindu kings, also used *bheda*. For instance, in 409 CE, Emperor Honorius used 10,000 Hunnic allies against the Goths.[299] When the structure of the armies became more loose, political treachery often decided the outcome of campaigns in

---

[296] Keppie, *Making of the Roman Army*, p. 39.
[297] Sandhu, *Military History of Ancient India*, p. 391.
[298] Ibid., pp. 376–7.
[299] Heather, 'The Huns and the End of the Roman Empire in Western Europe', pp. 14–17.

160   *Hinduism and the Ethics of Warfare in South Asia*

Western European history. Castinus' Roman force against the Vandals in Spain was crippled in 422 CE, when the former's Gothic confederates deserted.[300]

Mounted archery was absent in south India because before the thirteenth century CE the south Indian kingdoms never encountered the mounted archery of the steppe nomads. For the discontinuation of horse archery in post-Gupta north India, Sandhu blames the chairborne *sastric* teachers. The Brahmin teachers hated any sort of change, hence they resisted all innovation and particularly disliked the imposition of the *mlechcha* system of mounted archery.[301] An additional reason was the ecology of India. Despite the fact that the Central Asian nomadic tribes with their mounted archery ran roughshod over the armies of the Hindus, mounted archery was never a prominent theme either for Manu or for Kamandaka. Since south India had no experience with mounted archers, the *Kural* does not mention it. After the fall of the Guptas, India forgot all about horse archery, and the Hindu *rajas* continued to wage internecine warfare with elephants, as advocated by Kamandaka. However, by the tenth century CE, the elephant-centric armies of the Hindus in north-west India were facing disaster against the mounted archery of the Islamic nomads.

[300] Liebeschuetz, 'The End of the Roman Army in the Western Empire', p. 267.
[301] Sandhu, *Military History of Ancient India*, pp. 391, 529.

5

Hindu Militarism under Islamic Rule

900–1800 CE

INTRODUCTION

The entry of Islam onto the subcontinent began when the Arabs, between 710 and 714 CE, occupied Sind from a Hindu dynasty led by King Dahir. After the Arab conquest of Sind, due to the resistance of the Grujara-Pratiharas, Islam failed to expand into the interior of the subcontinent. From the eleventh century onwards, warlords from Afghanistan who had embraced Islam invaded India. At that time, north India was divided into several intermediate-sized principalities. These polities were ruled by the Kshatriya landed elements known as *thakurs*, who later came to be known as Rajputs. Initially, the Islamic military raids from Afghanistan (like those of Mahmud of Ghazni, who ruled from 999 to 1030 CE) were geared for pillage and plunder. But by the thirteenth century, the Turko-Afghan warlords had established the Delhi Sultanate, which lasted from 1206 until 1526. The military personnel of the Delhi Sultanate were mostly Afghan adventurers, especially horse dealers who had moved into Hindustan for loot and better careers in the military and administrative apparatus of the newly established Muslim polities in India.[1] By the early sixteenth century, the Delhi Sultanate was declining, and the Chaghtai Turks under Zahir-ud-din Babur established the Mughal Empire in 1526. In Jos Gommans's formulation, the Mughal Empire, like the Ottoman and Manchu empires, was a post-nomadic frontier state. The nomadic rulers from central Eurasia, taking advantage of the agrarian expansion of the sedentary societies,

---

[1] Raziuddin Aquil, *Sufism, Culture, and Politics: Afghans and Islam in Medieval North India* (New Delhi: Oxford University Press, 2007), p. 43.

161

162   *Hinduism and the Ethics of Warfare in South Asia*

created powerful cavalry armies with a longer reach, which enjoyed clout in the agrarian societies along the borders of the central Eurasian steppe zone.[2] However, the nomadic regimes were also dependent on the talents and services of various indigenous communities. The Rajputs, albeit from a subordinate position, played an important role in the functioning of the Mughal Empire. But the Mughals failed to co-opt the Marathas (the resurgent Hindu peasantry in west India). The Marathas challenged the Mughal Empire during late seventeenth century. The Mughal Empire, though in terminal decline from the 1720s, continued to function until the mid eighteenth century, when the East India Company started on its road towards political dominance of the subcontinent.

The Hindu response to Islamic Turkish domination occurred at two levels, theoretical and practical, and its objectives were twofold: contestation as well as accommodation with the Muslim rulers. Here, we will analyze some of the Hindu texts and try to contextualize them vis-à-vis the political and military backgrounds in order to see how Hinduism met the challenge of Islam from a subordinate position. Aziz Ahmad writes that Muslim rule in India gave rise to two literary genres: a Muslim epic of conquest in Persian language and a Hindu epic of resistance and rejection of Islam in Hindi. The Muslim epic and Hindu counter-epic emerged in challenge-response dynamic: Muslim epic literature emphasizes the glory of Muslim victories, while Hindu counter-epic works emphasize resistance and repudiation of Islam. Aziz continues that these works reflect historical attitudes rather than history.[3] Azis's statement is partly true with respect to the literature in Sanskrit and in vernaculars other than Hindi that emerged in reaction to Muslim domination. As we shall see, the Hindu theoretical tracts emerged in interaction with changing political circumstances and Islamic political and military theories propounded by various jurists.

THE POLITICAL AND MILITARY LANDSCAPE

The Turks were excellent horse archers. A skilled archer was able to aim and shoot at least six arrows per minute.[4] The Turkish nomads learnt to

---

[2] Jos Gommans, 'Warhorse and Post-Nomadic Empire in Asia, c. 1000–1800', *Journal of Global History*, vol. 2 (2007), pp. 1–21.

[3] Aziz Ahmad, 'Epic and Counter-Epic in Medieval India', *Journal of the American Oriental Society*, vol. 83, no. 4 (1963), p. 470.

[4] Andre Wink, *Al-Hind: The Making of the Indo-Islamic World*, vol. 2, *The Slave Kings and the Islamic Conquest, 11th–13th Centuries* (1997; reprint, New Delhi: Oxford University Press, 2001), p. 76.

use bows while riding horses from early childhood.[5] The mounted horse archers of the Seljuq Turks enabled them to conquer Anatolia from the Byzantine Empire during the eleventh century, following the Battle of Manzikert (26 August 1071 CE). The sword-wielding Armenians, who were capable of close-quarter combat, were destroyed from a distance by the mounted archery of the Seljuq Turks.[6] The Rajput warriors used bows made of cane whose range was shorter than that of the composite bows used by the Turkish mounted archers.[7] The Hindus used simple bows. Each such bow was made of a single piece of wood or bamboo. By contrast, the composite bows used by the Muslim horse archers were made of wood, horn and sinew.[8] The strings of the composite bows were made of hides.[9] The Turks also used *nawak*s (crossbows); the bolts from these bows were able to pierce armour.[10] Simon Digby writes that the Rajput archers, unlike the Turks, did not use thumb rings.[11] The Rajputs had stirrups made of rope or wood. By contrast, the Ghaznavids had metal stirrups, which enabled them to develop heavy cavalry geared to delivering shock charges on the battlefield.[12] The medieval Western European horsemen used long stirrups, which enabled riders to stand up while delivering an effective lance thrust.[13]

Andre Wink asserts that from the tenth century onwards, Hindu military theorists started attaching great importance to war horses. But the ecology of India, unlike that of Central Asia, was unsuitable for breeding good horses. The arid zone in Central Asia, with its extensive grassland, gave rise to good horses, while India lacked adequate pastures.[14] The Suleiman Mountains west of the Indus produced good horses. On the

---

[5] Douglas Streusand, 'The Process of Expansion', in Jos J. L. Gommans and Dirk H. A. Kolff (eds.), *Warfare and Weaponry in South Asia: 1000–1800* (New Delhi: Oxford University Press, 2001), p. 340.

[6] Walter Emil Kaegi, Jr., 'The Contribution of Archery to the Turkish Conquest of Anatolia', in John Haldon (ed.), *Byzantine Warfare* (Aldershot: Ashgate, 2007), pp. 237–49.

[7] Wink, *Al-Hind*, vol. 2, p. 82.

[8] Jean Deloche, *Military Technology in Hoysala Sculpture (Twelfth and Thirteenth Century)* (New Delhi: Sitaram Bhartia Institute of Scientific Research, 1989), p. 12.

[9] Simon Digby, 'The Problem of the Military Ascendancy of the Delhi Sultanate', in Gommans and Kolff (eds.), *Warfare and Weaponry in South Asia*, pp. 316–17.

[10] Peter Jackson, *The Delhi Sultanate: A Political and Military History* (Cambridge: Cambridge University Press, 1999), p. 16.

[11] Digby, 'The Problem of the Military Ascendancy of the Delhi Sultanate', p. 316.

[12] K. S. Lal, 'The Striking Power of the Army of the Sultanate', *Journal of Indian History*, vol. 60, Part II (Aug. 1977), pp. 95–6.

[13] Ian Pierce, 'Arms, Armour and Warfare in the Eleventh Century', in John France (ed.), *Medieval Warfare: 1000–1300* (Aldershot: Ashgate, 2006), p. 71.

[14] Wink, *Al-Hind*, vol. 2, pp. 80, 84.

164   *Hinduism and the Ethics of Warfare in South Asia*

upper Oxus, the lush valleys and upland pastures were breeding grounds for very good horses.[15] In the medieval era, the best horses were the Turki horses imported from Turan. Yabu horses were the offspring of Turki horses from an inferior breed. In strength and size, they were inferior to Turki horses. Tazi and Jangli horses were Indian breeds and inferior to Yabu horses.[16] Kalhana's *Rajatarangini* notes that the Turuska horsemen were a threat to the security of Kashmir. The *Rajatarangini* notes that the kings of Kashmir made desperate attempts to acquire horses from the region west of the Indus. Foreign horse dealers grew rich from the horse trade.[17] During the twelfth century, the south Indian powers imported Arabian and Turkish horses through Arab merchants. The Hoysala Dynasty's (west India) attempt to cross Arab mares with local breeds produced horses with thick legs and broad heads, which proved inferior to the Central and West Asian war horses.[18] The Palas (750–1175) and the Senas (1096–1225) of Bengal imported horses from north-west India, and when this source of supply was cut, mounts were imported from south China.[19] Moreover, the Hindus did not feed their horses properly. As a result, many horses fell sick and died.[20] Another limitation of the cavalry of the Hindu powers was that their horses were not shoed. Only during the second half of the thirteenth century was horse shoeing introduced in south India.[21] Jos J. L. Gommans notes that when cut off from external sources of supply, the Delhi Sultanate raised war horses in the sub-montane tract of the Siwalik Hills and the comparatively drier regions around the Sutlej River in Punjab.[22]

Feudalism in the medieval world was probably a global phenomenon. R. J. Barendse asserts in an article that the feudal process can be understood in the light of a world historic juncture at which peasant societies were subjugated by an aristocracy of mounted warriors, who became

[15] C. E. Bosworth, 'The Army of the Ghaznavids', in Gommans and Kolff (eds.), *Warfare and Weaponry in South Asia*, p. 169.

[16] S. Inayat A. Zaidi, 'Rozindar Troopers under Sawai Jai Singh of Jaipur (AD 1700–1743)', *Indian Historical Review*, vol. 10 (1983–4), p. 49.

[17] *Kalhana's Rajatarangini, A Chronicle of the Kings of Kashmir*, tr. with an Introduction, Commentary, and Appendices by M. A. Stein, 3 vols. (1900; reprint, New Delhi: Motilal Banarsidas, 1989), vol. 2, pp. 39–40, 70.

[18] Deloche, *Military Technology in Hoysala Sculpture*, p. 36.

[19] Ranabir Chakravarti, 'Early Medieval Bengal and the Trade in Horses: A Note', *Journal of the Economic and Social History of the Orient*, vol. 42, no. 2 (1999), pp. 194–211.

[20] Lal, 'Striking Power of the Army of the Sultanate', p. 93.

[21] Deloche, *Military Technology in Hoysala Sculpture*, p. 31.

[22] Jos Gommans, 'The Silent Frontier of South Asia, c AD 1100–1800', *Journal of World History*, vol. 9, no. 1 (1998), pp. 18–19.

more powerful than any central institution and increasingly appropriated jurisdiction over the peasants and thus the land revenue.[23] During the eleventh century, the Byzantine emperors paid the chiefs and their retainers by providing land, and many military chiefs became large landholders and semi-autonomous from the declining central government.[24] The great provincial landlords in the Byzantine Empire maintained their own armies with the revenues generated by the large landed estates at their disposal.[25] In Japan, during the mid tenth century, conscripted provincial armies had vanished; they were replaced by forces knit together from small war bands led by members of the provincial aristocracy. The embryonic warrior class of the eighth and ninth centuries became the *bushi* caste of medieval Japan. The court tried to co-opt the rising private military power by giving the elite provincial warriors (who were leaders of the private military organizations) rank, office and land in return for performance of assigned tasks.[26] In late medieval Japan, military service was provided in exchange for leases of land.[27]

The *samanta* (Hindu feudal lords/feudatories) system in India was a product of the disintegration of the central government and the emergence of the feudal complex. One characteristic feature of this system was the prevalence of land grants to administrators in lieu of a salary. This was due to the decline of urbanism, the paucity of trade and commerce, the shortage of money, and the resultant emergence of closed local economies. The fragmentation of political authority and the rise of the lord-vassal relationship shaped the political structure. The net result was the rise of several layers of hierarchical landed intermediaries with increasing rights and obligations to the land and the produce of the land. Owing to frequent religious and secular grants and an increasing tax burden, the peasantry was impoverished. Many among the free and middle peasantry were economically ruined and became unfree labourers.[28]

[23] R. J. Barendse, 'The Feudal Mutation: Military and Economic Transformations of the Ethnosphere in the Tenth to Thirteenth Centuries', *Journal of World History*, vol. 14, no. 4 (2003), p. 511.

[24] Paul Magdalino, 'The Byzantine Army and the Land: From *Stratiotikon Ktema* to Military *Pronoia*', in Haldon (ed.), *Byzantine Warfare*, pp. 180–2.

[25] Barendse, 'The Feudal Mutation', p. 509.

[26] Karl Friday, 'Teeth and Claws: Provincial Warriors and the Heian Court', in Harald Kleinschmidt (ed.), *Warfare in Japan* (Aldershot: Ashgate, 2007), pp. 57, 59.

[27] Harald Kleinschmidt, 'Introduction', in Kleinschmidt (ed.), *Warfare in Japan*, p. xvii.

[28] B. N. S. Yadava, 'Problem of the Interaction between Socio-Economic Classes in the Early Medieval Complex', *Indian Historical Review*, vol. 3, no. 1 (1976), pp. 43–56.

166   *Hinduism and the Ethics of Warfare in South Asia*

A more nuanced argument as regards the formation of decentralized states and the emergence of the *samanta*s in early medieval India is provided by Brajadulal Chattopadhyaya. He argues that due to the spread of agriculture and brahmanism, tribes became peasants, and state formation occurred at the local level. Brahmanism spread by appropriation and integration of the local cults and customs.[29] The *samanta*s were landed aristocracy with military obligations to their overlords. They represented a focus of quasi-autonomous political power. During the twelfth and thirteenth centuries, a hierarchy emerged among the *samanta*s, and we find terms like *mahasamanta*, *samanta*, *ranaka*, *rauta*, and so on. They later were known as *rajapurusa*s or Rajputs.[30]

The Rajputs, originally known as *rajaputra*s (literal meaning 'sons of the king'), by the twelfth century had come to be known by the former term. They were a mixed caste consisting mostly of small chiefs possessing estates. Gradually, these chieftains bought the tribal territory under their control, and pastoralism was replaced by an agrarian economy. In Rajasthan during the seventh and eighth centuries, due to the use of irrigation, agriculture spread and strengthened the position of the Rajput lineages. The Rajputs also strengthened themselves in local society by suppressing various tribes like the Bhils, Ahirs, and so on and colonizing the new areas. With the disintegration of central government in polities like Gurjara-Pratiharas in Rajasthan and north India, their *samanta*s became independent and proclaimed their *rajaputra* status by establishing independent kingdoms. Inter-clan marriage among the *rajaputra*s further strengthened the Rajput identity. By the end of the thirteenth century, the term 'Rajput' conveyed both political status and an element of heredity.[31] In medieval India, writes Stewart Gordon, 'Rajput' was a descriptive term for men on horseback who disdained agriculture and pursued honour and social mobility through

---

[29] B. D. Chattopadhyaya, 'Introduction: The Making of Early Medieval India', in Chattopadhyaya, *The Making of Early Medieval India* (1994; reprint, New Delhi: Oxford University Press, 2005), p. 16.

[30] B. D. Chattopadhyaya, 'Political Processes and Structure of Polity in Early Medieval India', in Chattopadhyaya, *Making of Early Medieval India*, p. 217.

[31] B. D. Chattopadhyaya, 'Origin of the Rajputs: The Political, Economic and Social Processes in Early Medieval Rajasthan', *Indian Historical Review*, vol. 3, no. 1 (1976), pp. 59–82; Chattopadhyaya, 'Introduction' and 'Early Memorial Stones of Rajasthan: A Preliminary Analysis of Their Inscriptions', in Chattopadhyaya, *Making of Early Medieval India*, pp. 22, 128–9.

military service.[32] According to another theory, the Rajputs were the products of intermarriage between the Central Asian conquerors (like the Sakas, Parthians, and Huns) who had settled in the subcontinent and the Kshatriyas of India.[33]

The Rajput state was initially based on a sort of *bhai-bhant*, in which the nobles considered themselves the co-sharers of the state, and the ruler was almost a *primus inter pares*. However, this system was replaced by the *pattadari* system. Raja Sur Singh (ruled 1596–1619) introduced the *pattadari* system at Jodhpur, and Raja Rai Singh introduced it at Bikaner around 1625 CE. The *sanad* or *patta* was roughly equivalent to the *jagir*, which authorized the holder to collect land revenue (*rekh*, i.e., assessed revenue) and other taxes. This changed the relationship between the nobles and the ruler. From being sharers in the patrimony of the state, the Rajput chieftains were reduced to a position of subordination. They were forced to accept certain obligations of *chakri* (service) and in return were granted *pattas*.[34]

The Rajputs were roughly equivalent to the warrior class of medieval Japan, who were known as *bushi/Samurai*. The *bushi* were also known as *chusei* (between the tenth and fourteenth centuries), and the warrior bands were referred to as *bushidan*. The term *bushi* refers to men of military background who specialized in martial arts and combat. The intention of the *bakufu* was to make archery, swordsmanship and horsemanship – the major martial skills of the warrior class – the exclusive attribute of those of *bushi* status.[35] A mounted *bushi* was supposed to supply the services of his *matamono* (personal retainers) to his *daimyo* as a military duty in compensation for the fief that he received from the *daimyo*. The number of *matamono* that the *bushi* was expected to supply was determined by the size of the fief/stipend he received.[36] The

---

[32] Stewart Gordon, 'Zones of Military Entrepreneurship in India, 1500–1700', in Gordon, *Marathas, Marauders, and State Formation in Eighteenth-Century India* (1994; reprint, New Delhi: Oxford University Press, 1998), p. 184.

[33] G. N. Sharma, 'Rajasthan', in Mohammad Habib and Khaliq Ahmad Nizami (eds.), *A Comprehensive History of India*, vol. 5, Part II, *The Delhi Sultanate: 1206–1526* (1970; reprint, New Delhi: People's Publishing House, 2000), p. 783.

[34] R. K. Saxena, 'The Mughal and Rajput Armies', in S. N. Prasad (ed.), *Historical Perspectives of Warfare in India: Some Morale and Materiel Determinants* (New Delhi: Centre for Studies in Civilizations, 2002), p. 303.

[35] Susumu Ishi, 'The Formation of *Bushi* Bands (*Bushidan*)', in Kleinschmidt (ed.), *Warfare in Japan*, pp. 77–9.

[36] Shosaku Takagi, '"Hideyoshi's Peace" and the Transformation of the *Bushi* Class – The Dissolution of the Autonomy of the Medieval *Bushi*', in Kleinschmidt (ed.), *Warfare in Japan*, pp. 126–7.

168 Hinduism and the Ethics of Warfare in South Asia

Kamakura Shogunate (1192–1333) placed the landholding professional warriors (*bushi/Samurai*) above the commoners (*bonge*). Ultimately, the *bushi* evolved from being a class of professional warriors in the service of the central government to become a group of provincial lords.[37]

The mounted troops of Western Europe were known as *milites* (knights). By 1400, a small proportion of the mounted troops were knighted, and they constituted an elite group.[38] Until the fifteenth century, in Western Europe, the armies were comprised of lords leading their vassals. The vassals owed military service to their lords. Each lord was the chief of the lineage. A principality of an overlord was comprised of several lineages. Claude Gaier notes that 'lineage' refers to a super-family grouping of all the individuals who claimed a common ancestor directly or by alliance. The members showed a solidarity that was strengthened by social equality and a convergence of interests.[39]

HINDU RESPONSE TO TURKISH DOMINATION

Pope Leo IV (847–55) and Pope John VIII (872–882) stated that those who died defending the church and Christendom would be granted absolution and receive heavenly rewards. Yuri Stoynov asserts that these notions gradually contributed to the development and eventual formalization of the Crusade idea and the sanctification of holy war by the Catholic Church. The Byzantine Church delegated the conceptualization and practice of warfare to the secular imperial government, trying on occasion to check unwarranted imperial demands such as rewarding holy military martyrdom. Wars were declared, led and conducted by the emperor, a secular and public authority entrusted to maintain the defence and unity of the imperial state. The conceptualization of Byzantine warfare was to a great extent a continuation of the Roman just war tradition, which meant defending the state and regaining lost territory. However, the late Roman just war tradition underwent Christianization during the Byzantine period. Constantinople became the New Rome, and the Christianized just war tradition became an integral part of the Byzantine imperial

---

[37] Kleinschmidt, 'Introduction', p. xviii.

[38] Michael Prestwich, '*Miles in Armis Strenuus*: The Knight at War', in France (ed.), *Medieval Warfare*, p. 185.

[39] Claude Gaier, 'Analysis of Military Forces in the Principality of Liege and the County of Looz from the Twelfth to the Fifteenth Century', in France (ed.), *Medieval Warfare*, pp. 105–6, 109.

Hindu Militarism under Islamic Rule 169

ideology.[40] The Byzantine just war ideology, which states that the purpose of all war is establishment of peace, is an older, secular idea. The notion that the purpose of all war is the establishment of peace was first introduced by Aristotle. However, the assumption that man is by nature peace-loving is a Christian idea. This contributed in part to the Byzantine idea that only defensive war is just. Angeliki E. Laiou claims that while Western Christendom developed a more open-ended idea of just war, based on Saint Augustine, that avenges injustice, the Byzantine just war concept of Emperor Leo VI was more defensive in nature, that is, the protection of territory invaded by the enemy. Leo VI did not advocate preventive war or preemptive strikes. Nor, unlike some of the medieval Western European commentators, did the Byzantine just war concept demand total extirpation of the pagans.[41] Again unlike the Western European clergy, the Byzantine clergy did not actually participate in battle.[42]

A holy war can be declared by a competent religious authority: the pope or the *Caliph*. The objective is religious: protection or recovery of sacred shrines or forced conversion. And those who participate in the holy war are promised a spiritual reward such as remission of their sins or assurance of a place in paradise.[43] The medieval Western world clearly differentiated between just war and holy war, but these two concepts were fused within the Hindu concept of *dharmayuddha*. T. M. Kolbaba asserts that if the combatants understood that the command of god can come through his human servants, then the Crusades could be categorized as holy wars.[44]

In Wink's view, the Ghaznavids launched annual *jihad*s against India and also forced many defeated rulers and their subjects to accept Islam.[45] Amira Sonbol asserts that *jihad* has the meaning of 'strive', while in the Quran, the word *qatilu* means fighting, going to war. After the death

[40] Yuri Stoyanov, 'Norms of War in Eastern Orthodox Christianity', in Vesselin Popovski, Gregory Reichberg and Nicholas Turner (eds.), *World Religions and Norms of War* (Tokyo: United Nations University Press, 2009), pp. 170, 178.

[41] Angeliki E. Laiou, 'On Just War in Byzantium', and George T. Dennis, 'Defenders of the Christian People: Holy War in Byzantium', in Haldon (ed.), *Byzantine Warfare*, pp. 31–3, 78.

[42] T. M. Kolbaba, 'Fighting for Christianity: Holy War in the Byzantine Empire', in Haldon (ed.), *Byzantine Warfare*, p. 63.

[43] George T. Dennis, 'Defenders of the Christian People: Holy War in Byzantium', in Haldon (ed.), *Byzantine Warfare*, p. 71.

[44] Kolbaba, 'Fighting for Christianity', p. 51.

[45] Wink, *Al-Hind*, vol. 2, pp. 111–24.

170   *Hinduism and the Ethics of Warfare in South Asia*

of the Prophet Muhammad, the *hadith* literature (oral traditions relating to the words and deeds of the Prophet Muhammad) expanded the meaning of war and the reasons to wage just war. The *hadith* literature referred to *jihad* as a means of waging war. The *hadith*s conveyed the message that *jihad* was to be waged against the unbelievers until they accepted Islam. One of the duties of *jihad* was to convert *dar al Harb* into *dar al Islam*. During the thirteenth century, the sufis and some theologians divided *jihad* into greater *jihad* (a spiritual form of *jihad* of the self) and lesser *jihad* (holy war against Islam's enemies).[46] John Kelsay writes that the Prophet Muhammad had a concept of just war. A war is just in his eyes when there is a just cause and the presence of righteous intention, and when the war is directed by a legitimate authority. Further, in the paradigm of just war of Al Shaybani (died 804 CE), a thinker of the early Hanafi School, in a just war non-combatants are immune from harm.[47]

Rajat Datta warns that despite the many syncretic and inclusionist dimensions of medieval Indian cultures, for the Turkish conquerors and their ideologues Hindustan was a land of *kufr* (infidels).[48] During the first half of the sixteenth century, when the Mughals and the Afghans fought each other in north and east India, they did not use the term *jihad*. The term *jihad* was used only during campaigns against the Rajputs.[49] Before the Battle of Khanwa (1527) against Rana Sangram Singh, Babur gave the call for *jihad*.[50] The army of an Islamic ruler fighting the Hindus was known as *lashkar-i-Islam* (the army of Islam) and any campaign (i.e., offensive or defensive) for suppressing rebellious Rajput chieftains or to capture new Rajput territories was given the sanction of being a *jihad*.[51]

Datta continues that with the exception of Akbar (emperor from 1565 to 1605) in his later years, the Mughals were devout Muslims,

---

[46] Amira Sonbol, 'Norms of War in Sunni Islam', in Popovski, Reichberg and Turner (eds.), *World Religions and Norms of War*, pp. 282–98.

[47] John Kelsay, 'Al-Shaybani and the Islamic Law of War', *Journal of Military Ethics*, vol. 2, no. 1 (2003), pp. 69, 72.

[48] Rajat Datta, 'Introduction: Indian History from Eighth to Eighteenth Centuries: Problems, Perspectives, and Possibilities', in Datta (ed.), *Rethinking a Millennium: Perspectives on Indian History from the Eighth to the Eighteenth Centuries, Essays for Harbans Mukhia* (New Delhi: Aakar, 2008), p. 4.

[49] Aquil, *Sufism, Culture, and Politics*, p. 65.

[50] R. K. Saxena, 'Islamic and Rajput War: Concepts and Strategies', in Prasad (ed.), *Historical Perspectives of Warfare in India*, p. 286.

[51] Aquil, *Sufism, Culture and Politics*, p. 218.

and the demands of Islam loomed large in the governance of a country where the majority of subjects were non-Muslims.[52] The *shariat* (Islamic law) did not entirely replace secular or customary law. The Muslim rulers were expected to maintain a delicate balance between the two. Publicly, the Muslim rulers declared respect and adherence to the *shariat*. The rulers rushed to the Sufis during the succession crises for blessings and prayer.[53] Raziuddin Aquil and Sunil Kumar question the very concept of liberal Sufis functioning as bridge builders between the Hindu and Muslim communities, in contrast to the orthodox *ulemas*.[54] The Sufis were interested in conversion.[55] Aquil concentrates on the fourteenth-century chronicler and political theorist Khwaja Ziya al-Din Barani. Barani praised Sultan Mahmud, whose objective in the former's eye was to destroy the Hindu religion. Barani noted that it is incumbent upon a good sultan to wage *jihad*. Barani advocated that 2–300,000 Brahmins be killed and that the rest of the Hindus be given the option of either death or Islam.[56] However, Barani also realized the distinction between what was ideal and what was real. He noted that total annihilation of the opponents and of the *shariat* was not possible. At best, the Hindus could be oppressed, disgraced and barred from high offices as they, in his eyes, posed a grave threat to Islam.[57] Aquil continues that Barani was no lone fanatic. His contemporaries and near-contemporaries like Sayyid Ali Hamadani and Fakhr-i Mudabbir offered similar formulations.[58] The *ulemas* functioned as paid servants of the state. They generally interpreted the *shariat* to suit the policies of the sultan. They were employed in the administration as religious advisors and judges in order to project the image among Muslim subjects that the polity was an Islamic state. They also legitimized the ruler's campaigns against non-Muslim chieftains by characterizing them as *jihad*.[59]

[52] Rajat Datta, 'Harbans Mukhia: A Historian's Journey through a Millennium', in Datta (ed.), *Rethinking a Millennium*, p. 372.

[53] Aquil, *Sufism, Culture and Politics*, pp. 118, 180.

[54] Sunil Kumar, 'Politics, the Muslim Community and Hindu-Muslim Relations Reconsidered: North India in the Early Thirteenth Century', in Datta (ed.), *Rethinking a Millennium*, pp. 139–67.

[55] Aquil, *Sufism, Culture, and Politics*, p. 166.

[56] Raziuddin Aquil, 'On Islam and *Kufr* in the Delhi Sultanate: Towards a Reinterpretation of Ziya al-Din Barani's *Fatawa-i Jahandari*', in Datta (ed.), *Rethinking a Millennium*, pp. 169–79.

[57] Aquil, *Sufism, Culture and Politics*, p. 120.

[58] Aquil, 'On Islam and *Kufr* in the Delhi Sultanate', p. 180.

[59] Aquil, *Sufism, Culture, and Politics*, p. 122.

172   *Hinduism and the Ethics of Warfare in South Asia*

Many Hindu and Muslim soldiers after leaving military service became ascetics. In fact, many ascetic orders of both communities were militarized. Medieval society believed in the paranormal power of religious disciples. Several Sufis at various times also wore military uniforms. A large number of Sufi saints participated in the *lashkar-i-Islam*, either as soldiers equipped with swords or by providing moral support and legitimacy. Further, the *barkat* of the presence of the Sufis strengthened the motivational spirit of the Muslim soldiers.[60] W. G. Orr asserts that Hindu ascetic orders became militarized in response to the Islamic intrusion. The Islamic armies brought with them a large number of religious adventurers like *faqir*s and *dervishe*s (Islamic holy men) equipped with spears and battle axes. They roamed throughout Hindustan, murdering and pillaging at will. In response, the *yogi*s (Hindu ascetics) and the Naths (followers of Goraknath) also took to arms in order to save themselves.[61] It would be wrong to argue that militarist Hindu ascetics emerged only in response to the intrusion of Islam. Even before the advent of the Muslims on the subcontinent, Hindu militant monks were active. Bana's *Harsacharita*, composed before the entry of Islam into South Asia, tells us that Hindu monks from Thaneshwar in north India participated in warfare. These ascetics did not renounce the world but indulged in sex, gained political power, amassed wealth and worshipped *shakti* (violence, destruction). Nevertheless, the advent of Islam in South Asia radicalized the situation and resulted in the emergence of a larger number of more aggressive Hindu monks. The *guru*s trained their *chela*s (retainers) at the *akhara*s. The militarist *sadhu*s (Hindu saints) were equipped with swords, bows, arrows, *charka*s (throwing discs with sharp pointed spikes) and, during the late medieval era, even with handguns.[62] The Naga *sanyasis*, who excelled as wrestlers and swordsmen, made use of *bhang*, opium and intoxicating liquors before attacking the enemy.[63] At times, temples were used as defensive fortifications. Kalhana, in *Rajatarangini*, notes: 'As the [refugees] stayed in the temple courtyard which was protected by massive wooden ramparts and gates, the assailants could neither capture nor kill them.'[64]

---

[60] Ibid., pp. 105, 196, 218.

[61] W. G. Orr, 'Armed Religious Ascetics in Northern India', in Gommans and Kolff (eds.), *Warfare and Weaponry in South Asia*, pp. 186–7.

[62] William R. Pinch, *Warrior Ascetics and Indian Empires* (Cambridge: Cambridge University Press, 2006), pp. 59, 116, 207, 211, 255.

[63] Orr, 'Armed Religious Ascetics in Northern India', p. 197.

[64] *Kalhana's Rajatarangini*, vol. 2, Book 8, no. 974, p. 77.

Hindu Militarism under Islamic Rule 173

David N. Lorenzen writes that around 600 CE, a corpus of myths about the gods and goddesses, codified in the epics (*Ramayana* and *Mahabharata*) and in the early *Purana*s, was completed. All the Hindu movements after this date were based on *bhakti* and, at least in their initial stages, were led by poet saints who sang songs and recited stories about these gods and goddesses.[65] According to Sheldon Pollock, the Hindu kings of the last thousand years commissioned a large number of dramas and other forms of narrative on the Rama theme in Sanskrit, Prakrit and other regional languages.[66] In Merutunga's *Prabandhachintamani* of 1304 CE and in Jayanaka's *Prithvirajavijaya*, written between 1178 and 1193 CE, King Jayasima Siddharaja of Gujarat (1094–1143 CE) and King Prithviraja Chauhan of Ajmer (died 1193 CE) are identified with Rama and their Turkish opponents with Rama's demon opponents.[67] Aziz Ahmad asserts that *Prithvirajavijaya*, composed between 1178 and 1200 CE, accuses the Muslims of oppressing the Brahmins and confiscating the charity lands granted to them.[68] Rama is presented in these works as a righteous ruler with a curved bow (the composite bow used effectively by the Turkish cavaliers against the Rajputs?) and Ravana as the arch-villain who makes the world weep and fills the earth with terror.[69] The Sisodiya Rana Jagat Singh (ruled 1638–52) commissioned an illustrated *Ramayana* under the direction of the artist Sahib Din. In this work, Ravana and his entourage are depicted in Mughal-style tents.[70]

Brajadulal Chattopadhyaya cautions that the popularity of the concepts of Rama and *Ramrajya* were not merely a reaction to Muslim invasions but part of a wider historical process that started during the post-Gupta era. Large Hindu kingdoms tried to legitimize kingship and authority over the non-sedentary tribal people using the ideological constructs of Rama and *Ramrajya*.[71] Suvira Jaiswal claims that the Rama cult became popular in north India during the fifth and sixth centuries CE. The Chola rulers, after gaining victories during the ninth and

---

[65] David N. Lorenzen, 'Introduction', in Lorenzen (ed.), *Religious Movements in South Asia, 600–1800* (2004; reprint, New Delhi: Oxford University Press, 2006), pp. 16–17.

[66] Sheldon Pollock, '*Ramayana* and Political Imagination in India', in Lorenzen (ed.), *Religious Movements in South Asia*, p. 155.

[67] Lorenzen, 'Introduction', p. 30.

[68] Ahmad, 'Epic and Counter-Epic in Medieval India', p. 473.

[69] Pollock, '*Ramayana* and Political Imagination in India', p. 157.

[70] Catherine B. Asher, 'Excavating Communalism: Kachhwaha *Rajadharma* and Mughal Sovereignty', in Datta (ed.), *Rethinking a Millennium*, p. 229.

[71] Brajadulal Chattopadhyaya, 'Anachronism of Political Imagination', in Lorenzen (ed.), *Religious Movements in South Asia*, pp. 209–26.

tenth centuries, constructed Rama temples. The Rama cult was designed to suppress the Sudras and to maintain the dominant position of the Brahmins. During the fifteenth and the sixteenth centuries, the Rama cult became popular among different regional language groups due to the spread of the *bhakti* movement.[72] Protest occurred not only against Islam but also against the spread of brahmanism. For instance, the massive social following of Virasaivism in Deccan was actually a protest against the *varna* hierarchy and the economic and social dominance of the Brahmins.[73]

In a similar vein, Romila Thapar criticizes scholars who have posited two monolithic religions, Hinduism and Islam, coming face to face during the second millennium CE. Thapar says that the people of India did not perceive the new arrivals as a homogeneous community going by the name 'Muslim'. The terms used by the Indians to describe the outsiders were *Turuska*s, *mlechcha*s (unclean) and *yavana*s. The term *yavana*s, derived form the word *yona* (referring to the Ionians/Greeks), was also used after the beginning of the Common Era to refer to the Greeks who invaded India from Bactria.[74] K. M. Shrimali says that in Indian literature, the term *mlechcha*s is used to designate indigenous tribes, the Sudras as well as foreigners.[75] Thapar continues that India before the invasion of Islam did not comprise one single Hindu religion. Rather, Indian society was an amalgam of various sects and cults with beliefs and rituals ranging from atheism to animism.[76] Richard M. Eaton writes that it was customary for a victorious Hindu king to desecrate the temple containing the state deity of the defeated enemy ruler.[77] Hence, it was not only the Muslim rulers who desecrated temples. Some of the Hindu kingdoms were indeed multi-religious entities. Kalhana's *Rajatarangini* tells us that in the first half of the twelfth century, in Kashmir, both the Buddhists and the Saivas were given royal patronage.[78]

[72] Suvira Jaiswal, 'Social Dimensions of the Cult of Rama', in Irfan Habib (ed.), *Religion in Indian History* (New Delhi: Tulika Books, 2007), pp. 71–101.

[73] Chattopadhyaya, 'Introduction', p. 20.

[74] Romila Thapar, 'Imagined Religious Communities? Ancient History and the Modern Search for a Hindu Identity', in Lorenzen (ed.), *Religious Movements in South Asia*, pp. 348–9.

[75] K. M. Shrimali, 'Religions in Complex Societies: The Myth of the "Dark Age"', in Habib (ed.), *Religion in Indian History*, p. 66.

[76] Thapar, 'Imagined Religious Communities?', p. 354.

[77] Richard M. Eaton, 'From Kalyana to Talikota: Culture, Politics, and War in the Deccan, 1542–65', in Datta (ed.), *Rethinking a Millennium*, p. 104.

[78] *Kalhana's Rajatarangini*, vol. 2, p. 9.

Hindu Militarism under Islamic Rule 175

Politics as well as religion determined state policies at various times. For instance, while the Shia Persian ruler Shah Tahmasp I gave refuge to Babur's son Humayun (who had been driven out by the Afghan warlord-turned-ruler Sher Shah), Sher Shah tried to conclude an alliance with the Sunni Ottoman Empire.[79] During the first half of the twelfth century, catapults were used in siege warfare in Kashmir. And Muslim military mercenaries were utilized by the Hindu kings of Kashmir, when campaigning against the rebels.[80] M. Habib writes that during the twelfth century, the Hindu rulers of north India employed Muslim mechanics skilled in manufacturing and operating *manjaniq*s (catapults).[81] Among the Muslim scholars who settled in India during the medieval era, the notion of India as a country with a composite culture gradually evolved. M. Athar Ali writes that Isami (who wrote during the mid fourteenth century) used the word *Hindian*, meaning *Hindis*, which included both the Hindus and the Muslims settled in India.[82] In the history of the medieval world, there are numerous instances of mercenary soldiers belonging to one religion taking service with monarchs belonging to another religion. For instance, the Latin mercenaries between the eleventh and thirteenth centuries took service with the Muslim monarchs of the Middle East and even with the Mongols. Simultaneously, large-scale warfare (Crusades) also occurred among the Muslim polities and the Latin states of the Middle East.[83] Overall, despite some Muslims serving with the Rajput monarchs, there was serious tension between the Muslims and the Hindus, as portrayed in medieval poems like *Prithvirajavijayamahakavya*.

PRITHVIRAJAVIJAYAMAHAKAVYA AND *RAJATARANGINI*: TWO TALES OF RAJPUT HEROISM AND VALOUR

In medieval Sanskrit literature, the genre known as *charita*s represents historical *kavya*s (poems). These *kavya*s were written by the elites and

---

[79] Naim R. Farooqi, 'Moguls, Ottomans, and the Pilgrims: Protecting the Routes to Mecca in the Sixteenth and Seventeenth Centuries', *International History Review*, vol. 10, no. 2 (1988), p. 202.

[80] *Kalhana's Rajatarangini*, vol. 2, pp. 132, 175.

[81] M. Habib, 'The Urban Revolution in Northern India', in Gommans and Kolff (eds.), *Warfare and Weaponry in South Asia*, p. 54.

[82] M. Athar Ali, 'The Perception of India in Akbar and Abu'l Fazl', in Irfan Habib (ed.), *Akbar and His India* (1997; reprint, New Delhi: Oxford University Press, 2002), pp. 216–17.

[83] Jean Richard, 'An Account of the Battle of Hattin referring to the Frankish Mercenaries in Oriental Moslem States', in France (ed.), *Medieval Warfare*, pp. 56–9.

176   Hinduism and the Ethics of Warfare in South Asia

for the elites. They highlight the exploits of the princely patrons of the poets and the patrons' immediate princely predecessors. A shortcoming of such poems is their panegyrical character. Since the poets were dependent on princely patronage, the poems do not recount the limitations of the poets' patrons. While Kalhana's *Rajatarangini* offers a connected narrative of the various dynasties that ruled Kashmir from the dawn of civilization until Kalhana's time, *Prithvirajavijayamahakavya* focuses on one particular king, the poet Jayanaka's patron. For the earlier period, Kalhana depends on legends and myths, and for the later history period of Kashmir, he uses written records. Kalhana was the son of a great Brahmin Kashmiri minister, Lord Canpaka. Canpaka was *dvarapati* (literal meaning, 'lord of the gate'), which means commandant of the frontier defence. Kalhana completed his work around 1148–9 CE; his patron was King Harsa (ruled 1089–1101 CE; not to be confused with Harsa Vardhana of Kanauj, the patron of the poet Bana). Both Kalhana and his father were Saivaites (worshippers of Lord Shiva and followers of Saivism). In Kalhana's paradigm, unfolding separate events are not phenomena to be traced back to respective causes but rather illustrate the religious, moral and legal maxims that together constitute *dharma*. Kalhana claims that the performance of both a 'nation' and an individual is dependent on *punya* (spiritual merit) gathered from previous births. Kalhana also emphasizes the importance of fate in shaping the course of history.[84] Both the *Rajatarangini* and the *Prithvirajavijayamahakavya* highlight the heroism and bravery of the Rajputs.

Prithvirajavijayamahakavya is comprised of 1,067 *slokas*. The poet Jayanaka (a Kashmiri) in this poem highlights the defeat of Muhammad Ghori (the ruler of Ghor in Afghanistan) by Prithviraja III Chauhan (the hero of the poem) in the First Battle of Tarain (1191 CE). However, Jayanaka does not mention the defeat of Prithviraja at the hands of Muhammad Ghori in the Second Battle of Tarain (1192 CE),[85] just as Bana in *Harsacharita* does not describe the defeat of his patron, Harsa of Kanauj, at the hands of the other potentates. The defeat of Prithviraja in the Second Battle of Tarain was important as Muslim victory in this battle led to the establishment of Ghorid rule. According to

---

[84] *Kalhana's Rajatarangini*, vol. 1, Introduction, pp. 3–4, 6–8, 18, 35–6.
[85] *Prithvirajavijayamahakavya, Aithihasik o Kavyik Parikrama*, by Sanjit Bhattacharya [in Bengali] (Kolkata: Asiatic Society, 2003), *Bhumika*, pp. 9–10, *Ditiya Adhaya*, p. 15. All translations from Bengali are by the author.

Jayanaka, between the tenth and the fourteenth centuries the Chauhans (or Chahamanas), from their capital at Ajmir, fought the Muslim invaders with the last drop of their blood. The early Chahamana rulers – including Arnoraja, Vigraharaja IV, Baghbhata, Hamira, Sathaldeva, and Kahurdeva – fought the Ghaznavid sultans. Prithviraja continued this tradition by fighting the Ghorids. In fact, *Maharajadhiraj* Arnoraja extended the boundary of his kingdom to Sind and the Saraswati River in the west and to Haryana in the north. Jayanaka writes that the blood of the dead Turkish soldiers reddened the soil of Ajmir, and the city celebrated Arnoraja's victory.[86]

Prithviraja ascended to the throne in 1177 CE. His chief secretary was the Rajput Kadambasa, who was also the *jagirdar* of south-east Punjab. Prithviraja III's realm extended from Thaneswar in the north to Mewar in the south.[87] During the twelfth and thirteenth centuries, the Nagda-Ahar lineages of the Guhilas created the Rajput state of Mewar.[88] Initially, when Prithviraja was young, Kadambasa maintained the kingdom through wisdom. Gradually, Prithviraja became skilled in both *sastra* (vedic *dharma*) and *astra-sastra* (weapons). Jayanaka writes that in order to maintain the brahmanical social order, Prithviraja send soldiers to different corners of his kingdom. The Brahmins chanted vedic *sloka*s under the protection of Prithviraja.[89] Prithviraja was not merely a skilled warlord but also a patron of the arts and literature. His court poets, besides Jayanaka, included Vidyapati Gaur, Baghisar Janardhana, and Biswarup. Jayanaka depicts Prithviraja as the incarnation of Vishnu.[90] The Chauhan inscriptions use the word *matanga* or *mlechcha*s, while Jayanaka uses the work *Turuskas* to designate the Turks. At times, Jayanaka uses the term 'Garjan *matanga*s' to designate the Ghaznavid Turks who were defeated by Ajoyraja Chauhan in 1112 CE.[91]

In Kashmir, Harsa or (Harsa-deva) plundered many temples and destroyed several idols. According to Kalhana, nemesis overtook him.[92] The various Rajput clans fought against each other. Due to the heavy fiscal extractions required for maintaining a luxurious court and for

---

[86] *Prithvirajavijayamahakavya, Ditiya Adhaya*, p. 11.
[87] *Prithvirajavijayamahakavya, Ditiya Adhaya*, p. 12, *Chaturtha Adhaya*, p. 93.
[88] Chattopadhyaya, 'Introduction', in p. 22.
[89] *Prithvirajavijayamahakavya, Chaturtha Adhaya*, pp. 93–4.
[90] *Prithvirajavijayamahakavya, Ditiya Adhaya*, pp. 13, 16.
[91] *Prithvirajavijayamahakavya, Tritiya Adhaya*, pp. 45, 49.
[92] R. K. Parmu, 'Kashmir: 1320–1586', in Habib and Nizami (eds.), *The Delhi Sultanat*, p. 735.

178   *Hinduism and the Ethics of Warfare in South Asia*

suppression of the *damara*s (landowning class) by the crown, the *damara*s rebelled under the leadership of the brothers Uccala and Sussala, two relatives of King Harsa of Kashmir of the Lohara Dynasty. Harsa was defeated in the struggle and subsequently murdered. A *dharmik* king, warns Kalhana, should avoid heavy fiscal exploitation of his subjects, as it might cause rebellion. And ill-gotten wealth should be distributed, especially among the Brahmins, in order to strengthen *dharma* in the realm. This assertion is in tune with Manu and Kamandaka's dictum. The king should maintain peace with the Rajput clans in his kingdom, writes Kalhana, by judiciously distributing administrative posts among the various Rajput clans.[93] Jayanaka also gives instances of *dharmayuddha* conducted by the *dharmik* Rajput kings. In 1151 CE, Vigraharaja defeated the Tomara Rajputs, occupied Indraprastha (Delhi) and made the Tomaras subordinate feudatories. The inscriptions issued by the Rajputs show that the Rajput rulers considered north India to be part of the *Aryavarta*.[94] For the Rajputs, internecine warfare was at times more important than fighting the Turks. The Rajputs indulged in raids for the purpose of stealing princesses from neighbouring Rajput polities.[95] A pan-Indian Rajput consciousness was probably not that strong. Prithviraja, on the advice of Kadambasa, remained neutral when Muhammad Ghori attacked the Chalukya ruler of Gujarat, Raja Bhimdeva. This was due to the ongoing Chalukya-Chauhan rivalry.[96] In 1178 CE, the *Rai* of Gujarat was able to defeat Muhammad Ghori.[97] When Muhammad Ghori occupied Nadol, Prithviraja III declared war against him.[98] The result was the two battles of Tarain.

ETHICS OF RAJPUT WARFARE

Fighting was the favourite game of the Rajputs, and they emphasized loyalty, devotion, valour, chivalry and death-defying rashness on the battlefield.[99] Before starting a battle, the Rajput chiefs consulted the

---

[93] *Kalhana's Rajatarangini*, vol. 1, Introduction, pp. 15, 36, 38.
[94] *Prithvirajavijayamahakavya, Tritiya Adhaya*, p. 63.
[95] Somadeva Bhatta, *Kathasaritsagara*, tr. by Hirendralal Biswas, Introduction by Sudhansghmohan Bandopadhyay (1981; reprint, Kolkata: Academic Publisher, 1982), vol. 5, *Pratham o Ditiya Taranga*, pp. 3–29. The *Kathasaritsagara* uses the term *Aryaputra*s, which is equivalent to Rajputs. All translations by the author.
[96] *Prithvirajavijayamahakavya, Chaturtha Adhaya*, p. 102.
[97] Habib, 'The Urban Revolution in Northern India', p. 55.
[98] *Prithvirajavijayamahakavya, Chaturtha Adhaya*, p. 101.
[99] Saxena, 'Islamic and Rajput War: Concepts and Strategies', p. 287.

Hindu *Militarism under Islamic Rule*

soothsayers.[100] The ideal of chivalry was an essential ingredient of the Rajput *Kshatradharma*. The bards fostered the growth of chivalrous literature. The chivalrous ethos emphasized the vanity of personal valour at the cost of neglecting policy and expediency.[101] The Rajputs emphasized single combat for the display of individual bravery rather than collective training to maneuver as a body on the battlefield.[102] Just before the Second Battle of Tarain, Muhammad Ghori launched a night attack and harried Prithviraja's army as it was retreating.[103] All these techniques in the Rajput paradigm of warfare comprised *kutayuddha*. John France claims that the culture of military individualism among the knights encouraged displays of personal courage on the battlefield rather than planning and strategy.[104] Like the Rajputs, the knights of Western Europe never stooped to employ stratagems but went straight ahead regardless of consequences. Exhibition of individual prowess rather than tactical finesse characterized the knights' behaviour in battle.[105] Rather than collective training, the knights, like the Rajputs, emphasized individual strength and stamina.[106]

The *bushi*'s ethical ideals of warfare were known as *budo*, which later came to be known as *bushido*.[107] Kenneth Dean Butler asserts that theorists like Yamaga Soko gave the finishing touch to the *bushido* code during the Tokugawa period in the seventeenth century.[108] However, the origins of the various elements that constituted the *bushido* code can be traced back much earlier. While *Kshatradharma* was derived from Hinduism, the ideology of the *bushi* was influenced by the Zen Buddhist tradition of 'mind-to-mind transmission' and Neo-Confucianism. Karl F. Friday notes the influence of Confucianism's infatuation with ritual and ritualized action. The Confucian assumption is that through action and practice, man fashions the conceptual frameworks that he uses to order

---

[100] R. K. Saxena, 'Appendix 2, The Battle of Tunga, 1787', in Prasad (ed.), *Historical Perspectives of Warfare in India*, p. 373.

[101] B. N. S. Yadava, 'Chivalry and Warfare', in Gommans and Kolff (eds.), *Warfare and Weaponry in South Asia*, pp. 66, 68.

[102] *Kalhana's Rajatarangini*, vol. 2, p. 16.

[103] Jackson, *The Delhi Sultanate*, p. 16.

[104] John France, 'Crusading Warfare and Its Adaptation to Eastern Conditions in the Twelfth Century', in France (ed.), *Medieval Warfare*, p. 456.

[105] Timothy S. Miller, 'Introduction', in Haldon (ed.), *Byzantine Warfare*, p. 7.

[106] Prestwich, '*Miles in Armis Strenuus*', p. 197.

[107] G. Cameron Hurst III, 'From Heiho to Bugei: The Emergence of the Martial Arts in Tokugawa Japan', in Klenschmidt (ed.), *Warfare in Japan*, p. 188.

[108] Kenneth Dean Butler, 'The *Heike Monogatari* and the Japanese Warrior Ethic', in Kleinschmidt (ed.), *Warfare in Japan*, p. 295.

and thereby comprehend the chaos or raw experience of life. Ritual is stylized action, sequentially structured, that leads those who follow it to wisdom. Those who seek knowledge and truth, then, must carefully cultivate the right kind of experience if they are to achieve the right kind of understanding. For the early Confucians, whose main interest was the proper ordering of state and society, this meant habitualizing themselves to the codes of what they saw as the perfect political organization. For *bugei* (school of traditional arts) students, it meant ritualized duplication of the acts of the past masters. Neo-Confucianism emphasized understanding the abstract through the concrete and the necessity of unifying knowledge and action.[109] The *bushi* fought for honour. Each military unit was identified by a bannerman selected for his bravery. These men proved to be targets of the enemy soldiers on the battlefield. The banners fostered a sense of group identity and were invested with emotional value. The warriors would attack rashly to retrieve lost flags on the battlefield. The display of individual prowess was the credo of the *bushi* just as it was for the knights and the Rajputs. Prior to the fourteenth century, the *bushi* warriors were praised for securing as many heads as possible by decapitating enemy soldiers.[110]

The core of the Rajput army was comprised of cavalry. Horses were symbols of prestige and position.[111] The troopers wore armour and helmets, and the horses were caparisoned with steel plates for the protection of their heads. By the fourteenth century, plate armour was used.[112] The *khanda* was central to the Rajput martial culture. When a young Rajput male was considered old enough to bear arms, he went through the ceremony of *kharg bandai*. The Rajputs worshipped swords because they believed that Visvakarma, the Hindu god in charge of making weapons, made the swords.[113] As the need for mounted archery diminished, swordsmanship became the primary martial art practiced by the warriors

---

[109] Karl F. Friday, 'Kabala in Motion: Kata and Pattern Practice in the Traditional Bugei', in Kleinschmidt (ed.), *Warfare in Japan*, pp. 202–3.

[110] Thomas Conlan, 'The Nature of Warfare in Fourteenth-Century Japan: The Record of Nomoto Tomoyuki', in Kleinschmidt (ed.), *Warfare in Japan*, pp. 316, 322–3.

[111] Norman P. Ziegler, 'Evolution of the Rathor State of Marvar: Horses, Structural Change and Warfare', in Karine Schomer, Joan L. Erdman, Deryck O. Lodrick and Lloyd I. Rudolph (eds.), *The Idea of Rajasthan: Explorations in Regional Identity*, vol. 2, *Institutions* (New Delhi: Manohar and American Institute for Indian Studies, 1994), p. 194.

[112] Ravindra Kumar Sharma, 'The Military System of the Mewar (Udaipur) State (ca. 800 to 1947 AD)', *Central Asiatic Journal*, vol. 30 (1986), p. 124.

[113] Robert Elgood, *Hindu Arms and Rituals: Arms and Armour from India, 1400–1865* (Ahmedabad: Mapin, 2004), p. 107.

Hindu Militarism under Islamic Rule

181

in Tokugawa Japan, especially during the seventeenth century. The idea that the sword is the soul of the *Samurai* became prevalent in medieval Japan.[114] The knights of medieval Western Europe also preferred to fight close-quarter combat with straight double-edged swords suitable for hacking and slashing.[115]

The knightly army was a loose structure comprised of the household retinues of the monarch and followers of the vassals.[116] Knights were rewarded by the crown with fiefs for military service. A military contingent under a Rajput chief was comprised of relatives (fathers, sons, uncles, nephews, etc.).[117] The Rajput soldiers were remunerated through land assignments. There were two types of assignments: patrimonial and prebendal. In the patrimonial domain, the kinship group inherits control over the land; in prebendal tenure, the assignment was issued to the soldier by the chief in return for military service.[118]

The Rajput chiefs employed *charan*s in their contingents. They motivated the soldiers by playing martial music during battles.[119] In the Kannada region, we find *viragal*s (commemorative stones) celebrating the heroism of men who died on the battlefield. The literature of the Hoysala period was marked by *vira-rasa* (heroic sentiment) that praises the men who sacrificed themselves for the king on the field of battle.[120] The *Rajatarangini* emphasizes the loyalty of vassals towards their lords.[121] Kalhana writes: 'Soldiers of noble race who had left their homes, as if in exultation, were carried away mutilated from the palace courts by their relatives.'[122] Kalhana continues: 'The two Rajaputras Sahadeva and Yudhistira there paid back in battle with their lives the debt [they owed] for their lord's favour.'[123] Those Rajput chiefs who betrayed their king and fought against him were designated as *dasyu*s by Kalhana.[124] It was

---

[114] Hurst III, 'From Heiho to Bugei', p. 190.

[115] Ian Pierce, 'Arms, Armour and Warfare in the Eleventh Century', in France (ed.), *Medieval Warfare*, p. 76.

[116] France, 'Crusading Warfare and Its Adaptation to Eastern Conditions in the Twelfth Century', p. 458.

[117] S. Inayat Ali Zaidi, 'Ordinary Kachawaha Troopers Serving the Mughal Empire: Composition and Structure of the Contingent of the Kachawaha Nobles', *Studies in History*, vol. 2, no. 1 (1980), p. 48.

[118] Ziegler, 'Evolution of the Rathor State of Marvar', p. 198.

[119] Zaidi, 'Rozindar Troopers under Sawai Jai Singh of Jaipur (AD 1700–1743)', p. 63.

[120] Deloche, *Military Technology in Hoysala Sculpture*, p. 38.

[121] *Kalhana's Rajatarangini*, vol. 2, p. 115.

[122] *Kalhana's Rajatarangini*, vol. 2, Book 8, no. 172, p. 16.

[123] *Kalhana's Rajatarangini*, vol. 2, Book 8, no. 198, p. 18.

[124] *Kalhana's Rajatarangini*, vol. 1, Introduction, p. 19.

182   Hinduism and the Ethics of Warfare in South Asia

believed that those who died on the battlefield were received into heaven by the *apsaras* (beautiful maidens).[125] Srivara, in *Zaina Rajatarangini*, writes: 'The Rajput princes ... laid down their lives in the sacrificial fire of the battlefield emitted by the war weapons making a bilva fruit of their body.'[126] The Rajputs conceived of battle as a sacrificial fire into which oblations in the form of dead soldiers were thrown. The bilva fruit is a favourite of Shiva (the god of destruction).

Jayanaka writes that while the duty of the Brahmins was to conduct *yagnas* and study the *vedas*, the duty of the Kshatriyas was to fight in order to protect the people. And the duty of the Sudras was to till the land.[127] This assertion was the same as that made by Manu in *Manava Dharmasastra*. In reality, the Brahmins occasionally took to arms. A Brahmin named Skand Nagar was the *Senapati* of Prithviraja III.[128] In Western Europe during the eleventh century, political theoreticians started talking about three orders of society: those who prayed (the bishops and the clergy), those who fought (the new knightly nobility), and those who worked (the peasants). The justification for the existence of the prerogatives of the nobility was its skill in the use of arms.[129] Nevertheless, several bishops and archbishops of Germany provided cavalry to the German Emperor Otto II.[130]

The Rajputs believed that to escape from the battlefield or to become a prisoner of war were fates worse than death. Their motto was victory or death on the battlefield.[131] During the battle with the Muslims, when the Rajputs found the battle going against them, they formed a death squad comprised of men armed with swords. When the Rajput forts were surrounded by the Muslims, the Rajput women performed *jauhar* (burning themselves on a pyre in order to prevent the enemy from dishonoring them), and the Rajput males came out to fight and die.[132] In 1296 CE, when Alauddin Khalji's (Delhi sultan from 1296 to 1316) army attacked Jaisalmer, 16,000 women committed *jauhar*, and Tilak Singh with 700

---

[125] *Kalhana's Rajatarangini*, vol. 2, p. 39.
[126] *Srivara's Zaina Rajatarangini*, English tr. and annotations by Kashi Nath Dhar (New Delhi: Indian Council of Historical Research and People's Publishing House, 1994), wave I, canto I, verse 155, p. 77.
[127] *Prithvirajavijayamahakavya, Sashtha Adhaya*, p. 119.
[128] Saxena, 'Mughal and Rajput Armies', p. 304.
[129] Miller, 'Introduction', p. 8.
[130] Gaier, 'Analysis of the Military Forces in the Principality of Liege and the County of Looz from the Twelfth to the Fifteenth Century', p. 113.
[131] *Prithvirajavijayamahakavya, Ditiya Adhaya*, p. 11.
[132] Aquil, *Sufism, Culture, and Politics*, pp. 152–3.

Hindu Militarism under Islamic Rule   183

of his clan members fell on the battlefield.[133] *Jauhar* was not performed during the internecine fighting among the Rajputs.

One of the most important duties of the Rajput king was to lead the army on the battlefield.[134] The duty of a *dharmik* king was to protect the kingdom and the subjects from external and internal enemies. Kalhana says that the duty of the king of Kashmir was to subjugate the 'unruly' non-Hindu hill tribes.[135] In 1179 CE, Prithviraja III led an army on the battlefield. Jayanaka writes that when Prithviraja participated in battle, he did not fear death. After gaining victory, Prithviraja returned all the wealth captured during the campaign to his defeated enemy.[136] This practice was in consonance with the code of *dharmayuddha*. Vigraharaja's campaigning against the Tomaras and then returning the kingdom to them is also an example of *dharmayuddha*. The objective of war in this paradigm becomes the display of heroism to prove one's manliness without resorting to fraud. The *Rajatarangini* notes the prevalence of *dharmayuddha* in Kashmir during the first half of the twelfth century: 'The king [Jayasimha, ruled 1128–49 CE], whose character was distinguished by its guileless generosity …. gave his own troops for his assistance [Somapala, who was driven out by his son Bhupala], and after humbling the pride of the enemy restored him to power.'[137] This was despite the fact that Somapala had previously proved to be disloyal to Jayasimha.

The Rajputs were influenced by neo-Vaishnavism, which focused on *bhakti*, that is, total devotion to god and lord.[138] Ramanuja in the eleventh century emphasized *bhakti* as the true path of knowledge and *karma*. During the thirteenth and fourteenth centuries, *bhakti* was emphasized as the only path to salvation and was addressed to the human incarnations of Vishnu, that is to Rama and Krishna. The cult of Rama *bhakti* was popularized by Ramanand in northern India during the fourteenth and fifteenth centuries.[139] From *bhakti*, the concept of *namak halali* (loyalty to the employer) was derived. One of the core values of the Rajputs

---

[133] R. K. Saxena, 'Medieval Forts, Logistics and Heraldry', in Prasad (ed.), *Historical Perspectives of Warfare in India*, p. 343.

[134] Sharma, 'The Military System of the Mewar (Udaipur) State (ca. 800 to 1947 AD)', p. 120.

[135] *Kalhana's Rajatarangini*, vol. 1, Introduction, pp. 37–8.

[136] *Prithvirajavijayamahakavya, Chaturtha Adhaya*, pp. 94–5.

[137] *Kalhana's Rajatarangini*, vol. 2, Book 8, nos. 2217–18, p. 171.

[138] Sharma, 'Rajasthan', p. 783.

[139] J. S. Grewal, *The New Cambridge History of India*, II:3, *The Sikhs of the Punjab* (1994; reprint, New Delhi: Foundation Books, 2002), p. 25.

184   *Hinduism and the Ethics of Warfare in South Asia*

was *namak halali*, that is, the soldier's obligation to fight to the death in return for eating the salt of his employer, that is, the overlord.[140] Like the Rajput code of honour, the Japanese warrior ethic emphasized the concepts of personal loyalty, a willingness to sacrifice one's life for one's lord and a determination to fight to an honourable death rather than surrendering to a superior foe.[141]

Dharmayuddha for the Rajputs was always defensive and never offensive and was geared to establishing hegemony rather than territorial annexation. Francisco de Vitoria (1492–1546), the Spanish Dominican, drawing on Thomas Aquinas's theory of just war, noted that enemy princes should not be deposed after each and every just war. The practice of the removal of the defeated enemy prince was reserved for the most extreme cases. Vitoria says that punishment should be reduced in favour of mercy, which was the rule not only of human law but also of natural law. So harm done by the enemy may be a sufficient cause for war, but it is not always sufficient to justify the extermination of the enemy kingdom and the deposition of its legitimate princes, which was considered altogether too savage and inhumane. Gregory M. Reichberg writes in an article that the mainstream just war theory in medieval Western Christendom did not permit the use of offensive force to forestall hostile acts if uncertainty remained as to the time and place of enemy attack. According to the postulates of the just war theory, offensive force is permissible only in reaction to a determinable wrongdoing.[142]

Several times during Sher Shah's (founder of the Suri Sultanate in north and central India) campaigns against the Rajputs in the 1540s, the former refused to take prisoners of war and executed all the Rajput males. Sher Shah gained legitimacy in the eyes of the Muslims by sending all the 'non-believers to hell'.[143] At least some medieval Western European Catholic Christian theologians conceived of just war as a sort of holy war that allowed forcible baptizing of unbelievers (Jews and Muslims).[144] This trend was completely absent in the medieval Rajput-Hindu discourse. The Muslims might be killed on the battlefield, but Muslim prisoners

---

[140] Gordon, 'Zones of Military Entrepreneurship in India', pp. 186–7.

[141] Butler, '*Heike Monogatari* and Warrior Ethic', p. 287.

[142] Gregory M. Reichberg, 'Preventive War in Classical Just War Theory', *Journal of the History of International Law*, vol. 9 (2007), pp. 15, 32–3.

[143] Aquil, *Sufism, Culture, and Politics*, pp. 154–5.

[144] Gregory M. Reichberg, 'Norms of War in Roman Catholic Christianity', in Popovski, Reichberg and Turner (eds.), *World Religions and Norms of War*, pp. 154–6.

could not be converted to Hinduism. Enslavement of non-Muslims during a military raid was accepted even in the Sufi literature of the thirteenth and the fourteenth centuries but became a matter of controversy during the fifteenth century,[145] due in part to the influence of non-Islamic philosophies. Vijayasena Suri, a Jain leader of Akbar's time, argued that Jain philosophy was very similar to the Samkhya philosophy of Hinduism. Vijayasena Suri advised Akbar that it is unjust to capture the personnel of the defeated party as prisoners of war after a battle.[146] The prisoners of war were sold as slaves. During 1562–3, Akbar prohibited the slave trade.[147]

GUNPOWDER AND HINDU MILITARY THEORIES

Let us now see how the various *nitisastras* of the Hindus tackled the issue of Muslim invasions and the use of gunpowder. The term *niti* is derived from the Sanskrit root word *ni*, meaning to lead, carry, bring forward, convey, guide. *Niti* therefore denotes guidance, right policy. *Nitisastras* are the ethics of statecraft.[148]

The Sanskrit word for gunpowder is *agnichurna*. The ingredients of gunpowder were easily available on the subcontinent. Saltpeter is found in Bengal. Especially after the rainy season, it is an efflorescence from the ground. The Sanskrit word for saltpeter is *suvarcilavana* (shining salt). Sulphur is found in Sind.[149] The *Nitiprakasika* (expounder of polity) contains eight *canto*s (chapters).[150] The author of the *Nitiprakasika* (composed around the sixteenth century) is probably Vaisampayana. Vaisampayana notes the importance of gunpowder. He speaks about *nalika*s (handguns) and the use of hand grenades. The latter were comprised of pots filled the with resin of the Sal tree, burning husks of corn, stones, iron spikes, and so on. Gustav Oppert opines that these smoke/fire bombs were used during

---

[145] M. Athar Ali, 'Elements of Social Justice in Medieval Islamic Thought', in Ali, *Mughal India: Studies in Polity, Ideas, Society and Culture* (New Delhi: Oxford University Press, 2006), p. 140.

[146] Pushpa Prasad, 'Akbar and the Jains', in Habib (ed.), *Akbar and His India*, p. 103.

[147] Ali, 'Elements of Social Justice in Medieval Islamic Thought', p. 140.

[148] Nand Kishore Acharya, *The Polity in Sukranitisara* (Bikaner: Vagdevi Prakashan, 1987), p. 13.

[149] Gustav Oppert, *On the Weapons, Army Organization, and Political Maxims of the Ancient Hindus, with Special Reference to Gunpowder and Firearms* (n.d.; reprint, Ahmedabad: New Order Book, 1967), p. 60.

[150] *Nitiprakasika*, ed. by Gustav Oppert (1882; reprint, New Delhi: Kumar Brothers, 1970), p. 4.

186 *Hinduism and the Ethics of Warfare in South Asia*

sieges.[151] The *Nitiprakasika* uses the term *surmi*, which can be translated as a blazing tube made of metal. Oppert translates *surmi* as a hollow tube. Another term used is *karnakavati*, which means a metallic cylinder with a hole inside, which could produce a blazing fire. The *Nitiprakasika* says that the *raksas* were destroyed by lead. Oppert opines that the *Nitiprakasika* is referring to leaden balls, which were fired from the hollow metallic cylinders with the aid of gunpowder.[152] However, Oppert's assertion that gunpowder was invented in India, long before its advocacy in Western Europe by Roger Bacon during the thirteenth century,[153] is untenable. The passages in the *Nitiprakasika* that refer to gunpowder and gunpowder weapons were definitely later additions, probably made during the later medieval period.

Srivara's *Zaina Rajatarangni*, which covers the history of Kashmir between 1459 and 1486 CE, mentions that ammunition balls and cartridges were manufactured by skilled artisans. Cannons were made of various metals cast together. Cannons were also imported from outside.[154] Some of the cannons were pulled by mules.[155] According to one author, Vijayanagara manufactured cannons as early as 1388 CE.[156] In 1442–3, the Sisodia clans among the Rajputs probably used cannons at Chitor against an invading army from Malwa.[157] In 1547, Rama Raya, the ruler of Vijayanagara, signed a treaty with the Portuguese for acquiring sulphur because gunpowder was required for fighting the Adil Shahi Sultanate.[158] One can conclude that during the thirteenth century the Mongols introduced gunpowder into north India from China.[159] And in south India, the Portuguese introduced gunpowder. In east India, gunpowder probably came from China via the overland route. The Afghans in Bengal before the entry of the Mughals used *ban*s (rockets) and not hand-held firearms.[160]

---

[151] Oppert, *On the Weapons, Army Organization, and Political Maxims of the Ancient Hindus*, pp. 32–3.

[152] *Nitiprakasika*, ed. by Oppert, pp. 11–12, 14.

[153] Oppert, *On the Weapons, Army Organization, and Political Maxims of the Ancient Hindus*, pp. 44–7.

[154] *Srivara's Zaina Rajatarangini*, wave I, canto I, verses 72–3, p. 37.

[155] *Srivara's Zaina Rajatarangini*, wave I, canto I, verse 75, p. 38.

[156] Elgood, *Hindu Arms and Ritual*, p. 51.

[157] Iqtidar Alam Khan, 'Early Use of Cannon and Musket in India: AD 1442–1526', in Gommans and Kolff (eds.), *Warfare and Weaponry in South Asia*, p. 336.

[158] Elgood, *Hindu Arms and Ritual*, p. 39.

[159] Iqtidar Alam Khan, 'Origin and Development of Gunpowder Technology in India: AD 1250–1500', *Indian Historical Review*, vol. 4, no. 1 (1977), p. 24.

[160] Khan, 'Early Use of Cannon and Musket in India', p. 328.

The *Sukranitisara* or *Sukraniti* was based on Kamandaka's *Nitisara*. We do not know any details about the author of *Sukranitisara*. In accordance with the tradition of Hindu classical writers, the author chose to remain anonymous by giving authorship to an ancient mythical *rishi*. The dating of the work is also uncertain. No ancient or medieval work refers to *Sukranitisara*. Nand Kishore Acharya writes that the council of ministers described in *Sukranitisara* bears a close resemblance to the Maratha King Shivaji's (died 1680) council of ministers. On the basis of this evidence, *Sukranitisara* could be placed between seventeenth and eighteenth centuries. However, *Sukranitisara* does not mention the *feranghis* (foreigners or Franks or Western Europeans). Hence, it must have been composed before the eighteenth century. The *Sukranitisara* discusses gunpowder. By the mid fifteenth century, gunpowder was used in India. The *Sukranitisara* (a practical guidebook for the ruler) was comprised of 2,500 *slokas*[161] and, combining elements of the earlier work of Sukracharya, was probably composed between the sixteenth and seventeenth centuries CE.

The *Sukranitisara* categorizes the Muslims as *yavanas*. It accepts the cardinal importance of the military in statecraft. The *Sukranitisara* says that 50 percent of the revenue of the state should be allocated to the army.[162] Krishnadevaraya, the ruler of the Vijayanagara Empire, ordered that 50 percent of the state's revenue be spent on the army.[163] Interestingly, the *Nitiprakasika* says that the king should take some of the bankers residing in his capital along with the army when campaigning. The *Nitiprakasika*, like the *Arthasastra*, emphasizes the importance of paying soldiers regularly in cash in order to motivate them to fight and die for their employer.[164] Here, one sees the connection between the bankers who financed warfare and the aggressive designs of a ruler.

The *Sukranitisara* states that a strong, just ruler is the incarnation of Vishnu.[165] It is to be noted that Jayanaka equates Prithviraja, his hero, with Vishnu. The *Sukranitisara* emphasizes two types of army: a standing army and a militia. The latter was raised during emergencies and functioned as a sort of second line of defence. The *Sukranitisara* introduces an organizational format for the army. In the *Sukranitisara*, the smallest unit of the army is the *patti*, which is comprised of five or six soldiers under a

---

[161] Acharya, *Polity in Sukranitisara*, pp. 13, 17, 18–20.
[162] Ibid., pp. 18, 161.
[163] Elgood, *Hindu Arms and Ritual*, p. 143.
[164] *Nitiprakasika*, ed. by Oppert, pp. 17, 26.
[165] Oppert, *On the Weapons, Army Organization, and Political Maxims of the Ancient Hindus*, p. 83.

188   *Hinduism and the Ethics of Warfare in South Asia*

chief known as a *pattipal*. The *Sukranitisara*'s *patti* (equivalent to a modern-day section) is thus different from the *Mahabharata*'s *patti,* which was comprised of fifty-five soldiers. Above the *pattipal,* the *Sukranitisara* mentions the *gaulmika,* the chief of thirty soldiers. A group of 100 soldiers is known as a *satanika* (equivalent to a company), and a group of over 1,000 soldiers is known as a *sahasrika* (equivalent to a battalion or regiment). The *ayutika* is the head of an *ayata,* a group of 10,000 soldiers (equivalent to a modern division).[166]

Vaisampayana writes that the efficiency of weapons depends on time and place. The effectiveness of a particular weapon also depends on the strength and skill of the user.[167] The importance of training and command is emphasized in the *Sukranitisara* in the following verses:

The efficient is eager for a good fight... the trained is clever in tactics....
One should increase the physical strength for pugilistic combat by diet and by athletic exercises and wrestling....
A king should always ... encourage bravery by tiger-hunts, by practice with weapons and arms....
He should keep up his military strength by good pay, but the strength of his weapons by ... practice.'[168]

While Thomas Aquinas differentiates between war (violence done by one independent nation against another) and sedition (violent acts committed against the internal order of a single nation),[169] the *Sukrantisara,* like Kautilya *Arthasastra,* fuses these two concepts. In the paradigm of *Sukranitisara,* the use of force for maintenance of the *varnasrama* society against internal rebellion or external invasion constitutes just war.[170] For both Kautilya and the *Sukranitisara, asurayuddha* is an extreme form of barbaric warfare. In the *Arthasastra, asurayuddha* means destruction of the enemy forces and annexation of the enemy kingdom. In such a war, the defeated ruler was executed, and his wives were violated, and his wealth was appropriated by the victor. Kalhana warns that a righteous king must follow the law of kings and should not exterminate members of the defeated royal family.[171] The *Sukranitisara* defines *asurayuddha* as a war fought mainly with mechanical devices (gunpowder

[166] Acharya, *Polity in Sukranitisara,* pp. 162, 165.
[167] Oppert, *On the Weapons, Army Organization, and Political Maxims of the Ancient Hindus,* p. 30.
[168] Quoted from ibid., pp. 84–5.
[169] Reichberg, 'Norms of War in Roman Catholic Chrisianity', p. 149.
[170] Acharya, *Polity in Sukranitisara,* pp. 203–4.
[171] *Kalhana's Rajatarangini,* vol. 2, p. 210.

Hindu Militarism under Islamic Rule 189

weapons?) and *manavayuddha* as one fought principally with hand-held weapons (swords, spears, etc.).[172] The mechanical devices that the *Sukranitisara* refers to might also include *maghribi*s (devices used for throwing stones, used in siege warfare), which were introduced into south India by Alauddin Khalji's general Malik Kafur.[173] Alauddin Khalji's forces tried unsuccessfully to mine the wall of Ranthambhor during 1299–1300 CE.[174] And in 1398 CE, Amir Timur used gunpowder for mining the Bhatnir fort.[175] Mining involved digging a hole near the wall of the fort and filling it with combustible materials. Then it was set on fire, which brought the wall down. The *Sukranitisara*'s concept of *asurayuddha* is thus different from that of Kautilya and Kalhana. In the *Sukranitisara*'s paradigm, *asurayuddha* becomes the most extreme form of warfare fought with 'barbaric' devices, that is, gunpowder and mechanical siege weapons. The *Sukranitisara* discusses various types of expeditions. The *sambhuya* expedition utilizes the forces of the feudatories. The *prasanga* expedition (involving guile and duplicity, hence a form of *kutayuddha*) begins against a particular enemy but proceeds against another enemy.[176]

In medieval south India, *virakkal* (commemorative hero stones) portraying dead warriors were made. A fifteenth-century hero stone, writes Robert Elgood, portrays an infantry soldier holding a sword like a dagger for stabbing the enemy.[177] The latter form of combat – that is, *manavayuddha* – is considered as more humane than *asurayuddha*. *Manavayuddha* is a sort of just war in *Sukranitisara*'s paradigm. The *nayaka*s (Hindu chieftains of south India) during the sixteenth century disdained firearms and guns. They regarded them as weapons of weaklings or cowards, for those who refused to face danger close-up. The *nayaka*s regarded swords and lances as honourable weapons, and death while fighting with such weapons, they believed, resulted in ascension to heaven. In south India the forest tribes, unlike the high caste *nayaka*s, adopted gunpowder weapons rapidly, and their leaders became powerful chieftains.[178] As regards medieval Japan, Shosaku Takagi writes that despite the effectiveness of

---

[172] Acharya, *Polity in Sukranitisara*, p. 170.
[173] Elgood, *Hindu Arms and Rituals*, p. 289.
[174] Saxena, 'Medieval Forts, Logistics and Heraldry', p. 341.
[175] Khan, 'Origin and Development of Gunpowder Technology in India', p. 21.
[176] Acharya, *Polity in Sukranitisara*, p. 172.
[177] Elgood, *Hindu Arms and Ritual*, p. 13.
[178] V. Narayana Rao, David Shulman and Sanjay Subrahmanyam, 'The Art of War under the Nayakas', in Gommans and Kolff (eds.), *Warfare and Weaponry in South Asia*, pp. 146–7.

190　　*Hinduism and the Ethics of Warfare in South Asia*

guns, various accounts of meritorious deeds and family histories written in and after the Sengoku period testify that the issue of a battle continued to depend on the final confrontation between cavalrymen armed with lances; to decapitate an enemy was regarded as the utmost military exploit.[179]

Kalhana's *Rajarangini* accepts that neither divine causation nor a righteous cause always leads to victory. Kalhana writes: 'What can man achieve by prowess ... when success depends on the strange ways of fate?'[180] However, the *Sukranitisara*, like Kautilya *Arthasastra*, asserts that fate at times could be overcome by practicing deceit. The *Sukranitisara* argues that the Rajput concept of *dharmayuddha* is too rigid for attaining victory against a wily enemy. Hence, the *Sukranitisara* states: 'Considering the ... expedients and designs of his enemy and his own, he should surely always kill his enemy by fair and unfair fighting.'[181] Instead of a frontal attack resulting in a decisive battle, the *Sukranitisara* preaches *asanayuddha*. This means cutting the enemy's supply line by attacking the non-combatants who provide wood, water and food to the enemy army.[182] The *Sukranitisara*, like Mao Tse-Tung, says that when the enemy is strong, it is necessary to retreat. One should then fall suddenly upon the enemy like a robber and plunder his belongings.[183] For the *Sukranitisara*, *asanayuddha* is a sort of attritional guerrilla warfare. The *Sukranitisara* also justifies the techniques of tactical retreat and flank attack as advocated in the format of *kutayuddha*: 'by attacking the enemy in front; by falling on him with the two wings, by retreating, in such a manner so far as the advantage of the ground favours the combat.'[184] The *Sukranitisara* is implying that in order to defend the homeland against the 'demonic' Muslims, *kutayuddha* may be practiced. And in such a context, *kutayuddha* becomes *dharmayuddha*. During the second half of the seventeenth century, under their warlord Shivaji, the Marathas practiced *asanayuddha* when the Mughals under Emperor Aurangzeb invaded Maharashtra.

---

[179] Takagi, '"Hideyoshi's Peace" and the Transformation of the *Bushi* Class', p.126.

[180] *Kalhana's Rajatarangini*, vol. 2, Book 8, no. 1274, p. 101.

[181] Quoted from Oppert, *On the Weapons, Army Organization, and Political Maxims of the Ancient Hindus*, p. 131.

[182] Acharya, *Polity in Sukranitisara*, p. 172.

[183] Jagadish Narayan Sarkar, *Some Aspects of Military Thinking and Practice in Medieval India* (Calcutta: Ratna Prakashan, 1974), p. 33.

[184] Quoted from Oppert, *On the Weapons, Army Organization, and Political Maxims of the Ancient Hindus*, p. 130.

Hindu Militarism under Islamic Rule

Many Sufis and *ulemas* accompanied Sher Shah's army in order to legitimize the use of force against the *kafirs*. One such religious leader, named Nimatullah Harawi, quoted a *hadith* and argued that treachery against the enemy (*al-hard khudat*) was legally valid. Hence, treacherous behaviour against non-believers during battle became part and parcel of what could be termed 'just' war.[185] The *Sukranitisara* was probably influenced by such strands of thought.

As regards the force structure, the *Sukranitisara* notes that a king should always maintain four times as many foot soldiers as horses. For logistical purposes, elephants, bulls and camels were also necessary. In addition, big guns should be placed on the chariots. In the *Sukranitisara*, 'chariots' probably refer to wagons on which the heavy field guns were placed. The *Sukranitisara* explains that the wagons were iron carriages with wheels, filled with weapons and drawn by good horses.[186]

The following details about the manufacture of gunpowder and handguns are available in the *Sukranitisara*:

After the gunpowder is placed inside, it is firmly pressed down with a ramrod. This is the small gun which ought to be carried by foot soldiers.

....

Five parts of saltpeter, one part of sulphur, one part of charcoal ... and is prepared in such a manner that the smoke does not escape.

If all this is taken after having been cleansed, is then powdered, and mixed together, one should squeeze it ... and dry it in the sun; having ground this like sugar, it will certainly become gunpowder.

....

The ball is made of iron, and has either small balls in its inside or is empty; for small tubular arms it should be of lead or of any other metal.

The tubular projectile weapon is ... of iron....

By the application of fire they throw the ball coming from the tube at the mark.[187]

During the second half of the sixteenth century, the Mughals manufactured handgun barrels by twisting a flat iron sheet continuously fired to fold rounds repeatedly in an elongated fashion with its edges overlapping one another, and then joining the twisted heated pieces over an iron rod to create a barrel. Thus, there were no weak joints in the barrel. This method produced a barrel of great strength, which could withstand high

---

[185] Aquil, *Sufism, Culture, and Politics*, p. 156.
[186] Oppert, *On the Weapons, Army Organization, and Political Maxims of the Ancient Hindus*, pp. 85, 88.
[187] Quoted from ibid., pp. 106–8.

192   *Hinduism and the Ethics of Warfare in South Asia*

explosive pressure. The ramrod is known as the *gaz*. Initially, the Mughals used matchlock guns; for firing them, a match (known as a *fatila*) was required. Later, for firing, the wheel-lock mechanism was introduced.[188] The artillery pieces in India during the fifteenth century were made of brass or bronze.[189]

Like Srivara's *Zaina Rajatarangini*, the *Sukranitisara* emphasizes the importance of guns and animals like mules and bullocks for logistical purposes. The *Nitiprakasika* also emphasizes the importance of constructing roads before ordering the army to march and the necessity of taking artisans along with the campaigning army.[190] Roads were necessary for dragging the carts carrying heavy cannons, and artisans were required for manufacturing and repairing the gunpowder weapons.

Compared to Kamandaka's *Nitisara*, the *Sukranitisara* gives less importance to the role of elephants in battle and highlights the importance of war horses and infantry.[191] This development might be due to the uselessness of the war elephants of the Rajputs against the mounted horse archers of Islam in the two battles of Tarain. The *Nitiprakasika* charts the linkage between terrain and the effectiveness of cavalry in the following words: 'A country without mire, without stumps, without stones, which can withstand the treading of the hoofs of horses ... is even, is esteemed a good country for horses.'[192] In South Asian warfare, the role of handgun-equipped infantry increased over time. Between 1526 and 1595, the number of foot musketeers under the direct control of the Mughal emperor rose from 1,200 to 35,000.[193] In 1647, while there were 200,000 cavalrymen under the Mughal imperial banner, there were also 40,000 infantry (matchlock men, gunners, men equipped with *ban*s, etc.).[194]

RAJPUTS AND MARATHAS UNDER THE MUGHALS

Akbar, the 'real' founder of the Mughal Empire, modified the character of the Mughal state by introducing certain measures. In 1579, Muslim

[188] Irfan Habib, 'Akbar and Technology', in Habib (ed.), *Akbar and His India*, pp. 142–3.
[189] Iqtidar Alam Khan, 'Gunpowder and Empire: Indian Case', *Social Scientist*, vol. 33, nos. 3–4 (2005), p. 55.
[190] *Nitiprakasika*, ed. by Oppert, p. 18.
[191] Acharya, *Polity in Sukranitisara*, p. 19; Oppert, *On the Weapons, Army Organization, and Political Maxims of the Ancient Hindus*, p. 86.
[192] *Nitiprakasika*, ed. by Oppert, p. 21.
[193] Khan, 'Gunpowder and Empire: Indian Case', p. 59.
[194] M. Athar Ali, 'Towards an Interpretation of the Mughal Empire', in Ali, *Mughal India*, p. 69.

Hindu Militarism under Islamic Rule

theologians were forced by Akbar to sign a document proclaiming that the position of a *sultan-i-adil* (just king) was higher than that of a *mujtahid* (interpreter of law).[195] In Akbar's *durbar* (court), under the leadership of the court intellectual, Abul Fazl, the reigning dogma was that all religions in essence were the same and differed only in form. Such a philosophy was well suited to a multi-religious and multi-ethnic country like India.[196] Akbar, in order to placate the Hindus, abolished the *jizya* (poll tax) and the pilgrimage tax. He discouraged cow slaughter and forcible conversion from one faith to another and extended state patronage to non-Muslim institutions and individuals.[197] Whether the influence of Hindu ideas was responsible for Akbar's cosmopolitan outlook is debatable. However, several Sanskrit works were translated in the Mughal *durbar*. Shaikh Bhawan, a Brahmin who converted to Islam in 1575, took up the task of translating the *Atharva Veda*. The translation of *Mahabharata* begun in 1582.[198] William R. Pinch asserts that Kautilya's *Arthasastra* was translated during Akbar's reign, and Kautilya's technique of using ascetics in the espionage department was eagerly copied by the Mughals. Badauni was ordered by Akbar to translate Valmiki *Mahabharata* into Persian.[199] Translations of Sanskrit works continued under Akbar's successors. Dara Shikoh, the eldest son of Mughal Emperor Shah Jahan (ruled 1628–58) translated the fifty-two *Upanishads* around 1657 CE.[200]

Akbar made extensive and effective use of the suzerain-vassal polity, by means of which a large number of non-Muslim chiefs were inducted into the Mughal nobility. The willing vassals were inducted into the nobility through the *mansabdari* system.[201] In 1595, the Hindus comprised 16.8 percent of the Mughal nobility.[202] Despite Emperor Aurangzeb (ruled 1658–1707) following an orthodox Islamic policy, between 1679 and 1707 one-sixth of all the Mughal nobles of 1,000 *zat* (personal rank in the imperial hierarchy) and above were Hindus (Rajputs and

---

[195] M. Athal Ali, '*Sulh-i Kul* and the Religious Ideas of Akbar', in Ali, *Mughal India*, p. 159.

[196] M. Athar Ali, 'The State in Islamic Thought in India', in Ali, *Mughal India*, p. 126.

[197] J. S. Grewal, 'The Sikh Movement during the Reign of Akbar', in Habib (ed.), *Akbar and His India*, p. 253.

[198] M. Athar Ali, 'Translations of Sanskrit Works at Akbar's Court', in Ali, *Mughal India*, pp. 174, 175.

[199] Pinch, *Warrior Ascetics and Indian Empires*, pp. 46, 216–17.

[200] M. Athar Ali, 'The Religious Environment under Shah Jahan and Aurangzeb', in Ali, *Mughal India*, p. 203.

[201] Grewal, 'The Sikh Movement during the Reign of Akbar', p. 252.

[202] Ali, '*Sulh-i-Kul* and the Religious Ideas of Akbar', p. 165.

194   *Hinduism and the Ethics of Warfare in South Asia*

Marathas).[203] Unlike the Western European fiefs, the *mansab*s (imperial offices) were not hereditary, and the *mansabdar*s (holders of *mansab*s) were transferred from one region to another. A military fief in the Ottoman Empire was known as a *timar*. In general, the *timariot* (holder of a *timar*) was not transferred as long as he bought troops, and the *timariot* was generally succeeded by his son. In the Safavid Empire, the equivalent of the military *jagir* was the *tuyul*. The holders of the *tuyul*s were generally given pieces of land along with the associated peasants for a lifetime; and the *tuyul*s were also inheritable.[204] The *mansab* system consumed about 80 percent of the Mughal Empire's land revenue.[205] Like the various grades of *mansabdar*s, there were different types of *Samurai*. Some *Samurai* might have large landholdings with thousands of warriors under them; others received small stipends and were attended by only a few military retainers.[206]

The Mughal Empire under Akbar was comprised of large number of semi-autonomous principalities ruled by hereditary chieftains styled as *raja*s, *rana*s, *rawat*s, *rai*s, and so on. The Persian chroniclers categorize them as *zamindar*s. Most of these chieftains of north India fell under the generic term 'Rajput'. Some of their principalities stretched over hundreds of kilometers. The number of cavalry commanded by some of them exceeded the strength of cavalry commanded by the highest grandees of the empire. Since these chieftains were not united, they posed only local threats to the empire. Many of them were coerced to join the Mughal Empire as *mansabdar*s. Many chieftains were also enrolled in the *mansabdari* service after being defeated in battles.[207]

To an extent, the recruitment of the Rajput chiefs into the Mughal army under Akbar was a reaction to the defeat of Humayun at the hands of the Afghans.[208] S. Inayat A. Zaidi asserts that Akbar followed a coherent policy towards the Rajput chiefs that represented a complete break

---

[203] M. Athar Ali, 'The Religious Environment under Shah Jahan and Aurangzeb', in Ali, *Mughal India*, p. 207.

[204] M. Athar Ali, 'Political Structures of the Islamic Orient in the Sixteenth and Seventeenth Centuries', in Ali, *Mughal India*, p. 100.

[205] Jos J. L. Gommans and Dirk H. A. Kolff, 'Introduction: Warfare and Weaponry in South Asia: 1000–1800 AD', in Gommans and Kolff (eds.), *Warfare and Weaponry in South Asia*, p. 23.

[206] Michael P. Birt, '*Samurai* in Passage: The Transformation of the Sixteenth-Century Kanto', in Kleinschmidt (ed.), *Warfare in Japan*, p. 338.

[207] Ahsan Raza Khan, 'Akbar's Initial Encounters with the Chiefs: Accident versus Design in the Process of Subjugation', in Habib (ed.), *Akbar and His India*, pp. 1–24.

[208] Zaidi, 'Ordinary Kachawaha Troopers Serving the Mughal Empire', p. 57.

Hindu Militarism under Islamic Rule

from the policy followed by the previous Islamic Turkish rulers of India. The conventional policy was to subjugate a local chief, exact a heavy sum of *peshkash* (offering or tribute) and then leave him free in his domain. But Akbar bought the Rajput chiefs into the fold of the empire and allowed them to serve as military commanders. Thus, they were treated on a par with the Irani and Turani nobles. For providing military service, the Rajput chiefs not only retained their traditional landholdings (known as *watan*s) but also were assigned *jagir*s in various parts of the empire outside their principalities. Besides assigning *jagir*s, the emperor also controlled the Rajput chiefs by interfering during the succession struggles. Though in theory succession of the legal heir to the throne of the principality was hereditary, it still had to be ratified by the emperor. If the emperor was dissatisfied with a disloyal chief, he could refuse to ratify the succession of the eldest son and instead support the candidacy of a younger brother or another male relative of the dead chieftain.[209] Like the Mughal emperors' bureaucrats, the *daimyo*s were able to survey their retainers' land and assigned a value to their incomes.[210]

A RAJPUT *MANSABDAR* ON *DHARMAYUDDHA* AND *KUTAYUDDHA*

Udairaj Munshi was the secretary of Mirza Raja Jai Singh, a *mansabdar* of the Mughal Emperor Aurangzeb. Jai Singh fought in Deccan. In 1667, Jai Singh died; Udairaj embraced Islam, and the emperor gave him the title Taleyar Khan. The military dispatches of Jai Singh were collected and edited by Taleyar Khan and published after Taleyar's death (1675) as *Insha-I-Haft Anjuman* in 1698–99.[211] Shivaji's sack of Port Surat in Gujarat resulted in Aurangzeb sending Jai Singh with 15,000 soldiers to attack him.[212] Jai Singh's campaign against Shivaji resulted in the Treaty of Purandar (June 1665). In accordance with the terms of this treaty, Shivaji surrendered twenty-three of his forts to the Mughals but retained twelve forts. Shivaji's son Sabhaji became a *panchhazari mansabdar* (5,000 *zat*),

---

[209] S. Inayat A. Zaidi, 'Akbar and the Rajput Principalities: Integration into Empire', in Habib (ed.), *Akbar and His India*, pp. 15–19.

[210] Birt, 'Samurai in Passage', p. 339.

[211] *The Military Despatches of a Seventeenth Century Indian General, Being an English Translation of the Haft Anjuman of Munshi Udairaj alias Taleyar Khan*, ed. by Jagadish Narayan Sarkar (Calcutta: Scientific Book Agency, 1969), Introduction, p. 3.

[212] Stewart Gordon, *The Marathas: 1600–1818* (1998; reprint, New Delhi: Foundation Books, 2000), pp. 71, 73.

196 *Hinduism and the Ethics of Warfare in South Asia*

and Shivaji agreed to render military service to the Mughals anywhere in the Deccan. However, Shivaji was exempted from personal attendance in the *durbar* of the Mughal Empire, and the Mughals agreed to assign *jagirs* in the Konkan region to him in lieu of military service. However, after the failure of the Bijapur campaign, Jai Singh began to retreat in October 1666.[213] Aurangzeb then recalled him from the Deccan. Jai Singh was a battlefield commander, so his dispatches give some idea of the attitudes and ethics of warfare of a Hindu commander in the Mughal service.

As Jai Singh advanced into Maharashtra, Shivaji send his agents to engage in diplomatic negotiations. Jai Singh wrote to Aurangzeb: 'After the arrival of the imperial army near Pabal, Shiva's agents began to visit me, and again up to my arrival at Pune they twice brought letters from him. But I gave no answer, and send them back in disappointment. I know that unless a strong hand was laid on him, his words and stories would not contain a particle of truth.'[214] Jai Singh was aiming to achieve the subjugation of Shivaji through the implementation of organized violence.

Sometime later, Jai Singh agreed to receive Shivaji's envoy. Jai Singh noted in his dispatches: 'I listened to what Shiva had written. Its purport was, "I am a useful servant of the imperial ... and many services can be secured from my humble self. If the Mughal Army turns to the invasion of Bijapur, such a course would be better than undergoing the many hardships (of campaigning) in this hilly region ... of difficult paths and stony soil."'[215] Shivaji was aware that his leverage depended on utilizing the difficult terrain of Maharashtra. Maharashtra is divided into three regions: the Konkan, the Ghats and the Desh. The steep Ghats rise sharply from the Konkan coast and are separated by peaks and a few passes. The mountains are wooded, and food and fodder were scarce, thus making it difficult to deploy a large army. The Ghats were also protected by numerous mountain forts. In addition, Shivaji commanded 10,000 soldiers and controlled several forts.[216] Shivaji's objective was to become a junior partner of the Mughal Empire in the Deccan or at least to buy time by making a temporary truce with the Mughals so that he could reorganize his army and realm and continue the struggle later.

Jai Singh responded to Shivaji in the following words: 'The imperial army, countless like the stars ... Do not put your faith in your hills and

[213] *Haft Anjuman*, pp. 8, 37.
[214] Ibid., p. 49.
[215] Ibid., p. 49.
[216] Gordon, *The Marathas*, pp. 12, 73.

stony country.... It will be trodden flat with the dust by the hoofs of the wind paced chargers of the imperial army. If you desire your own life and safety, place in your ear the ring of servitude to the slaves of the imperial court.'[217]

Jai Singh's strategic deployment of the army becomes clear in the following lines: 'And I divided my army, sending Daud Khan and Raja Rai Singh to plunder Shivaji's country, and appointing one party to guard the camp and to go rounds, and another party to forage and patrol – who were to remain constantly in the saddle.'[218] Jai Singh, in addition to possessing a mobile field army, also had a force with siege engines, which engaged in static siege warfare against Shivaji's forts.

Rather than engaging in a frontal battle in the style of Prithviraja III, Jai Singh enunciated a sophisticated from of warfare that included elements of *kutayuddha*. Jai Singh, in accordance with Kautilya's *kutayuddha*, resorted to bribery to win over Shivaji's supporters in order to weaken him before engaging in a battle. Jai Singh reported to Aurangzeb that while Shivaji's country was being plundered by the Mughal cavalry, his troops were simultaneously being seduced by the Mughals. The Mughals, by giving safety passes and bribes, encouraged desertions from Shivaji's army.[219]

Politics rather than religion determined the behaviour of both Hindu and Muslim rulers. The sultan of Bijapur was afraid that after subjugating Shivaji, the Mughals would turn their military machine against Bijapur. So the sultan was eager to aid Shivaji against the Mughals. Aurangzeb ordered simultaneous campaigns against both Shivaji and Bijapur. Jai Singh counselled caution in order to prevent the emergence of an anti-Mughal front by the triple powers (Marathas under Shivaji, Bijapur and the Golkunda sultanates) in Deccan. Jai Singh advised the emperor that to render Shivaji hopeless would only drive him into an alliance with Bijapur. When the Mughals attacked Bijapur, in order to prevent the sultan of Golkunda from joining Bijapur, Jai Singh followed a policy of moderation towards Golkunda. Jai Singh noted that it would be highly expedient to show excessive imperial favour to Qutb-ul-mulk, the ruler of Golkunda, for the purpose of putting him off guard and inducing him to give up the idea of joining the Bijapuris.[220]

---

[217] *Haft Anjuman*, pp. 49–50.
[218] Ibid., p. 50.
[219] Ibid., p. 50.
[220] Ibid., pp. 51, 84.

198   *Hinduism and the Ethics of Warfare in South Asia*

Jai Singh's policy was to balance *dharmayuddha* with *kutayuddha* and to use techniques of both in accordance with the demands of the context. Unlike Jayanaka, who emphasized only *dharmayuddha*, Jai Singh, for practical reasons, was willing to use at least some aspects of *kutayuddha* at certain times. Blatant *kutayuddha* would have left the Mughals without any allies for future campaigns. After capturing Purandar Fort, Jai Singh wrote that a demonstration of the power of the imperial army might make Shivaji eager to tread the path of submission.[221]

Mughal warfare did not consist merely of theatrics, spectacles and coercive diplomacy, as Jos Gommans argues.[222] Mughal warfare also involved bloodletting. About the siege of the Khadkala Fort, Jai Singh describes the use of artillery fire to demolish the gates and bastions.[223] In contradiction to *dharmayuddha*, Jai Singh was not averse to attacking and destroying the retreating enemy. Jai Singh was probably influenced by the thirteenth-century Persian work *Adab ul Harb,* by Fakhr-i Mudabbir, which, like *Arthasastra*, emphasizes conducting tactical retreat and attacking a retreating foe.[224] The Mughals used siege artillery in this encounter. In accordance with *Sukranitisara*'s paradigm, Jai Singh was waging *asurayuddha*.

At the commencement of the Bijapur campaign, Jai Singh, in his dispatches to Aurangzeb, stressed the importance of siege artillery. He noted that the fort of Bijapur was defended by many cannons. In order to render them useless, and to accomplish the task (of conquering Bijapur), Jai Singh demanded fifty cannons. Mounted musketeers also played an important role in the Mughal order of battle. Jai Singh pleaded with the emperor to increase their numbers in his army.[225]

Thus, we see the force structure of the contingents under the Rajput chiefs was changing with time. From a cavalry-centric army under Prithviraja III during the twelfth century, gunpowder weapons had become an integral part of warfare by the seventeenth century. Though gunpowder weapons initially were regarded as elements of *kutayuddha*,

---

[221] Ibid., p. 57.
[222] Jos Gommans, *Mughal Warfare: Indian Frontiers and High Roads to Empire, 1500–1700* (London/New York: Routledge, 2002).
[223] *Haft Anjuman*, pp. 57–8.
[224] Sarkar, *Some Aspects of Military Thinking and Practice in Medieval India*, pp. 5, 31, 33–5.
[225] *Haft Anjuman*, pp. 69–70.

Hindu Militarism under Islamic Rule

because of their combat effectiveness the Hindu generals in the Mughal army were willing to use them. Now, let us shift the focus to the Marathas, who could be categorized as the 'Rajputs of Deccan'.

TWO MARATHI POEMS AND ANTI-MUSLIM HEROIC RESISTANCE BY THE HINDUS

The term 'Maharashtra', writes Stewart Gordon, refers to the area in western India where Marathi was the dominant language. Though the term 'Maharashtra' was mentioned from first century CE, due to developments in the Marathi language the emergence of a definite linguistic region occurred between 800 to 1300 CE. The term 'Maratha' refers to the landholding castes who gained power, prestige and wealth because of service in the army and thus differed from the *kunbis*, who were cultivators, iron workers and tailors. Gordon asserts that there were certain similarities between the rise of the Rajput and Maratha warrior groups. By dint of service in the army and translating their service into land grants in local society, a family became Rajput. In order to strengthen their cultural identity, the Rajputs resorted to ending widow remarriage, changed their dress and eating patterns and provided patronage to the local shrines. Similarly, in Maharashtra, successful military service differentiated many families from the ordinary cultivators. *Imam* (tax free land grants) and *watan* (hereditary *jagir*s) grants further increased the power and status of these families at the local level. Simultaneously, a new ethic developed that emphasized a martial ethos, hunting, changes in dress (e.g., a more complicated turban) and diet patterns, the use of genealogists and restrictions on widow remarriage. Such caste behaviour, especially such things as seclusion of women and an elaborate turban, could not be emulated by poorer farmers. This in turn differentiated them from the Marathas. These changes were solidified into a kinship network. The rise of the Maratha gentry was further financed by wealth accumulated through grants of revenue farming. The families that held such service grants established their power in certain territories. Thus, they became a new landed elite and not merely a service elite. The various Maratha families did not develop territorial possessions with clearly defined borders. Families with clusters of nested rights often interpenetrated other families' rights. This resulted in tension and occasional fighting among the various families and also enabled an extra-regional power to manipulate the families against each other. For instance, during

200 *Hinduism and the Ethics of Warfare in South Asia*

the first half of the seventeenth century, Shivaji's mother's family joined the Mughal side.[226]

While the *Sivabharata* deals with the origins of Maratha power under Shivaji, the *Maharashtra Purana* describes the expansion of the Maratha Empire in eastern India. The Marathas are portrayed as heroes in the former poem but as somewhat villainous in the latter work. The *Sivabharata* does not mention the fact that many of the great Maratha families emerged because of their military service in the Muslim sultanates of Deccan.[227] The Marathas initially rose to fame under the Abyssinian Ahamdnagar noble Malik Ambar, who maintained 10,000 Maratha light cavalry in 1609.[228]

Shivaji, the second son of Shahji Bhonsle and Jijabai, was born in 1627 (or February 1630) in the hill fort of Shivner in the northern part of the Pune district of Maharashtra.[229] During the second half of the seventeenth century, Shivaji became the greatest threat to the Mughal Empire; Aurangzeb used to refer him as the 'mountain rat'. *Sivabharata* (*The Epic of Shivaji*) was written in Sanskrit and was in part a product of seventeenth-century Marathi culture. Shivaji employed a Marathi court poet named Kavindra Paramananda, who wrote the Sanskrit epic poem to record the history of his patron's rise to power.[230]

James W. Laine notes that the poem *Sivabharata* is an assertion of Hindu political identity in response to the cultural and political threat posed by Islam.[231] *Sivabharata* tell us:

> Here Shivaji fights with Turks,
> Whom he had descended to earth to strike.[232]

Laine says that *Sivabharata* is an example of 'vulgate epic'. This means that the poem represents the Hindu heroic legend of Shivaji's life by supplying numerous elements of pathos and tragic heroism, describing the death of a great warrior battling evil opponents in order to conserve

---

[226] Gordon, *The Marathas*, pp. 10, 15–17, 35, 59.

[227] Ibid., p. 17.

[228] Radhey Shyam, *Life and Times of Malik Ambar* (New Delhi: Munshirasm Manoharlal, 1968), pp. 146–8.

[229] *The Epic of Shivaji, Kavindra Paramananda's Sivabharata*, a translation and study by James W. Laine in collaboration with S. S. Bahulkar (New Delhi: Orient Longman, 2001), p. 88; Gordon, *The Marathas*, p. 59.

[230] *Sivabharata*, Introduction, pp. 1, 8, 43.

[231] Ibid., p. 10.

[232] *Sivabharata*, Canto One, p. 48.

Hindu Militarism under Islamic Rule 201

all things near and dear to Hinduism (cows, women, etc.) against the onslaught of the *mlechcha*s (Muslims).[233]

In S. S. Bahulkar's interpretation, *Sivabharata* is a historical *mahakavya* (great poem). The function of the *mahakavya* is to describe the heroic acts of the kings (who are at times compared to the deities) or of the Kshatriya heroes who achieved kingship. Despite erotic and heroic elements, the story is generally drawn from history. The structure of the *mahakavya* can be described as *sargabandha*, which means a composition consisting of several cantos. A canto comprises anywhere from 30 to 200 stanzas.[234] The poem is comprised of one hundred thousand verses.[235] Bahulkar notes that instead of calling the poem *Sivacharita* (Life of Shivaji), the poem is called *Sivabharata*, since Paramananda's model was the *Mahabharata*. The *Mahabharata* begins with a dialogue between a bard and a Brahmin *rishi*; *Sivabharata* begins with Paramanda describing Shivaji's exploits to the Brahmin *pundit*s at Kasi (Benaras).[236] While *Mahabharata* tells the story of the King Bharata and his descendants, *Sivabharata* describes the story of King Shivaji.[237]

Paramananda claims that Shivaji decided to fight the Muslims because Lord Shiva appeared to him in a dream and ordered him to get rid of the Muslims, who were demons in their previous births and had acquired power through *tapas*.[238] Paramananda, the panegyrist of Shivaji, portrays the struggle between his patron and the Bijapur Sultanate's Muslim General Afzal Khan as the war between good and evil.[239] Afzal Khan is portrayed by Paramananda as the embodiment of *adharma*:

> He is like a mountain of sin,
> Completely a man of passion,
> Determined to obstruct
> The path of caste-*dharma*....
> He is the opponent of all *dharma*s,
> And supporter of all *adharma*s.[240]

---

[233] *Sivabharata*, Introduction, p. 23.

[234] *Sivabharata*, 'The *Sivabharata* in the Context of Classical *Mahakavya* Literature', S. S. Bahulkar, pp. 34–5.

[235] *Sivabharata*, p. 67.

[236] *Sivabharata*, 'The *Sivabharata* in the Context of Classical *Mahakavya* Literature', Bahulkar, p. 36.

[237] Ibid., p. 37.

[238] *Sivabharata*, p. 126.

[239] *Sivabharata*, Introduction, p. 11.

[240] *Sivabharata*, Canto Eighteen, p. 234.

202   *Hinduism and the Ethics of Warfare in South Asia*

In 1659, Afzal Khan, the commander of the Bijapur army, entered the Ghats with 10,000 troops to crush Shivaji. Afzal Khan desecrated the Hindu places of pilgrimage, especially Pandharpur, while advancing to meet Shivaji. This reflected the growth of sectarian orthodoxy in the declining Bijapur Sultanate. The above-mentioned act by Azfal Khan alienated the local *deshmukh*s (high-caste Hindu landlords of Maharashtra), who could have provided local knowledge about the terrain and Shivaji's hideouts as well as supplies for the Bijapur army. From May to November, both Afzal Khan's and Shivaji's forces maneuvered. Shivaji retreated to the Pratapgad Fort and stationed his forces in the jungles of Javli. Afzal Khan's army, comprised of heavy cavalry, was suited for a decisive battle in the plains and could not deploy effectively in the narrow mountainous passes. Further, Afzal Khan lacked siege equipment. So Afzal Khan surrounded Pratapgad and waited. Both sides faced difficulties. While Shivaji was not getting supplies from outside the fort, Afzal also was unable to procure supplies from the surrounding countryside. Shivaji agreed to meet Afzal at the walls beneath Pratapgad, in a clearing in the dense forest whose trails were known only to Shivaji's followers. In this locale, Afzal Khan could bring only 1,500 of his followers. The meeting was set up under an agreement that the two leaders would meet alone. A decade earlier, Afzal had used such a truce to imprison a Hindu general. Both men came armed. Shivaji wore chain mail under his clothes and a metal skull protector under his turban and carried a sword plus sharpened *baghnak*s (iron claws). The two men fought, and Shivaji disemboweled Afzal with his iron claws. Then, at a signal from Shivaji, his followers fell upon Afzal Khan's unsuspecting guards. The death of Afzal and the surprise attack of the Marathas resulted in the complete defeat of the Bijapuri army.[241]

Laine writes that Shivaji's killing of Azfal Khan represents violent sacrifice and demon slaying that had its origins in the vedic literature. When Shivaji clashed with the Mughals, the former is portrayed in the poem as Rama fighting Ravana (Aurangzeb).[242] Shivaji, like Prithviraja III, is also regarded as the incarnation of Lord Vishnu, deputed to cleanse the earth from the domination of the *mlechcha*s.[243] The Muslims are depicted as both *mlechcha*s and *yavana*s in *Sivabharata*. Paramananda writes:

---

[241] Gordon, *The Marathas*, pp. 67–8.
[242] *Sivabharata*, Introduction, pp. 13, 18.
[243] *Sivabharata*, 'The *Sivabharata* in the Context of Classical *Mahakavya* Literature', Bahulkar, p. 37.

The glories of King Shivaji
Blot out the stain of the *Kali Yuga* (Dark Age).[244]

Paramananda describes the duties of the *dharmik* King Shivaji in the following words:

And without fear remained devoted
To the great destruction of Muslims.[245]

Protecting the state from internal and external enemies is the duty of a just king. *Sivabharata* narrates:

Dharma is declared to be
The very self of the seven membered Kingdom.
....
The rise of enemies ... *adharma*;[246]

Shivaji, in Paramananda's view, was immersed in classical Hinduism. About his education, *Sivabharata* tells us:

Clever and knowledgeable in many subjects:
Mythology and scripture, politics and classics,
Mahabharata and *Ramayana*.[247]

As regards both external and internal policies, Shivaji, claims Paramananda, followed policies flavoured with 'Hinduism'. Shivaji wrote a letter to Jai Singh asking him to desert Aurangzeb in order to protect Hinduism.[248] Before Shivaji crowned himself as king, he made a pilgrimage to the shrines of Prasurama and Bhavani Goddess at Pratapgad. Shivaji believed in the classical Hindu *Saptanga* theory. *Sivabharata* tells us the kingdom's bodily members are seven:

First the king, then the prime minister,
Then realm and great wealth,
Then allies, forts and armies.
....
The head is the king,
The mouth, the prime minister,
Wealth and the army
Are (the body's) two arms,

---

[244] *Sivabharata*, Canto One, p. 46. Parenthetical material is my own.
[245] *Sivabharata*, Canto Sixteen, pp. 217–18.
[246] Ibid., p. 215.
[247] *Sivabharata*, Canto Ten, p. 139.
[248] *Sivabharata*, Introduction, p. 19.

204   *Hinduism and the Ethics of Warfare in South Asia*

> The realm is the rest of the body,
> With allies for firm joints,
> And forts for the strongest of bones.[249]

As far as the organization of his realm was concerned, Shivaji 'Sanskritized' his administration, giving Sanskrit instead of Persian names to his ministers. Shivaji's cabinet was comprised of eight ministers who were called *asta-pradhan*s.[250] Gordon claims that due to the demands of reality on the ground, Shivaji was not totally anti-Muslim. He welcomed Muslim recruits into his army (probably due to their technical skill in gunnery and horse riding). The Pathans from Bijapur joined Shivaji's army. This was probably an act of *realpolitik* taken by Shivaji in order to weaken the neighbouring Muslim monarchies. During the confrontation with Afzal Khan, Siddi Ibrahim supported Shivaji. Another Muslim commander in Shivaji's army was Nurkhan Beg. And Muslim *qazi*s (judges) continued to function in the regions occupied by Shivaji.[251]

Paramananda draws several parallels between Shivaji and the Pandavas. Paramananda portrays Shivaji as a warrior saint like Arjuna; though performing violent acts, Shivaji remained in control of his senses like a *yogin*.[252] Shivaji, the warrior *yogi* like Arjuna, is both *pratapi* (brave and heroic) and *vijitendriya* (having control over the senses) and a *mahatapi* (ascetic).[253] Paramananda writes that he was born an *avatar* (incarnation), like the second Arjuna.[254] Shivaji's escape from the Mughal *durbar* at Agra to Deccan in 1665 in the guise of a mendicant in order to escape Aurangzeb's guards is compared to the wandering of the Pandavas in the forest in order to escape Duryodhana's force. Ultimately, writes Laine, a Hindu hero achieves the pinnacles of heroism by sacrificing his own life, that is, by dying in battle.[255] This is equivalent to achieving *viragati* for the Rajputs.

After the death of Shivaji, the Marathas spilled into north and east India. The *Maharashtra Purana* is an eighteenth-century Bengali poem of 716 lines that discusses the Maratha invasions of Mughal Bengal. The Maratha incursions into Bengal started in April 1742, when Raghuji Bhonsle, the Maratha *sirdar* (chieftain) of Nagpur, sent his general Bhaskar

---

[249] *Sivabharata*, Canto Sixteen, p. 215.
[250] *Sivabharata*, Introduction, p. 25.
[251] Gordon, *The Marathas*, p. 66.
[252] *Sivabharata*, Introduction, p. 13.
[253] *Sivabharata*, p. 45.
[254] *Sivabharata*, Canto One, p. 49.
[255] *Sivabharata*, Introduction, pp. 21, 25.

Pandit (also known as Bhaskar Pant Kolhatkar) to collect *chauth* (one-fourth of land revenue as a tax) from Bengal.[256] At that time, Bengal was under *Nawab* Alivardi Khan. Alivardi was initially the governor of Bihar. In 1739, he rebelled against his master, *Nawab* Sarfaraz Khan, and seized power by killing Sarfaraz in battle. Alivardi proceeded to Murshidabad (the capital of Bengal *Subah*) with a strong army on the pretext of having an interview with Sarfaraz. Sarfaraz, unaware of Alivardi's treachery, went out to meet him with a small force and was killed in a battle in 1740. Alivardi ruled from 1740 to 1756.[257] The *Maharashtra Purana* tells us that Alivardi, after campaigning against some rebels in Orissa, was returning to his capital, Murshidabad, when the Maratha cavalry surrounded him near Burdwan city, some seventy miles from Calcutta. What actually happened was that after the death of Sarfaraz, Murshid Quli Khan (not to be confused with Murshid Quli Khan, the first *Nawab* of Bengal), the son-in-law of Shuja-ud-Daulah and governor of Orissa, declared war against Alivardi. Alivardi defeated Murshid at Balasore, and Murshid Quli escaped to Deccan and took refuge with Asaf Jah, the *Nawab* of Hyderabad. Mir Habib Ardistani, the *Bakshi* (paymaster) of Murshid Quli, went to Raghuji and encouraged him to attack Bengal under Alivardi.[258] In May 1751, after repeated invasions by the Marathas, Alivardi signed a treaty with Raghuji under which he agreed to give Orissa to the former and also agreed to pay Rs 1,200,000 annually as *chauth*. The *Maharashtra Purana* covers the early part of the story until the treacherous murder of Bhaskar by Alivardi.[259]

The author of the *Maharashtra Purana* is a poet named Gangaram, a Bengali Hindu, but we do not have any details about his background. Edward C. Dimock Jr. and Pratul Chandra Gupta assert that the poet not only lived during the time of Maratha depredations but also seems to be familiar with the districts (Burdwan, Bankura and Birbhum) that were ravaged by the Marathas. In addition to the *Maharashtra Purana*,

---

[256] *The Maharashtra Purana, An Eighteenth Century Bengali Historical Text*, tr., annotated, and with an Introduction by Edward C. Dimock, Jr., and Pratul Chandra Gupta (1965; reprint, Hyderabad: Orient Longman, 1985), Introduction, p. 1. All translations are by the author.

[257] *Maharashtra Purana*, p. 19; *The Maathir-ul-umara, Being Biographies of the Muhammadan and Hindu Officers of the Timurid Sovereigns of India from 1500 to about 1780*, by Nawab Samsam-ud-Daulah Shah Nawaz Khan and his son Abdul Hayy, tr. by H. Beveridge, revised, annotated and completed by Baini Prashad, vol. 1 (1941; reprint, Delhi: Low Price Publications, 1999), p. 206.

[258] The *Maathir-ul-umara*, vol. 1, pp. 206–7.

[259] *Maharashtra Purana*, Introduction, pp. 2–3.

206   *Hinduism and the Ethics of Warfare in South Asia*

there exists an earlier Sanskrit poem titled *Citracampu* written in 1744 by Vanesvara Vidyalankara, the court poet of the *Maharaja* of Burdwan. Compared to *Citracampu*, which is more concerned with poetic effect, the *Maharashtra Purana* gives more accurate, rich and thick historical descriptions of the Maratha raids into Bengal. For instance, the *Citracampu* states that the superior mobility of the Marathas gave them an advantage over the *nawab*'s troops and that the Maratha cavalry could travel a hundred *yojana*s (one *yojana* is equivalent to eight miles) in a day. So, instead of accurate description of the speed of Maratha cavalry, the *Citracampu* focuses more on metaphorical effect. However, both the *Citracampu* and the *Maharashtra Purana* emphasize the negative effects of the Marathas' pillage and plundering on Bengal's civil society. Another poet, Bharatchandra Ray (1712–60), in his *Annandamangal*, writes that Raghuji sent Bhaskar Pandit with fierce troopers from Maharashtra and Saurashtra for the purpose of ravaging Bengal. Interestingly, Bharatchandra, like Gangaram, came from Burdwan, which was ravaged by the Marathas.[260]

Both Bharatchandra and Gangaram accepted the idea that the Maratha raids occurred as punishment for sins committed by the people and the ruler of Bengal. Bharatchandra's assertion is more communal as he writes that the misconduct of Alivardi's Muslim army at Bhubaneshwar (a Hindu holy place of pilgrimage in Orissa associated with Lord Shiva and his consort, Goddess Durga) caused the Maratha raids as divine retribution. Gangaram, however, puts the blame on the immoral conduct of the common people of Bengal, which generated sin and brought about the Maratha depredations as divine punishment.[261]

Raja Sahu was the grandson of Shivaji. He had been a Mughal prisoner and was freed after Aurangzeb's death in 1707. Under Sahu, the *peshwa* (prime minister) became powerful, and the Maratha Empire continued to expand until Sahu's death in 1749. The *Maharashtra Purana* notes that on Lord Brahma's (creator of the world) advice, Lord Shiva told his agent Nandi to enter the body of *Raja* Sahu, who would cleanse the earth of the sins.[262] The *Maharashtra Purana* continues:

> Raja Sahu ordered Raghuji,
> To collect the *chauth* from Bengal.
> An envoy was sent to Delhi,

---

[260] Ibid., pp. 3–7.
[261] Ibid, p. 7.
[262] *Maharashtra Purana*, p. 16.

Hindu Militarism under Islamic Rule

For getting *chauth* from Bengal.

....

When the Emperor received the letter from Raja Sahu's envoy,
He gave it to his *Wazir*.

....

The Emperor ordered the Wazir,
To write to Raja Sahu,
That a rebel by killing the Subadar had usurped the throne,
And is not paying the revenues to Delhi.
We do not have an army to chastise the rebel,

....

But, the rebel is enjoying the *Suba* of Bengal for two years.

....

Then Raja Sahu decided to collect *chauth* by force,

....

When Raja Sahu gave his assent,
Raghuji sent ... Bhaskar.[263]

Gangaram says that the Mughal emperor, due to the rebellious activities of Alivardi Khan (who had killed the legal Mughal *subadar*), encouraged the Marathas to attack Bengal. Raghuji attacked Bengal for several reasons. The gradual weakening of the Mughal government in Delhi encouraged the Marathas to expand into Bengal. Also, Asaf Jah, the *Nawab* of Hyderabad, encouraged Raghuji to attack Bengal in order to divert Maratha pressure away from the northern frontier of Hyderabad.[264]

Raghuji send Bhaskar with 40,000 troopers.[265] The *Maharashtra Purana* explains:

... the Marathas reached Cuttack.
From countryside, the troopers were assembled,
At Nagpur.

....

Bhaskar enquired from his envoy, about the location of the *nawab*.

....

At Burdwan city, near Rani Dighi,
Was the camp of the *nawab* located.[266]

Keeping Birbhum on their left, the army of Bhaskar reached Burdwan and quickly surrounded the *nawab*'s camp. *Nawab* Alivardi Khan

---

[263] Ibid., pp. 42–3. *Chauth* is one-fourth of land revenue demanded by the Marathas.
[264] Ibid., Introduction, p. 9.
[265] Ibid., Introduction, p. 8.
[266] Ibid., p. 44.

208   *Hinduism and the Ethics of Warfare in South Asia*

ordered Rajaram Singh, the head of his espionage department, to ascertain the strength of Bhaskar's force. The *Maharashtra Purana* notes that Rajaram's department was caught at a loss due to the sudden intrusion of Bhaskar's cavalry. The *bargi* force suddenly surrounded the *nawab*'s camp without any advance warning by his *harkara*s (spies).[267]

Initially, some commanders of the *nawab*'s army were eager for a fight with the Marathas. The *Maharashtra Purana* depicts their enthusiasms in the following lines:

> ... the *nawab* said,
> The Marathas are asking for *chauth*.
> The *sirdar*s present replied,
> Instead of giving the money to the Marathas, it should be distributed among the soldiers.
> We all present, should kill the *bargis* (Maratha light cavalry).[268]

Fighting the *bargis* was easier said than done. The *bargis* cut off all the supply lines to the *nawab*'s camp. Not only his army, but the *nawab* himself suffered from food shortages. The *bargis*, equipped with swords, attacked the rear of the *nawab*'s camp and plundered his baggage. Bhaskar's force was conducting *asanayuddha* as propounded by *Sukranitisara*. Mir Habib, one commander of the *nawab*, deserted to the Marathas. The *nawab* and his depleted army somehow survived relying on supplies send by boats one of his subordinates, Haji Sahib.[269]

Though the *nawab* and his army somehow escaped, there was no escape for the common folks. Gangaram provides a vivid description of the desolation caused among the common people. The farmers with their seeds and bullocks, the *shaikh*s, the Mughals and the Pathans all suffered at the hands of the raiding *bargi*s. The *Maharashtra Purana* depicts the large-scale abduction and rape of women by the Marathas.[270] The Maratha depredations gave rise to folk memories that still exist in the countryside of Bengal. Mothers frighten their kids by recounting the fear of the *bargi* invasion. One folk tales goes:

> *Khoka ghumalo, para juralo,*
> *Bargi alo deshe.*
> (Everybody is sleeping in the deep of night,
> And suddenly the *bargis* burst upon the towns and the countryside.)

[267] Ibid., pp. 19, 44.
[268] Ibid., p. 46. Parenthetical material is my own.
[269] Ibid., pp. 23–5.
[270] Ibid., pp. 26–7.

Hindu Militarism under Islamic Rule   209

The *bargi*s ravaged Burdwan district and then reached the bank of the Bhagirathi River.[271] The Maratha raids in Bengal continued until the British conquest of Bengal as a result of the Battle of Plassey (23 June 1757).

CONCLUSION

The concept of just war and holy war in medieval Hinduism should be judged by its own standards and not with reference to Western European Latin Christian traditions. To an extent, Western Christendom's concepts of open-ended just war and Crusade are similar to *jihad*. And the more limited Byzantine concept of just war, which advocated only defensive war, is similar to the Rajput concept of *dharmayuddha*. There is no clear differentiation among the Hindus between just war and holy war. The Hindus of the medieval era tried to incorporate the new trends in warfare (both conceptual and material) into their bipolar concepts of *dharmayuddha* and *kutayuddha*. And these two concepts are also quite open-ended and changed with the context. Interestingly, during the medieval period, in the theoretical frame of many Hindus, depending on the context, *kutayuddha* became *dharmayuddha*. Due to the impact of the Islamic invasions from the eleventh century onwards, the Rajput concept of *dharmayuddha* was partially replaced by the *Sukranitisara*'s more practical approach, which introduced elements of *kutayuddha*. From the fifteenth century onwards, the Hindu theorists of warfare tried to accommodate gunpowder weapons within their framework of *dharmayuddha* against the *mlechchas*.

Marxist historians like Brajadulal Chattopadhyaya, Suvira Jaiswal and Romila Thapar underrate the religious, political and military confrontations between Hinduism and Islam during the medieval era. Their interpretation is in consonance with their secular political agenda, which is to check the spread of communalism in present-day Indian society. Hinduism in medieval India was obviously an umbrella religion for various cults and sects but at the same time was quite distinct from Islam. The Aligarh School (comprising historians like Irfan Habib, M. Athar Ali, etc.) downplays the Muslim identity of the Mughal rulers and harps on the role played by Hindu-Muslim unity in running the Mughal Empire. To an extent, their assertion holds water. For instance, in Jai Singh's paradigm, combat with both Hindu and Muslim polities that opposed the

---

[271] Ibid., p. 28.

Mughal Empire was just because the Rajput Jai Singh's *dharma* as a *mansabdar* was to fight gallantly for the Mughals in accordance with the concept of *namak halili*. And Jai Singh did not desert Mughal service to join the Hindu warlord Shivaji. However, when political difference and religious difference coincided (as in the case of the Marathas), the result was an explosive compound.

6

Hindu Militarism and Anti-Militarism in British India

1750–1947

The British officers who served in colonial India as well as most modern scholars assert that the British-Indian Empire was a secular political entity. Hence, the British period of Indian history is considered to be a break with the past, as pre-colonial India had experienced only non-secular political entities like the Hindu Gupta Empire of classical antiquity and medieval Islamic empires like the Delhi Sultanate and the Mughal Empire. In reality, despite the claim that the British Empire in South Asia ushered in secular modernity, the British used various religions, albeit in a nuanced way, in order to establish their control. The first section of this chapter focuses on the British use of religion (here we will be concerned only with the use of Hinduism and not with Sikhism or Islam) in constructing a loyal army from the human resources of the subcontinent. As the anti-colonial struggle intensified during the early twentieth century, Indian nationalists also used two forms of Hinduism, aggressive and passive, for attacking the *Raj*. Now, let us focus on the use of religion, especially Hinduism, in the sepoy army.

HINDUISM AND THE CONSTRUCTION OF THE BRITISH-INDIAN ARMY

Peter Van Der Veer claims that religion had been crucial in the formation of national identities both in India and in supposedly secular Britain. During the first half of the nineteenth century, while the Utilitarians tried to define modernity in terms of utility and rationality, the evangelicals attempted to define it in terms of Christian morality. Veer contends that even during the Industrial Revolution, religious expansion occurred

212   *Hinduism and the Ethics of Warfare in South Asia*

simultaneously with secularization. Moreover, the impact of scientific discoveries, especially the evolutionary theories of Darwin, on the decline of religion as a belief system must not be exaggerated. The separation of church and state did not lead, claims Veer, to a decline in the social and political importance of religion. In Veer's view, the Indians did not look upon the colonial state as a secular entity but as a fundamentally Christian one.[1]

During the seventeenth century, the East India Company (hereinafter EIC) was a minor power in South Asia. The EIC's small forces were repeatedly defeated by the indigenous powers. However, the scenario started changing rapidly beginning in the 1750s. From coastal enclaves, the EIC started projecting power into the interior of the subcontinent. One after other, the indigenous powers were defeated and destroyed. By 1849, the EIC had gained political dominance on the subcontinent. The EIC's military success was not merely the result of importing the military institutions that had emerged in Western Europe. One of the principal factors behind British military success on the subcontinent was the use of Indian military manpower for imperial purposes. The EIC had to utilize indigenous military manpower because the demographic resources of Britain were inadequate for conquering India. Further, Indian manpower was not only cheaper but also more effective in the terrain and climate of South Asia.[2]

During the late seventeenth century, the land forces maintained by the EIC were in a sorry state. In 1664, the EIC's garrison at Bombay numbered 400 men.[3] In 1699, the EIC's military force in Bengal numbered 130 men plus some artillerymen.[4] Gradually, the size of the colonial military establishment rose. This was made possible by effective utilization of South Asian manpower. In 1773, the EIC possessed 9,000 European and 45,000 Indian soldiers.[5] In 1813, there were 21,940 British troops and

---

[1] Peter Van Der Veer, *Imperial Encounters: Religion and Modernity in India and Britain* (2001; reprint, New Delhi: Permanent Black, 2006), pp. 3, 7, 15, 20, 23.

[2] Kaushik Roy, *Brown Warriors of the Raj: Recruitment and the Mechanics of Command in the Sepoy Army, 1859–1913* (New Delhi: Manohar, 2008), p. 20.

[3] Sue Pyatt Peeler, 'Land Forces of the English East India Company in the Seventeenth Century', *Journal of Indian History*, Golden Jubilee Volume (1973), p. 552.

[4] Lieutenant F. G. Cardew, *A Sketch of the Services of the Bengal Native Army to the Year 1895* (1903; reprint, Faridabad: Today and Tomorrow's Printers & Publishers, 1971), p. 3.

[5] General George Chesney, *Indian Polity: A View of the System of Administration in India* (1894; reprint, Delhi: Metropolitan Books, 1976), p. 209.

179,632 Indian troops in South Asia organized into three armies: those of Bengal, Madras and Bombay.[6]

The EIC's Indian military personnel were long-term volunteers who served willingly for about twenty-five years. Because of South Asia's huge demographic resources, military service had always been voluntary. Between 1600 and 1800, the population of the subcontinent rose from 150 million to about 200 million.[7] Younger sons of small farmers joined the army in order to supplement their family income, especially after the harvest was over. Moreover – unlike the situation in eighteenth-century Britain, where military service was unpopular[8] – in India there were several communities who regarded military service, under any power broker, as honourable. National consciousness did not exist among the Indians at that time.[9] The attractions of regular pay and a pension pulled Indians into the EIC's forces. The British officers won the trust of the sepoys by showing deference to their religious and cultural sensibilities. Language training for communication with the sepoys and sowars was part of British officers' professional expertise.[10] On 22 August 1806, the commander-in-chief of India ordered the British officers to become thoroughly acquainted with the 'native' languages[11] in order to effectively command the *Purbiya*s of the Bengal army.

The Mughal government recruited musketeers from the high castes (Brahmins and Rajputs) of Awadh and Buxar. They were known as *Purbiya*s (men from Purab, i.e., east India).[12] The *Purbiya*s joined the

---

[6] *Parliamentary Papers, Reports from the Select Committees on the Affairs of the East India Company with Appendices, Colonies, East India, Sessions 1805–10* (Shannon: Irish University Press, 1971), pp. 112, 131.

[7] John F. Richards, 'Early Modern India and World History', *Journal of World History*, vol. 8, no. 2 (1997), p. 207.

[8] Victor E. Neuburg, 'The British Army in the Eighteenth Century', *Journal of the Society for Army Historical Research*, vol. 61, no. 245 (1983), p. 44.

[9] In pre-modern India, the tradition of *bhrata bala*s (military mercenaries) was quite common. And the EIC effectively tapped into this tradition. V. R. Ramachandra Dikshitar, 'Indian Martial Tradition', *Journal of the Ganganath Jha Research Institute*, vol. 3, nos. 3–4 (1946), pp. 263–77.

[10] Lorenzo M. Crowell, 'Military Professionalism in a Colonial Context: The Madras Army, circa 1832', *Modern Asian Studies* (hereinafter *MAS*), vol. 24, no. 2 (1990), pp. 249–73; Raymond Callahan, *The East India Company and Army Reform: 1783–98* (Cambridge, Massachusetts: Harvard University Press, 1972).

[11] Lieutenant-Colonel W. J. Wilson, *Historical Record of the Fourth Prince of Wales' Own Regiment Madras Light Cavalry* (Madras: Government Office, 1877), p. 35.

[12] Jadunath Sarkar, *Fall of the Mughal Empire*, vol. 2, *1754–71* (1934; reprint, New Delhi: Orient Longman, 1991), pp. 20, 32.

214 Hinduism and the Ethics of Warfare in South Asia

Maratha *campoo*s (brigades comprised of infantry armed and trained in Western style by European mercenaries). The *Dal Khalsa* of Ranjit Singh also recruited the *Purbiya*s and the Gurkhas into the infantry. These communities were also tapped by the EIC. In the 1820s, most of the sepoys of the Bengal army were *Purbiya*s. This was partly because the British officers believed that tall yeomen peasantry made the best infantry recruits and that the higher the caste, the more respectable and well-behaved were the men.[13] The *Purbiya*s were five feet eight inches tall, hence the British officers liked to recruit them.[14] In 1823, the commander-in-chief of India extended the recruiting base of the Bengal army's infantry to Allahabad, Meerut, Bundelkhand and Rohilkhand.[15] In 1825, the Brahmins and the Rajputs constituted 80 percent of the Bengal army, and Muslims constituted another 10 percent. These three communities came from Awadh, Bihar and Rohilkhand.[16] Most of the Hindu sowars were Rajputs and Marathas. The low castes were not recruited due to the hostility of the high castes who had joined the EIC's units.[17]

The EIC was cautious in introducing Western dress for the sepoys. The introduction of leather cockades along with declining service conditions sparked the Vellore Mutiny among the sepoys in the Madras Army in 1806. According to high-caste Hindu soldiers' cultural mores, the use of leather resulted in a loss of caste.[18] Feeding a multi-ethnic army made the logistical task complex. The EIC had to take care of the dietary preferences of their indigenous soldiers, which in turn were shaped by culture. Among the South Asian military personnel, the Gurkhas and the Muslims consumed beef. Most of the high-caste Hindu soldiers were vegetarians. The Madras army's sepoys consumed rice.[19] In the Bengal army's infantry regiments, dominated by Brahmins, messing was impossible. The caste rule was that a Brahmin could not touch food that had not been prepared by himself or his relatives or by members of his own *gotra* (sub-division

---

[13] Court of Enquiry into the Barrackpur Mutiny, Minutes of Evidence, 1824, vol. 11, p. 479, National Archives of India (henceforth NAI), New Delhi.

[14] Captain A. H. Bingley and Captain A. Nicholls, *Caste Handbooks for the Indian Army: Brahmins* (Simla: Government Central Office, 1897), p. 48.

[15] General Order by the Commander-in-Chief, no. 197, 4 December 1823, NAI.

[16] Douglas M. Peers, '"The Habitual Nobility of Being": British Officers and the Social Construction of the Bengal Army in the Early Nineteenth Century', *MAS*, vol. 25, no. 3 (1991), p. 549.

[17] Wilson, *Fourth Prince of Wales' Own Regiment Madras Light Cavalry*, pp. 1, 3, 92–3.

[18] James W. Hoover, *Men without Hats: Dialogue, Discipline and Discontent in the Madras Army, 1806–7* (New Delhi: Manohar, 2007).

[19] Brigadier Humphry Bullock, *History of the Army Service Corps*, vol. 1, *1760–1857* (1952; reprint, Delhi: Sterling Publishers, 1976), p. 25.

Hindu Militarism and Anti-Militarism in British India   215

within a caste). So messing was not possible for the Brahmins, and each Brahmin soldier prepared his own food (rice, *ghee* [clarified butter] and vegetables) and ate alone. However, during campaigns, they depended on *puris* (fried bread made of wheat) and *laddus* (sweetmeats), which they prepared and carried in haversacks.[20]

The British-officered Indian army was used before the 1857 uprising to annex the various independent kingdoms of the subcontinent. After 1859, the British-led Indian army was used for internal policing, that is, for guarding India against the Indians on behalf of the white masters. To an extent, the Indian army was also used to protect the *Raj* from a Russian invasion of India through Afghanistan. Before World War I, the Indian army was comprised of 128,854 sepoys and about 25,036 sowars. The Imperial Service Troops (British-commanded armies of the Indian princes) numbered about 22,479 men.[21] The British garrison in India numbered 75,000 personnel.[22] During the two world wars, the Indian army was used as an imperial reserve. Between 1914 and 1918, 877,068 combatants were recruited from India.[23] Between 1919 and 1930, the percentage of recruits supplied by Punjab and North-West Frontier Province rose from 46 percent to 58.5 percent. The percentage of Nepal, Garhwal and Kumaun rose from 14.8 percent to 22 percent for the same period.[24] Through voluntary enlistment, the Indian army between September 1939 and August 1945 expanded from 189,000 to 2,500,000 men.[25]

One of the reasons behind the revolt of the Brahmins and Rajputs of the Bengal army in 1857 was the fact that they did not like the British policy of overseas deployment. The British frequently used the Bengal army as an imperial reserve, but the high-caste soldiers believed that crossing the *kalapani* (sea) resulted in loss of caste. During the pre-1857 era, the British relied on caste categories to recruit selected communities

---

[20] Bingley and Nicholls, *Brahmins*, pp. 15, 43.

[21] S. D. Pradhan, 'Indian Army and the First World War', in DeWitt Ellinwood and S. D. Pradhan (eds.), *India and World War I* (New Delhi: Manohar, 1978), pp. 51–3; *The Army in India and Its Evolution including an Account of the Establishment of the Royal Air Force in India* (1924; reprint, New Delhi: Anmol Publications, 1985), p. 156.

[22] *India's Contribution to the Great War* (Calcutta: Superintendent of Govt. Printing, 1923), p. 79.

[23] Kaushik Roy, 'The Construction of Martial Race Culture in British-India and Its Legacies in Post-Colonial South Asia', in Kausik Bandopadhyay (ed.), *Asia Annual 2008: Understanding Popular Culture* (New Delhi: Manohar, 2010), p. 250.

[24] Nirad C. Chaudhuri, 'The Martial Races of India', Part II, *Modern Review*, vol. 48, no. 285 (1930), p. 296.

[25] Nandan Prasad, *Expansion of the Armed Forces and Defence Organizations: 1939–45* (New Delhi: Govt. of India, 1956), p. 53.

216   *Hinduism and the Ethics of Warfare in South Asia*

into the army. However, the 1857 mutiny of the Bengal army resulted in the replacement of a policy of categorizing Indian communities by caste with a policy based on race.[26] For the British, there was much similarity between caste and race. Religious, occupational and hereditary factors determined the nature of a caste/race in British eyes.[27] Important scholar-officials of the *Raj* like W. W. Hunter and Herbert Risley conceived of castes as ethnologically based races.[28] From the late nineteenth century, the Martial Race theory shaped recruitment policy.

According to the Martial Race theory, only selected communities on the subcontinent, for biological and cultural reasons, were capable of bearing arms. The father figure of the Martial Race theory was Lord Roberts (the commander-in-chief of India from 1885 to 1893). In 1882, Roberts, then commander-in-chief of the Madras army, argued that the people inhabiting west and south India lacked courage and possessed inferior physiques.[29] He believed that the fighting races of the subcontinent were the Sikhs, Gurkhas, Dogras, Rajputs and Pathans.[30] The Dogras recruited from eastern Punjab and the hills of Jammu and Kashmir were actually Rajputs who inhabited the mountainous regions of the above-mentioned provinces.[31] The imperial belief was that the *vedas* designated the Rajputs as warriors.[32] Table 6.1 shows that the 'martial races' dominated the British-led Indian army just prior to World War I. Roberts's concept influenced the British officers even during the Second World War. For instance, in July 1943, Lieutenant-General G. N. Molesworth noted that the virile races were the Sikhs, Punjabi Muslims, Rajputs, Dogras, Pathans and Jats.[33]

---

[26] David Omissi, '"Martial Races": Ethnicity and Security in Colonial India, 1858–1939', *War & Society*, vol. 9, no. 1 (1991), pp. 6–7.

[27] Peers, '"Habitual Nobility"', p. 548.

[28] Chandar S. Sundaram, '"Reviving a Dead Letter": Military Indianization and the Ideology of Anglo-Indians, 1885–91', in P. S. Gupta and Anirudh Deshpande (eds.), *The British Raj and Its Indian Armed Forces: 1857–1939* (New Delhi: Oxford University Press, 2002), p. 51.

[29] Brian Robson (ed.), *Roberts in India: The Military Papers of Field-Marshal Lord Roberts, 1876–1893* (Stroud: Sutton, 1993), p. 256.

[30] Roberts to Kitchener, 1904, 11/36, Roberts to the secretary of state, 12 Sept. 1897, Kitchener Papers, Roll no. 2, M/F, NAI, New Delhi.

[31] John Gaylor, *Sons of John Company: The Indian and Pakistan Armies, 1903–91* (1992; reprint, New Delhi: Lancer, 1993), p. 188.

[32] Captain A. H. Bingley, *Handbook on Rajputs* (1899; reprint, New Delhi: Low Price Publications, 1999), p. 26.

[33] Recruitment in India, Appendix 19, Note by General Molesworth on Indian Army Recruitment, 21 July 1943, L/WS/1/136, IOR, BL, London.

Hindu Militarism and Anti-Militarism in British India   217

Table 6.1. Religious Composition of the Indian Army in 1912

Religious Category	Communities	Number	Percentage
Sikhs		32,702	20.5
Muslims	Punjabi Muslims + Pathans + Hindustani Muslims + Other Muslims	25,299 + 12,202 + 9,054 + 8,717	16 + 7.7 + 5.7 + 5.5 = 34.5 (approximately)
Hindus	Gurkhas + Rajputs + Dogras and Garhwalis + Other Hindus (Ahirs, Gujars, Mers, Mians, Bhils, Pariahs and Tamils) + Jats + Marathas + Brahmins	18,100 + 12,051 + 10,421 + 10,252 + 9,670 + 5,685 + 2,636	11.5 + 7.7 + 6.1 + 6.5 + 6 + 3 + 1.7 = 42 (approximately)
Christians		1,800	1.2
Total		158,603	

Source: Proceedings of the Army in India Committee, 1912 (Simla: Govt. Central Branch Press, 1913), vol. 1-A, *Minority Report*, p. 156.

The colonial discourse on the 'martial races' emphasized the subcontinent's ethnic diversity in order to make the point that India was not a nation.[34] The process of categorization and classification was part of the larger Enlightenment endeavour. The objective was to observe and study the world outside Europe in order to understand it. An urge to count and classify the various things the British encountered, writes Thomas R. Metcalf, characterized much of the Victorian intellectual programme.[35] DeWitt Ellinwood says that the British belief in racial distinctions was amalgamated with India's social distinctions – especially differences of caste, religion, and occupation – and the product was the Martial Race theory.[36] Philip Constable asserts that the Martial Race theory was not

---

[34] Tapan Raychaudhuri, *Perceptions, Emotions, Sensibilities: Essays on India's Colonial and Post-colonial Experiences* (1999; reprint, New Delhi: Oxford University Press, 2005), p. 217.

[35] Thomas R. Metcalf, *The New Cambridge History of India*, III:4, *Ideologies of the Raj* (1998; reprint, New Delhi: Foundation Books, 2005), p. 113.

[36] DeWitt Ellinwood, 'Ethnicity in a Colonial Asian Army: British Policy, War, and the Indian Army, 1914–18', in Ellinwood and Cynthia H. Enloe (eds.), *Ethnicity and the Military in Asia* (New Brunswick/London: Transaction Books, 1981), pp. 91–2.

218 Hinduism and the Ethics of Warfare in South Asia

merely an 'Orientalist' invention by the British officers for the purpose of strategic recruitment and hegemonic control, but also incorporated the indigenous social differentiation of Kshatriya identity.[37] Let us look closely at the construction of the Gurkha 'martial race' by the British.

Brigadier-General C. G. Bruce noted in 1927 that the term 'Gorkha'/'Goorkha' (later 'Gurkha') was actually a construction of the British. The term originally referred to a small state in the Kathmandu Valley. The ruler of this state unified Nepal during the late eighteenth century. The subjects of this kingdom, who were an amalgam of Mongolian hill tribes, Newars, Rajputs, Brahmins and other menial clans, were called Gorkhalis after their patron saint, Gorakh Nath. The British used the term 'Gurkhas' to refer to the conglomeration of 'military races' found mostly in central Nepal and parts of west and east Nepal.[38] During the mid nineteenth century, the British obtained recruits from Kumaun and Garhwalis, and they were also categorized as Gurkhas.[39] Thus, 'Gurkha' was never a homogeneous category. Linguistic and cultural boundaries divided the men from Nepal who joined the British-Indian army.[40]

The *Raj*'s policy makers accepted the theory of an Aryan invasion of India. It was believed that the Aryans, the original martial race, after conquering the land of the Dravidians, had settled in north India. For occupational purposes, three groups emerged within the Aryans: Brahmins, Kshatriyas or Rajputs, and Vaisyas. The second group had provided hereditary warriors to the subcontinent from time immemorial. In the 1920s, Professor R. L. Turner argued that during the medieval age, when pressed by the Muslim invasion of India, many Aryan groups like the Rajputs had migrated from north India into Nepal. These Rajputs intermarried with the Mongoloid tribes of Nepal, and their offspring inherited the martial instincts of their Rajput forefathers.[41] They were the Gurkhas of the Sepoy army.

---

[37] Philip Constable, 'The Marginalization of a *Dalit* Martial Race in Late Nineteenth- and Early Twentieth-Century Western India', *Journal of Asian Studies*, vol. 60, no. 2 (2001), p. 443.

[38] W. Brook Northey and C. J. Morris, *The Gurkhas* (1927; reprint, New Delhi: Cosmo Publications, 1987), Foreword, pp. xv–xvi.

[39] Colonel L. W. Shakespear, *History of the 2nd King Edward's Own Goorkha Rifles (The Sirmoor Rifles)* (Aldershot: Gale and Polden, 1912), pp. 67, 73.

[40] Lionel Caplan, *Warrior Gentleman: "Gurkhas" in the Western Imagination* (Providence/Oxford: Berghahn Books, 1995), p. 52.

[41] R. L. Turner, 'The People and Their Languages', in Northey and Morris, *The Gurkhas*, pp. 64, 68–9.

The Martial Race theory, in the view of Heather Streets, was not merely an instrument of colonial control. The Martial Race theory also operated in the case of the British army. For instance, the Scottish Highlanders were regarded as a martial race like the Sikhs and the Gurkhas. Edmund Candler, a military commentator who wrote during the early twentieth century, emphasized that the Gurkhas had the nerve of a Highlander. Heather Streets say that the British military elites used the Martial Race theory to manage global imperial politics.[42] The British media popularized the racial and gendered constructs of the savage martiality of certain communities in the guise of the Martial Race theory. In Streets's view, the Martial Race stereotype represented an idealized version of masculinity.[43]

Thus, we have seen that the colonial state used religion in a subtle way. Probably in reaction, the anti-colonial movement also utilized religious ethos and religious symbols. The anti-colonial movement drew on both popular devotional practices and brahmanical ideas for sustaining its struggle against the *Raj*.

MOHANDAS KARAMCHAND GANDHI'S ANTI-MILITARISM

The Indian National Congress (henceforth INC) was set up as a 'safety valve' in 1887 by a liberal British named A. O. Hume.[44] In 1907, the INC was divided into moderate and extremist wings.[45] In January 1915, M. K. Gandhi returned to India from South Africa.[46] By 1919, Gandhi was controlling the INC.[47] Demonstrations and a massive procession organized by the Home Rule League were held in connection with the Rowlatt *Satyagraha* in 1919 at Aligarh. The charisma of Gandhi encouraged people from both the Hindu and Muslim communities to join the movement

---

[42] Heather Streets, *Martial Races: The Military, Race and Masculinity in British Imperial Culture, 1857–1914* (Manchester: Manchester University Press, 2004), p. 1; Edmund Candler, *The Sepoy* (London: John Murray, 1919), p. 18.

[43] Streets, *Martial Races*, pp. 2, 12.

[44] John R. Mclane, 'The Early Congress, Hindu Populism, and the Wider Society', in Richard Sisson and Stanley Wolpert (eds.), *Congress and Indian Nationalism: The Pre-Independence Phase* (New Delhi: Oxford University Press, 1988), p. 50.

[45] Rajat Kanta Ray, 'Moderates, Extremists, and Revolutionaries: Bengal, 1900–1908', in Sisson and Wolpert (eds.), *Congress and Indian Nationalism*, p. 62.

[46] C. H. Philips and Mary Doreen Wainwright, 'Introduction', in Philips and Wainwright (eds.), *The Partition of India: Policies and Perspectives, 1935–47* (London: George Allen and Unwin, 1970), p. 34.

[47] Eleanor Zelliot, 'Congress and the Untouchables, 1917–50', in Sisson and Wolpert (eds.), *Congress and Indian Nationalism*, pp. 182–4.

220 *Hinduism and the Ethics of Warfare in South Asia*

and boycott government institutions.[48] However, Gandhi's alliance with the Muslims through cooperation with the *Khilafat* movement leaders (i.e., the Ali brothers) soon collapsed. The *Khilafat* leaders were actually demonstrating grievances against the British following the abolition of the *caliphate* in Turkey in the aftermath of World War I. In response to India's contribution of men and materials to the British Empire during World War I, and also to appease the rising nationalist forces, the British Government decided to offer some political concessions to the Indians. In 1917, the Montagu Declaration promised Indians 'responsible' government. The 1919 Government of India Act (based on the Montagu-Chelmsford reforms) introduced *dyarchy* (joint rule) in provincial and central government. In 1928, the INC demanded dominion status. In response, to ward off agitation, on 31 October 1929, Viceroy Lord Irwin issued his dominion status declaration. In 1930, Gandhi launched the salt march at Dandi. The stated grievance was that the Indians refused to pay salt tax to an alien government; it was the inviolable right of every Indian to make salt from sea water.[49] Following Gandhi's civil disobedience campaign, the British government passed the Government of India Act, which allowed the Indian political parties to form ministries at the provinces. In 1942, Gandhi launched his last and greatest mass movement, called 'Quit India'. Ultimately, in 1947, British India was divided into two independent states, India and Pakistan. In 1948, Gandhi was assassinated by a Hindu fundamentalist named Nathuram Godse.[50] The British government accused the INC of being a Hindu body and not representative of the 'Indian nation'. There were some elements of truth in the British accusation.

There were about eighty million Muslims in South Asia, and Muslims constituted about 25 percent of British India's population in the early twentieth century.[51] Political and social developments within India widened the rift between the Hindu and Muslim communities. In 1867, Hindu leaders

---

[48] Zoya Hasan, 'Congress in Aligarh District, 1930–46: Problems of Political Mobilization', in Sisson and Wolpert (eds.), *Congress and Indian Nationalism*, p. 331.

[49] R. J. Moore, 'The Making of India's Paper Federation', in Philips and Wainwright (eds.), *Partition of India*, p. 56; Denis Judd, *The Lion and the Tiger: The Rise and Fall of the British Raj* (New Delhi: Oxford University Press, 2004), p. 203; D. A. Low, 'The Imprint of Ambiguity: Britain and India in the Early 1930s', in Mushirul Hasan and Narayani Gupta (eds.), *India's Colonial Encounter: Essays in Memory of Eric Stokes* (1993; reprint, New Delhi: Manohar, 2004), p. 472.

[50] Judd, *The Lion and the Tiger*, p. 204.

[51] Mumtaz Hasan, 'The Background of the Partition of the Indo-Pakistan Subcontinent', in Philips and Wainwright (eds.), *Partition of India*, pp. 325, 358.

demanded the replacement of Urdu with Hindi in the United Provinces. The *Arya Samaj* was established in Bombay in 1875 and in Lahore in 1877. Similarly, an Islamic seminary was established at Deoband. The net result was consolidation of the religious identities of both Hindus and Muslims on the subcontinent. Millions of people who had lived under tribal and folk traditions and outside the influence of the scriptures of the great religious traditions (rigid scriptural Islam, Brahmanism, etc.) were persuaded to make their identities and their commitments clear. As a result, these 'outsiders' now began to move towards the different great religious traditions. This, in turn, resulted in a hardening of religious boundaries and identities. Iswar Chandra Vidyasagar (born 1820), an ardent Bengali nationalist and social reformer, proclaimed himself at one level a humanist and an atheist but at another level, for the purpose of reforming the 'decadent' Hindu society, he justified rationalism on the basis of classical Hindu texts. The *shuddhi* (purification) movement of the *Arya Samaj* also aggravated Hindu-Muslim tensions. To give an example, during 1923–4, in the Agra-Mathura region, the *Arya Samaj* persuaded 150,000 Muslims to convert to Hinduism.[52] Towards the end of the nineteenth century, *ganapati* festivals and a cow protection movement by Marathi Hindu leaders like B. G. Tilak further inflamed the situation. At the local level in north India, the idiom of discourse was vernacular and religious, and the rhetoric of local politics among the lower classes was Hindu in content.[53] Nationalist leaders like Bal Gangadhar Tilak, Lala Lajpat Rai, Bipin Chandra Pal and Aurobindo Ghosh, who belonged to the extremist wing of the INC, equated the nation with the Hindu community, and Hindu religion became the natural paradigm for describing the national ethos.[54] As a reaction, in 1906, the Muslims demanded separate electorates from the viceroy.[55] The Morley-Minto reforms of 1908–9 gave Indians some representation in provincial and central government. The British, in order to prevent the emergence of a joint Hindu-Muslim opposition, went ahead with the introduction of separate electorates in the Indian Councils Act of 1909.[56] From then onwards, Hindu and

---

[52] Satish Saberwal, *Spirals of Contention: Why India Was Partitioned in 1947* (London/New York/New Delhi: Routledge, 2008), pp. xxiii, xxxii–xxxiii, 45.

[53] Mclane, 'The Early Congress, Hindu Populism, and the Wider Society', p. 56.

[54] William Gould, *Hindu Nationalism and the Language of Politics in Late Colonial India* (New Delhi: Foundation Books, 2005), p. 38.

[55] M. A. H. Ispahani, 'Factors Leading to the Partition of British India', in Philip and Wainwright (eds.), *Partition of India*, pp. 333–6.

[56] Stanley Wolpert, 'The Indian National Congress in Nationalist Perspective', in Sisson and Wolpert (eds.), *Congress and Indian Nationalism*, p. 24.

Muslim leaders could look only to their co-religionists for winning elections. William Gould asserts that the widening of communalism in public life was encouraged by the INC leaders' representation of the national polity using Hindu symbols.[57] The INC's dependence on Hindu religious symbols and on Hindu organizations like the *Mahasabha* and the *Arya Samaj* for mobilizing Hindus further alienated the Muslims, who perceived that the INC's goal was Hindu *raj*.[58] Throughout the early 1930s, the INC leaders in the United Provinces organized meetings during religious festivals and bathing fairs. The vernacular newspapers associated with the 'leftist' and 'secular' Congress position also used Hindu religious imagery.[59] In the 1937 election, the INC was able to secure only 5.4 percent of the total Muslim seats. In the elections of 1945–6, the Muslim League won 427 of the 507 Muslim seats and formed ministries in the two Muslim-majority provinces, Bengal and Sind. In the provincial elections held in February 1946, the Muslim League won 88.8 percent of the Muslim seats.[60] The failure of the INC to carry the Muslims was due in part to Gandhi's techniques of mass mobilization, which involved concepts like *satyagraha, swaraj, sarvodaya, ahimsa, harijan, Ramrajya,* and so on. All these idioms were derived from Hinduism, as the following discussion shows.

Much of Gandhi's philosophy could be culled from *Hind Swaraj,* which was written in November 1909. Gandhi's objective was to transmit the 'mighty message of *ahimsa*' to the rest of the world through the English language. Anthony J. Parel writes that *Hind Swaraj* was addressed to the British living in India and Britain and also to expatriate Indians who were attracted to terrorism, and also to the extremist wing of the INC.[61] The underground Bengal revolutionaries were supported by the Ramakrishna Mission. The Ramakrishna Mission was organized by Swami Vivekananda during 1897–1902. Its central message was rejection of Western material superiority and assertion of the spiritual superiority of Hinduism.[62] Interestingly, Gandhi's philosophy

---

[57] Gould, *Hindu Nationalism and the Language of Politics in Late Colonial India,* p. 29.

[58] Hasan, 'Congress in Aligarh District, 1930–46', pp. 337–8.

[59] Gould, *Hindu Nationalism and the Language of Politics in Late Colonial India,* pp. 12, 31–2.

[60] S. R. Mehrotra, 'The Congress and the Partition of India', and Z. H. Zaidi, 'Aspects of the Development of Muslim League Policy, 1937–47', in Philip and Wainwright (eds.), *Partition of India,* pp. 190, 217, 253, 272.

[61] M. K. Gandhi, *Hind Swaraj and Other Writings,* ed. by Anthony J. Parel (1997; reprint, New Delhi: Foundation Books, 2004), Editor's Introduction, pp. xiii–xv.

[62] Ray, 'Moderates, Extremists, and Revolutionaries', p. 63.

Hindu Militarism and Anti-Militarism in British India 223

also reflected these trends. In 1921, Gandhi recalled that during his 1909 visit to London, he came in contact with several Indian 'anarchists' and felt the need to write a book in response to their 'immoral' demand for political violence.[63]

In *Hind Swaraj*, Gandhi linked the moral regeneration of India with its political emancipation from British rule. Gandhi made a distinction between *swaraj* as self-rule/self-government or the quest for home rule and establishment of a 'good' (i.e., righteous) state and *swaraj* as the quest for self-improvement. Gandhi's concept is similar to the concepts of inner/greater *jihad* (self-purification of the Muslims) and inferior/lesser external *jihad* (expanding *Dar al Islam* into *Dar al Harb*). Gandhi pushed the argument that modern civilization posed a greater threat than colonialism and that the latter was the product of modern civilization. Basically, *Hind Swaraj* pushed twin interlinked ideas: that worldly pursuits should give way to ethical living, and that there is no room for violence against any human being. Later, in his collected works, Gandhi noted that one cannot build non-violence on factory civilization; *ahimsa* could be built only on the basis of self-contained villages. Gandhi's aim was also rapprochement between the Indians and the British.[64] Gandhi critiqued the idea of the extremists and the revolutionaries that expulsion of the British and retention of their political, military and economic institutions would result in *swaraj*. Gandhi noted that they want the structure of British rule without the British personnel. Then it will not be Hindustan but Englistan, and he is against this sort of *swaraj*.[65] On 1 November 1921, Gandhi wrote that for him, attaining *swaraj* is a part of the striving for *moksha*.[66]

In Gandhi's philosophy there is no religious act without political implications and no political act without religious overtones.[67] Gandhi believed that politics is part of *dharma* and that political power is a means and not end.[68] On 12 May 1920, Gandhi claimed:

I have been experimenting with myself and my friends by introducing religion into politics. Let me explain what I mean by religion. It is not the Hindu religion, which I certainly prize above all other religions, but the religion which transcends

---

[63] Gandhi, *Hind Swaraj*, Editor's Introduction, p. xv.
[64] Ibid., pp. xiv–xvi.
[65] Gandhi, *Hind Swaraj*, pp. 26–8.
[66] *The Essential Writings of Mahatma Gandhi*, ed. by Raghavan Iyer (1993; reprint, New Delhi: Oxford University Press, 2007) (hereinafter *EWMG*), p. 29.
[67] *The Writings of Gandhi: A Selection*, edited and with an Introduction by Ronald Duncan (1971; reprint, Calcutta: Rupa, 1990), Introduction, p. 29.
[68] *EWMG*, Introduction, p. 16.

Hinduism, which changes one's very nature, which binds one indissolubly to the truth within and which even purifies... It was in that religious spirit that I came upon *hartal*. I wanted to show that it is not a knowledge of letters that would give India consciousness of herself, or that would bind the educated together.[69]

On 3 April 1924, Gandhi expounded that his patriotism is a stage in his journey to the land of eternal freedom and peace. In his paradigm, there are no politics devoid of religion. Politics bereft of religion, warned Gandhi, are a death-trap because they kill the soul.[70]

Gandhi once stated that there was adequate space in Hinduism for both Islam and Christianity.[71] On 11 August 1920, Gandhi wrote that his life was dedicated to the service of India through the religion of non-violence, which according to him is the root of Hinduism.[72] Gandhi believed that the ancient epics and the vedic literature preached *ahimsa*. Gandhi explained:

Even in 1888–9, when I first became acquainted with the *Gita*, I felt that it was not an historical work, but that under the guise of physical warfare, it described the duel that perpetually went on in the hearts of mankind, and that physical warfare was brought in merely to make the description of the internal duel more alluring.... I do not regard the *Mahabharata* as an historical work in the accepted sense.... The author of the *Mahabharata* has not established the necessity of physical warfare; on the contrary he has proved its futility.[73]

In an article in *Harijan* (the newspaper published by Gandhi) dated 3 October 1936, Gandhi wrote that the epic describes the eternal duel between the forces of darkness and of light.[74]

On 3 October 1936, in an article published in *Harijan*, Gandhi clarified his modification of Hinduism as regards *ahimsa*. Gandhi acknowledged that no Hindu 'prophet' before him had ever condemned violence in such strong language. Further, Hinduism, in his eyes, is always evolving. The fact that, unlike the Koran and the Bible, there is no single book in Hinduism gives it the scope and flexibility, wrote Gandhi, to adapt to the demands of the time.[75]

Gandhi claimed that he derived his concept of *dharma* from the *Bhagavad Gita* and the *Ramayana*. In Gandhi's view, the *Gita* and the

[69] *EWMG*, p. 46.
[70] Ibid., p. 33.
[71] Gould, *Hindu Nationalism and the Language of Politics in Late Colonial India*, p. 38.
[72] *EWMG*, p. 239.
[73] *The Writings of Gandhi*, ed. by Duncan, p. 33.
[74] Ibid., p. 41.
[75] Ibid., p. 40.

Hindu Militarism and Anti-Militarism in British India 225

Tulsidas *Ramayana* preaches *dharma*, which means concern for the welfare of others, and this leads to *ramrajya*.[76] Gandhi's concept of the force of love is derived from Tulsidas *Ramayana*. Gandhi notes in *Hind Swaraj* that the poet Tulsidas said that pity or love is the root of religion.[77]

Gandhi's concept of *anasakti yoga* (selfless, disinterested action) was influenced by disinterested action for the greater good as preached by Lord Krishna in the *Bhagavad Gita*.[78] Gandhi noted that the solution for most, if not all, problems is renunciation of the fruits of action. This is the core around which the *Bhagavad Gita* is woven.[79] On 21 December 1925, Gandhi had written:

When, thousands of years ago, the battle of Kurukshetra was fought, the doubts which occurred to Arjuna were answered by Shri Krishna in the *Gita*; but that battle of Kurukshetra is going on, will go on, for ever within us, the Prince of Yogis, Lord Krishna, the universal *atman* dwelling in the hearts of us all, will always be there to guide Arjuna, the human soul, and our Godward impulses represented by the Pandavas will always triumph over the demoniac impulses represented by the Kauravas.[80]

On 16 March 1945, Gandhi wrote that fate is the fruition of *karma*. Fate may be good or bad. Human effort consists in overcoming adverse fate or reducing its impact. There is a continuous struggle between fate and human effort. Who can say which of them really wins? So we human beings must continue with our work and leave the result to God.[81] Gandhi linked his concept of *anasakti yoga* to *ahimsa* in the following manner. He declared that when there is no desire for fruit, there is no temptation for untruth or *himsa*.[82]

To an extent, Buddhism and Christianity also influenced Gandhi. On 12 May 1920, Gandhi wrote that Buddha would have died resisting the priesthood if the majesty of his love had not proved equal to the task of bending the priesthood. And Christ died on the Cross with a crown of thorns on his head defying the might of the Roman Empire. Gandhi admitted that he had learnt the message of non-violence, in part, from these great masters.[83]

---

[76] Gandhi, *Hind Swaraj*, Editor's Introduction, pp. xvi–xvii.
[77] Gandhi, *Hind Swaraj*, pp. 88–9.
[78] *EWMG*, Introduction, p. 21.
[79] *The Writings of Gandhi*, ed. by Duncan, p. 34.
[80] *EWMG*, pp. 33–4.
[81] Ibid., p. 184.
[82] *The Writings of Gandhi*, ed. by Duncan, p. 37.
[83] *EWMG*, p. 48.

226   *Hinduism and the Ethics of Warfare in South Asia*

Gandhi made a distinction between Eastern and Western civilization, and he claimed that the latter was predominantly based on force. Gandhi made a distinction between the humanistic Christian civilization and the modern Western civilization based on barbarism.[84] In *Hind Swaraj*, Gandhi describes the modern barbaric Western civilization as one that, according to the teachings of Prophet Muhammad, could be considered a satanic civilization. And Hinduism calls it the Black Age.[85]

Gandhi believed in the use of force in some context. The *Hind Swaraj* tells us that a petition, without the backing of force, is useless. However, Gandhi made a distinction between soul force and brute force.[86] Gandhi says in the *Hind Swaraj*:

Two kinds of force can back petitions. 'We will hurt you if you do not give this' is one kind of force; it is the force of arms, whose evil results we have already examined. The second kind of force can thus be stated: 'If you do not concede our demand, we will be no longer your petitioners. You can govern us only so long as we remain the governed; we shall no longer have any dealings with you.' The force implied in this may be described as love-force, soul-force or, more popularly but less accurately, passive resistance. This force is indestructible.[87]

The Gujarati word for passive resistance is *satyagraha*, a word derived from *sadagraha* (firmness in a good cause).[88] *Satyagraha* could be defined as non-violent resistance. So *satyagraha* is a sort of 'just' technique for waging just war. *Satyagraha* means truth-force, that is, the power of truth directed towards the promotion of social welfare. Injustice and the attendant hostility could be confronted through an appeal to conscience. However, *satyagraha* is also a policy of action and non-violent resistance.[89] Gandhi's non-violence requires active resistance to evil.[90] Gandhi advanced an alternate view of heroism for the purpose of conducting non-violent struggle. He believed that heroism is a quality of heart, free from every trace of fear and anger, and geared to exact instant atonement for every breach of honour. Heroism can enable a person to stand alone in times of trial and isolation.[91]

---

[84] Gandhi, *Hind Swaraj*, Editor's Introduction, p. xxii.
[85] Gandhi, *Hind Swaraj*, pp. 37–8.
[86] Ibid., pp. 79, 84.
[87] Ibid., p. 85.
[88] Ibid., p. 85.
[89] *EWMG*, Introduction, pp. 5–6, 8.
[90] Gandhi, *Hind Swaraj*, p. 86.
[91] *EWMG*, Introduction, p. 6.

Gandhi can conceive of getting *swaraj* only by applying soul force because he believed in an inviolable connection between ends and means. Gandhi elaborates in the *Hind Swaraj* that only fair means can produce fair results. There is harm in the exercise of brute force, never in that of pity.[92] Gandhi in *Hind Swaraj* quotes the Gospel of St. Matthew: 'Those that wield the sword shall perish by the sword.'[93] On 11 August 1920, Gandhi further explained his position. He claimed that he is not a visionary but a practical idealist. The religion of non-violence is not meant merely for the *rishis* and saints. It is meant for the common people as well. Non-violence is the law of our species as violence is the law of the brute. The spirit lies dormant in the brute, who knows no law but that of physical might. The dignity of man requires obedience to a higher law – to the strength of the spirit. On 8 November 1926, in the newspaper titled *The Hindu*, Gandhi wrote that the trait that distinguishes man from all other animals is his capacity to be non-violent.[94]

Gandhi believed that soul force is much superior to brute force. In the *Hind Swaraj*, Gandhi writes that the force of arms is powerless when matched against the force of love or the soul.[95] On 11 August 1920, in *Young India*, Gandhi wrote:

I do believe that where there is only a choice between cowardice and violence I would advise violence.... I would rather have India resort to arms in order to defend her honour than she should in a cowardly manner become or remain a helpless witness to her dishonour. But I believe that non-violence is infinitely superior to violence, forgiveness is more manly than punishment. *Kshama virasya bhushanam*. 'Forgiveness adorns a soldier.' But abstinence is forgiveness only when there is the power to punish; it is meaningless when it pretends to proceed from a helpless creature.... But I do not believe India to be helpless. I do not believe myself to be a helpless creature. Only I want to use India's and my strength for a better purpose. Let me not be misunderstood. Strength does not come from physical capacity. It comes from an indomitable will.[96]

Gandhi claimed that he would tolerate neither organized violence by the government nor unorganized violence by the people.[97] After the first civil disobedience movement (1919–22), Gandhi asserted his inability to

---

[92] Gandhi, *Hind Swaraj*, pp. 81, 84.
[93] Ibid., p. 89.
[94] *EWMG*, pp. 238, 240.
[95] Gandhi, *Hind Swaraj*, p. 85.
[96] *EWMG*, p. 237.
[97] S. Bhattacharya, 'Swaraj and the Kamgar: The Indian National Congress and the Bombay Working Class, 1919–31', in Sisson and Wolpert (eds.), *Congress and Indian Nationalism*, p. 244.

228   Hinduism and the Ethics of Warfare in South Asia

conduct a successful campaign of civil disobedience unless a completely non-violent spirit were generated among the people.[98] On 1 November 1928, Gandhi declared that he could not lead India again until the people were ready to pursue a policy of non-violence.[99] Gandhi aimed at moral regeneration. He pointed out that the application of violence does not improve the behaviour of the target group or the applicant. However, the exercise of *daya* (benevolence) results in the moral uplift even of the culprit. For acquiring *swaraj*, the people should follow *satya* (truth) and *dharma* (duties).[100] For Gandhi, *sat* (truth) is equivalent to God.[101] On 1 October 1931, Gandhi, in *Young India*, wrote that his daily experience is that every problem would lend itself to a solution if we were determined to make the law of truth and non-violence the law of life. For truth and non-violence are two sides of the same coin.[102] In 1932, Gandhi noted that the pursuit of truth is true *bhakti* (devotion). It is the path that leads to God, and therefore there is no place in it for cowardice, no place for defeat. It is the talisman by which death itself becomes the portal to life eternal.[103] In February 1946, when the Indian ratings of the Royal Indian Navy rebelled against British authority at Bombay, Madras and Karachi, Gandhi did not approve because the rebellion was wedded to violence.[104]

Linked to the concept of *satyagraha* is the idea of *sarvodaya*. Gandhi pushed the idea of civil humanism and broadened the concept of *dharma* to include notions of citizenship, cooperation, equality, liberty and fraternity.[105] Gandhi believed that human beings could incarnate their latent divinity by deliberately and joyously putting their abilities and assets to practical use for the sake of all (known as *sarvodaya*). *Sarvodaya* means universal welfare. Gandhi, unlike the socialists, did not favour 'revolution from above', which involved state violence. Gandhi's *sarvodaya* and his attendant concept of *ahimsa* made class war distasteful and unnecessary. Raghavan Iyer claims that the fundamental presupposition behind *sarvodaya* is non-violent socialism, which is as old as the communal sharing preached by Buddha and Christ.[106] Gandhi was opposed to the use of

---

[98] Quoted from ibid., p. 224.
[99] *EWMG*, pp. 38–9.
[100] Gandhi, *Hind Swaraj*, pp. 82, 84.
[101] *EWMG*, Introduction, p. 1.
[102] *EWMG*, p. 243.
[103] *The Writings of Gandhi*, ed. by Duncan, p. 42.
[104] Om Nagpal, 'Naval Revolt – The Last Blow on the British Raj', *Oracle*, vol. 1, no. 4 (1979), pp. 22–5; Judd, *The Lion and the Tiger*, pp. 172–3.
[105] Gandhi, *Hind Swaraj*, Editor's Introduction, p. xvi.
[106] *EWMG*, Introduction, pp. 1–2, 6, 11–12.

Hindu Militarism and Anti-Militarism in British India   229

violence for achieving social revolution. In 1934, when the left wing of the INC, under the leadership of Jawaharlal Nehru, was arguing for radical social change, Gandhi defended the zamindari system and talked of trusteeship.[107]

One of the crucial components of *satyagraha* is self-sacrifice. Gandhi indulged in daily acts of *tapas* (spiritual exercise and meditation/voluntary sacrifice) while engaged in social and political activities. Gandhi felt that leaders must always share the trials and travails of the human condition; he felt that ubiquitous suffering is the common predicament of humanity, while earthly pleasures and intellectual joys are ephemeral and deceptive.[108] On 11 August 1920, Gandhi noted: 'For *satyagraha* and its off-shoots, non-cooperation and civil resistance, are ... new names for the law of suffering. The *rishis*, who discovered the law of non-violence in the midst of violence ... were themselves greater warriors than Wellington. Having themselves known the use of arms, they realized their uselessness and taught a weary world that its salvation lay ... through non-violence.'[109]

In 1942, Gandhi wrote that non-violence in its dynamic condition means conscious suffering.[110] As D. G. Dalton notes, fasting was the ultimate weapon of *satyagraha*, employed when the other means failed.[111] However, Gandhi at the same time was aware of the limitations of fasting as a political weapon. He once said that you cannot fast against a tyrant.[112] D. A. Low rightly says that the British Empire during the interwar period was not looking forward to giving independence to India, though the British ruling elites assumed that sometime in the distant future, a grant of independence might become necessary. And the British, while devolving power to the Indians at the local and regional levels, simultaneously strengthened their control at the national level. The British were prepared to suppress mass movements but did not aim to eliminate the nationalist leaders. In other words, the British Empire in India was not as oppressive as the Dutch and French colonial empires. If the Conservatives under Winston Churchill had been in power in the 1930s, the British Empire in

---

[107] K. N. Chaudhuri, 'Economic Problems and Indian Independence', in Philips and Wainwright (eds.), *Partition of India*, p. 299.
[108] *EWMG*, Introduction, pp. 4–5.
[109] *EWMG*, p. 238.
[110] *The Writings of Gandhi*, ed. by Duncan, p. 49.
[111] D. G. Dalton, 'Gandhi during Partition: A Case Study in the Nature of Satyagraha', in Philips and Wainwright (eds.), *Partition of India*, p. 234.
[112] Quoted from ibid., p. 243.

230 Hinduism and the Ethics of Warfare in South Asia

India might have become like the French and Dutch colonial empires.[113] In such a scenario, Gandhi would have been replaced by the hard-liners who spoke of armed revolutions, terrorism and direct violent action against the *Raj*.

In fact, in Gandhi's framework, *ahimsa* is an integral part of *yajna* (sacrifice), a practice rooted in the ancient Indian belief in a benevolent cosmic order maintained by human self-purification and self-examination. *Ahimsa*, for Gandhi, is based on *anasakti* (selfless action). *Ahimsa* in a passive manner means refusal to do harm, and in a positive/active form means the largest amount of love leading to large-scale charity.[114] On 2 May 1935, Gandhi claimed that love has no boundary. My nationalism, noted Gandhi, includes the love of all the nations of the earth, irrespective of creed.[115] However, not every nationalist leader accepted Gandhi's message of love, peace and non-violence. The greatest challenge emerged from the Bengali politician Subhas Chandra Bose (1897–1945).

SUBHAS CHANDRA BOSE AND HINDU MILITARISM

While Gandhi believed that the struggle for independence was a *dharmayuddha* and that in *dharmayuddha*, physical force can never be applied, Subhas Bose believed that the end justifies the means. Since the object of independence is a *dharmik* (noble) aim, unfair means (i.e., the use of physical force, alliance with the enemy's enemy, etc.) were well justified in order to achieve the righteous end. In an article printed in the *Azad Hind* (the official bi-monthly journal of the Netaji's Free India Centre in Europe) dated June 1942, Bose bluntly wrote: '[N]on-violent civil disobedience cannot secure the expulsion of the British from India.... Tell the Indian people that if passive resistance fails to secure the liberation of the country, they should be ready to take up arms in the final struggle.'[116] In another article dated October 1942, which appeared in the *Azad Hind*, Bose posed a more trenchant criticism of Gandhian philosophy in the following words:

---

[113] Low, 'The Imprint of Ambiguity', pp. 467–70.
[114] *EWMG*, Introduction, pp. 6–7.
[115] *EWMG*, p. 245.
[116] *Azad Hind: Writings and Speeches, 1941–43*, eds. Sisir Kumar Bose and Sugata Bose, in *Netaji Collected Works*, vol. 11 (New Delhi: Permanent Black, 2002), p. 128. See also Introduction, p. 2.

Hindu Militarism and Anti-Militarism in British India   231

But now that the British are engaged in a war with other powers and have been considerably weakened thereby, it has become possible for the Indian people to work up a revolution which will end British rule once for all. But, it is necessary for the Indian people to take up arms in their struggle and to cooperate with those powers that are fighting Britain today. This task, Gandhi will not accomplish – hence India now needs a new leadership.[117]

Since Bose demanded violent rather than non-violent struggle, he warned his countrymen about the necessary bloodletting. In a broadcast from Berlin on 7 December 1942, he asserted: 'Two years and one hundred thousand lives! We must be prepared to voluntarily sacrifice one hundred thousand lives in the course of the struggle. If we do so freedom will be ours once and for all.'[118] In January 1943, Tokyo decided to bring Bose from Germany to Japan to lead the anti-British struggle in India from Southeast Asia.[119] Before Bose departed for Japan in a German U-boat on 8 February 1943, he prepared a speech that was broadcast over *Azad Hind* Radio in Berlin on 13 April 1943. In this speech, Bose reminded his listeners of the Jallianwala Bagh massacre and argued, 'The blood of the martyr is the price that must be paid for liberty.'[120] On 6 July 1944, in a broadcast to Gandhi on Rangoon Radio, Bose emphasized: 'These men and women honestly feel that the British Government will never surrender to persuasion or moral pressure or non-violent resistance.'[121]

Bose's concept of history was coloured by Western secular freedom fighters and socialism, as well as by Hinduism. Bose was influenced by Aurobindo Ghosh (1872–1950), who advocated combating British violence with indigenous violence. Like Balgangadhar Tilak, Aurobindo realized the necessity of setting up secret societies for carrying out violent revolutionary struggle.[122] Aurobindo used Kali (the fearsome Tantric goddess) worship as an instrument to promote revolutionary terrorism in Bengal. *Tantra* is an esoteric system that heroically subverts social norms in order to confront death and suffering and achieve

---

[117] *Azad Hind: Writings and Speeches*, p. 149.
[118] Ibid., p. 179.
[119] Lieutenant-General Isoda Saburo, 'Netaji: The Man', *Oracle*, vol. 17, no. 4 (1995), p. 17.
[120] *Azad Hind: Writings and Speeches*, p. 202.
[121] 'Netaji's Broadcast Address to Mahatma Gandhi over the Rangoon Radio on 6 July 1944', *Oracle*, vol. 16, no. 1 (1994), p. 1.
[122] Joyce Chapman Lebra, *Women against the Raj: The Rani of Jhansi Regiment* (Singapore: ISEAS, 2008), pp. 10–11.

232   Hinduism and the Ethics of Warfare in South Asia

liberation and worldy empowerment simultaneously.[123] Some background information about Bose is necessary to contextualize his political philosophy.

In 1938, Bose was appointed president of the INC. Bose demanded direct action against the *Raj*.[124] Due to pressure from Gandhi, Bose resigned from the post of president of All India Congress Committee and in May 1939 formed the Forward Bloc in order to consolidate the left forces under its banner. In March 1941, Bose escaped from Calcutta to Kabul. In March 1941, at Kabul, Bose met Alberto Quaroni, the Italian minister, at the Italian legation in Kabul.[125] On 9 April 1941, in a secret memorandum send to Berlin, Bose noted:

> The overthrow of British power in India can, in its last stages, be materially assisted by Japanese foreign policy in the Far East. If Japan decides on expansion southwards it will lead to an open clash with Great Britain.... A defeat of the British Navy in the Far East including smashing up of the Singapore base, will automatically weaken British military strength and prestige in India.[126]

After arriving in Berlin, Bose organized the Free India Centre and started broadcasting on *Azad Hind* Radio to India and East Asia in order to undermine British war efforts.[127] From the Indian soldiers captured by the Afrika Korps while fighting the British forces in North Africa, Bose created the 3,000-strong Indian Legion. However, Germany's failure to reach India through Egypt or south Russia meant that this body of troops could not be utilized directly for invasion of India.[128] In fact, Nazi Germany's plan was that, after the successful conclusion of the Russian campaign, German forces would advance into Afghanistan and then into north-west India.[129] On 1 May 1942, Bose, in a broadcast from Berlin, exhorted: 'On the 10th day of that month in the year 1857, began India's first war of independence. In May 1942, 85 years later, has begun India's

---

[123] Rachael Fabish, 'The Political Goddess: Aurobindo's Use of Bengali *Sakta* Tantrism to Justify Political Violence in the Indian Anti-Colonial Movement', *South Asia: Journal of South Asian Studies*, vol. 30, no. 2 (2007), pp. 269, 273.

[124] Johannes H. Voigt, 'Co-operation or Confrontation? War and Congress Politics, 1939–42', in D. A. Low (ed.), *Congress and the Raj: Facets of the Indian Struggle 1917–47* (London: Heinemann, 1977), p. 351.

[125] *Azad Hind: Writings and Speeches*, pp. 13, 21, 34.

[126] Ibid., p. 49.

[127] Masayoshi Kakitsubo, 'Netaji as I Knew Him', *Oracle*, vol. 17, no. 4 (1995), p. 24.

[128] Peter Ward Fay, 'Partners against the *Raj*: Netaji and the Indian National Army', *Oracle*, vol. 17, no. 2 (1995), p. 8.

[129] Milan L. Hauner, '1942: The Decisive War Year in India's Destiny', *Oracle*, vol. 8, no. 1 (1986), pp. 38–9.

Hindu Militarism and Anti-Militarism in British India 233

last war of independence.'[130] On 15 November 1943, the Provisional Free Indian Government was announced at Berlin in the presence of Nazi Foreign Minister Joachim Von Ribentrop, Japanese Ambassador to Berlin Oshima and the Italian Ambassador Anfuso. A. C. N. Nambiar was deputized in the absence of Bose, who at that time was in Southeast Asia organizing the Indian National Army/*Azad Hind Fauj* (henceforth INA) for liberating India from the yoke of the British.[131]

In July 1943, the INA was resurrected by Bose. Even before the advent of Bose, the Japanese government from 1939 onwards had been collaborating with another Bengali revolutionary named Rash Behari Bose to organize an anti-British front using Indian prisoners of war (hereafter POWs) and the Indian diaspora in Southeast Asia. After the surrender of the Allied forces at Singapore on 15 February 1942, the Indian POWs were handed over to an Indian military officer named Captain Mohan Singh. With the aid of the Japanese and Rash Behari (head of the Indian Independence League), Mohan Singh formed the INA.[132] Due to differences with the Japanese, Mohan Singh was soon removed from command of the INA. On 25 August 1943, Bose became the supreme commander of the INA.[133] On 5 July 1943, Bose, in his first address to the INA at Singapore, emphasized: 'Throughout my public career I have always felt that though India is otherwise ripe for independence in every way, she has lacked one thing; namely, an army of liberation. George Washington of America could fight and win freedom, because he had his army. Garibaldi could liberate Italy because he had his armed volunteers behind him.'[134] Bose's objective was to raise an army of about 300,000 volunteers from the Indian POWs in Japanese hands as well as from the three million Indian civilians settled in Southeast Asia.[135]

When addressing an assembly of Indians at Singapore on 9 July 1943, Bose used the phrase 'Total Mobilization'.[136] Despite the opposition

---

[130] *Azad Hind: Writings and Speeches*, p. 98.

[131] 'Celebration of the Foundation of the Provisional Government of Free India, Berlin, 15 November 1943', *Oracle*, vol. 15, no. 4 (1993), p. 11.

[132] Colonel P. K. Sehgal, 'The Indian National Army', *Oracle*, vol. 15, no. 1 (1993), pp. 7–10; Voigt, 'Co-operation or Confrontation?', p. 366.

[133] Colonel P. K. Sahgal, 'My INA Odyssey', *Oracle*, vol. 7, no. 2 (1985), p. 4.

[134] Subhas Chandra Bose, 'First Address to Indian National Army, Singapore, 5 July 1943', *Oracle*, vol. 15, no. 3 (1993), pp. 7–8.

[135] J. K. Banerji, 'Subhas Chandra Bose in East Asia', *Oracle*, vol. 15, no. 4 (1993), pp. 22–3; Subhas Chandra Banerjee, 'Indian National Army: Social Background and Training', *Oracle*, vol. 8, no. 3 (1986), p. 25.

[136] M. L. Bhargava, 'Netaji Subhas Chandra Bose in South-East Asia and India's Liberation War, 1943–45', *Oracle*, vol. 8, no. 3 (1986), p. 9.

234   *Hinduism and the Ethics of Warfare in South Asia*

of the Japanese and some conservative Indians, Bose decided to set up an all-female military regiment called the Rani of Jhansi Regiment and appointed Lakshmi Sahgal as commander of this unit.[137] She was later given the rank of colonel. The philosophy behind setting up this regiment was elaborated in the inaugural address that Bose delivered at the Rani of Jhansi Training Camp at Singapore on 22 October 1943:

India could not have produced a heroine like the Rani of Jhansi if she did not have a glorious tradition. The history of the great women in India is as ancient as the Vedic period. The greatness of Indian womanhood had at its roots in those early days when India had its Sanskrit culture. The same India which produced great women in the past also produced the Rani of Jhansi at a grave hour in India's history. And today while we are facing the gravest hour in our history, I have confidence that Indian womanhood will not fail to rise to the occasion. If for the war of independence of Jhansi, India had to produce and it did produce a Lakshmi Bai, today for the war of independence of the whole of India, to liberate 38 crores of Indians, India had to produce and shall produce thousands of Rani of Jhansi.... We have the inspiring examples of Ahalyabai of Maharashtra, Rani Bhawani of Bengal, Raziya Begum and Nur Jahan, who were shining administrators in recent historic times prior to British rule in India.[138]

Bose's concept of women actively participating in armed struggle was shaped by the Hindu Mother Goddess (Durga, Kali, etc.) paradigm. The Mother is the most powerful Hindu feminine prototype. The Mother Goddess is backed up by the cosmic power of the universe, *shakti*, which is also female. According to Joyce C. Lebra, Bose was also influenced by Vivekananda, who argued that women should be trained in physical exercise and also with weapons. By contrast, in Gandhi's framework, Indian women would be like submissive Sita, the epitome of loyalty, chastity and courage. Both Gandhi and Bose demanded sacrifice from women. Sacrificial ritual was, after all, a central part of vedic religious observance. In fact, the women who joined revolutionary terrorist groups in Bengal during the 1920s and 1930s as well as the personnel of the Rani Jhansi Regiment were imbued with the motivation of sacrificing themselves for *Bharat Mata* (Mother India).[139] Carol Hills and Daniel C. Silverman write that Bose's philosophy – as evident from his setting up of the Rani of Jhansi Regiment, which demanded that women, instead of accepting

---

[137] Sahgal, 'My INA Odyssey', p. 5.
[138] 'Inaugural Address at the Rani of Jhansi Training Camp, Singapore, 22 October 1943', *Oracle*, vol. 15, no. 4 (1993), p. 7.
[139] Lebra, *Women against the Raj*, pp. 13, 15–16, 22–9.

Hindu Militarism and Anti-Militarism in British India 235

a Sita-like role, take Goddess Durga as their role model – represented a fusion of aggressive Hindu nationalism and feminism.[140]

During August 1943, at Singapore, Bose met some Japanese military officers and discussed a possible joint invasion of north-east India by the Imperial Japanese Army and the INA. In February 1944, in a meeting with the Japanese military officers of the Fifteenth Army at Maymyo in Burma, Bose urged that if the Japanese were to break through into Manipur, a large-scale uprising of Indians would start in Assam. Further, seeing the INA in action, Bose hoped that the Indian soldiers in the British-Indian army would desert and join the INA in large numbers.[141] On 8 March 1944, the Japanese invasion of Manipur started.[142] In July 1944, Bose elaborated his strategic concept in a speech:

> So far as I am concerned after twenty years' experience of public service in India, I came to the conclusion that it was impossible to organize an armed resistance in the country without some help from outside, help from our countrymen abroad, as well as from some foreign power or powers.... In 1940 I read my history once again, and once again, I came to the conclusion that history did not furnish a single instance where freedom had been won without help of some sort from abroad.[143]

During November 1944, when Bose visited Tokyo, he tried to meet the Soviet ambassador. Bose's strategy was to turn to the USSR to conduct the anti-British struggle in case Japan failed in the war. However, the Soviet ambassador refused to meet Bose.[144] On 17 August 1945, Bose left Saigon Airport to go to the USSR via Manchuria. However, he died in an aircraft accident.[145]

CONCLUSION

Which communities would be recruited into the British-Indian army, and in what percentages, was to a great extent shaped by imperial policies. The British construction of 'martial races' was tinged with religious

---

[140] Carol Hills and Daniel C. Silverman, 'Nationalism and Feminism in Late Colonial India: The Rani of Jhansi Regiment, 1943–45', *MAS*, vol. 27, no. 4 (1993), pp. 741–60.

[141] Lieutenant-General Iwaichi Fujiwara, 'My Memories of the INA and Netaji', *Oracle*, vol. 17, no. 4 (1995), pp. 5–8; Sahgal, 'Indian National Army', p. 16.

[142] Fujiwara, 'My Memories of the INA and Netaji', p. 9.

[143] 'Netaji's Broadcast Address to Mahatma Gandhi over the Rangoon Radio on 6 July 1944', p. 3.

[144] Kakitsubo, 'Netaji as I Knew Him', p. 26.

[145] Saburo, 'Netaji: The Man', p. 19.

236 *Hinduism and the Ethics of Warfare in South Asia*

fervour. As the Gurkha case showed, the imperialists used the Hindu religion to create a loyal warrior 'race' from the 'natives' of Nepal. Thanks to the British 'divide and rule' policy, relations between Hindus and Muslims were not that good from the late nineteenth century onwards. Between 1923 and 1927, there were 112 major communal riots on the subcontinent.[146] The logical culmination of communal politics was the Muslim League's Direct Action Day on 16 August 1946.[147] If anything, Gandhi's use of Hindu cultural symbols further aggravated the situation and made the partition of British India in 1947 inevitable. Overall, one million Indians lost their lives in the violence that accompanied the mass migrations during and just after independence and partition.[148] Stanley Wolpert rightly asserts that Gandhi made the most effective use of Hindu symbols, translating the *yogic*-Jain 'fast unto death' into his political weapon, blending traditional Hindu faith in *satya* and *ahimsa* into a modern movement of *satyagraha* and thus winning the hearts of rural Hindus. Gandhi deliberately divested himself of material possessions while consciously courting suffering (*tapasya*) through monastic vows of celibacy and poverty, which helped him to gain the stature of a great soul (*mahatma*). But this very image prevented large-scale entry of the Muslim elites and the Muslim masses into the fold of the Gandhian INC.[149] However, one could argue that Gandhi was caught 'between the devil and the deep blue sea'. The only way to mobilize the illiterate Hindu peasant masses was to use Sanskritized Hindu symbols. And this in turn deepened the rift between Hindus and Muslims. Bose, as compared to Gandhi, was more secular in his operating style. He was influenced by a totalitarian philosophy somewhat tinged with aggressive Hinduism. The military failure of the Axis powers and Bose's accidental death cast his INA project into oblivion. As the British departed from South Asia in 1947, Gandhi's 'blue-eyed boy', Jawaharlal Nehru, inherited Gandhi's legacy and position. His thoughts, actions and legacies are the focus of the next chapter.

---

[146] Hasan, 'The Background of the Partition of the Indo-Pakistan Subcontinent', p. 322.
[147] Judd, *The Lion and the Tiger*, p. 177.
[148] Saberwal, *Spirals of Contention*, p. xvi; Judd, *The Lion and the Tiger*, p. 188.
[149] Wolpert, 'Indian National Congress in Nationalist Perspective', p. 24.

7

The Hindu Military Ethos and
Strategic Thought in Post-Colonial India

With the British departure from India in 1947, British India was partitioned into India and Pakistan. Though India officially claims to be a secular state, Hinduism continues to influence statecraft. At the beginning of the new millennium, India is a rising power, if not a mini-superpower. India's economy is growing at an annual rate of 6 percent, and it is the fourth-largest economy, after the United States, China and the European Union.[1] India's land frontiers exceed 15,000 km, and it shares land frontiers with seven countries. India's coastline is 7,600 km long, and its exclusive economic zone is over two million square km. The island territories in the east are 1,300 km away from the mainland. India shares a maritime boundary with five countries.[2]

And the Indian army, with more than a million men, is the fourth-largest in the world. This chapter shows the influence of the Hindu ethos in four areas: grand strategy, conventional warfare, unconventional warfare and the nuclear issue.

HINDUISM AND INDIA'S GRAND STRATEGY

Jawaharlal Nehru (1889–1964, independent India's first prime minister 1947–64) believed in the civilizational inheritance of India. He wrote: 'There seemed to me something unique about the continuity of

---

[1] Bharat Karnad, *Nuclear Weapons and Indian Security: The Realist Foundations of Strategy* (New Delhi: Macmillan, 2002), p. xx.
[2] *Ministry of Defence Government of India Annual Report* (hereinafter *MODAR*), 2000–2001, p. 2.

a cultural tradition through five thousand years of history, of invasion and upheaval, a tradition which was widespread among the masses and powerfully influenced them. Only China had such a continuity of tradition and cultural life.'[3] However, he did not overlook differences in India. Rather, he emphasized, 'cultural unity amidst diversity'.[4] Nehru continues: '... a country with a long cultural background and a common outlook on life develops a spirit that is peculiar to it and that it impressed on all its children, however much they differ among themselves.'[5] Here Nehru is expressing something similar to the approach of the strategic culture theorists.

However, Nehru differs from the strategic culture theorists when, unlike the latter, he assumes that the civilizational ethos of Bharat is not confined to a mere handful of elites but has imbued even the common masses through the ages. Nehru noted: '... for our ancient epics and myths and legends, which they knew so well, had made them familiar with the conception of their country, and there were always some who had traveled far and wide to the great places of pilgrimage situated at the four corners of India.'[6]

Nehru is not alone in identifying a civilizational ethos of India. Jaswant Singh, who served as deputy chairman of the Planning Commission and also as foreign minister in the Bharatiya Janata Party (i.e., the BJP, the Hindu right-wing party of independent India) government (1998–2004), like Nehru and Gandhi accepted the idea that the accommodating capacity is one of the principal characteristics of Hinduism. The strength of India's civilization, in Nehru's paradigm, lies in its capacity to adapt and assimilate.[7] In Jaswant Singh's words: '*Sanatan* is "for all"; it is the ultimate of inclusiveness, it is *sanatan* that subscribes to the noble concept of "*sarvapath sambhav*".'[8] Singh asserts that India is accommodative and tolerant because of Hinduism. Unlike the case of countries with Judaic religions, in India other religions have flourished. In Jaswant Singh's paradigm, unlike that of Nehru, the Hindu influence is grossly represented.

---

[3] *The Essential Writings of Jawaharlal Nehru*, ed. by S. Gopal and Uma Iyengar, 2 vols. (New Delhi: Oxford University Press, 2003) (hereinafter *EWJN*), vol. 1, p. 5.

[4] *EWJN*, vol. 1, p. 22.

[5] Ibid., p. 7.

[6] Ibid., p. 8.

[7] Ibid., p. 34.

[8] Jaswant Singh, *A Call to Honour: In Service of Emergent India* (New Delhi: Rupa, 2006), p. 87.

Jaswant Singh claims that there is only one culture in India. It is Indian/Hindu/*Bharatiya*.[9]

Jaswant Singh notes the negative effect of Hinduism on India's grand strategy:

The ethos of the Indian state was crippled by another failing. Not just occasional, often an excessive, and at times ersatz pacifism, both internal and external, has twisted India's strategic culture into all kinds of absurdities. Many influences have contributed to this: an accommodative and forgiving Hindu milieu; successive Jain, Buddhist, and later Vaishnav-Bhakti influences resulting in excessive piety and, much later, in the twentieth century *ahimsa*.... An unintended consequence of all these influences, spread over many centuries, has been a near total emasculation of the concept of state power, also its proper employment as an instrument of state policy, in service of national interests.[10]

The core concept of Nehru's foreign policy was the *Panchsheel* (five principles), which Nehru explained to the Lok Sabha (the Lower House of the Parliament) on 17 September 1955. The first principle is recognition by countries of their own and each other's independence, sovereignty and territorial integrity. The second is non-aggression; the third is non-interference with each other; the fourth is mutual respect and equality; and the fifth is peaceful coexistence.[11] Jaswant Singh judges Nehru's *Aussenpolitik* harshly. He writes that the core of Nehru's position on China, '*Hindi-Chini Bai Bhai*' and '*Panchsheel*', perished on the bleak heights of the Aksai Chin and the high passes of north-east India in the late autumn of 1962. And these two significant foreign policy errors were the direct outcome of Nehru's idealistic romanticism.[12]

One modern Indian analyst notes that even the policy of *ahimsa* followed by Gandhi, which to an extent influenced Nehru, has elements of realism inherent in it. He justifies Nehru's 'peaceful' policy towards China through the lens of realism. He claims that in the 1950s, the Indian army was going through a process of reorganization. At that time, it was no match for the People's Liberation Army of China. Hence, Nehru had recourse to *Panchsheel*.[13] Despite the rhetoric, Nehru also tried to attain

---

[9] Singh, *A Call to Honour*, pp. 88–9.

[10] Jaswant Singh, *Defending India* (Houndmills, Basingstoke: Macmillan, 1999), p. 13.

[11] *EWJN*, vol. 2, p. 163.

[12] Singh, *Defending India*, p. 34.

[13] Waheguru Pal Singh Sidhu, 'Of Oral Judgements and Ethnocentric Judgements', in Kanti P. Bajpai and Amitabh Mattoo (eds.), *Securing India, Strategic Thought and Practice: Essays by George K. Tanham with Commentaries* (New Delhi: Manohar, 2006), pp. 176–7.

240 *Hinduism and the Ethics of Warfare in South Asia*

a hegemonic position for India. As early as 1948, Nehru wrote that India is the natural leader of Southeast Asia, and perhaps of some other parts of Asia as well. This is because there was no other possible leadership in Asia, and any foreign leadership would not be tolerated.[14] Under Nehru's stewardship, when India tried to follow such a course, it resulted in conflict with China.

When necessary, Nehru was not averse to utilizing Kautilya's dictum: 'my enemy's enemy is my friend'. Just one year after independence, Nehru observed:

... as a result of Pakistan coming into existence and the growth of an Islamic sentiment, the Middle Eastern countries will tend to become somewhat hostile to India.... Our general policy in regard to them should be one of friendship as well as firmness.... Afghanistan being anti-Pakistan, automatically is a little more friendly to India. We should take full advantage of this fact. Turkey also is not very much affected by the Islamic sentiment.[15]

Tension between Afghanistan and Pakistan over the Durand line, in Nehru's eyes, was to be used as diplomatic leverage by India. Another streak of Nehru's realism is evident in the letter of advice he wrote to U. Nu of Burma in 1949. Nehru wrote that any attempt to fight on all fronts is not likely to succeed and may well end in serious losses. In politics as in warfare, Nehru advised U. Nu, one takes up one's enemies one by one.[16]

C. Raja Mohan, an Indian foreign policy analyst, offers a realist interpretation of Nehru's non-aligned movement. India's treaty-based relations with Nepal and Bhutan were security alliances whereby New Delhi promised to protect these states against external threats. This constituted India's inner circle. In the next concentric circle, which comprised India's extended neighbourhood, New Delhi's policy was determined more by balance-of-power considerations than by ideological ones. India refused to join the non-aligned bandwagon against the Soviet Union's intervention in Afghanistan in the early 1980s. This is because from the 1970s onwards the USSR had been India's steadfast ally. At the global level, the third concentric circle, India's alignment with the Soviet Union was shaped by considerations of national interest. Throughout the Cold War, India determinedly sought to reduce Chinese influence in Southeast Asia. There is nothing, then, in the history of India's non-aligned policy that suggests a fundamental aversion to playing power politics, including

[14] *EWJN*, vol. 2, p. 237.
[15] Ibid., pp. 237–8.
[16] Ibid., p. 251.

Hindu Military Ethos in Post-Colonial India

alliances.[17] Both Raja Mohan and George K. Tanham (an American analyst) accept the idea that Kautilya's *mandala* policy continues to shape India's grand strategy.[18]

In the last decade of the twentieth century, India's strategic policy represented both change and continuity. The imperatives for change were the disappearance of the USSR and the fiscal crisis that led the Narasimha Rao–led INC government in the 1990s to start the process of globalization.[19] Tanham, taking a leaf from Samuel Huntington's clash of civilizations scenario, portrays India's strategic landscape in the following words:

India continues to see Islam as a ... threat. Having been invaded by different Muslim peoples for several centuries, then ruled by the Mughals for about 200 years, Indians are understandably sensitive to perceived Islamic threats. Today, they are surrounded on their land borders by seven Muslim countries. Pakistan's destabilizing efforts in India, supported by other Muslim nations is the clearest and nearest and most important Islamic threat. The recent formation of five independent republics in Central Asia, all with large Muslim populations, is seen as the latest manifestation of the Muslim presence.[20]

Even with potentially hostile neighbours, India's policy is to seek cooperation first, if possible, with some, if not with all; the last option is war. Swarna Rajagopalan asserts that India's policy of seeking strategic cooperation with its neighbours is shaped by the ethical security politics derived from the *Ramayana*. One of the principle themes of the *Ramayana* is strategic cooperation for the purpose of tackling the enemy. This is evident in Rama's strategic alliance with the *vanara*s for the purpose of tackling Ravana.[21]

HINDUISM AND INDIA'S CONDUCT OF CONVENTIONAL WARFARE

On 9 May 1929, M. K. Gandhi declared:

This I know that if India comes to her own demonstrably through non-violent means, India will never want to carry a vast army, an equally grand navy and a

---

[17] C. Raja Mohan, *Impossible Allies: Nuclear India, United States and the Global Order* (New Delhi: India Research Press, 2006), pp. 267–8.

[18] George K. Tanham, 'Indian Strategic Thought: An Interpretive Essay', in Bajpai and Mattoo (eds.), *Essays by George K. Tanham with Commentaries*, pp. 47–72.

[19] George K. Tanham, 'Indian Strategy in Flux?', in Bajpai and Mattoo (eds.), *Essays by George K. Tanham with Commentaries*, pp. 113–15, 134.

[20] Ibid., p. 129.

[21] Swarna Rajagopalan, 'Security Ideas in the *Valmiki Ramayana*', in Rajagopalan (ed.), *Security and South Asia: Ideas, Institutions and Initiatives* (London/New York/New Delhi: Routledge, 2006), pp. 24–53.

242 *Hinduism and the Ethics of Warfare in South Asia*

grander air force. If her self-consciousness rises to the height necessary to give her a non-violent victory in her fight for freedom, the world values will have changed and most of the paraphernalia of war would be found to be useless.[22]

While Gandhi advocated abolishing the armed forces in free India, Nehru demurred. The latter may not have been interested in matters military but did not completely neglect them. In 1937, Nehru noted:

There is no doubt that India can build up an efficient defence apparatus.... We live in an abnormal world, full of wars and aggression, when international law has ceased to be and treaties and undertakings have no value, and an unabashed gangsterism prevails among nations.... The only thing to be done to protect one-self is to rely on one's strength as well as to have a policy of peace.[23]

Despite the Nehruvian policy of apathy as regards projection of power overseas, India has been very sensitive as far its borders are concerned and has not hesitated to start conventional operations when its borders have been threatened. Tanham offers an explanation:

Independent India sees itself as continuing the tradition of non-aggression and non-expansion outside the subcontinent. Nehru's foreign policy rested on these principles, and subsequent leaders have followed suit. The tradition of non-aggression, however, has never applied internally. Warfare within the subcontinent has been the norm for centuries. States fought to gain power and wealth, to establish empires, or to destroy them. This seeming paradox with regard to non-aggression arises from the Indian view of the subcontinent as a single strategic area that coincides with Indian national interests. This belief justified India's taking much more aggressive measures – to protect its interest in the subcontinent.[24]

Air Marshal R. K. Nehra asserts that post-1947 India's military response to its hostile neighbours like Pakistan and China has been passive owing to the pervasive influence of the Hindu mindset. Too much focus on *ahimsa* and *shanti* (peace) is seen by Nehru as the root cause of India's fragmented approach to matters military. The focus on non-violence in Hinduism, argues Nehra, is due to the pervasive influence of Buddhism. In original Hinduism, martial valour was emphasized. Nehra cites the sloka: '*Vira bhoga Vasundhara*', that is, the mighty heroes will enjoy the earth.[25] In a similar vein, Brigadier Kuldip Singh notes, in a monograph

---

[22] *The Essential Writings of Mahatma Gandhi*, ed. by Raghavan Iyer (1993; reprint, New Delhi: Oxford University Press, 2007) (hereinafter *EWMG*), p. 275.
[23] *EWJN*, vol. 1, p. 41.
[24] Tanham, 'Indian Strategic Thought', p. 77.
[25] Air Marshal R. K. Nehra, *Hinduism and Its Military Ethos* (New Delhi: Lancer, 2010), p. 325.

Hindu Military Ethos in Post-Colonial India 243

published in 2011, that ancient Hinduism emphasized just militarism. He continues:

India's military mind is as pristine, resplendent and advanced as its longstanding civilization. Its inherent philosophy of life and statecraft accorded exalted primacy to warfare, as evident from the *veda*s, the *epic*s, *Arthasastra* and other classics.... Indians were not only men of thought alone, but men of action too. The aggressive combative spirit of ancient Bharata is exemplified by its confederated military might, which evicted the Greeks, Kushan and Hun invaders from the Indian soil.[26]

The retired Indian Lieutenant-General S. C. Sardeshpande writes that India's passive defence policy throughout its history is a product of the 'inward looking self-satisfied attitude' of the people. This is due in part to the geographical features of India. High mountains in the north and jungle-filled hills in the east, with sea and ocean along the western and southern borders, has resulted in India being an 'inward-looking geographical entity.' Hence, the people are satisfied with their natural geographical frontiers. Throughout history, Indians have not exhibited any extra-territorial ambitions.[27] This geographical inwardness has been further strengthened by cultural passivity. Sardeshpande notes: 'Preoccupation with spiritualism, theorizing, complacency and plentitude led Indian militarism away from geographical planes to the peculiar planes of glory, honour, sport and kind of ritual.'[28] The net result throughout history has been a sort of non-lethal warfare. He continues: 'But perhaps because of cultural identity and stress on spiritualism, wars seldom attained cruel, fanatic or exterminatory proportions. By and large wars remained far less inhuman as compared to those in European and American continents.'[29]

As regards Indian politicians' attitude towards the armed forces, Nehra comments: '... the new rulers of the country suffered from an overdose of *ahimsa*, which has become a part of their mental make-up; it was lodged in their subconscious. Most of them felt apologetic about militarism. There was a visible lack of enthusiasm about the armed forces in the political class.'[30] For instance, in 1955, Nehru declared that India's symbols throughout its long history had never been great military

---

[26] Brigadier K. Kuldip Singh, *Indian Military Thought: Kurukshetra to Kargil and Future Perspectives* (New Delhi: Lancer, 2011), p. 592.

[27] Lieutenant-General S. C. Sardeshpande, *War and Soldiering* (New Delhi: Lancer, 1993), p. 126.

[28] Ibid., p. 127.

[29] Ibid.

[30] Nehra, *Hinduism and Its Military Ethos*, p. 329.

244   *Hinduism and the Ethics of Warfare in South Asia*

commanders but men like Buddha and, in our own time, Gandhi, both of whom were messengers of goodwill and peace.[31] Kuldip Singh warns politicians about the importance of military strength for national security in the following words: 'India's inherent depth and vitality of *dharma*, spirituality and wealth of knowledge and natural resources, on their own, could not protect its frontiers. The case of Emperor Asoka bears out how India's neglected defence system led to national humbling and foreign intrusion, in spite of its otherwise established civilizational grandeur during his time.'[32]

Because politicians have neglected defence since Independence, claim several military officers, the armed forces have become demoralized. The performance of the Indian army during the 1965 war with Pakistan was below average owing to a defensive mindset and a lack of an aggressive attitude and killer spirit. Nehra gives an instance of the defeatist Hindu mindset prevailing even among the top officers of the armed forces. In 2009, Admiral Suresh Mehta, the chief of the naval staff and chairman of the Chiefs of Staff Committee, publicly stated that India could never catch up with China and that the gap between the two would only widen with time.[33] Kuldip Singh warns: 'We need to change the attitude and recognize that war undertaken for a noble cause, and as the last resort, it is the highest worship of God.'[34]

Both civilian commentators and military officers suggest that the epics could impart lessons for the modern military. For instance, Waheguru Pal Singh Sidhu claims that the *Mahabharata* highlights the strategy for breaking into and breaking out of a *chakravyu* (enemy encirclement).[35] Brigadier G. D. Bakshi writes that principles of war could be gleaned from the *Mahabharata*. Despite changes in technology, the tactical and strategic principles of warfare remain constant. He comments that the Mahabharata War was a high-intensity war of short duration; it lasted for only eighteen days. All the conventional wars fought by India with Pakistan and China were also of short duration. For instance, the Second India-Pakistan War (1965) lasted for twenty-two days, and the Third India-Pakistan War (1971) lasted for fourteen days. Again, the *Mahabharata* notes that the campaigning season lasts from November to March. Bakshi notes that independent India's wars, like the 1962 China-India War, occurred during

---

[31] *EWJN*, vol. 2, p. 289.
[32] Singh, *Indian Military Thought*, p. 593.
[33] Nehra, *Hinduism and Its Military Ethos*, pp. 331, 337, 351.
[34] Singh, *Indian Military Thought*, p. 599.
[35] Sidhu, 'Of Oral Traditions and Ethnocentric Judgements', p. 175.

November–December. Later, the 1971 India-Pakistan War occurred during November and December. The *Mahabharata* emphasizes that wars are to be fought with large numbers of regular soldiers, and the Indian army is comprised of long-service volunteer soldiers from the 'martial races'.[36]

Bakshi notes that in the *Mahabharata* one finds two military approaches: the traditional direct approach, enunciated by Bhisma, and the indirect approach as practiced by Lord Krishna and Dronacharya's son Ashwathama. The latter approach finds its logical culmination in Kautilya's *kutayuddha*. The former approach dominates the Indian military mind. The direct approach of conducting *dharmayuddha* – emphasizing restraint, chivalry, a sporting mentality, symmetrical responses, and so on – is responsible for the inefficiency of Indian tactics. Bakshi continues that in accordance with the *dharmayuddha* tradition, Indian armour was used during the India-Pakistan conflicts only against enemy armour in a tank-killer role. Indian armour was not used against enemy infantry or for deep penetration of the enemy's vulnerable flanks due to the ethics of *dharmayuddha*.[37] For instance, during the 1965 India-Pakistan War, an Indian armoured division was ordered to seek out and engage Pakistan's First Armoured Division in a classic tank-versus-tank battle. It was an attrition-oriented paradigm, and the Indian generalship was further hamstrung by over-cautiousness and rigidity.[38] It is part of our inheritance, Bakshi continues, that chariots must only attack chariots.[39] Here, Bakshi is referring to the *Mahabharata* and *Manusamhita*'s concept of *dharmayudha*.

After analyzing the three India-Pakistan Wars, Bakshi notes in an article:

By historical legacy, we are an attrition oriented army. This legacy goes back to the era of the Mahabharata War in 1200 BC. Today, we need to grow beyond tactical frontal pushes at the corps level. Our Operational Art must be enhanced in sophistication to include single and double envelopment pincer movements and turning movements.... What we need to recognize is the ... level of Operational Art in the context of limited or unlimited wars in the subcontinent and the dire necessity of outgrowing attrition mindset (which incidentally is a legacy of the Mahabharat War).[40]

---

[36] Lieutenant-Colonel G. D. Bakshi, *Mahabharata: A Military Analysis* (New Delhi: Lancer, 1990), pp. 72–3.

[37] Bakshi, *Mahabharata: A Military Analysis*, pp. 73–4.

[38] G. D. Bakshi, 'Operational Art in the Indian Context: An Open Sources Analysis', *Strategic Analysis*, vol. 25, no. 6 (2001), p. 728.

[39] Bakshi, *Mahabharata: A Military Analysis*, p. 74.

[40] Bakshi, 'Operational Art in the Indian Context', pp. 732–3.

246   *Hinduism and the Ethics of Warfare in South Asia*

In Bakshi's eyes, the absence of intelligence-oriented covert operations is a weakness of the Indian military system. He writes:

Kutayuddha methods were despised by 'honourable' Indian soldiers of the Mahabharata period. The tragedy is that even today our Indian regular soldiers still tend to despise these methods as unethical or unsoldierly. Notice the fact that officers of our intelligence corps have no bright career opportunities *vis-à-vis* the other arms. It appears intelligence and covert operations are second rate side shows for which only second grade officers can or need be spared. This attitude has been further reinforced by our British heritage.[41]

Bakshi's observation is supported by a fellow officer, Kuldip Singh, in the following words: 'The poor showing of India's intelligence system has been an interminable story of unmitigated disaster. The importance of having an effective intelligence organization is highlighted in not only the *epic*s, but also the *Arthashastra* constitutes an ageless masterpiece on surveillance and spying, in both peace and war.'[42] Bakshi claims that the *acharya*s of the *Mahabharata* were experts in conducting psychological war. Their main aim at all times was to attack the mind of the enemy commander.[43]

If necessary on the basis of historical study, certain aspects of Hinduism, write some officers, need to be revised. Kuldip Singh concludes that the failure of the Hindus during the medieval era was due to passive defence. The medieval Hindu rulers' failed to pre-empt Islamic invasions and also did not carry the battle to the invaders' bases. Hence, all the battles were fought deep inside India. Singh is probably referring to Prithviraja Chauhan and the two battles of Tarain with Muhammad Ghori. Aggressive defence and pre-emptive action could have saved the Hindus. And, Kuldip Singh emphasizes, we should learn from such mistakes.[44]

C. Coker claims that the principal lesson of *Arthasastra* is asymmetric warfare. In 1988, the office of the U.S. secretary of defence concluded that India would seek to deny the U.S. Navy uncontested control over the Indian Ocean and that New Delhi would use asymmetric sufficiency as a counter. In Indian coastal warfare, subsurface weapons could function as a deterrent.[45]

---

[41] Bakshi, *Mahabharata: A Military Analysis*, p. 74.
[42] Singh, *Indian Military Thought*, p. 593.
[43] Bakshi, *Mahabharata: A Military Analysis*, pp. 74–5.
[44] Singh, *Indian Military Thought*, pp. 593–4.
[45] Christopher Coker, *Waging War without Warriors? The Changing Culture of Military Conflict* (Boulder, Colorado: Lynne Rienner, 2002), pp. 142–3.

POST-COLONIAL INDIA'S CONDUCT OF
UNCONVENTIONAL WARFARE

The late twentieth century was characterized by the proliferation of unconventional warfare. The latter term refers to intra-state rather than inter-state war. In recent times, the term 'insurgency' has connoted an organized movement aimed at the overthrow of a constituted government through the use of subversion and armed conflict.[46] Lieutenant-Colonel Vivek Chadha of the Indian army makes a distinction between terrorism and insurgency. In his framework, terrorist movements are based in urban areas, whereas insurgencies establish their bases in rural areas and then graduate to urban regions.[47] Chadha's definition is somewhat similar to James D. Fearon and David D. Laitin's view. They write: 'Insurgency is a technology of military conflict characterized by small, lightly armed bands practicing guerrilla warfare from rural base areas.'[48] Insurgency includes both guerrilla warfare and terrorism. Insurgency and responses to it by the polity concerned (known as counter-insurgency or COIN) together constitute unconventional warfare. A high level of insurgency and COIN in a country create a civil war.

A group of Western scholars argue that civil wars occur more frequently in countries with substantial populations belonging to different ethnic, linguistic and religious groups.[49] India has eighteen officially recognized languages, twelve ethnic groups and seven religious groups that are further subdivided into various sects, castes and sub-castes.[50] Somewhat like Stephen Peter Rosen, Jaswant Singh notes that the culture of divisive politics within India prevents the state from the generating surplus military power needed for power projection outside the country. Jaswant Singh writes that India's strategic culture has become internalized, fixated upon curbing dissent within the subcontinent rather

---

[46] Emily Spencer and Bernd Horn, 'Introduction', in Spencer (ed.), *The Difficult War: Perspectives on Insurgency and Special Operations Forces* (Ontario: Dundurn Press, 2009), p. 13.

[47] Lieutenant-Colonel Vivek Chadha, *Low Intensity Conflicts in India: An Analysis* (New Delhi: Sage, 2005), p. 25.

[48] James D. Fearon and David D. Laitin, 'Ethnicity, Insurgency, and Civil War', *American Political Science Review* (hereinafter *APSR*), vol. 97, no. 1 (2003), p. 75.

[49] Havard Hegre, Tanja Ellingsen, Scott Gates and Nils Petter Gleditsch, 'Towards a Democratic Civil Peace? Democracy, Political Change, and Civil War, 1816–1992', *APSR*, vol. 95, no. 1 (2001), p. 37.

[50] Satish Kumar, 'Sources of Democracy and Pluralism in India', in Vice-Admiral K. K. Nayyar and Jorg Schultz (eds.), *South Asia Post 9/11: Searching for Stability* (New Delhi: Rupa, 2003), p. 74.

248   *Hinduism and the Ethics of Warfare in South Asia*

than combating external dangers, and has thereby created a yawning chasm of mutual suspicion between the state and the citizen. This in turn has prevented India from developing its true power, that is, its capability to project power beyond the boundaries of India.[51] In a similar vein, Sardeshpande claims that geographic compartmentalization within South Asia has resulted in political fragmentation despite cultural unity. The net result has been a long tradition of intense internecine warfare within South Asia.[52]

Tanham notes that Kautilya long ago warned against the intrigues of foreign kings as a threat to one's own security, even though the *Arthasastra* accepted intrigue and the use of internal spies as legitimate self-defence measures. The Indians suffer from a pervasive fear of 'foreign hands' at work among India's unstable neighbours and within India.[53] In Kautilya's format, the principal threat to the *rashtra* encompassing the whole subcontinent comes from *kopa*. This is also the view of various Indian military officers.[54] Like Kautilya, Chadha writes that with external support, an ongoing insurgency can escalate into a regular war between the states.[55] The Pakistani army and especially the Inter-Services Intelligence (ISI) have been supporting insurgents since the mid-1980s with money, equipment and training. The objective is to exhaust India by giving a 'thousand cuts' with the aid of the insurgents.[56] Pakistan's strategy is to give moral and material assistance to groups like Hizb-ul-Mujahidin, which aim at the secession of Kashmir from India through armed struggle and then merger with Pakistan.[57] The transnational connection is also apparent in Kashmir's case. Al-Qaeda connects sub-national organizations with a trans-national network.[58] Osama Bin Laden declared a *jihad*

---

[51] Singh, *Defending India*, p. 13; Stephen Peter Rosen, *Societies and Military Power: India and Its Armies* (New Delhi: Oxford University Press, 1996).

[52] Sardeshpande, *War and Soldiering*, p. 126.

[53] Tanham, 'India's Strategic Thought', p. 53.

[54] Colonel Harjeet Singh, *Doda: An Insurgency in the Wilderness* (New Delhi: Lancer, 1999), p. 141.

[55] Chadha, *Low Intensity Conflicts in India*, pp. 405–6, 419.

[56] Amelie Blom, 'A Patron-Client Perspective on Militia-State Relations: The Case of the Hizb-ul-Mujahidin of Kashmir', in Laurent Gayer and Christophe Jaffrelot (eds.), *Armed Militias of South Asia: Fundamentalists, Maoists and Separatists* (New Delhi: Foundation, 2009), pp. 136–7.

[57] V. G. Patankar, 'Insurgency, Proxy War, and Terrorism in Kashmir', in Sumit Ganguly and David P. Fidler (eds.), *India and Counterinsurgency: Lessons Learned* (Oxon: Routledge, 2009), p. 68.

[58] Claudia Haydt, '"New" Terrorism: Guidelines for Security Policies', in Nayyar and Schultz (eds.), *South Asia Post 9/11*, p. 15.

Hindu Military Ethos in Post-Colonial India

in Kashmir in 1989 and extended support to the Harkat-ul-Mujahideen, Harkat-ul-Jihad-Islami, Harkat-ul-Ansar, Lashkar-e-Toiba and Jaish-e-Mohammed *tanzeem*s (militant outfits).[59] In 1989, about 400,000 personnel (from the Indian army and the various paramilitary forces) were deployed in Kashmir.[60]

The most serious insurgency that India has to face is the Islamic insurgency in Kashmir. Monica Duffy Toft claims that the proportion of civil wars in which religion has become a central issue has increased over time. Further, religious civil wars are much more destructive than wars fought over other issues. Toft goes on to say that religious civil wars last longer and result in more combatant and especially non-combatant deaths, because while nationalism by nature tends to be a local issue, religion tends to be trans-national.[61] One aspect of the rebellion in Mizoram, the insurgents claim, is protection of the Christian religion against the 'Hindu' Indian state despite the post-independence Indian government's professed secular approach to politics.[62] In north-east India, more than forty insurgent groups are operating.[63] In 1982, more than 200,000 military personnel were deployed in north-east India.[64] Between 1986 and 1996, the Indian army suffered a total of 2,467 dead and 14,359 wounded in its various COIN missions.[65]

Kautilya and the Indian military officers following him note that initiating or destroying *kopa* is a time-consuming affair. Walter C. Ladwig III writes that analysis of India's COIN policies shows that India has the patience, determination and resources to outlast the insurgents.[66] Both in India and Nepal, the Maoists conceive their armed violence against the state as a sort of *dharmayuddha*. The violence they resort to is positive for the well-being of the community and in reaction to

[59] K. Santhanam, Sreedhar, Sudhir Saxena and Manish, *Jihadis in Jammu and Kashmir: A Portrait Gallery* (New Delhi: IDSA and Sage, 2003), p. 25.

[60] Sumit Ganguly, 'Explaining the Kashmir Insurgency: Political Mobilization and Institutional Decay', *International Security*, vol. 21, no. 2 (1996), p. 76.

[61] Monica Duffy Toft, 'Getting Religion? The Puzzling Case of Islam and Civil War', *International Security*, vol. 31, no. 4 (2007), pp. 98, 101, 103.

[62] Vivek Chadha, 'India's Counterinsurgency Campaign in Mizoram', in Ganguly and Fidler (eds.), *India and Counterinsurgency*, pp. 32–3.

[63] R. S. Grewal, 'Ethno Nationalism in North Eastern India', *Journal of the United Service Institution of India* (henceforth *JUSII*), vol. 133, no. 552 (2003), p. 268.

[64] Jerrold F. Elkin and W. Andrew Ritezel, 'Military Role Expansion in India', *Armed Forces & Society*, vol. 11, no. 4 (1985), p. 495.

[65] Singh, *Doda*, p. 245.

[66] Walter C. Ladwig III, 'Insights from the Northeast: Counterinsurgency in Nagaland and Mizoram', in Ganguly and Fidler (eds.), *India and Counterinsurgency*, p. 50.

250   *Hinduism and the Ethics of Warfare in South Asia*

the corruption, inefficiency and misrule of the rich against the poor.[67] Both the *Mahabharata* and the *Arthasastra* dislike tyrants. Kautilya says that while tyrants are interested in self-aggrandizement, efficient 'just' monarchs are more concerned with the interests of the *rashtra*. Kautilya warns the king to use *danda* with a sense of discrimination and by steering a middle course. Kautilya repeatedly emphasizes good governance to prevent *kopa*. He urges that, if necessary, then righteous customs should be initiated and unrighteous customs abolished. Kautilya notes that the government should be attentive to the cultural sensibilities of people inhabiting troubled regions. The state's policies should respect the dress, language and cultural behaviour of the people in order to win and retain their loyalty.[68] Proper respect should be shown by the government to the fairs and festivals of people in a disturbed zone, and punishment should be moderate. Kautilya advocates replacement of corporal punishment with monetary fines and opposes exorbitant monetary fines that might alienate subjects who have erred slightly. During natural calamities, in order to prevent the anger of the people from crossing the threshold and resulting in *kopa*, Kautilya warns that state officials must initiate large-scale relief measures to alleviate the sufferings of people in the disturbed zone.[69]

The Indian army frequently provides aid to civil operations during natural calamities. Some examples will suffice. On 29 March 1999, an earthquake occurred in the Garhwal region. In response, the Indian army distributed food packets, blankets and tents, and the affected civilians were treated by the army's medical units. During 17–18, October 1999, a cyclone from the Bay of Bengal caused devastation in the coastal areas of Andhra Pradesh and Tamil Nadu. In response, more than 5,000 army personnel were deployed to the affected areas. They rescued marooned civilians, distributed food packets and provided medical aid. About 22,288 civilians were evacuated; 33,722 civilians were medically treated; 4,259 tons of food items were distributed; and 2,48,000 litres of drinking water was provided.[70]

---

[67] Marie Lecomte-Tilouine, 'Fighting with Ideas: Maoist and Popular Conceptions of the Nepalese People's War', in Gayer and Jaffrelot (eds.), *Armed Militias of South Asia*, pp. 67–8.

[68] *The Kautilya Arthasastra* (hereinafter *KA*), Part II, *An English Translation with Critical and Explanatory Notes*, by R. P. Kangle (1972; reprint, New Delhi: Motilal Banarasidas, 1992), pp. 491, 493.

[69] *The Kautilya Arthasastra* (hereinafter *KA*), Part III, *A Study*, by R. P. Kangle (1965; reprint, New Delhi: Motilal Banrasidas, 2000), pp. 234, 236–9, 261.

[70] *MODAR: 1999–2000*, pp. 110, 113.

Hindu Military Ethos in Post-Colonial India   251

For the COIN forces, Colonel Harjeet Singh (who served in the Sikh Light Infantry and in the Army Training Command before his retirement in 1998) notes what he calls the Ten Commandments: (i) no rape, (ii) no molestation, (iii) no torture resulting in death or maiming, (iv) no military disgrace, (v) no meddling in civil administration, (vi) competence in platoon/company tactics, (vii) willingness to conduct civic actions, (viii) developing interaction with the media, (ix) respect for human rights, and finally (x) fearing only God and upholding *dharma*. Harjeet Singh defines *dharma* as the ethical mode of life that leads to the path of righteousness. Here, Harjeet Singh is obliquely referring to the *dharmayuddha* concept inherent in Hinduism. And the latter part of the last commandment refers to *nishkakarma*, that is, doing one's own duty without looking for any tangible reward. This is a concept lifted from the *Bhagavad Gita*. The eighth commandment is elaborated so as to use the media as a force multiplier rather than a force degrader.[71] In case of a popular uprising (Kautilya's *kopa*), the personalities of the leaders and public opinion constitute, for Kautilya and Clausewitz, the centre of gravity.[72] Public opinion is an integral part of democracy, especially in a country like India. In 2005, Chadha asserted that in insurgencies the idea is more important than arms.[73] Lieutenant-General Depinder Singh (who served with the Indian Peace Keeping Force [IPKF] in Sri Lanka in the 1980s) focuses on psychological warfare and public relations as part of COIN operations.[74] Harjeet Singh's third commandment finds support in the *Arthasastra*. The *Arthasastra* warns that prison officials should not harass or torture prisoners; especially as regards female prisoners, there should be no sexual harassment, as such a policy is destructive of the legitimacy of the state in the long run.[75] As a point of comparison, the U.S. torture of Iraqi prisoners in 2003 at Abu Ghraib Prison resulted in Iraqi and international public opinion turning against the American forces stationed in that country.[76]

The Indian army, following Kautilya and Kamandaka, believes that no insurgency can be settled by military force alone. Rather, the

---

[71] Singh, *Doda*, Appendix D.

[72] Michael I. Handel, *Masters of War: Classical Strategic Thought* (1992; reprint, London: Frank Cass, 1996), p. 45.

[73] Chadha, *Low Intensity Conflicts in India*, p. 19.

[74] Lieutenant-General Depinder Singh, *Indian Peacekeeping Force in Sri Lanka* (Dehra Dun: Natraj Publishers, 2001), p. 112.

[75] *KA*, Part III, by Kangle, p. 242.

[76] Warren Chin, 'Examining the Application of British Counterinsurgency Doctrine by the American Army in Iraq', *Small Wars & Insurgencies*, vol. 18, no. 1 (2007), p. 4.

application of military force should prepare the ground for holding elections that will result in the formation of a democratic government.[77] Harjeet Singh opines that insurgency cannot be defeated or even contained by military power alone.[78] Depinder Singh notes in his autobiography: 'I was quite clear in my mind that no insurgency has ever been or can ever be settled militarily. Therefore, a political solution had to be found.... On the military plane we had to mount unrelenting pressure against the insurgents to force them to negotiate at some point in the future.'[79] In fact, Chadha claims that the only solution to insurgency is a decentralized federal system in the spirit of self-governance.[80] W. Ladwig III claims that India's flexibility and willingness to redefine internal borders and political arrangements in order to satisfy the preservationist as well as the reformist goals of the insurgents, is praiseworthy.[81]

Nevertheless, COIN cannot be conducted without military coercion. The *Arthasastra* tells us that military operations should be conducted taking into consideration *desa* (terrain) and *kala* (season). Kautilya notes that government troops should be ready to fight in mountainous or wooded regions and that they should conduct operations with adequate flank guards and a reserve force stationed behind the attacking units. Nocturnal commando attacks, says Kautilya, are to be launched in order to surprise the rebels.[82] The Indian army has recently accepted the doctrine: 'Fight the guerrilla like a guerrilla'.[83] Rajesh Rajagolan writes that successful COIN requires small, highly mobile offensive patrolling units moving deep inside guerrilla territory. Large-unit cordon and search operations are useless. In fact, moving large numbers of security forces to the sensitive areas alerts the insurgents and allows them to escape the security cordon into the wilderness.[84] In 2004, an American analyst of COIN strategy in Iraq emphasized small-unit operations and careful intelligence work.[85]

---

[77] Rajesh Rajagopalan, *Fighting like a Guerrilla: The Indian Army and Counterinsurgency* (New Delhi: Routledge, 2008), p. 107.

[78] Singh, *Doda*, p. 141.

[79] Singh, *Indian Peacekeeping Force in Sri Lanka*, p. 107.

[80] Chadha, *Low Intensity Conflicts in India*, p. 412.

[81] Ladwig III, 'Insights from the Northeast', pp. 46, 48.

[82] *KA*, Part III, by Kangle, pp. 257–9.

[83] *MODAR: 1999–2000*, p. 94.

[84] Rajagopalan, *Fighting like a Guerrilla*, pp. 56, 108.

[85] Austin Long, *On "Other War": Lessons from Five Decades of RAND Counterinsurgency Research* (Santa Monica, California: RAND Corporation, 2006), p. 44.

Hindu Military Ethos in Post-Colonial India

Kautilya repeatedly emphasizes the need for integrating the views of different sorts of spies (roving spies, stationary spies, double agents, etc.) and those of the state bureaucracy in order to generate a clear and unified picture of the intelligence landscape. Interestingly, Caleb M. Bartley writes that Sun Tzu also emphasizes the importance of spies and psychological operations.[86] In 1970, Brigadier S. K. Sinha noted that sound intelligence is the bedrock for success in COIN operations.[87] Rajagopalan asserts that long-range patrols by small units are necessary in order to gather real-time intelligence about the insurgents.[88] Similarly, Depinder Singh asserts that good and secure intelligence functioning is a force multiplier in COIN campaigns.[89]

Integration of the various intelligence agencies is something Indian military officers demand, but the Indian state is yet to construct unified, integrated machinery for collating intelligence acquired from the various intelligence agencies. As a result, the Indian COIN strategy suffers. For instance, one reason for the Sri Lankan imbroglio was the fact that the Research and Analysis Wing and the Ministry of External Affairs intelligence agencies did not cooperate with the military intelligence agency of the Indian army. The net result was that the IPKF remained in the dark about the strength and intentions of the LTTE and the Sri Lankan armed forces.[90]

Al-Qaeda and the other successful terrorist networks around the world heavily utilize spies, and the focus is on human intelligence (HUMINT).[91] Rather than technology, Kautilya focuses on HUMINT and urges that spies be conversant with the culture of the region in which they are deployed. Jaswant Singh emphasizes:

India needs to reorganize, reorient and integrate its intelligence sources. It must also update its methodology. The technological revolution underway since the last decade now provides the tools to acquire real-time intelligence of value and give time to plan ahead. Electronic (ELINT) and Signal (SIGINT) intelligence has proved more reliable than simply the routine human intelligence (HUMINT). That, however, does not in any sense dilute the primacy still accorded to HUMINT.

---

[86] Caleb M. Bartley, 'The Art of Terrorism: What Sun Tzu Can Teach Us about International Terrorism', *Comparative Strategy*, vol. 24 (2005), pp. 237–51.

[87] S. K. Sinha, 'Counter Insurgency Operations', *JUSII*, vol. 100, no. 420 (1970), p. 267.

[88] Rajagopalan, *Fighting like a Guerrilla*, p. 109.

[89] Singh, *Indian Peacekeeping Force in Sri Lanka*, pp. 191–2.

[90] Gautam Das and M. K. Gupta-Ray, *Sri Lanka Misadventure: India's Military Peace-Keeping Campaign, 1987–1990* (New Delhi: Har-Anand, 2008), p. 60.

[91] Bartley, 'What Sun Tzu Can Teach Us about International Terrorism', p. 245.

254   *Hinduism and the Ethics of Warfare in South Asia*

And for good reason, for besides being the oldest form, it is also of the most high value kind.[92]

From both the British and Kautilya, independent India inherited a 'divide and rule' policy. In accordance with Kautilya's dictum, the Indian state followed *bheda* against the insurgents. One example: in October 1968, encouraged by the Indian state, the Sema tribal Nagas broke from the Naga Federal Government of Z. A. Phizo and made peace with the central government.[93] One strategy of the Indian state is to tire out insurgent militias by provoking internal strife and co-opting some members of the *tanzeem*s.[94] In 2003, George Fernandez, the defence minister in the BJP's government, initiated a project within the Defence Ministry aimed at inculcating Kautilya's *kutayuddha* as part and parcel of India's unconventional warfare strategy. Fernandez went on record saying that Kautilya's principles should be followed much more systematically when fighting insurgents.[95]

To sum up, the Hindu ethic made India's COIN policy somewhat humane. As a point of comparison, one author argues that the Protestant ethic (emphasizing chivalry, individual sensibilities, etc.) shaped the British COIN policy of using only minimum force against insurgents during the nineteenth and twentieth centuries. By contrast, the Calvinist values of the Americans indirectly emphasized brutality in American COIN policy.[96]

'HINDU' INDIA AND NUCLEAR POLITICS

On 25 April 1947, Gandhi declared: 'I hold that he who invented the atom bomb has committed the gravest sin in the world of science. The only weapon that can save the world is non-violence.'[97] On August 1948, the Atomic Energy Commission of India was set up, with Homi Bhabha, a nuclear physicist, as the first chairman. In 1974, India blasted a nuclear device at Pokhran but did not follow up. India conducted a series of

---

[92] Singh, *Defending India*, p. 289.
[93] Anil A. Athale, 'Insurgency and Counter-Insurgency in Modern India: An Overview', in S. N. Prasad (ed.), *Historical Perspectives of Warfare in India: Some Morale and Materiel Determinants* (New Delhi: Centre for Studies in Civilizations, distributed by Motilal Banarasidas, 2002), p. 403.
[94] Kanti P. Bajpai, 'State, Society, Strategy', in Bajpai and Mattoo (eds.), *Essays by George K. Tanham with Commentaries*, p. 151.
[95] J. Singh, *Indian Defence Yearbook* (DehraDun: Natraj, 2003), p. 575.
[96] Rod Thornton, 'The British Army and the Origins of Its Minimum Force Philosophy', *Small Wars & Insurgencies*, vol. 15, no. 1 (2004), pp. 83–106.
[97] *EWMG*, p. 268.

Hindu Military Ethos in Post-Colonial India 255

five nuclear tests at Pokhran in Rajasthan on 11 and 13 May 1998. In response, on 28 and 30 May 1998, at Chagai Hills in Baluchistan, Pakistan conducted a series of nuclear tests.

There has always been a pro-bomb lobby and an anti-bomb lobby in India comprised of intellectuals, politicians, bureaucrats and scientists. The anti-bomb lobby pointed to the economic burden of becoming a nuclear power as well as to Nehruvian internationalism and the Gandhian ideology of non-violence. The pro-bomb lobby in the 1960s pointed to the threat from China. By the late 1980s, in addition to China, India also faced a nuclear threat from Pakistan. From the 1990s, the pro-bomb lobby has had two wings. The moderate wing influenced by Kenneth Waltz (proliferation results in deterrence stability) believes that a small number of nuclear weapons in the hands of India would stabilize the regional scenario.[98] The extreme/radical wing demands a triad (nuclear weapons–equipped air, land and sea-based platforms) in order to achieve great power status. The two immediate factors behind the 1998 tests were Western (especially American) diplomatic pressure for signing NPT and CTBT, and the rise of the BJP to power. At present, the moderate pro-bomb lobby is pressing for a minimum deterrent, while the extreme wing of the pro-bomb lobby advocates developing a credible deterrent and overt weaponization.

Kanti P. Bajpai, in one article, analyzes the Hindu roots behind the BJP's ideology. The ideological father figure of the BJP is M. S. Golwalker. His view of inter-state relations is similar to the Hobbesian/Darwinian realist interpretation. Golwalker, following Kautilya and the *Panchatantra*, believed that in this world there are no permanent friends but only permanent enemies. Alliance with strong powers will result in enslavement. Hence, in order to survive, a nation must be strong and self-reliant. With Pakistan in mind, Golwalker said that it is always the Muslim who strikes first and it is the Hindu who bears the brunt.[99]

In Stephen P. Cohen's analysis, the BJP's bomb programme is a product of domestic politics. Cohen writes:

One of the major reasons why the BJP and many secular Indians supported a nuclear weapons programme was to destroy the image of India as a "Gandhian" or non-violent country. More practically, the BJP sought to undo Nehru's legacy,

---

[98] Stephen P. Cohen, *India: Emerging Power* (2001; reprint, New Delhi: Oxford University Press, 2003), p. 189.

[99] Kanti Bajpai, 'Hinduism and Weapons of Mass Destruction: Pacifist, Prudential, and Political', in Sohail H. Hashmi and Steven P. Lee (eds.), *Ethics and Weapons of Mass Destruction: Religious and Secular Perspectives* (Cambridge: Cambridge University Press, 2004), pp. 313–15.

256   *Hinduism and the Ethics of Warfare in South Asia*

with its emphasis on disarmament, peace talks, and its special opposition to nuclear weapons. By supporting the very weapons that the Congress party of Nehru and Gandhi had for so long opposed, the BJP was attempting to redefine India's political identity along new lines.[100]

Jaswant Singh critiques the INC's nuclear policy by saying that for thirty years (1969 to 1999) an overtly moralistic but simultaneously ambiguous nuclear policy and self-restraint have paid no measurable dividends.[101] Similarly, Raja Mohan praises the BJP's 1998 decision to go for nuclear blasts and simultaneously offers a critique of the INC's (especially the Nehruvian) nuclear policy:

Thanks to India's nuclear vacillations in the 1960s, India found itself outside the NPT, which by the turn of the millennium had near universal membership barring India, Israel and Pakistan. India's refusal to sign the treaty had little to do with the in-built discrimination in the NPT, an argument that Indians would go hoarse in presenting the world and themselves.... If India had conducted a nuclear test before the treaty was drafted, it would have automatically become a nuclear weapon power like China. Having failed to test in time, India had no option but to stay out if it wanted to preserve its nuclear option.... With the nuclear tests of May 1998, Delhi ended the self-created confusion about its nuclear status.[102]

At present, the anti-nuclear lobby in India, influenced by Mahatma Gandhi's *ahimsa* philosophy, wants India to sign the CTBT and to stop testing and weaponizing nukes.[103] The Noble prize–winning Indian economist Amartya Sen notes: 'Nuclear restraint strengthens rather than weakens India's voice.... But making nuclear bombs, not to mention deploying them, and spending scarce resource on missiles and what is euphemistically called "delivery" can hardly be seen as sensible policy.'[104]

Bharat Karnad, a hyper-realist, asserts that *ahimsa* is not integral to Hinduism. Rather, true Hinduism, he says, like the military officer Nehra, is aggressive and ultra-realist. He believes that nuclear weapons (*brahmastra* in *Mahabharata*) are weapons for winning a war and not merely symbolic 'dangerous toys' for gaining political prestige and deterring potential enemies.[105] He writes:

[100] Cohen, *India*, p. 195.
[101] Singh, *A Call to Honour*, p. 113.
[102] Raja Mohan, *Impossible Allies*, pp. 219–20.
[103] Karnad, *Nuclear Weapons and Indian Security*, p. xxii.
[104] Amartya Sen, 'India and the Bomb', in M. V. Ramanna and C. Rammanohar Reddy (eds.), *Prisoners of the Nuclear Dream* (New Delhi: Orient Longman, 2003), p. 187.
[105] Cohen, *India*, p. 183.

... the Hinduism of the *veda*s – the ancient Sanskrit texts that are the wellsprings of the Indic religion and culture, far from inculcating passivity, is suffused with the spirit of adventure and daring, of flamboyance and vigour, and of uninhibited use of force to overcome any resistance or obstacles.... These texts also conceptualize a Hindu *Machtpolitik* that is at once intolerant of any opposition, driven to realize the goal of supremacy for the nation and State by means fair and foul, and is breathtaking in its amorality.[106]

Post-1998 India's nuclear policy also receives praise from Raja Mohan: 'As a nuclear power India becomes stronger economically and acquires greater confidence in pursuing its manifest destiny on the global stage, the *moralpolitik* that overwhelmed the public discourse for decades has given some space to *realpolitik*.... India has begun to rediscover the roots of realist statecraft in its own long history.'[107] Raja Mohan goes on to say that for all the claims that India has always represented the idealist traditions of foreign policy, its own texts – *Mahabharata*, *Panchatantra* and *Arthasastra* – are steeped in an appreciation of power politics.[108]

Jaswant Singh believes that a nuclear-equipped China has surrounded India on all sides. In the north, nuclear-tipped ballistic missiles stationed in Tibet target India. In the west, Pakistan is China's ally. And in the south, in the Indian Ocean, China maintains submarines equipped with ballistic missiles. And Burma (Myanmar) in India's east is also an ally of China.[109] In his eyes, China, like a *vijigishu* of Kautilya's paradigm, is following *mandala* policy in order to contain India. The effective response for India could be to adopt a counter-*mandala* policy in order to break out of China's encirclement.

Both Karnad and Raja Mohan, like Jaswant Singh, favor using the realist *kutayuddha* tradition when conducting nuclear diplomacy. Karnad asserts that India needs a strategic nuclear arsenal in order to deter foreign countries from intervening in its internal affairs. In his framework, the United States poses a latent threat, and China is the more immediate and principal threat. Karnad wants India to follow the Kautilyan dictum: 'My enemy's enemy is my friend'. He notes that just as China has armed Pakistan with conventional and nuclear weapons in order to distract and deter India, India should arm Vietnam with strategic nuclear weapons in order to threaten China's position in Southeast Asia. An Indian presence in Southeast Asia would also neutralize China's position in Myanmar. If

[106] Karnad, *Nuclear Weapons and Indian Security*, p. xxvi.
[107] Raja Mohan, *Impossible Allies*, p. 282.
[108] Ibid., pp. 282–3.
[109] Singh, *Defending India*, p. 251.

258   *Hinduism and the Ethics of Warfare in South Asia*

necessary, India should cooperate with the United States to aid Taiwan in order to threaten Beijing.[110]

In a similar vein, Raja Mohan writes that Bhisma, the great grandee in the *Mahabharata*, preached to the victorious Pandavas at the end of a great destructive war on the essence of alliances. For Bhisma, there is no condition that permanently deserves the name of either friendship or hostility. Both friends and foes arise from considerations of interest and gain. Friendship can turn into enmity in the course of time, and a foe can become a friend. It is the force of circumstances that creates friends and foes.[111]

Neo-realist nuclear theorists like Karnad and Raju G. C. Thomas are wary of any intimate relationship with the United States. Somewhat influenced by *Panchatantra*, they accept that real friendship can occur only among the equals. However, in the changed circumstances, limited cooperation with the world's sole superpower is necessary.[112] To an extent, India seems to be following the policy of cooperating with the United States in order to balance China. For example, despite India's traditional good relations with Iran, in 2005 India voted with the United States at the IAEA Board of Governors meeting to declare Iran to be noncompliant with the Non-Proliferation Treaty.[113]

In 1999, nuclear weapons–equipped India and Pakistan came very close to war at Kargil. Mohammed Ayoob claims that Pakistan's test firing of an intermediate-range Ghauri missile (range 1,500 km) on 6 April 1998 was the immediate trigger that led to India's second series of nuclear tests at Pokhran.[114] In 1998, Pakistan got the medium-range No Dong missile from North Korea and renamed it the Ghauri. This missile was named after Muhammad Ghori, the ruler of Ghor in Afghanistan, who repeatedly invaded Rajput-dominated India during the late twelfth century. Pakistan's other missile, the Abdali, was named after an Afghan ruler who invaded Mughal India in the first half of the eighteenth century. The nomenclature of the weaponry accumulating in Pakistan thus keeps

---

[110] Karnad, *Nuclear Weapons and Indian Security*, pp. xiv–xviii.

[111] Raja Mohan, *Impossible Allies*, p. 283.

[112] Raju G. C. Thomas, 'India's Nuclear and Missile Programmes: Strategy, Intentions, Capabilities', in Thomas and Amit Gupta (eds.), *India's Nuclear Security* (New Delhi: Vistaar, 2000), pp. 100–1.

[113] Breena E. Coates, 'Modern India's Strategic Advantage to the United States: Her Twin Strengths in *Himsa* and *Ahimsa*', *Comparative Strategy*, vol. 27, no. 2 (2008), p. 143.

[114] Mohammed Ayoob, 'India's Nuclear Decision: Implications for Indian-US Relations', in Thomas and Gupta (eds.), *India's Nuclear Security*, pp. 131–2.

Hindu Military Ethos in Post-Colonial India 259

alive, on both sides, vengeful and largely mythologized memories from earlier periods.[115]

Pakistan is the only Muslim state with a nuclear capability. This fact heightens the prestige of Pakistan in the anti-Western Muslim world.[116] The crisis at Kargil erupted when Pakistan send 3–4,000 soldiers of the Northern Light Infantry (henceforth NLI) across the line of control (LOC) to the Kargil-Drass region. The military planners at Islamabad thought that due to Pakistan's possession of nuclear weapons, India would not dare to launch a massive conventional attack along the LOC, unlike the situation, in 1965. They calculated that after consolidating the Kargil heights, Pakistan would be able to internationalize the Kashmir issue and negotiate with India from a position of strength.[117] Initially, Pakistan maintained the fiction that these intruders were *mujahideen*s fighting for the liberation of Kashmir from 'Hindu' India's yoke. The war was fought for two months at altitudes ranging from 12,000 to 17,000 feet.[118] In 1999, unlike in 1965, India did not escalate horizontally by launching attacks elsewhere along the LOC but did initiate vertical escalation at Kargil by using artillery and airpower to evict the 'intruders'.[119] Most of the NLI personnel were armed with rifles, machine-guns and light mortars (81-mm). They were not equipped with heavy weapons suitable for major offensive operations.[120] On 7 June 1999, India's 56th Brigade, supported by Bofors howitzers counter-attacked the heights of Tololing.[121] By July, due to intervention by the United States and Indian military pressure, the intruders retreated from Kargil.

As regards the future of India's nuclear programme, Cohen concludes that India went for the bomb for reasons of 'national prestige'. India's

---

[115] Strobe Talbott, *Engaging India: Diplomacy, Democracy and the Bomb* (New Delhi: Penguin, 2004), pp. 21–2.

[116] Sanjay Badri-Maharaj, *The Armageddon Factor: Nuclear Weapons in the India-Pakistan Context* (New Delhi: Lancer, 2000), pp. 45–6.

[117] John H. Gill, 'Military Operations in the Kargil Conflict', in Peter R. Lavoy (ed.), *Asymmetric Warfare in South Asia: The Causes and Consequences of the Kargil Conflict* (Cambridge: Cambridge University Press, 2009), pp. 94–5.

[118] Peter R. Lavoy, 'Introduction: The Importance of the Kargil Conflict', and C. Christine Fair, 'Militants in the Kargil Conflict: Myths, Realities, and Impacts', in Lavoy (ed.), *Asymmetric Warfare in South Asia*, pp. 1, 6, 231, 235.

[119] Feroz Hassan Khan, Peter R. Lavoy and Christopher Clary, 'Pakistan's Motivations and Calculations for the Kargil Conflict', in Lavoy (ed.), *Asymmetric Warfare in South Asia*, p. 72.

[120] Gill, 'Military Operations in the Kargil Conflict', p. 97.

[121] Praveen Swami, 'The Impact of the Kargil Conflict and Kashmir on Indian Politics and Society', in Lavoy (ed.), *Asymmetric Warfare in South Asia*, p. 258.

260   *Hinduism and the Ethics of Warfare in South Asia*

'trophy' nuclear arsenal will not deter China, nor will it solve the con-undrum vis-à-vis Pakistan regarding Kashmir. Cohen goes on to say that just as India was never entirely 'Gandhian,' it has not entirely rejected the Mahatma. Gandhi argued that Indians have a special obligation to resist evil by nonviolent means; the greatest sin for Gandhi was the use of vio-lence. If the development of an Indian nuclear weapon fails to provide security against putative threats from Pakistan, China, and the United States, then enthusiasm for its development and deployment will wane. The nuclear advocates will have to continually jack up the external threat in order to win support for additions to the nuclear arsenal and argue that there is no other way to resist this 'international evil.' Furthermore, if non-nuclear threats continue to increase, whether in the form of interna-tional pressure or terrorism, Indians will have to examine the relevance of nuclear weapons to threats that must be 'resisted,' in Gandhian terms.[122]

CONCLUSION

Nehru's grand strategy was an amalgam of realism and idealism couched in the mould of moderate Hinduism. Some Indian military officers are aware of a new necessity to reject or modify certain aspects of moderate Hinduism. Both the insurgents and the state's elites use religion in order to legitimize their actions and policies. The Indian Army's COIN doctrine has been shaped to a great extent by the *Arthasastra*. In Kashmir, the Islamic insurgency continues. The Indian army would do better to cull further lessons from the *Arthasastra* rather than looking at the newfan-gled Western COIN theories of New War. As regards the nuclear question, those Indian experts who consider themselves realists perceive a great threat to the *Bharat Mata*. To an extent, the rise of the BJP was a reaction to the emergence of Islamic fundamentalism in Pakistan. The BJP high-lights the threat as well as magnifying it; its stated response is aggressive *kutayuddha*. To conclude, some American state officials overemphasize the danger of nuclear war between India and Pakistan. Despite being por-trayed by the political managers of India and Pakistan as a Hindu bomb and a Muslim bomb for domestic mass consumption, the small nuclear arsenals of these two countries, as Kargil shows, have brought stability in South Asia by deterring a conventional war.

---

[122] Cohen, *India*, pp. 196–7.

Conclusion

There are certain limitations inherent in drawing conclusions from a text-based study, especially when such 'high texts' could be categorized as 'construction' by the Orientalists. It cannot be denied that in pre-modern India, with its low rate of literacy, iconography was more important than the written word as a means of communicating ideas. For instance, one might argue that analysis of Hindu iconography might be more valuable than examining written texts for the purpose of throwing light on Hindu attitudes towards warfare. The most serious problem in the history of ideas is to prove/show a direct connection between certain concepts expressed in different texts and their execution/implementation in reality by strategic/military managers.

However, this book puts to rest the banal assertion of modern scholars that India has no pre-modern text except Kautilya *Arthasastra*.[1] It is difficult to chisel out direct linkages between classical Indian tradition and modern Indian strategic-military thought for several reasons. Most modern Indian intellectuals and generals have been educated in Western-model schools and universities. So most of them try to mould their thought to conform to the liberal/realist paradigms. They are anxious to avoid highlighting the connection between ancient Hindu theories and modern strategic thinking in order to avoid the stigma of being a communal right-wing Hindu. Especially among academicians, the intellectual milieu has been shaped by Marxism and then post-modernism. Any

---

[1] See, for instance, the assertion of Kanti Bajpai in 'Indian Strategic Culture and the Problem of Pakistan', in Swarna Rajagopalan (ed.), *Security and South Asia: Ideas, Institutions and Initiatives* (London/New York/New Delhi: Routledge, 2006), pp. 54–79.

scholar trying to trace out the legacies of ancient Hinduism in modern-day statecraft will be marginalized by the mainstream academic community. Because Muslims constitute about 23 percent of India's population, and because of the influence of 'liberal' Hindus (especially in the media) among the electorate, politicians (except those belonging to the BJP) are also wary of carrying the baggage of Hinduism in modern India. Hence, Indian intellectuals, generals and most Indian politicians avoid referring overtly to the Hindu influence on their thought and practice. At best, we can speculate about indirect connections between modern India's strategic discourse and ancient Hindu thought.

One author rightly states that the meaning of culture is not always confined to an autonomous text but is also the product of social interaction and institutional processes.[2] Hence, this book has attempted to historicize the various Hindu traditions. This book does not discuss in detail the nuances of doctrinal debates relating to morality and *karma* theory. Nor have I discussed the complex ideas propounded in the *Upanishad*s. This is in part because the focus of this monograph remains mainstream Hinduism. Moreover, neither the rulers/politicians nor the *senapati*s/ generals cared and care much for the intricacies of religious doctrines. They pick and choose from the shelf the ideas/concepts available to them. But what is available on the shelf is also constrained by the evolution of 'national' culture. To give an example from Western history, the German generals during their interrogations after World War II admitted that Clausewitz's *On War* is foggy, messy and very complex, suited for reading by professors. Nevertheless, the *panzer* knights knew the broad outlines of Clausewitz's ideas.

Gandhi and the BJP's proponent Jaswant Singh, as well as Nehru (in a more sophisticated manner), claimed that India is Hindu and that Hinduism is the king of all religions and can accommodate and absorb all other religions. Whether the Mahabharata war is mythical or not is not the issue. The fact is that several Hindu rulers of medieval India and military officers and civilian analysts of independent India have been influenced by the concepts in the epics. Similarly, famous Indian political figures like Gandhi, Aurobindo, and others have been influenced by the *vedas* and the *Bhagavad Gita*. Both the moderates/pacifists (like Gandhi and the present anti-nuclear lobby) and the aggressive/extremists (e.g., Subhas Chandra Bose and hyper-realist nuclear theorists like Karnad)

---

[2] Tim Hallett, 'Symbolic Power and Organizational Culture', *Sociological Theory*, vol. 21, no. 2 (2003), p. 141.

Conclusion 263

package their ideas using interpretations of Hinduism. While the former lobby asserts that real Hinduism is pacific, the latter claims that the true essence of Hinduism is aggressive and martial. An instrumental interpretation would be that the spokesmen of both lobbies use religious imagery and metaphors merely to legitimize their opposing claims in the public sphere. A more nuanced interpretation would be that religious ideas (Hinduism, in our case) have not only legitimized but also shaped the ideas and worldviews of the country's strategic managers throughout history. After all, we live in a world that is partially 'constructed' through our worldviews, which to an extent are shaped by inherited culture.

To assume that the *ahimsa* tradition is purely idealistic and devoid of realism would be simplistic. Alastair Ian Johnston cautions that many miss the dominant hard *realpolitik* tendencies in Chinese strategic culture when they emphasize the elements of inherent defensiveness and anti-militarism of the Confucian brand of strategic thought.[3] Asoka and Gandhi gave a twist to statecraft by emphasizing *ahimsa* as a component of the *dharmayuddha* tradition. It could be argued that the policy of *ahimsa*, as followed by Asoka and Gandhi, and which influenced Nehru, was a sort of 'weapon of the weak'. *Ahimsa* justifies non-action by the weaker party against a strong adversary. In addition, it provides the weak state with the high moral ground. We can conclude by saying that the Hindu ethos not only shapes the mental world of Indian policymakers and military officers but also allows them to legitimize their views and opinions. While the *dharmayuddha* tradition aids the liberals, the *kutayuddha* tradition comes in handy for the realists/hard-liners. This ongoing dialectic has shaped India's strategic and military tradition for the last two millennia.

Can we speak of a Hindu strategic and military tradition that has unfolded throughout the last two thousand years? Despite political fragmentation, can we speak of cultural continuity? After all, both Arjuna and Gandhi speak of *tapas* for the greater good. Defensive military doctrine and the Martial Race theory continue to hold sway even in the new millennium. Despite these and other similarities, one cannot speak of a monolithic and homogeneous Indian Way of Warfare. At best, this monograph shows that Hinduism in various guises has structured the thought processes of India's strategic managers and military officers.

This volume argues that warfare and the politics associated with it cannot be explained merely by referring to realist/neo-realist theories.

---

[3] Alastair Iain Johnston, 'Thinking about Strategic Culture', *International Security*, vol. 19, no. 4 (1995), p. 55.

264   *Hinduism and the Ethics of Warfare in South Asia*

However, it would be simplistic to claim that a coherent Indian Way of Warfare has operated over two millennia. Examining the very evolution of the *dharmayuddha* and *kutayuddha* concepts, the contradictions present within Hinduism, the development of its traditions and its interactions with the changing historical scenario, has been the objective of this volume. Military traditions cannot be explained merely by realism, nor do I want to fall into the trap of claiming, like Hanson, that unique national characteristics of warfare can identified in the *longue duree*.[4]

Warfare (its origins, conduct and consequences) is certainly shaped by cultural traits, and culture is also partially shaped by organized violence and the material setting. The paradigm of culture varies from region to region. This book has more or less followed the approach that political scientists would brand the First Generation Strategic Culture approach. Proponents of the First Generation approach focus on three levels of input into a polity's strategic culture: the macro-environmental level (geography, ethno-cultural characteristics, historical experience, etc.), the societal level (society, economy and political structures) and the micro level (military institutions and civil-military relations). As regards the shortcomings of First Generation theorists, Alastair Ian Johnston writes that they have little appreciation of the instrumentality of strategic culture, its potential for conscious manipulation in order to justify the competence of decision makers, deflect criticism, suppress dissent and limit access to the decision-making process. By contrast, so-called Third Generation Strategic Culture proponents claim that culture is rooted in recent experience and not in ancient historical practice as posited by First Generation theorists. The Third Generation approach focuses more on the autonomy of the culture and places more emphasis on the role of the domestic political context in shaping the country's politico-military culture.[5] Third Generation scholars claim that the military culture rather than the broader strategic culture has shaped national ways of war.[6]

I refuse to accept the idea that the military culture is completely separate from the wider culture or that contemporary military traditions are merely the product of domestic politics. At least in the Indian case, military organizations have been subordinated to the wider cultural ethos, which to an extent is shaped by Hinduism. The connection between

---

[4] Victor Davis Hanson, *Carnage and Culture: Landmark Battles in the Rise of Western Power* (New York: Doubleday, 2001).

[5] Johnston, 'Thinking about Strategic Culture', pp. 37–42.

[6] Lawrence Sondhaus, *Strategic Culture and Ways of War* (London/New York: Routledge, 2006), p. 11.

Conclusion 265

organizational culture and the broader culture is shown by Tim Hallett. He writes that organizational culture is a negotiated order that emerges through the formal and informal interactions among organizational actors, an order influenced by people with symbolic power, that is, the power to define the situation. Embedded in the context, valued practice become the basis of legitimacy that the negotiators deploy as symbolic power to define the situation and influence future practices, interactions and the ongoing negotiated order. People bring their culturally inscribed dispositions and tool kits with them into an organization, linking organizational culture to the broader social order.[7]

Despite Lawrence Sondhaus's warning that the true utility of strategic culture lies in how it can help us to understand observed behaviour in the present rather than to predict future behaviour,[8] one can ask the question: how will the future unfold? One thing is sure. Because both the *dharmayuddha* and *kutayuddha* traditions critique the *senapati*s taking over the reins of power from the monarch and their Brahmin advisors (along with many other factors), the possibility of a military coup is extremely remote in India. The classical Hindu tradition accepts the idea that an inefficient and incompetent ruler can be replaced by a *mantri* or *amatya*, but never by a *senapati*. So frequent Cabinet reshufflings and increases in the power of the civilian bureaucracy are established features of modern-day Indian statecraft, but the possibility of brass hats replacing the frock coats is remote.[9] If India's current economic growth rate continues and New Delhi is able to manage internal rebellion, at best an anglicized worldview laced with moderate Hinduism will prevail. Then India may have the luxury to speak about the *dharmayuddha* tradition, which in turn will generate strategic and military restraint on India's part. If, on the other hand, India's economy goes into a downswing and internal rebellion gets out of control, an increasingly insecure India will probably take solace in the exclusive fundamentalist brand of Hinduism, that is, *kutayuddha*.

---

[7] Hallett, 'Symbolic Power and Organizational Culture', pp. 129–31, 136.
[8] Sondhaus, *Strategic Culture and Ways of War*, p. 13.
[9] Kaushik Roy, 'Good Governance versus Bad Governance in South Asia: Civil-Military Relations in India and Pakistan, 1947–2000', *Asian Studies*, vol. 18, nos. 1–2 (2000), pp. 82–99.

Select Bibliography

Primary Sources

Azad Hind: Writings and Speeches, 1941–43, ed. by Sisir Kumar Bose and Sugata Bose, in *Netaji Collected Works*, vol. 11 (New Delhi: Permanent Black, 2002).

Bhatta, Somadeva, *Kathasaritsagara*, tr. from Sanskrit into Bengali by Hirendralal Biswas, Introduction by R. C. Majumdar, 5 vols. (1975; reprint, Kolkata: Academic Publishers, 1983).

Bingley, Captain A. H., *Handbook on Rajputs* (1899; reprint, New Delhi: Low Price Publications, 1999).

Bingley, Captain A. H. and Nicholls, Captain A., *Caste Handbooks for the Indian Army: Brahmins* (Simla: Government Central Office, 1897), p. 48.

Buck, William, *Mahabharata*, with an Introduction by B. A. van Nooten (1981; reprint, New Delhi: Motilal Banarasidas, 2006).

Candler, Edmund, *The Sepoy* (London: John Murray, 1919).

Cardew, Lieutenant F. G., *A Sketch of the Services of the Bengal Native Army to the Year 1895* (1903; reprint, Faridabad: Today and Tomorrow's Printers & Publishers, 1971).

Chesney, General George, *Indian Polity: A View of the System of Administration in India* (1894; reprint, Delhi: Metropolitan Books, 1976).

Clausewitz, Carl Von, *On War*, ed. and tr. by Michael Howard and Peter Paret (1984; reprint, Princeton, New Jersey: Princeton University Press, 1989).

Court of Enquiry into the Barrackpur Mutiny, Minutes of Evidence, 1824, vol. 11, NAI.

Das, Gautam and Gupta-Ray, M. K., *Sri Lanka Misadventure: India's Military Peace-Keeping Campaign, 1987–1990* (New Delhi: Har-Anand, 2008).

Gandhi, M. K., *Hind Swaraj and Other Writings*, ed. by Anthony J. Parel (1997; reprint, New Delhi: Foundation Books, 2004).

General Order by the Commander-in-Chief of British-India, NAI.

India's Contribution to the Great War (Calcutta: Superintendent of Govt. Printing, 1923).

268   *Select Bibliography*

Journal of the United Service Institution of India (various issues).
Kalhana's Rajatarangini: A Chronicle of the Kings of Kashmir, tr. with an Introduction, Commentary, and Appendices by M. A. Stein, vols. 1 and 2 (1900, reprint, New Delhi: Motilal Banarasidas, 1989).
Kautilya, *The Arthasastra*, ed., rearranged, tr. and introduced by L. N. Rangarajan (New Delhi: Penguin, 1992).
Kitchener Papers, M/F, NAI, New Delhi.
Machiavelli, Niccolo, *The Prince*, tr. with an Introduction by George Bull (1961; reprint, Harmondsworth, Middlesex: Penguin, 1981).
Mahakabi Kalidas Birachitam Raghuvamsam, Pratham Sarga to Chaturdash Sarga, Mallinath krita Tikapetam, Gurunath Vidhyanithi Bhattacharyamanudithancha, edited by Ashok Kumar Bandopadhyay (Kolkata: Sanskrit Pustak Bhandar, 1411).
Manu's Code of Law, A Critical Edition and Translation of the Manava-Dharmasastra, by Patrick Olivelle, with the editorial assistance of Suman Olivelle (2005; reprint, New Delhi: Oxford University Press, 2006).
Ministry of Defence Government of India Annual Reports, 1999–2000, 2000–2001.
Narayana, *The Hitopadesa*, tr. from the Sanskrit with an Introduction by A. N. D. Haksar (New Delhi: Penguin, 1998).
Nitiprakasika, ed. by Gustav Oppert (1882; reprint, New Delhi: Kumar Brothers, 1970).
Northey, W. Brook and Morris, C. J., *The Gurkhas* (1927; reprint, New Delhi: Cosmo Publications, 1987).
Oracle (various issues).
Parliamentary Papers, Reports from the Select Committees on the Affairs of the East India Company with Appendices, Colonies, East India, Sessions 1805–10 (Shannon: Irish University Press, 1971).
Prasad, Nandan, *Expansion of the Armed Forces and Defence Organizations: 1939–45* (New Delhi: Govt. of India, 1956).
Prithvirajavijayamahakavya, Aithihasik o Kavyik Parikrama, by Sanjil Bhattacharya (in Bengali) (Kolkata: Asiatic Society, 2003).
Recruitment in India, Appendix 19, Note by General Molesworth on Indian Army Recruitment, 21 July 1943, L/WS/1/136, IOR, BL, London.
Reichberg, Gregory M., Syse, Henrik and Begny, Endre (eds.), *The Ethics of War: Classic and Contemporary Readings* (Malden, MA and Oxford: Blackwell, 2006).
Robson, Brian (ed.), *Roberts in India: The Military Papers of Field-Marshal Lord Roberts, 1876–1893* (Stroud: Sutton, 1993).
Shakespear, Colonel L. W., *History of the 2nd King Edward's Own Goorkha Rifles (The Sirmoor Rifles)* (Aldershot: Gale and Polden, 1912).
Singh, Lieutenant-General Depinder, *Indian Peacekeeping Force in Sri Lanka* (DehraDun: Natraj Publishers, 2001).
Singh, Colonel Harjeet, *Doda: An Insurgency in the Wilderness* (New Delhi: Lancer, 1999).
Singh, J., *Indian Defence Yearbook* (DehraDun: Natraj, 2003).

Select Bibliography

Singh, Jaswant, *A Call to Honour: In Service of Emergent India* (New Delhi: Rupa, 2006).

Srimad Valmiki-Ramayana (with Sanskrit Text and English Translation), Part I *[Balakanda, Ayodhaykanda, Aryanyakanda and Kiskindhakanda]* (1969; reprint, Gorakhpur: Gita Press, 2001).

Srivara's Zaina Rajatarangini, English tr. and annotations by Kashi Nath Dhar (New Delhi: Indian Council of Historical Research and People's Publishing House, 1994).

The Army in India and Its Evolution including an Account of the Establishment of the Royal Air Force in India (1924; reprint, New Delhi: Anmol Publications, 1985).

The Art of War in World History from Antiquity to the Nuclear Age, ed. by Gerard Chaliand (Berkeley/Los Angeles: University of California Press, 1994).

The Bhagavad Gita, tr. from the Sanskrit with an Introduction by Juan Mascaro (London: Penguin, 1962).

The Epic of Shivaji, Kavindra Paramananda's Sivabharata, tr. and study by James W. Laine in collaboration with S. S. Bahulkar (New Delhi: Orient Longman, 2001).

The Essential Writings of Jawaharlal Nehru, ed. by S. Gopal and Uma Iyengar, 2 vols. (New Delhi: Oxford University Press, 2003).

The Essential Writings of Mahatma Gandhi, ed. by Raghavan Iyer (1993; reprint, New Delhi: Oxford University Press, 2007).

The Harsacharita by Banabhatta, tr. by E. P. Cowell and P. W. Thomas, ed. by R. P. Shastri (New Delhi: Global Vision, 2004).

The Harshacarita of Banabhatta with Exclusive Notes (Uchchhvasas I–VIII), ed. with an Introduction and Notes by P. V. Kane (New Delhi: Motilal Banarasidas, 1965).

The Kautilya Arthasastra, Part II, *An English Translation with Critical and Explanatory Notes*, by R. P. Kangle (1972; reprint, New Delhi: Motilal Banarasidas, 1992).

The Kautilya Arthasastra, Part III, *A Study*, by R. P. Kangle (1965; reprint, New Delhi: Motilal Banrasidas, 2000).

The Laws of Manu, with an Introduction and Notes, tr. by Wendy Doniger with Brian K. Smith (New Delhi: Penguin, 1991).

The Maathir-ul-umara, Being Biographies of the Muhammadan and Hindu Officers of the Timurid Sovereigns of India from 1500 to about 1780, by Nawab Samsam-ud-Daulah Shah Nawaz Khan and his son Abdul Hayy, tr. by H. Beveridge, revised, annotated and completed by Baini Prashad, vol. 1 (1941; reprint, Delhi: Low Price Publications, 1999).

The Maharashtra Purana, An Eighteenth Century Bengali Historical Text, tr., annotated, and with an Introduction by Edward C. Dimock, Jr., and Pratul Chandra Gupta (1965; reprint, Hyderabad: Orient Longman, 1985).

The Military Despatches of a Seventeenth Century Indian General, Being an English Translation of the Haft Anjuman of Munshi Udairaj alias Taleyar Khan, ed. by Jagadish Narayan Sarkar (Calcutta: Scientific Book Agency, 1969).

270   *Select Bibliography*

The Nitisara by Kamandaki, ed. by Rajendra Lala Mitra, revised with English translation by Sisir Kumar Mitra (1849; reprint, Calcutta: The Asiatic Society, 1982).

The Panchatantra, tr. from the Sanskrit by Arthur W. Ryder (1949; reprint, Mumbai: Jaico, 2003).

The Ramayana of Valmiki: An Epic of Ancient India, vol. 1, *Balakanda*, Introduction and tr. by Robert P. Goldman (1984; reprint, Delhi: Motilal Banarasidas, 2007).

The Rig Veda: An Anthology, One Hundred and Eight Hymns, selected, tr. and annotated by Wendy Doniger O' Flaherty (1981; reprint, New Delhi: Penguin, 1994).

The Seven Military Classics of Ancient China, tr. and Commentary by Ralph D. Sawyer with Mei-chun Sawyer (Boulder/San Francisco: Westview Press, 1993).

The Writings of Gandhi: A Selection, edited and with an Introduction by Ronald Duncan (1971; reprint, Calcutta: Rupa, 1990).

Tiruvalluvar, The Kural, tr. from the Tamil with an Introduction by P. S. Sundaram (New Delhi: Penguin, 1990).

Tzu, Sun, *Art of War*, tr. with an Historical Introduction by Ralph D. Sawyer (Boulder, Colorado: Westview, 1994).

Tzu II, Sun, *The Lost Art of War*, tr. with Commentary by Thomas Cleary (San Francisco: HarperCollins, 1996).

Wilson, Lieutenant-Colonel W. J., *Historical Record of the Fourth Prince of Wales' Own Regiment Madras Light Cavalry* (Madras: Government Office, 1877).

Secondary Sources

Acharya, Nand Kishore, *The Polity in Sukranitisara* (Bikaner: Vagdevi Prakashan, 1987).

Agrawal, Ashvini, *Rise and Fall of the Imperial Guptas* (Delhi: Motilal Banarasidas, 1989).

Ali, M. Athar, *Mughal India: Studies in Polity, Ideas, Society and Culture* (New Delhi: Oxford University Press, 2006).

Allen, Nick, 'Just War in the *Mahabharata*', in Richard Sorabji and David Rodin (eds.), *The Ethics of War: Shared Problems in Different Traditions* (Aldershot: Ashgate, 2006), pp. 138–49.

Aquil, Raziuddin, *Sufism, Culture, and Politics: Afghans and Islam in Medieval North India* (New Delhi: Oxford University Press, 2007).

Athale, Anil A., 'Insurgency and Counter-Insurgency in Modern India: An Overview', in S. N. Prasad (ed.), *Historical Perspectives of Warfare in India: Some Morale and Materiel Determinants* (New Delhi: Centre for Studies in Civilizations, distributed by Motilal Banarasidas, 2002), pp. 389–423.

Ayoob, Mohammed, 'India's Nuclear Decision: Implications for Indian-US Relations', in Raju G. C. Thomas and Amit Gupta (eds.), *India's Nuclear Security* (New Delhi: Vistaar, 2000), pp. 123–44.

Select Bibliography

Badri-Maharaj, Sanjay, *The Armageddon Factor: Nuclear Weapons in the India-Pakistan Context* (New Delhi: Lancer, 2000).

Bailey, Greg, 'Introduction: An Empirical Approach to the *Ramayana*', in Greg Bailey and Mary Brockington (eds.), *Epic Threads: John Brockington on the Sanskrit Epics* (2000; reprint, New Delhi: Oxford University Press, 2002), pp. vii–xxv.

Bajpai, Kanti P., 'State, Society, Strategy', in Kanti P. Bajpai and Amitabh Mattoo (eds.), *Securing India, Strategic Thought and Practice: Essays by George K. Tanham with Commentaries* (New Delhi: Manohar, 2006), pp. 140–59.

'Indian Strategic Culture and the Problem of Pakistan', in Swarna Rajagopalan (ed.), *Security and South Asia: Ideas, Institutions and Initiatives* (London/New York/New Delhi: Routledge, 2006), pp. 54–79.

Bakshi, Lieutenant-Colonel G. D., *Mahabharata: A Military Analysis* (New Delhi: Lancer, 1990).

'Operational Art in the Indian Context: An Open Sources Analysis', *Strategic Analysis*, vol. 25, no. 6 (2001), pp. 723–36.

Bartley, Caleb M., 'The Art of Terrorism: What Sun Tzu Can Teach Us about International Terrorism', *Comparative Strategy*, vol. 24 (2005), pp. 237–51.

Barua, Pradeep P., *The State at War in South Asia* (Lincoln/London: University of Nebraska Press, 2005).

Bhandare, Shailendra, 'Numismatics and History: The Maurya-Gupta Interlude in the Gangetic Plain', in Patrick Olivelle (ed.), *Between the Empires: Society in India 300 BCE to 400 CE* (2006; reprint, New York: Oxford University Press, 2007), pp. 67–112.

Bhat, G. N., 'Means to Fill the Treasury during a Financial Crisis – Kautilya's Views', in Dr. Michael (ed.), *The Concept of Rajadharma* (New Delhi: Sundeep Prakashan, 2005), pp. 148–58.

Bhat, Sumitra V., 'Ethical Values in the *Ramayana*: A Reflection', in K. B. Archak (ed.), *Ethics for Modern Man in Sanskrit Literature* (New Delhi: Sundeep Prakashan, 2007), pp. 27–33.

Bhattacharya, Pachugopal, *Ramayana Yuddhabidhya* [in Bengali] (Kolkata: Sanskrit Pustak Bhandar, 1399).

Blom, Amelie, 'A Patron-Client Perspective on Militia-State Relations: The Case of the Hizb-ul-Mujahidin of Kashmir', in Laurent Gayer and Christophe Jaffrelot (eds.), *Armed Militias of South Asia: Fundamentalists, Maoists and Separatists* (New Delhi: Foundation, 2009), pp. 135–56.

Brekke, Torkel, 'Wielding the Rod of Punishment – War and Violence in the Political Science of Kautilya', *Journal of Military Ethics*, vol. 3, no. 1 (2004), pp. 40–52.

'Between Prudence and Heroism: Ethics of War in the Hindu Tradition', in Torkel Brekke (ed.), *The Ethics of War in Asian Civilizations* (London/New York: Routledge, 2006), pp. 113–44.

Brockington, John, 'Stereotyped Expressions in the *Ramayana*', in Greg Bailey and Mary Brockington (eds.), *Epic Threads: John Brockington on the Sanskrit Epics* (2000; reprint, New Delhi: Oxford University Press, 2002), pp. 98–125.

Select Bibliography

'Religious Attitudes in Valmiki's *Ramayana*', in Greg Bailey and Mary Brockington (eds.), *Epic Threads: John Brockington on the Sanskrit Epics* (2000; reprint, New Delhi: Oxford University Press, 2002), pp. 218–49.

'*Ramo dharmabhrtam varah*', in Greg Bailey and Mary Brockington (eds.), *Epic Threads: John Brockington on the Sanskrit Epics* (2000; reprint, New Delhi: Oxford University Press, 2002), pp. 250–64.

'Fashions in Formulae: Sanskrit Epic Tradition III', in Greg Bailey and Mary Brockington (eds.), *Epic Threads: John Brockington on the Sanskrit Epics* (2000; reprint, New Delhi: Oxford University Press, 2002), pp. 339–52.

Bullock, Brigadier Humphry, *History of the Army Service Corps*, vol. 1, *1760–1857* (1952; reprint, Delhi: Sterling Publishers, 1976).

Callahan, Raymond, *The East India Company and Army Reform: 1783–98* (Cambridge, Massachusetts: Harvard University Press, 1972).

Caplan, Lionel, *Warrior Gentleman: "Gurkhas" in the Western Imagination* (Providence/Oxford: Berghahn Books, 1995).

Chadha, Lieutenant-Colonel Vivek, *Low Intensity Conflicts in India: An Analysis* (New Delhi: Sage, 2005).

'India's Counterinsurgency Campaign in Mizoram', in Sumit Ganguly and David P. Fidler (eds.), *India and Counterinsurgency: Lessons Learned* (Oxon: Routledge, 2009), pp. 28–44.

Chakravarti, P. C., *The Art of War in Ancient India* (1941; reprint, New Delhi: Low Price Publications, 1989).

Chattopadhyaya, B. D., 'Origin of the Rajputs: The Political, Economic and Social Processes in Early Medieval Rajasthan', *Indian Historical Review*, vol. 3, no. 1 (1976), pp. 59–82.

The Making of Early Medieval India (1994; reprint, New Delhi: Oxford University Press, 2005).

'Anachronism of the Political Imagination', in David N. Lorenzen (ed.), *Religious Movements in South Asia, 600–1800* (2004; reprint, New Delhi: Oxford University Press, 2006), pp. 209–26.

Chousalkar, Ashok S., *A Comparative Study of Theory of Rebellion in Kautilya and Aristotle* (New Delhi: Indological Book House, 1990).

Coates, Breena E., 'Modern India's Strategic Advantage to the United States: Her Twin Strengths in *Himsa* and *Ahimsa*', *Comparative Strategy*, vol. 27, no. 2 (2008), pp. 133–47.

Cohen, Stephen P., *India: Emerging Power* (2001; reprint, New Delhi: Oxford University Press, 2003).

Coker, Christopher, *Waging War without Warriors? The Changing Culture of Military Conflict* (Boulder, Colorado: Lynne Rienner, 2002).

Connor, W. R., 'Early Greek Land Warfare as Symbolic Expression', in Everett L. Wheeler (ed.), *The Armies of Classical Greece* (Aldershot: Ashgate, 2007), pp. 83–109.

Crowell, Lorenzo M., 'Military Professionalism in a Colonial Context: The Madras Army, circa 1832', *Modern Asian Studies*, vol. 24, no. 2 (1990), pp. 249–73.

Dange, Sindhu S., 'Ethical Codes in the Vedic Literature', in K. B. Archak (ed.), *Ethics for Modern Man in Sanskrit Literature* (New Delhi: Sundeep Prakashan, 2007), pp. 17–26.

Select Bibliography

Datta, Rajat (ed.), *Rethinking a Millennium: Perspectives on Indian History from the Eighth to the Eighteenth Centuries, Essays for Harbans Mukhia* (New Delhi: Aakar, 2008).

Davis, G. Scott, 'Introduction: Comparative Ethics and the Crucible of War', in Torkel Brekke (ed.), *The Ethics of War in Asian Civilizations* (London/New York: Routledge, 2006), pp. 1–36.

Dawson, Doyne, *The First Armies* (London: Cassell, 2001).

Deegalle, Mahinda, *Popularizing Buddhism: Preaching as Performance in Sri Lanka* (New York: State University of New York Press, 2006).

Deloche, Jean, *Military Technology in Hoysala Sculpture (Twelfth and Thirteenth Century)* (New Delhi: Sitaram Bhartia Institute of Scientific Research, 1989).

Studies on Fortification in India (Pondicherry: Institut Francais De Pondicherry and Ecole Francaise D'Extreme Orient, 2007).

Devahuti, D., *Harsha: A Political Study* (Oxford: Clarendon Press, 1970).

Digby, Simon, 'The Problem of the Military Ascendancy of the Delhi Sultanate', in Jos J. L. Gommans and Dirk H. A. Kolff (eds.), *Warfare and Weaponry in South Asia: 1000–1800* (New Delhi: Oxford University Press, 2001), pp. 311–20.

Dikshitar, V. R. Ramachandra, 'Indian Martial Tradition', *Journal of the Ganganath Jha Research Institute*, vol. 3, nos. 3–4 (1946), pp. 263–77.

Dundas, Paul, 'The Non-Violence of Violence: Jain Perspectives on Warfare, Asceticism and Worship', in John R. Hinnells and Richard King (eds.), *Religion and Violence in South Asia: Theory and Practice* (London/New York: Routledge, 2007), pp. 41–61.

Duyvesteyn, Isabelle, *Clausewitz and African War: Politics and Strategy in Liberia and Somalia* (Oxon: Routledge, 2005).

Elgood, Robert, *Hindu Arms and Rituals: Arms and Armour from India, 1400–1865* (Ahmedabad: Mapin, 2004).

Fair, C. Christine, 'Militants in the Kargil Conflict: Myths, Realities, and Impacts', in Peter R. Lavoy (ed.), *Asymmetric Warfare in South Asia: The Causes and Consequences of the Kargil Conflict* (Cambridge: Cambridge University Press, 2009), pp. 231–57.

Ferguson, John, *War and Peace in the World Religions* (New York: Oxford University Press, 1978).

Ferguson, W. S., 'The Zulus and the Spartans: A Comparison of Their Military Systems', in Everett L. Wheeler (ed.), *The Armies of Classical Greece* (Aldershot: Ashgate, 2007), pp. 45–82.

Fussman, Gerard, 'Central and Provincial Administration in Ancient India: The Problem of the Mauryan Empire', *Indian Historical Review*, vol. 14, nos. 1–2 (1988), pp. 43–72.

Gabriel, Richard A., *The Great Armies of Antiquity* (Westport, Connecticut: Praeger, 2002).

Gaylor, John, *Sons of John Company: The Indian and Pakistan Armies, 1903–91* (1992; reprint, New Delhi: Lancer, 1993).

Gethin, Rupert, 'Buddhist Monks, Buddhist Kings, Buddhist Violence: On the Early Buddhist Attitudes to Violence', in John R. Hinnells and Richard King (eds.),

Religion and Violence in South Asia: Theory and Practice (London/New York: Routledge, 2007), pp. 62–82.

Gill, John H., 'Military Operations in the Kargil Conflict', in Peter R. Lavoy (ed.), *Asymmetric Warfare in South Asia: The Causes and Consequences of the Kargil Conflict* (Cambridge: Cambridge University Press, 2009), pp. 92–129.

Gommans, Jos J. L. and Kolff, Dirk H. A., 'Introduction: Warfare and Weaponry in South Asia: 1000–1800 AD', in Gommans and Kolff (eds.), *Warfare and Weaponry in South Asia: 1000–1800* (New Delhi: Oxford University Press, 2001), pp. 1–42.

Gommans, Jos, *Mughal Warfare: Indian Frontiers and High Roads to Empire, 1500–1700* (London/New York: Routledge, 2002).

'Warhorse and Post-Nomadic Empire in Asia, c. 1000–1800', *Journal of Global History*, vol. 2 (2007), pp. 1–21.

Goodman, M. D. and Holladay, A. J., 'Religious Scruples in Ancient Warfare', in Everett L. Wheeler (ed.), *The Armies of Classical Greece* (Aldershot: Ashgate, 2007), pp. 131–51.

Gordon, Stewart, *Marathas, Marauders, and State Formation in Eighteenth-Century India* (1994; reprint, New Delhi: Oxford University Press, 1998).

The Marathas: 1600–1818 (1998; reprint, New Delhi: Foundation Books, 2000).

Gould, William, *Hindu Nationalism and the Language of Politics in Late Colonial India* (New Delhi: Foundation Books, 2005).

Grewal, J. S., *The New Cambridge History of India*, II:3, *The Sikhs of the Punjab* (1994; reprint, New Delhi: Foundation Books, 2002).

Habib, Irfan (ed.), *Akbar and His India* (1997; reprint, New Delhi: Oxford University Press, 2002).

Habib, Irfan, *A People's History of India*, vol. 2, *The Indus Civilization* (New Delhi: Tulika, 2002).

Habib, Irfan and Jha, Vivekanand, *A People's History of India*, vol. 4, *Mauryan India* (New Delhi: Tulika Books, 2004).

Habib, Irfan and Thakur, Vijay Kumar, *A People's History of India*, vol. 3, *The Vedic Age and the Coming of Iron, c. 1500–700 BC* (New Delhi: Tulika Books, 2003).

Habib, Mohammad and Nizami, Khaliq Ahmad (eds.), *A Comprehensive History of India*, vol. 5, Part II, *The Delhi Sultanate: 1206–1526* (1970; reprint, New Delhi: People's Publishing House, 2000).

Handel, Michael I., *Masters of War: Classical Strategic Thought* (1992; reprint, London: Frank Cass, 1996).

Hanson, Victor Davis, *The Wars of the Ancient Greeks* (1999; reprint, London: Cassell, 2000).

Carnage and Culture: Landmark Battles in the Rise of Western Power (New York: Doubleday, 2001).

Haydt, Claudia, '"New" Terrorism: Guidelines for Security Policies', in Vice-Admiral K. K. Nayyar and Jorg Schultz (eds.), *South Asia Post 9/11: Searching for Stability* (New Delhi: Rupa, 2003), pp. 14–20.

Heathcote, T. A., *The Military in British India: The Development of British Land Forces in South Asia, 1600–1947* (Manchester: Manchester University Press, 1995).

Select Bibliography

Heuser, Beatrice, *Reading Clausewitz* (London: Pimlico, 2002).

Hills, Carol and Silverman, Daniel C., 'Nationalism and Feminism in Late Colonial India: The Rani of Jhansi Regiment, 1943–45', *Modern Asian Studies*, vol. 27, no. 4 (1993), pp. 741–60.

Hoover, James W., *Men without Hats: Dialogue, Discipline and Discontent in the Madras Army, 1806–7* (New Delhi: Manohar, 2007).

Indra, *Ideologies of War and Peace in Ancient India* (Hoshiarpur: Vishveshvaranand Institute Publications, 1957).

Jackson, Peter, *The Delhi Sultanate: A Political and Military History* (Cambridge: Cambridge University Press, 1999).

Jain, Kailash Chand, *Lord Mahavira and His Times* (1974; reprint, Delhi: Motilal Banarasidas, 1991).

Jaiswal, Suvira, 'Social Dimensions of the Cult of Rama', in Irfan Habib (ed.), *Religion in Indian History* (New Delhi: Tulika Books, 2007), pp. 71–101.

Jha, D. N., *Early India: A Concise History* (New Delhi: Manohar, 2004).

Johnston, Alastair Iain, 'Thinking about Strategic Culture', *International Security*, vol. 19, no. 4 (1995), pp. 32–64.

Judd, Denis, *The Lion and the Tiger: The Rise and Fall of the British Raj* (New Delhi: Oxford University Press, 2004).

Kane, P. V., *History of Dharmasastra (Ancient and Medieval Religious and Civil Law in India)*, vol. 1, Part 1 (1930; reprint, Poona: Bhandarkar Oriental Research Institute, 1968).

Kane, Thomas M., *Ancient China on Postmodern War: Enduring Ideas from the Chinese Strategic Tradition* (London/New York: Routledge, 2007).

Karnad, Bharat, *Nuclear Weapons and Indian Security: The Realist Foundations of Strategy* (New Delhi: Macmillan, 2002).

Keith, A. Berriedale, *A History of Sanskrit Literature* (1920; reprint, New Delhi: Oxford University Press, 1973).

Khan, Feroz Hassan, Lavoy, Peter R. and Clary, Christopher, 'Pakistan's Motivations and Calculations for the Kargil Conflict', in Peter R. Lavoy (ed.), *Asymmetric Warfare in South Asia: The Causes and Consequences of the Kargil Conflict* (Cambridge: Cambridge University Press, 2009), pp. 64–91.

Khan, Iqtidar Alam, 'Early Use of Cannon and Musket in India: AD 1442–1526', in Jos J. L. Gommans and Dirk H. A. Kolff (eds.), *Warfare and Weaponry in South Asia: 1000–1800* (New Delhi: Oxford University Press, 2001), pp. 321–36.

Kosambi, D. D., *The Culture and Civilisation of Ancient India in Historical Outline* (n.d.; reprint, New Delhi: Vikas, 2001).

Krentz, Peter, 'Fighting by the Rules: The Invention of the Hoplite *Agon*', in Everett L. Wheeler (ed.), *The Armies of Classical Greece* (Aldershot: Ashgate, 2007), pp. 111–27.

'Casualties in Hoplite Battles', in Everett L. Wheeler (ed.), *The Armies of Classical Greece* (Aldershot: Ashgate, 2007), pp. 349–56.

Kulkarni, Nirmala, 'Daily Routine of a King in Kautilya *Arthasastra*', in Dr. Michael (ed.), *The Concept of Rajadharma* (New Delhi: Sundeep Prakashan, 2005), pp. 140–7.

Select Bibliography

Kumar, Satish, 'Sources of Democracy and Pluralism in India', in Vice-Admiral K. K. Nayyar and Jorg Schultz (eds.), *South Asia Post 9/11: Searching for Stability* (New Delhi: Rupa, 2003), pp. 73–88.

Ladwig III, Walter C., 'Insights from the Northeast: Counterinsurgency in Nagaland and Mizoram', in Sumit Ganguly and David P. Fidler (eds.), *India and Counterinsurgency: Lessons Learned* (Oxon: Routledge, 2009), pp. 45–62.

Lebra, Joyce Chapman, *Women against the Raj: The Rani of Jhansi Regiment* (Singapore: ISEAS, 2008).

Lecomte-Tilouine, Marie, 'Fighting with Ideas: Maoist and Popular Conceptions of the Nepalese People's War', in Laurent Gayer and Christophe Jaffrelot (eds.), *Armed Militias of South Asia: Fundamentalists, Maoists and Separatists* (New Delhi: Foundation, 2009), pp. 65–89.

Lewis, Mark E., 'The Just War in Early China', in Torkel Brekke (ed.), *The Ethics of War in Asian Civilizations* (London/New York: Routledge, 2006), pp. 185–200.

Long, Austin, *On "Other War": Lessons from Five Decades of RAND Counterinsurgency Research* (Santa Monica, California: RAND Corporation, 2006).

Low, D. A., 'The Imprint of Ambiguity: Britain and India in the early 1930s', in Mushirul Hasan and Narayani Gupta (eds.), *India's Colonial Encounter: Essays in Memory of Eric Stokes* (1993; reprint, New Delhi: Manohar, 2004), pp. 465–84.

Mahapatra, Ranganayaki, Bhanumathi, P. and Chakrabarti, Sukla (eds.), *Studies in Tirukkural* (Calcutta: Calcutta University Press, 1996).

Mahulikar, Gauri, 'Ethical Teachings in the *Santiparva* of the *Mahabharata*', in K. B. Archak (ed.), *Ethics for Modern Man in Sanskrit Literature* (New Delhi: Sundeep Prakashan, 2007), pp. 34–42.

Majumdar, Bimal Kanti, *The Military System in Ancient India* (1955; reprint, Calcutta: Firma KLM, 1960).

Malinar, Angelika, *The Bhagavadgita: Doctrines and Context* (Cambridge: Cambridge University Press, 2007).

Mclane, John R., 'The Early Congress, Hindu Populism, and the Wider Society', in Richard Sisson and Stanley Wolpert (eds.), *Congress and Indian Nationalism: The Pre-Independence Phase* (New Delhi: Oxford University Press, 1988), pp. 47–61.

Mehendale, M. A., *Reflections on the Mahabharata War* (Shimla: Indian Institute of Advanced Study, 1995).

Metcalf, Thomas R., *The New Cambridge History of India*, III:4, *Ideologies of the Raj* (1998; reprint, New Delhi: Foundation Books, 2005).

Mital, Surendra Nath, *Kautilya Arthasastra Revisited* (2000; reprint, Centre for Studies in Civilizations, distributed by Munshiram Manoharlal: New Delhi, 2004).

Mohanraj, V. M., *The Warrior and the Charioteer: A Materialist Interpretation of the Bhagavad Gita* (New Delhi: Left Word, 2005).

Mookerji, R. K., *Chandragupta Maurya and His Times* (n.d.; reprint, New Delhi: Motilal Banrasidas, 1960).

The Gupta Empire (1973; reprint, Delhi: Motilal Banarasidas, 1997).

Select Bibliography

Mott IV, William H. and Kim, Jae Chang, *The Philosophy of Chinese Military Culture* (Houndmills, Basingstoke: Macmillan, 2006).

Naidu, W. Prahlada, 'Narayana Pandita's *Hitopadesa* and Ethics', in K. B. Archak (ed.), *Ethics for Modern Man in Sanskrit Literature* (New Delhi: Sundeep Prakashan, 2007), pp. 150–69.

Negi, J. S., *Some Indological Studies*, vol. 1 (Allahabad: Panchananda Publications, 1966).

Nehra, Air Marshal R. K., *Hinduism and Its Military Ethos* (New Delhi: Lancer, 2010).

Oppert, Gustav, *On the Weapons, Army Organization, and Political Maxims of the Ancient Hindus, with Special Reference to Gunpowder and Firearms* (n.d.; reprint, Ahmedabad: New Order Book, 1967).

Orr, W. G., 'Armed Religious Ascetics in Northern India', in Jos J. L. Gommans and Dirk H. A. Kolff (eds.), *Warfare and Weaponry in South Asia: 1000–1800* (New Delhi: Oxford University Press, 2001), pp. 185–201.

Pant, G. N., *Indian Archery* (1978; reprint, Delhi: Agam Kala Prakashan, 1993).

Patankar, V. G., 'Insurgency, Proxy War, and Terrorism in Kashmir', in Sumit Ganguly and David P. Fidler (eds.), *India and Counterinsurgency: Lessons Learned* (Oxon: Routledge, 2009), pp. 65–78.

Patton, Laurie L., 'Telling Stories about Harm: An Overview of Early Indian Narratives', in John R. Hinnells and Richard King (eds.), *Religion and Violence in South Asia: Theory and Practice* (London/New York: Routledge, 2007), pp. 11–40.

Pinch, William R., *Warrior Ascetics and Indian Empires* (Cambridge: Cambridge University Press, 2006).

Pollock, Sheldon, '*Ramayana* and Political Imagination in India', in David N. Lorenzen (ed.), *Religious Movements in South Asia, 600–1800* (2004; reprint, New Delhi: Oxford University Press, 2006), pp. 153–208.

Pradhan, S. D., 'Indian Army and the First World War', in DeWitt Ellinwood and S. D. Pradhan (eds.), *India and World War I* (New Delhi: Manohar, 1978), pp. 49–67.

Rajagopalan, Rajesh, *Fighting like a Guerrilla: The Indian Army and Counterinsurgency* (London/New York/New Delhi: Routledge, 2008).

Rajagopalan, Swarna, 'Security Ideas in the *Valmiki Ramayana*' in Rajagopalan (ed.), *Security and South Asia: Ideas, Institutions and Initiatives* (London/New York/New Delhi: Routledge, 2006), pp. 24–53.

Rajamohan, C., *Impossible Allies: Nuclear India, United States and the Global Order* (New Delhi: India Research Press, 2006).

Rajendran, C., '*Rajadharma* according to *Mahabharata*', in Dr. Michael (ed.), *The Concept of Rajadharma* (New Delhi: Sundeep Prakashan, 2005), pp. 31–40.

Rao, V. Narayana, Shulman, David and Subrahmanyam, Sanjay, 'The Art of War under the Nayakas', in Jos J. L. Gommans and Dirk H. A. Kolff (eds.), *Warfare and Weaponry in South Asia: 1000–1800* (New Delhi: Oxford University Press, 2001), pp. 133–52.

Raychaudhuri, Tapan, *Perceptions, Emotions, Sensibilities: Essays on India's Colonial and Post-colonial Experiences* (1999; reprint, New Delhi: Oxford University Press, 2005).

278 *Select Bibliography*

Reichberg, Gregory M., 'Norms of War in Roman Catholic Christianity', in Vesselin Popovski, Gregory M. Reichberg and Nicholas Turner (eds.), *World Religions and Norms of War* (Tokyo/New York: United Nations University Press, 2009), pp. 142–65.

Revathy, S., 'The Ethics of the *Bhagavad Gita*', in K. B. Archak (ed.), *Ethics for Modern Man in Sanskrit Literature* (New Delhi: Sundeep Prakashan, 2007), pp. 43–52.

Ridley, Ronald T., 'The Hoplite as Citizen: Athenian Military Institutions in Their Social Context', in Everett L. Wheeler (ed.), *The Armies of Classical Greece* (Aldershot: Ashgate, 2007), pp. 153–93.

Rosen, Stephen Peter, *Societies and Military Power: India and Its Armies* (New Delhi: Oxford University Press, 1996).

Rosen, Steven J., *Krishna's Song: A New Look at the Bhagavad Gita* (Westport, Connecticut: Praeger, 2007).

Roy, Kaushik, 'Good Governance versus Bad Governance in South Asia: Civil-Military Relations in India and Pakistan, 1947–2000', *Asian Studies*, vol. 18, nos. 1–2 (2000), pp. 82–99.

Brown Warriors of the Raj: Recruitment and the Mechanics of Command in the Sepoy Army, 1859–1913 (New Delhi: Manohar, 2008).

'The Construction of Martial Race Culture in British-India and Its Legacies in Post-Colonial South Asia', in Kausik Bandopadhyay (ed.), *Asia Annual 2008: Understanding Popular Culture* (New Delhi: Manohar, 2010), pp. 241–56.

Saberwal, Satish, *Spirals of Contention: Why India Was Partitioned in 1947* (London/New York/New Delhi: Routledge, 2008).

Sandhu, Major-General Gurcharn Singh, *A Military History of Ancient India* (New Delhi: Vision Books, 2000).

Santhanam, K., Sreedhar, Saxena, Sudhir and Manish, *Jihadis in Jammu and Kashmir: A Portrait Gallery* (New Delhi: IDSA and Sage, 2003).

Sardeshpande, Lieutenant-General S. C., *War and Soldiering* (New Delhi: Lancer, 1993).

Sarkar, Amal, *A Study on the Ramayanas* (Kolkata: Ridhi, 1987).

Sarkar, Jadunath, *Fall of the Mughal Empire*, vol. 2, 1754–71 (1934; reprint, New Delhi: Orient Longman, 1991).

Sarkar, Jagadish Narayan, *Some Aspects of Military Thinking and Practice in Medieval India* (Calcutta: Ratna Prakashan, 1974).

Saxena, R. K., 'Islamic and Rajput War: Concepts and Strategies', in S. N. Prasad (ed.), *Historical Perspectives of Warfare in India: Some Morale and Materiel Determinants* (New Delhi: Centre for Studies in Civilizations, 2002), pp. 284–300.

'The Mughal and Rajput Armies', in S. N. Prasad (ed.), *Historical Perspectives of Warfare in India: Some Morale and Materiel Determinants* (New Delhi: Centre for Studies in Civilizations, 2002), pp. 301–13.

'Medieval Forts, Logistics and Heraldry', in S. N. Prasad (ed.), *Historical Perspectives of Warfare in India: Some Morale and Materiel Determinants* (New Delhi: Centre for Studies in Civilizations, 2002), pp. 336–56.

Schmithausen, Lambert L., 'Aspects of the Buddhist Attitude towards War', in Jan E. M. Houben and Karel R. Van Kooij (eds.), *Violence Denied: Violence,*

Non-Violence and the Rationalization of Violence in South Asian Cultural History (Leiden: Brill, 1999), pp. 45–67.

Sen, Amartya, 'India and the Bomb', in M. V. Ramanna and C. Rammanohar Reddy (eds.), *Prisoners of the Nuclear Dream* (New Delhi: Orient Longman, 2003), pp. 167–88.

Sensarma, P., *Military Thoughts of Tiru Valluvar* (Calcutta: Noya Prakash, 1981).

Sharma, R. S., 'Material Background of the Origin of Buddhism', in Bhairabi Prasad Sahu (ed.), *Iron and Social Change in Early India* (New Delhi: Oxford University Press, 2006), pp. 42–8.

Shaugnessy, Edward L., 'Historical Perspectives on the Introduction of the Chariot into China', in Peter Lorge (ed.), *Warfare in China to 1600* (Aldershot: Ashgate, 2005), pp. 1–39.

Shrimali, Krishna Mohan, *A People's History of India*, 3A, *The Age of Iron and the Religious Revolution, c. 700–c. 350 BC* (New Delhi: Tulika Books, 2007).

   'Religions in Complex Societies: The Myth of the "Dark Age"', in Irfan Habib (ed.), *Religion in Indian History* (New Delhi: Tulika Books, 2007), pp. 36–70.

Shyam, Radhey, *Life and Times of Malik Ambar* (New Delhi: Munshirasm Manoharlal, 1968).

Sidhu, Waheguru Pal Singh, 'Of Oral Judgements and Ethnocentric Judgements', in Kanti P. Bajpai and Amitabh Mattoo (eds.), *Securing India, Strategic Thought and Practice: Essays by George K. Tanham with Commentaries* (New Delhi: Manohar, 2006), pp. 174–90.

Sil, Narasingha P., *Kautilya's Arthasastra: A Comparative Study* (Calcutta/New Delhi: Academic Publishers, 1985).

Singh, Brigadier K. Kuldip, *Indian Military Thought: Kurukshetra to Kargil and Future Perspectives* (New Delhi: Lancer, 2011).

Singh, G. P., *Political Thought in Ancient India* (1993; reprint, New Delhi: D. K. Printworld, 2005).

Singh, Jaswant, *Defending India* (Houndmills, Basingstoke: Macmillan, 1999).

Sinha, Manoj Kumar, 'Hinduism and International Humanitarian Law', *International Review of the Red Cross*, vol. 87, no. 858 (2005), pp. 285–94.

Sircar, D. C., *Inscriptions of Asoka* (1957; reprint, New Delhi: Publications Division, 1998).

Smith, Hugh, *On Clausewitz: A Study of Military and Political Ideas* (Houndmills, Basingstoke: Palgrave, 2005).

Snodgrass, A. M., 'The "Hoplite Reform" Revisited', in Everett L. Wheeler (ed.), *The Armies of Classical Greece* (Aldershot: Ashgate, 2007), pp. 3–17.

Solomon, Norman, 'The Ethics of War in Judaism', in Torkel Brekke (ed.), *The Ethics of War in Asian Civilizations* (London/New York: Routledge, 2006), pp. 39–80.

Sonbol, Amira, 'Norms of War in Sunni Islam', in Vesselin Popovski, Gregory M. Reichberg and Nicholas Turner (eds.), *World Religions and Norms of War* (Tokyo/New York: United Nations University Press, 2009), pp. 282–302.

Sondhaus, Lawrence, *Strategic Culture and Ways of War* (London/New York: Routledge, 2006).

280

Select Bibliography

Srivastava, A. K., *Ancient Indian Army: Its Administration and Organization* (New Delhi: Ajanta Publications, 1985).

Stein, Burton, *A History of India* (1998; reprint, New Delhi: Oxford University Press, 2004).

Stoyanov, Yuri, 'Norms of War in Eastern Orthodox Christianity', in Vesselin Popovski, Gregory M. Reichberg and Nicholas Turner (eds.), *World Religions and Norms of War* (Tokyo/New York: United Nations University Press, 2009), pp. 166–219.

Strachan, Hew, *Clausewitz's On War: A Biography* (New York: Atlantic Monthly Press, 2007).

Streets, Heather, *Martial Races: The Military, Race and Masculinity in British Imperial Culture, 1857–1914* (Manchester: Manchester University Press, 2004).

Streusand, Douglas, 'The Process of Expansion', in Jos J. L. Gommans and Dirk H. A. Kolff (eds.), *Warfare and Weaponry in South Asia: 1000–1800* (New Delhi: Oxford University Press, 2001), pp. 337–64.

Sundaram, Chandar S., 'Reviving a "Dead Letter": Military Indianization and the Ideology of Anglo-Indians, 1885–91', in P. S. Gupta and Anirudh Deshpande (eds.), *The British Raj and Its Indian Armed Forces: 1857–1939* (New Delhi: Oxford University Press, 2002), pp. 45–97.

Sundaram, J., 'Warfare in South India – The Background', in S. N. Prasad (ed.), *Historical Perspectives of Warfare in India: Some Morale and Materiel Determinants* (New Delhi: Motilal Banarasidas, 2002), pp. 167–83.

'Chola and Other Armies – Organization', in S. N. Prasad (ed.), *Historical Perspectives of Warfare in India: Some Morale and Materiel Determinants* (New Delhi: Motilal Banarasidas, 2002), pp. 184–208.

Swami, Praveen, 'The Impact of the Kargil Conflict and Kashmir on Indian Politics and Society', in Peter R. Lavoy (ed.), *Asymmetric Warfare in South Asia: The Causes and Consequences of the Kargil Conflict* (Cambridge: Cambridge University Press, 2009), pp. 258–79.

Swamy, M. R. V., 'Vedic *Rajadharma*', in Dr. Michael (ed.), *The Concept of Rajadharma* (New Delhi: Sundeep Prakashan, 2005), pp. 13–24.

Talbott, Strobe, *Engaging India: Diplomacy, Democracy and the Bomb* (New Delhi: Penguin, 2004).

Tanham, George K., 'Indian Strategic Thought: An Interpretive Essay', in Kanti P. Bajpai and Amitabh Mattoo (eds.), *Securing India, Strategic Thought and Practice: Essays by George K. Tanham with Commentaries* (New Delhi: Manohar, 2006), pp. 28–111.

'Indian Strategy in Flux?', in Kanti P. Bajpai and Amitabh Mattoo (eds.), *Securing India, Strategic Thought and Practice: Essays by George K. Tanham with Commentaries* (New Delhi: Manohar, 2006), pp. 112–39.

Thapar, Romila, *Asoka and the Decline of the Mauryas* (1963; reprint, New Delhi: Oxford University Press, 1989).

From Lineage to State: Social Formations in the Mid-First Millennium BC in the Ganga Valley (1984; reprint, New Delhi: Oxford University Press, 1990).

The Mauryas Revisited (1987; reprint, Calcutta: K. P. Bagchi & Company, 1993).

Select Bibliography

The Penguin History of Early India from the Origins to AD 1300 (2002; reprint, New Delhi: Penguin, 2003).

'Imagined Religious Communities? Ancient History and the Modern Search for a Hindu Identity', in David N. Lorenzen (ed.), *Religious Movements in South Asia, 600–1800* (2004; reprint, New Delhi: Oxford University Press, 2006), pp. 333–59.

Thapliyal, U. P., 'War in Ancient India – Concepts', in S. N. Prasad (ed.), *Historical Perspectives of Warfare in India: Some Morale and Materiel Determinants* (New Delhi: Motilal Banarasidas, 2002), pp. 45–67.

'Military Organization in the Ancient Period', in S. N. Prasad (ed.), *Historical Perspectives of Warfare in India: Some Morale and Materiel Determinants* (New Delhi: Motilal Banarasidas, 2002), pp. 68–103.

'Weapons, Fortifications and Military Training in Ancient India', in S. N. Prasad (ed.), *Historical Perspectives of Warfare in India: Some Morale and Materiel Determinants* (New Delhi: Motilal Banarasidas, 2002), pp. 104–35.

'Early Indian Heraldry and Ceremonials', in S. N. Prasad (ed.), *Historical Perspectives of Warfare in India: Some Morale and Materiel Determinants* (New Delhi: Motilal Banarasidas, 2002), pp. 136–55.

Thomas, Raju G. C., 'India's Nuclear and Missile Programmes: Strategy, Intentions, Capabilities', in Thomas and Amit Gupta (eds.), *India's Nuclear Security* (New Delhi: Vistaar, 2000), pp. 87–121.

Thornton, Rod, 'The British Army and the Origins of Its Minimum Force Philosophy', *Small Wars & Insurgencies*, vol. 15, no. 1 (2004), pp. 83–106.

Trautmann, Thomas R (ed.), *The Aryan Debate* (New Delhi: Oxford University Press, 2005).

Tripathi, Ramashankar, *History of Ancient India* (1942; reprint, New Delhi: Motilal Banarasidas, 1999).

Tritle, Lawrence A., 'Hector's Body: Mutilation of the Dead in Ancient Greece and Vietnam', in Everett L. Wheeler (ed.), *The Armies of Classical Greece* (Aldershot: Ashgate, 2007), pp. 335–48.

Trundle, Matthew F., 'Identity and Community among Greek Mercenaries in the Classical World: 700–322 BCE', in Everett L. Wheeler (ed.), *The Armies of Classical Greece* (Aldershot: Ashgate, 2007), pp. 481–91.

Veer, Peter Van Der, *Imperial Encounters: Religion and Modernity in India and Britain* (2001; reprint, New Delhi: Permanent Black, 2006).

Voigt, Johannes H., 'Co-operation or Confrontation? War and Congress Politics, 1939–42', in D. A. Low (ed.), *Congress and the Raj: Facets of the Indian Struggle 1917–47* (London: Heinemann, 1977), pp. 349–74.

Wheeler, Everett L. 'Introduction', in Wheeler (ed.), *The Armies of Classical Greece* (Aldershot: Ashgate, 2007), pp. xi–lxiv.

'Ephorus and the Prohibition of Missiles', in Wheeler (ed.), *The Armies of Classical Greece* (Aldershot: Ashgate, 2007), pp. 19–44.

Wink, Andre, *Al-Hind: The Making of the Indo-Islamic World*, vol. 2, *The Slave Kings and the Islamic Conquest 11th–13th Centuries* (1997; reprint, New Delhi: Oxford University Press, 2001).

Witzel, Michael, 'Brahmanical Reactions to Foreign Influences and to Social and Religious Change', in Patrick Olivelle (ed.), *Between the Empires: Society* in India 300 BCE to 400 CE (2006; reprint, New York: Oxford University Press, 2007), pp. 457–99.

Wood, Neal, 'Xenophon's Theory of Leadership', in Everett L. Wheeler (ed.), *The Armies of Classical Greece* (Aldershot: Ashgate, 2007), pp. 447–80.

Yadava, B. N. S., 'Problem of the Interaction between Socio-Economic Classes in the Early Medieval Complex', *Indian Historical Review*, vol. 3, no. 1 (1976), pp. 43–56.

'Chivalry and Warfare', in Jos J. L. Gommans and Dirk H. A. Kolff (eds.), *Warfare and Weaponry in South Asia: 1000–1800* (New Delhi: Oxford University Press, 2001), pp. 66–98.

Zydenbos, Robert J., 'Jainism as the Religion of Non-Violence', in Jan E. M. Houben and Karel R. Van Kooij (eds.), *Violence Denied: Violence, Non-Violence and the Rationalization of Violence in South Asian Cultural History* (Leiden: Brill, 1999), pp. 185–210.

Index

Abu Ghraib (prison), 251
acharyas, 1, 6, 7, 10, 11, 12, 106–7, 159, 246
Agrawal, Ashvini, 124
ahimsa (non-violence), 30, 38, 42, 47, 54, 239, 243, 263
(*see also* Mohandas Karamchand Gandhi)
Akbar (Mughal emperor), 47, 185, 192, 193, 194
Al Qaeda, 248
apate (surprise attack), 27
Aquinas, Thomas, 188
Aristotle, 33, 75, 76
Arthasastra, 12, 52, 57, 58–9, 60, 61, 64–6, 67, 68, 70, 73–4, 75, 76, 82, 83, 94, 100, 103, 118–19, 137, 188, 246, 248, 251, 257, 260
  adhikarnas, 60
  army, 82, 83
  divine origin, 76
  duty of rulers, 100, 103
  karmasandhi, 67
  objectives of war, 64
  predecessors of Kautilya 59, 61, 70
  realism in *Arthasastra*, 64–6
  revenue, 94
  rules of war, 57
Arya Samaj, 221
Aryabarta, 178
Aryans, 16, 20–1
asanayuddha, 190

Asoka (Maurya emperor), 12, 39, 40, 42, 47, 48, 49, 50, 51, 53, 54–5, 56
  animal protection, 42, 55
  army, 51
  hunting, 56
  Kalinga expedition, 50
  new religion (*dhamma*), 12, 40, 48, 49, 51, 56
  prisoners' welfare, 53
  rock and pillar edicts, 48, 49, 51, 53, 55
Assyrian army, 20, 22, 25
asurayuddha (*see also kutayuddha*)28, 188, 198
asvamedha/rajasuya, 54, 123
Atharva Veda, 24, 193
Attila, 126
Aurangzeb (Mughal emperor), 193
Azad Hind (newspaper), 230
Azad Hind Fauj (Indian National Army), 231, 233, 234, 235

Babur, 161
Banabhatta (also Bana), 12, 126–9, 135
bargi, 208–9 (*see also* Marathas)
Barua, Pradeep P., 19
Battle of Hydaspes, 80–1, 83, 121
Bhagavad Gita (*see also* Krishna)4, 11, 15, 22, 24, 28, 31, 33–4, 44, 78, 124, 262
  Sanjaya, 31

283

Index

Bhagavad Purana, 59
Bharatiya Janata Party (BJP), 238, 262
Bhattacharya, Pachugopal, 22
Bhisma, 28, 29, 35, 258
Bibhisana, 38
Black, Jeremy, 3
Booth, Ken, 2, 3
Bose, Subhas Chandra, 230–5
Brahma, 33
Brekke, Torkel, 9, 27–8, 38, 72
Brhadaranyaka Upanishad, 31
Brihaspati Sutra, 137
Brockington, John, 13, 14, 18
Buddha, 42 (*see also* Buddhism)
buddhi, 33
Buddhism, 2, 8, 12, 40, 41, 42–4, 47,
    49, 55, 64
  moksha, 64
bushi, 180
Byzantine Empire, 165

cakravartin (*see also vijigishu*)52–4
caste system 10, 18, 29, 30, 38, 39,
    64, 76
Chadha, Lieutenant-Colonel Vivek (
    see also insurgency)247, 251
Chakravarti, P. C., 79
Chanakya, *see* Kautilya
Chandragupta Maurya, 58, 59, 61
Chandragupta Vikramaditya (or II),
    124, 137
chara (spy), 35–6, 93, 105
chariot (*ratha*), 20, 21, 22–3, 25, 81,
    121
chaturanga bala, 19, 20, 25, 140
  patti, 20
China-India conflict, 240, 257
Chinese infantry, 135
Chinese military philosophy, 5, 7, 8,
    27, 50, 51, 52, 86, 87, 88, 89, 93,
    98, 102, 107
  Mott IV, William H., 7, 8
  Ssu-ma Fa, 50
  T'ai-Kung, 51
  Taoism, 87
  Wei Liao-Tzu, 52
  Yi bing, 27
Christian just war, 5, 11, 107, 130,
    169
Clausewitz, Carl von, 1, 2, 6, 77–80
Coker, Christopher, 4, 246

communalism, 220, 236, 255
concept of reincarnation (*karma*
    theory), 32–3, 39
Confucius, 47, 52, 53, 56
Connor, W. R., 26, 27
counter-insurgency (COIN), 247, 249
    (*see also* terrorism)

dana, 18, 29
danda, 29, 67, 75
dar al Harb, 170
Dark Age (Greece), 13, 20
darsana, 2
Darwin's theory of evolution, 212
Dasarajna, 21
Datta, Rajat, 170
dervishes, 172
dharma, 2, 11, 29
dharmasastra, 11, 47, 109
dharmayuddha, 1, 2, 4, 5, 11, 28,
    29–31, 32, 35, 37, 39, 121–2,
    129, 148, 169, 183, 184, 185,
    245, 251
  Hindu just war, 28, 32, 35, 148,
    251
  holy war and just war, 169, 184
  treatment of defeated ruler, 129,
    183, 184, 185
Digby, Simon, 163
Dravidian, 16
duta, 29
dvairatha, 20

East India Company's army, 212, 213,
    214–15, 216 (*see also* Martial
    Race theory)
Eastern way of warfare, 6
Eaton, Richard M., 174
elephants in warfare, 23, 24, 116, 133,
    143
Elgood, Robert, 189
Enlightenment, 97

Ferguson, R. Brian,, 107
forts, 94, 118–19, 120, 152, 157
    (*see also* siege warfare)
Fourth Generation Warfare (4GW),
    95, 96

Gabriel, Richard, A., 20
gadas, 22, 36

Index

Gandhi, Mohandas Karamchand, 11, 12, 40, 219, 220, 222, 223–30, 241
  Dandi March, 220
  ideology, 223–30 (*see also* Hind Swaraj)
  influence of the epics 224
Ganga, 15
Gat, Azar, 4
Gautama Dharmasutra, 41
Gnirs, Andrea M., 8, 27
gopa/gopati, 17
Greek warfare (ancient), 6, 20, 24, 26, 35
gunpowder (*agnichurna*), 185–6, 189, 191
Gupta Empire, 122–6, 159
Gurkhas, 218

hadith, 170
Han Empire, 133
Handel, Michael I., 6
Harijan (newspaper), 224
Harsa of Kanauj (Harsa Vardhana), 126, 138, 176
  (*see also* Harsacharita)
Harsacharita, 12, 122–3, 126, 132–3, 136, 137
Hastinapur, 15
Herodotus, 7, 82
Hind Swaraj, 222–3 (*see also* Gandhi)
Hindian, 175
Hindu Mahasabha, 222
Hitopadesa, 7, 12, 144, 151–2
Hiuen Tsang, 129
Homer, 7, 13, 26
Homi Bhaba, 254
horse in warfare, 82, 124–5, 133, 163, 164
Humayun, 175
Huns, 122–3 (*see also* steppe nomads)

Imperial Service Troops, 215
India Office Records, 12
Indian army, 250
Indian Council Act (1909), 221
Indian National Congress, 219–22
Indian Peace Keeping Force, 251
Indian way of warfare, 243, 244, 245–6, 264
Indra, 32, 34

Indrajit, 37, 39
Indraprastha, 15
Indus Valley Civilization, 16, 25
information warfare, 84
insurgencies, 247, 249–54
  (*see also* counter-insurgencies)
Inter-Services Intelligence, 248
Isocrates, 26

Jainism, 2, 11, 12, 45, 46, 52, 55
Jamuna, 15
Janaka, 17
janapada, 17
  (*see also* mahajanapadas)
jauhar, 182–3
Jayadratha, 35
Jayanaka, 182
Jha, D. N., 49, 58, 61
jihad, 5, 169–71, 223, 248
Johnston, Alastair Ian, 263–4
Judaism and warfare, 27

Kadambari, 127
Kalapani, 215
Kalhana's *Rajatarangini*, 164, 172, 174, 176, 178, 181, 188
  taxation, 178
  vassal-king relationship, 181, 188
Kali Purusha, 32
Kalidasa, 123–4
kama, 75–6
Kamandaka, 1, 6, 7, 8, 137–44, 192
  exercise of troops 138
  importance of horse, 192
  on rulers, 139, 141, 143
  on war economy, 142
  surprise attack, 144
Kambojas, 24
Kane, P. V., 58–9, 137
Kant, Immanuel, 51
Kanva Dynasty, 110
karma, 32–3, 38, 39
Kathasaritsagara, 12, 145
  (*see also* Somadeva)
Kautilya, 1, 6, 7, 8, 10, 12, 57, 58, 66–8, 101, 102, 128, 137–8, 241, 250 (*see also* Arthasastra)
kopa, 1, 10
Kelsay, John, 170
Khilafat movement, 220
Kosambi, D. D., 82

Index

Krishna, 29, 31, 32, 33, 34, 36
  (*see also Bhagavad Gita*)
Kshatriya, 18, 29, 30, 31, 33
kuladharma, 32
Kural, 12, 151–2, 153, 155, 156, 160
  (*see also* Tamil military theory)
Kushana, 108, 118
Kutayuddha, 1, 2, 5, 11, 12, 28,
  34, 36, 61, 74–5, 76, 77, 92,
  121, 129, 131, 135, 140, 145,
  146, 147–8, 179, 197–8, 245
  (*see also* Kautilya)
  aniti, 36
  bheda, 28
  economic destruction, 148
  realpolitik, 5
  self-defence, 146
  silent war, 145
  unjust war, 28

Laden, Osama Bin, 248
lashkar-i-Islam, 170, 172
Legalism, 86, 88
loka, 2
Lokayata, 2

Machiavelli, Niccolò, 66, 70, 71,
  72–4, 99–101
Magadha, 24
Mahabharata, 2, 11, 13, 14, 15, 18,
  26, 27, 28–9, 31, 32, 34–6, 39,
  68, 244–5, 262
  Aswathama, 35, 36
  composition 14
  Dhritarashtra, 31
  Drona, 35, 36
  Duryodhana, 29, 32
  influence on India's strategic theory,
    244
  Kuru-Pandava battle, 13, 14, 15, 29
  shantiparva, 68
  udyogparva, 28, 32
mahajanapadas, 40–1, 60
Maharashtra Purana, 204–9
  (*see also* Marathas)
Mahavira, 42
Majumdar, Bimal Kanti, 19
Malinar, Angelika, 15, 31, 32
Manavadharmasastra (*Laws of Manu
  or Manusamhita*), 2, 11, 12, 109,
  110
manavayuddha, 189

mandala theory, 67, 113, 117, 240,
  241 (*see also* Kautilya)
mantrasakti, 72
mantrayuddha, 37, 91
Manu, 1, 7, 8, 110–11, 112–21
Maoist, 249
Marathas, 162, 199, 205, 206, 207
  (*see also Maharashtra Purana*;
  Shivaji)
Martial Race theory, 216–19, 235
  (*see also* East India Company's
  army)
Maurya Empire, 6, 62–4, 108
Maurya warfare, 25–6, 57
mayayuddha, 37
Megasthenes, 50, 59, 62
Meghnad, *see* Indrajit
Mehendale, M.A., 28–30
mlechchas, 146
Mohanty, Jitendra Nath, 8
Montagu Declaration (1917), 220
Muhammad Ghori, 176
Muslim League, 222

Narayana, 7
National Archives of India, 12
Nehru, Jawaharlal, 11, 236,
  240, 242
New War, 96
nirvana, 49
niti, 12
Nitiprakasika, 185
Nitisara, 12, 137, 139, 140, 142, 192
  (*see also* Kamandaka)
nripati, 12
nuclear weapons, 12, 254–5, 256,
  257, 258, 260

Panchatantra, 144, 148, 149, 152
Panis, 21
Parasurama, 19
People's Liberation Army of China,
  239
Persian, 34, 48, 80
Plato, 26, 33, 50, 75
polis, 26, 27, 30
Prithviraja, 177

qatilu, 169

Raghuvamsa see Kalidasa
Raja Mohan, C., 240, 241, 258

Index

287

rajadharma, 29, 109
Rajagopalan, Rajesh, 9
rajan, 17 (*see also nripati*)
Rajput warfare, 162, 178, 179, 180,
 184 (*see also* Rajputs)
Rajputs, 161, 166–7, 178, 179, 181,
 218
Rajyavardhana, 133
raksas, 30, 37
Rama, 14, 18, 22, 29, 30, 31, 37, 38,
 173–4 (*see also Ramayana*)
 narach, 22
Ramayana, 2, 11, 13, 14, 17, 18, 19,
 22, 24, 25, 26, 27, 29–30, 31, 32,
 33, 34, 37, 39, 241
 Dasaratha, 24
 heroic fighting, 19
 Janaka, 17
 Lakshmana, 31
 Ravana, 19, 22
 Sugriva, 37
 Tulsidas, 14, 18
 upholder of *dharma*, 30
 Valmiki, 14
Ramkrishna Mission, 222
Rand, Christopher C., 107
rashtra, 8, 248
Rig Veda, 13, 18, 22, 31, 34
rishis, 21
rita, 30
Roberts, Lord, 216
Roman just war tradition, 168
Rosen, Stephen, Peter, 3, 10, 247
Rosen, Steven, J., 15
Russo-Japanese War (1905),
 136

sakti, 10
samanta, 165
Samkhya, 8, 33, 185
Sanchi, 124
sanghas, 41, 49
Sarkar, Amal, 34
sastras, 32
Satavahanas, 113
satyagraha, 40, 226
Second Punic War, 120
Schmithausen, Lambert, 54
Scobell, Andrew, 5
Sehgal, Lakshmi, 234
Shang Empire, 64
shariat, 171

Shiva (god of destruction), 182
Shiva Dhanurveda, 21
Shivaji, 187, 190, 195–204
 (*see also* Marathas)
shuddhi, 221
siege warfare, 25, 38, 95, 175, 189
 (*see also* forts)
Sikhism, 11
Singh, Upinder, 48
Sita, 17, 29, 30
Sivabharata, 202–4
Smith, Rupert, 96, 100
Snyder, Jack, 2
Socrates, 51
Solomon, Norman, 27
Somadeva, 145–7, 148
 (*see also Kathasaritsagara*)
Spartans, 31
Sri Lanka, 34
St. Augustine, 7
Stein, Burton, 49
steppe nomads, 121–6 (*see also*
 Huns)
strategic culture, 264
 (*see also* Tanham, George K.)
Subedi, Surya P., 5
Sudasa, 18
Sukraniti/Sukranitisara, 187–92,
 208
Sun Tzu, 6, 7, 87–91, 99, 104,
 114 (*see also* Chinese military
 philosophy)
Sunga Dynasty, 110
sutra literature, 109
Syse, Henrik, 50

Tamil military theory, 152–8
Tanham, George K., 5, 10, 241
Tantra, 10
terrorism (insurgency), 1, 247, 248–9
 (*see also* counter-insurgency)
Thapar, Romila, 16, 47, 63, 64,
 109
Thapliyal, U. P., 19
The Hindu (newspaper), 227
The Prince (Machiavelli), 70–2, 74
 (*see also* Machiavelli)
Thucydides, 7, 69–70, 73
Tilak, B. G., 221
Trautmann, Thomas, 58
Tripathi, R. S., 24
Turkish archers, 162, 163

Index

ulema, 171

Vaisampayana, 188
Valin, 37
Valluvar, 152–7
Valmiki, 13, 14 (*see also*
   Ramayana)
Varahamihira, 137
vedanta, 8, 10
vedas, 13
veeraswarga, 32
Vidyasagar, Iswar Chandra, 221
vigraha, 1, 10
vijigishu, 61, 64, 67, 68, 73–4,
   82, 103, 114, 138–40, 257
   (*see also Arthasastra*; Kautilya)
Vindhya Mountain, 34, 147
vis, 17

Viswakarma, 25, 180
Vyasa, 13
vyuha, 19, 83, 140

Western way of warfare, 4–5, 6
Wheeler, Everett L., 26, 31

Xenophon, 34

Yajur Veda, 23
Yama, 139
yavanas, 24, 123, 187
yogin, 33
yojana, 25
Young India (newspaper), 227

Zaina Rajatarangini, 186, 192